THE HISTORY OF KOREA

The History of Korea

By
Woo-keun Han

Translated by
Kyung-shik Lee

Edited by
Grafton K. Mintz

University of Hawaii Press
Honolulu

Originally published by the Eul-Yoo
    Publishing Co., Ltd. 1970
Published by East-West Center Press 1971
Paperback edition published by University
    of Hawaii Press 1974, 1980, 1988

All rights reserved
Library of Congress Catalog Card Number 72–186011
ISBN 0–8248–0334–5
Manufactured in the United States of America

Preface

It has long been a popular demand that the history of Korea be written in a new way. It is said that Korean histories should outgrow dynastic-centered description of history, correct historical facts that were distorted by government-patronized scholars during the Japanese colonial rule, and be written from an objective point of view.

I entirely agree with this. Korean histories should shake off their old shell and be built on an entirely new plan with a new system. It is not just one or two points that need reinterpretation.

It is true to say that research on Korean history has been actively carried out at home and abroad and has achieved tangible results in many ways for the last 20 years or so. With the help of these results, I present here a new history of Korea, in which I have attempted, among other things, to uncover the social structures of the past and have exerted my best efforts especially on the modern period. But I know I am not quite satisfied with my work. I only hope that my work will be of some help to readers in gaining a proper understanding of Korean history.

I wish to express my sincere and deep gratitude first and foremost to the translator, Mr. Lee Kyung-shik, assistant Professor in English literature, College of Liberal Arts and Sciences, Seoul National University, and also to

Mr. and Mrs. Merrill Kaitz and Mr. and Mrs. Philip Melzer who untiringly helped the translator with valuable comments. I also owe thanks to Mr. Han Yong-u, my assistant, for his help.

I am sincerely thankful to Mr. Chong Chin-suk, president of the Eul-Yoo Publishing Co., and Mr. An Ch'un-gun, director, without whose active interest, encouragement, and financial help I could not have done this work.

H. W. K.

December 1969
Seoul, Korea

Editor's Note

This book was originally written in the Korean language for Korean readers. It was therefore felt that straightforward translation into English would not be sufficient to make the book comprehensible and interesting to Western readers. There were, for example, numerous allusions which most Koreans would easily recognize but which few others would. Knowledge of matters such as the Buddhist religion was taken for granted. For these reasons, the publishers asked me to undertake a revision of the translation and the result is presented here. While making the needed changes, I have done my best to preserve the spirit of Professor Han's original text as very ably translated by Professor Lee.

G. K. M.

Contents

Maps

Illustrations

PART ONE

The Primitive and Tribal Societies

Chapter 1

Primitive Society

The date at which human beings first came to Korea has not yet been determined. Animal fossils from the holocene epoch of the quaternary period have been found on the peninsula, notably those of the mammoth (Elephas Primigenius) near the Tumen River in the northeast and those of a primitive species of cattle on Cheju Island in the south. In other areas of north Asia such as north China, Manchuria, Siberia and Japan, similar fossils have been found associated with human remains and artifacts from paleolithic and midlithic times. It seems a reasonable assumption, then, that the Korean peninsula was also inhabited by man at this time. This assumption is further strengthened by geological findings which seem to indicate that Korea was not invaded by glaciers during the ice age, as were other areas of north Asia.

Some time before World War II stone artifacts were found in the region of the Tumen River, which forms the northeast boundary of present-day Korea. Some scholars have claimed that these artifacts are of paleolithic provenance. However, since the surrounding region abounds in neolithic remains, the paleolithic argument cannot be considered conclusive. But as recently as 1963, pebble-chopping tools of undoubtedly paleolithic provenance were discovered during the excavation of a shell mound in North Hamgyong Province, in present north Korea. Similar paleolithic artifacts were subsequently found in South

Ch'ungch'ong Province, on the upper reaches of the Kum River in north central south Korea. A piece of charred wood from the sixth level of the paleolithic layer of that particular excavation has been found by the radiocarbon dating method to be 30,690 years old, which places it in the later paleolithic age. Similar remains were found in a cavern near the excavation.

All this appears to be fairly conclusive proof that man had come to Korea at least by the later paleolithic age, about thirty thousand years ago. The evidence so far discovered indicates that these paleolithic men were hunters and gatherers, living in the open or in caves. Though this evidence is rather sketchy, continued research in this field will undoubtedly give us a more detailed picture of the life of paleolithic man in Korea.

In contrast to the evidence for earlier times, neolithic remains are relatively abundant in Korea. Exact dating has not so far been possible, but most such remains can be placed roughly between 3,000 and 2,000 B. C. It is fairly certain that the makers of these neolithic artifacts were the ancestors of the present Korean people.

It is in these neolithic remains that we first encounter large quantities of pottery, best friend of the archeologist. The pottery of neolithic Korea is of a characteristic sort, being decorated with incised lines or scratches resembling those made by passing the teeth of a comb over the wet clay before firing. This type of pottery is therefore called combware, and the culture which produced it the combware culture.

Combware of various types has been found associated with neolithic cultures in many parts of northern Europe and north Asia. It has been found on the Scandinavian peninsula, in north Germany, and in Siberia and Mongolia. While there is some dispute over the exact lineage of the Korean combware culture, it is clear that Korean combware is closely related to that of Siberia. It is also generally agreed that combware unearthed in western Japan is also related to Korean combware.

These relationships of pottery types correspond, interestingly enough, to relationships of language. The Korean language belongs to the Altaic language family of north Asia, which includes Turkish, Mongolian, Tungusic and Japanese. This is a fairly good indication that the Korean people have a common racial origin with other peoples of north Asia, especially the Siberian tribes, the Mongols and the Manchus. It is quite possible that combware came to Japan by way of Korea, for it is almost certain that it came from Siberia to the western shore of Korea by way of Mongolia.

Combware from the western and southern shores of Korea is made of a sort of sandy clay called *sajilt'o* in Korean. The bottoms of the pots are either pointed or rounded. But combware from the northeastern shore is composed of a different material, a very sticky clay mixed with fine gravel. These pots are flat-bottomed and rather rough and crude in comparison to those from the south and west.

The fact that most combware has been found on the Korean seacoasts indicates that early neolithic Koreans were primarily fishermen. In the later neolithic period, however, we begin to find stone agricultural implements such as ploughshares and sickles. Millstones and saddle querns are also found in the later period, but fishhooks and nets persist, indicating that the combware people did not wholly abandon fishing. Stone knives and arrowheads are also found, indicating that hunting was also practiced.

We can now form a rough idea of the development of neolithic combware culture in Korea. During the early part of the neolithic age the primary economic activity was fishing, and most settlements were along the coasts.

Agriculture began to develop during the later period, with fishing and hunting continuing as supplementary activities.

Evidence about the dwellings of these people is not conclusive thus far. It is conjectured that they lived in caves or hollows dug into the seashores or river banks. Such shelters could easily be made without sophisticated tools. Some traces of fireplaces have been found at the bottoms of such hollows.

Toward the end of the neolithic age, the combware people began to move inland along the banks of rivers, still living in natural or artificial caves. Bone needles and spinning wheels have been found, showing that they at first used animal hides for clothing, but later began to weave cloth. Simple personal ornaments made from shells and gems have also been found.

From archeological evidence, supplemented by folklore, mythology, and early historical records, it is possible to form an idea of the society in which these neolithic people lived. From the evidence at hand, it seems to have been rather similar to many primitive societies known today.

The people were divided into clans—at first, perhaps, simply extended family groups, but later becoming more complex as collateral families were included with the original family to form the clan. These clans were mostly communal, owning property in common and performing labor in common. The notion of private property was not fully developed. Each clan lived on a territory which was jealously guarded. One of the chief causes of conflict in these early times was the encroachment by one clan on the territory of another.

Each clan was headed by a patriarch who held his position by right of age and descent. But his rule was by no means absolute. Especially on such important matters as war with another clan, the unanimous consent of all mature males was required. We find in the records of the ancient Silla kingdom (traditional founding date 57 B. C.) mention of a unanimous-decision system called *Hwabaek*, which may well be a survival into historical times of this primitive custom.

The powers and duties of the patriarchs differed in different areas. While the custom of requiring unanimous decision on such vital matters as war and food supply was observed in most places, we find the matter of religious duties varied. Among the Silla clans in early historical times, the patriarch was called *ch'ach'aung*, which signifies a shaman in Korean, an indication that he combined political and religious functions. Among the Han people of the south, however, there was a special official called a *ch'on'-gun* ("heavenly priest"), in addition to the patriarch, whose duties seem to have been exclusively religious, the patriarch presumably confining himself to secular matters.

But it is perhaps a mistake to make too sharp a distinction between the religious and the secular in discussing this primitive clan society. The religion of this society, like those of many other primitive societies, was an all-pervading thing, affecting all aspects of life. Two characteristics which this religion shares with other primitive religions were animism and totemism.

Animism is the belief that natural objects and the forces of nature are inhabited or controlled by spirits. All natural events are attributed to these spirits, and they are also believed to be able to influence human lives and fortunes. In Korea rivers, brooks, rocks, trees and mountains especially were believed to be inhabited by spirits. To this day, most Korean Buddhist temples include a small pavilion dedicated to the "mountain spirit," usually decorated with a painting of an old man and a tiger.

One of the most powerful spirits was, of course, that of the sun, especially important to an agricultural community. We find several traces of sun-worship from very early times, often associated with the legends of clan ancestors, like the sun-goddess myth of Japan. The sun was also frequently associated with mountains, and many mountains still retain names meaning "bright" or "white," as in the name *Paeksan* ("white mountain"), a very common name for mountains in Korea.

Animism is closely related to totemism, which in turn was important in the clan (and later tribal) system of ancient Korea. Primitive man often did not regard himself as something apart from the natural world, but as a creature like other creatures. Hence it was possible for him to believe that his clan was descended from an animal or a bird, or even a heavenly body like the sun or the moon, as already mentioned. Thus many ancient legends which have come down to us describe various clans as being descended from bears, horses, birds, and so on. These creatures were therefore regarded by clan members as sacred, and there were various taboos to be observed in connection with them.

Animism led to the development of shamanism. The word *shaman* is Siberian, and designates a person supposed to have especially intimate contact with or power over the spirits. Shamans are found in many primitive societies, both ancient and modern. In Korea they appeared fairly early. It is possible, for example, that the *ch'on'gun* priests mentioned in connection with the Han clans may have had a shamanistic function. The early shamans may thus have been men, although later Korean custom confined the practice to women, as it does to this day.

The ancient clans appear to have been mostly exogamous, prohibiting marriage within the clan. This ancient practice, which has also persisted until modern times, was one of the factors which mitigated the strife between rival clans, and helped to form the tribal society which was the next stage of Korean social development.

Chapter 2

The Formation of Tribal Society

The frequent peaceful contacts between clans resulting from exogamy led to a gradual softening of the fierce exclusiveness which had at first characterized them. Exchange of technological information and ideas, especially in the vital areas of farming and fishing, began to take place. Gradually, larger regional groups began to emerge, each composed of several clans.

This process was accelerated by the arrival of bronze-making from Siberia by way of Manchuria. The appearance of bronze weapons especially enabled certain clans to dominate others, so that the formation of tribes was also characterized by the emergence of a ruling class.

The bronze techniques thus introduced were not those of ancient China, where bronze-making had been known since well before 1,000 B. C., but the Scytho-Siberian techniques, which had developed among the tribes of central and north Asia. Moreover, bronze tools did not immediately replace stone. Stone agricultural implements continued to be used for a considerable period, bronze being reserved for weapons and ceremonial objects.

With the beginning of the bronze age in Korea, a new kind of pottery emerges, replacing the earlier combware. Called undecorated earthenware from its plainness, it was made of the same sticky clay mixed with fine gravel which was used for the northern combware of the previous period. The pots were ovoids with flat but very small bottoms, which gave them a rather unsteady look.

There is a possibility that the undecorated earthenware represents a different culture, and hence a different group of people, from that represented by combware. Whereas combware is found mostly along the coasts, undecorated earthenware is found mostly in the mountainous interior of the peninsula. The earliest examples were produced in about the seventh or sixth century B. C., by which time the undecorated earthenware people had developed agriculture. They made their dwellings like the combware people, by digging caves in the hillsides, but added an outer extension by erecting posts at the entrance to support a tent-like roof. Rice culture had been introduced from China by this time, as the many agricultural implements found on undecorated earthenware sites testify.

The development of tribal communities and the consequent emergence of ruling classes was not at first universal in Korea. Clans such as the Tong-Okcho and Ye on the eastern coast and Han in the south remained unaffiliated with tribes. Moreover, the clans did not disappear, but continued to function as units within the tribe.

Since bronze culture was first introduced in the north, it was in this area that tribal communities first developed, and hence genuine political institutions first appeared. Koguryo, which became the first of the three kingdoms of Korea, was one such northern tribe, as was Puyo, which gave its name to the capital of the Paekche kingdom.

One strong indication of the development of a ruling class is the appearance of dolmens in the bronze age. Dolmens are found in many primitive cultures, and have mostly been used as tombs. Typically, they consist of boulders or stone slabs laid out in a rectangular pattern, with a flat stone slab on top. There are two types in Korea, the southern type, which is rather low, often a simple slab without supporting stones, and the northern type, which uses large, flat stones of some height and a flat covering stone, so that it is larger and more definite in shape than the southern type.

Dolmens have usually been used as tombs for important persons. Curiously enough, human remains have never been found in Korean dolmens, although numerous artifacts, mostly small ornaments, tools and the like, presumably the personal possessions of the dead person, have been found in them. In any case, the existence of these structures, difficult and time-consuming to build and serving no practical purpose, is good evidence of the rise of a ruling class able to command the energies of the population for its own ends. Almost a hundred of these dolmens have been discovered along the upper reaches of the rivers that empty into the Yellow Sea. The earliest ones are estimated to have been built in the third century B. C. Menhirs, free-standing monoliths, are also found in considerable numbers throughout the country, some of them in association with dolmens.

Also dating from the tribal period are stone-box tombs, often containing Scytho-Siberian style copper and bronze artifacts. The stone-box type of burial may well have come to Korea by way of southern Manchuria.

The distribution of the dolmens and other structures indicates, as might have been expected, that tribes and ruling classes first emerged in the north, and hence it was in the north that larger political units, the tribal leagues, first emerged.

Chapter 3

The Tribal Leagues

I. Ancient Choson

It must be remembered that the line of the Tumen and Yalu Rivers has not always formed the northern limit of Korea. This was especially true in the ancient period with which we have now to deal.

As has already been stated, bronze culture first appeared in the north, and stimulated the development of tribes, and subsequently of tribal leagues. The first of these, now called Ancient Choson (to distinguish it from *Choson,* the name later used to designate Korea as a whole), dominated the territory between the Liao River in southern Manchuria and the Taedong River in central north Korea. The dominant clan, which hence furnished most of the rulers, was the bear totem family, whose legendary founder was Tan'gun-wanggom, the mythical progenitor of the Korean people.

Ancient Choson came into being during the fourth century B.C., and appears to have remained powerful until about the end of the third. It was thus contemporary with the Warring States period in China, which persisted until all China was unified by the Ch'in dynasty about 220 B.C. Ancient Choson was evidently on a par with at least some of these states, for ancient records show that it was able to compete successfully with the state of Yen, just to the west of the Liao River and hence its neighbor.

Taking the Chinese title of King, the ruler of Ancient Choson forestalled an attack by Yen forces and was able to consolidate his power in the Liao River basin.

The rise of the Huns, or Hsiung-nu, a group of nomadic tribes from the steppes of northern Asia, created a new situation in the Korean peninsula. These tribes became roughly unified during the Warring States period in China, and began pressing down into Manchuria and raiding the Chinese border states. This situation resulted in numerous refugees pouring southward through Manchuria and into Korea. These dislocations continued until China was unified under the short-lived Ch'in and subsequent Han dynasties.

Although Ancient Choson had at first been successful in resisting the attacks of Yen, the advantage ultimately passed to the attackers. Finally Ch'in K'ai, a general serving under King Chao of Yen (312–279 B.C.) succeeded in wresting the Liao River basin from Ancient Choson and annexing it to Yen.

One factor in the ability of the Chinese states to resist the Hsiung-nu and to defeat neighboring states such as Ancient Choson was the introduction of iron. Iron-using spread from China proper to the northern areas during the fourth and third centuries B.C., reaching Korea at about this time. Its route is fairly clear from the Yen coins that have been discovered at various sites between the Liao River and northwestern Korea. Ironware was thus not introduced into Korea by sea, but from the north, following the courses of the Yalu, Ch'ongch'on and Taedong Rivers.

Iron quickly replaced bronze in Ancient Choson in both weapons and tools and the refugee groups who brought it from the north established themselves as part of the ruling class. This ruling class rode horse-drawn coaches, and used iron swords and bows and arrows. Moreover, their bronze weapons were not mere imitations of those the Koreans had first seen, but original, unique designs peculiar to Korea.

This mixed iron and bronze culture of northwestern Korea spread southward both by land and by sea, mixing with the undecorated earthenware culture of inland Korea and ultimately reaching Japan, where it contributed to the so-called Yayoi culture in that country.

Partly owing to the introduction of iron, this was a period of significant change in the ancient Koreans' mode of life. The hillside and river-bank dugouts in which they had formerly lived were gradually giving place to wooden houses which their new iron tools made comparatively easy to build. At the same time, *ondol*, the unique Korean heating system, was being developed. The *ondol* system consists of parallel flues under a stone floor, leading from a fireplace on one side of the room to a chimney on the other.

Burial customs were also changing. The use of dolmens died out, and in their place two new kinds of burial appeared. The *t'ogwang-myo* seems to have been simply a mound of earth covering the corpse. The *onggwan-myo*, of which some examples have survived, consisted of several ceramic pot-shaped sections fitted together to form a coffin.

It was during this period that Korea began to be influenced significantly by events in China. Since this Chinese influence was to become all-pervasive and was to continue down to modern times, it will frequently be necessary, in order to understand Korean history, to refer to China. Let us now turn our attention to events in that country during the period under consideration.

It will be recalled that Ancient Choson appeared during the era known in Chinese history as the Warring States period. The Chou dynasty had lost all real political power some centuries before the appearance of Ancient Choson, and China had broken up into several rival kingdoms in a state of chronic conflict. Toward the end of the third century B.C., one of these states, Ch'in, managed to conquer all the others, and China was once more unified.

This new unity did not last long, however. Ch'in rule was harsh and cruel and the old kingdoms still yearned for independence. The first Ch'in emperor made the mistake of ordering the destruction of all the Confucian classics, an action for which he has been execrated by Chinese historians ever since. When he died and his son succeeded him, many of the kingdoms rose in revolt.

Out of the resulting political chaos arose the Han dynasty, founded by one of the leaders of the marauding armies that had first defeated the Ch'in government and then fought each other for supremacy. But the Han dynasty did not have an easy time either. The new emperor made many of his henchmen rulers of the old kingdoms, and it was not very long before several of them felt an itch for independence. This time, however, the new government was able to crush the revolts that followed.

The significance of all this for Korea was that several of these revolts against Han occurred in northern states within easy reach of the peninsula. When the revolts were crushed, refugees from the states of Yen (which we have encountered before), Ch'i and Chao poured into Ancient Choson. Among these refugees was one Wiman (Wei Man in Chinese), who had been in the service of the state of Yen. He was evidently a person of some importance, and is said to have brought about a thousand followers with him.

Chun, the king of Ancient Choson, at first attempted to neutralize this alien force within his kingdom by making Wiman the military defender of his western border. Wiman, however, took advantage of this appointment to gather strength among the refugees until he was powerful

enough to usurp the throne around 190 B.C. King Chun
fled southward to the state of Chin, where he called himself
King Han.

It may be appropriate here to clear up a rather confusing
matter of nomenclature. We have already had occasion to
mention certain clans of southern Korea who called themselves "Han." This word *Han* has been used at various times
to designate Korea, and is a part of the proper name of the
present republic—*Taehan Min'guk,* "Great Han People's
Country." It is a different word from the *Han* used to
designate the Chinese dynasty we have just been discussing,
and is written with a different Chinese character.

One of the factors which enabled Wiman to seize power
was, of course, the superior iron weapons which the refugees
brought with them. But this alone would not have enabled
him to establish firm control of the country. Ancient Choson had been expanding just prior to Wiman's usurpation,
and several clans had recently come under its control. It
seems likely that Wiman and his followers made common
cause with the patriarchs of these clans in their revolt
against the king. Wiman would thus have had loyal
followers among the Korean population of Ancient Choson, so that his rule was at least partly supported by his
subjects and thus did not appear completely alien.

At the time of Wiman's usurpation, the newly-founded
Han dynasty was fully occupied, not only with internal
revolt but also with serious incursions by the nomadic
Hsiung-nu. The Han emperor was in no position to extend
his power over neighboring states, and was in fact obliged
to seek their help against the barbarians. Wiman was thus
able to secure military and economic support from the
Han empire, which helped him both to solidify his control
of Ancient Choson and to conquer some of the neighboring
tribes.

Although Ancient Choson was culturally more advanced

1. Ruins of Ondol Floor Heating System: Made of stone. Songp'yong-dong, Unggi-up, North Hamgyong Province. Prehistoric period.

2. Dolmen: Unyul-gun, Hwanghae Province. H. about 2.4m, L. about 6.1m. Prehistoric period.

3. Paleolithic Artifacts: Later Paleolithic period. (a) Felstone and quartz porphyry. Rolled gravel pebble. 94.6mm × 79.4mm × 60mm. (b) Flake. Rolled gravel pebble. 73.2mm × 158.3mm × 38.8mm.

4. Neolithic Artifacts: Excavated in North Hamgyong Province. A little less than a third actual size. Prehistoric period, not earlier than 1000 B.C.

5. *Earthenware:* Neolithic period. (a) Combware pot. (b) Undec-orated earthenware. (c) Red-painted earthenware, surface whetted.

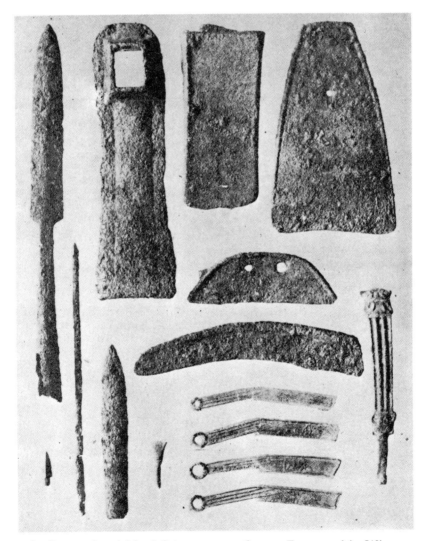

6. *Dagger-shaped Metal Coins, Iron and Copper:* Excavated in Wiwon, North P'yongan Province. (Bottom) Dagger-shaped metal coins of ancient China. Tribal period, 3rd-4th century B.C. (Upper left) Copper arrowhead. (Upper right) Iron axe.

7. *Mortuary Slabs Portraying Tan'gun Legend:*
Tomb of Wu Liang-tz'u, Shantung Province,
China. Han dynasty, 206 B.C. to A.D. 220.
H. 1.4m, L. 1.12m.

8. *Eight-pronged Ornament:*
Copper. Excavated from
the Naktong River basin.
About half actual size.
Tribal period, 1st-3rd cen-
tury B.C.

10. *Belt Hooks:* Bronze. Excavated in North
Kyongsang Province. L. horse 16.5cm; tiger
20.3cm. Tribal period, 1st-3rd century B.C.
National Museum of Korea.

9. *Mirror:* Bronze. Excavated in South Ch'ungch'ong
Province. D. 11.4cm. Tribal period, 1st-3rd century
B.C.

than other tribal communities in Korea, particularly in its use of bronze and iron, its political and social institutions remained primitive, so far as we can tell. Information concerning customs and daily life is scanty. Some records mention eight laws, of which three are actually recorded: murderers were punished by immediate execution; the victim's family had to be compensated in grain by the murderer's family; and thieves were made to serve the owners of the property they stole as slaves. Prohibitions of adultery, sacrilege and witchcraft may also have been observed.

These laws are evidence of a considerable development since the days of the primitive clans. The old communal life is gone, as is shown by the laws concerning thievery. The concept of private property is firmly established, and this means the formation of social classes and a widening gulf between rich and poor. The "laws" mentioned, however, should not be thought of as part of a fully developed legal system. They came out of tribal custom and were deduced by the observers who recorded them rather than having been consciously established as laws in the modern sense.

Wiman and his descendants were able to enjoy peaceful rule of Ancient Choson for over eighty years. During the reign of his grandson Ugo, however, the political situation in China again began to affect Korea.

The Han empire had by this time become firmly established. The internal rebellions which had plagued its earlier years had been successfully suppressed, and the imperial government was now ready to attempt a permanent solution to the problem of the Hsiung-nu nomads, who remai ed a constant threat to China's frontiers. The Han emperor of the time, whose reign title was Wu Ti ("martial emperor") mounted a series of large-scale military expeditions deep into Hsiung-nu territory to crush the military power of the nomads once and for all.

One way to control the barbarians, the Wu Ti emperor saw, was to outflank their territory by seizing control of northern Korea. When Ancient Choson attempted to monopolize trade with the Han empire, denying it to the southern Korean tribes, the emperor took advantage of the dispute by sending an army to invade the peninsula. In 109 B.C. an army of sixty thousand men and a navy of seven thousand attacked Wanggom-song, the capital.

This attack was successfully beaten off and the Han forces were obliged to retire. But the Wu Ti emperor was a determined man, and the following year a second expedition was sent against Ancient Choson, and this succeeded. The Korean forces surrendered and Wiman's grandson Ugo was assassinated.

The new rulers proceeded to organize the conquered territory into counties, in an attempt to integrate it into the administrative system of the Han empire. The counties were then subdivided into prefectures, and Chinese officials placed in control. The four counties were named Nangnang, Chinbon, Imdun and Hyont'o.

This attempt to integrate conquered northwestern Korea into China was, for the most part, unsuccessful. Of the four new counties, three were presently abandoned, and only one, Nangnang (Lo-lang in Chinese) achieved any real permanence, lasting until 313 A.D. Not even the exact locations of the others are definitely known, and we have only an approximate notion of the boundaries of Nangnang. Some scholars assert that the four colonies were all within Korea proper, north of the Han River. But it seems more logical to suppose that they coincided with the territory of Ancient Choson, which would put them partly in northwestern Korea, and partly in the Liaotung peninsula and the Liao River basin.

It is significant that even thus early in their history,

before the concept of nationhood had had time to develop, the Koreans put up such a strenuous resistance to foreign domination. Even then, the tribal communities seem to have been firmly organized and not amenable to alien customs or methods. Even after they were conquered, the people of Ancient Choson and of the other communities in the peninsula continued to resist, so that it was only with the greatest difficulty that the Chinese maintained their foothold in Nangnang, and they were gradually forced to abandon their other counties, Chinbon and Imdun in 82 B.C. and Hyont'o in 75 B.C.

Another problem confronting the Chinese authorities was migration. Since they were unable to oust the Chinese conquerors by force, thousands of the people of Ancient Choson went south, to the area then dominated by the Han tribes. (It will be recalled that this Han is different from the name of the Chinese dynasty.)

The fortunes of Nangnang, naturally enough, fluctuated with the fortunes of the Han dynasty. In the confusion attendant upon its fall, at the end of the third century A.D. a family named Kung-sun, from the Liaotung district, took over Nangnang and attempted to rule it as an independent kingdom. They even attempted to expand their territory, establishing Taebang-gun to the south in 204 A.D.

The Kung-sun family was able to do this because the Chinese administration had become largely ineffective, owing to political chaos at home. Officials from the central government were very frequently changed. Finally the Later Han dynasty ceased to exist altogether, and China was divided into three kingdoms. The northernmost of these, the state of Wei, destroyed the Kung-sun family and took over the rule of Nangnang. But Wei itself was eventually overthrown, and a successor-state named Chin assumed power.

The constant political turmoil in China and consequent frequent shift of rulers in Nangnang weakened Chinese control of the colony. At the same time the power of the Koguryo tribes in the northeast was rapidly growing, and they began to exert pressure on the Chinese rulers. Open conflict broke out, and in 313 A.D. the Koguryo tribes routed the Chinese and put an end to their 400-year rule of Ancient Choson. The Chinese retreated into Manchuria.

The establishment of a Chinese administration in the territory of Ancient Choson was facilitated by the fact that many Chinese already lived there. It will be recalled that Wiman was himself Chinese, or at any rate had served the government of a Chinese state, and that he brought many followers with him. In addition, as we have already noted, numerous political refugees had entered Ancient Choson at various times during the Warring States period in China. There was thus a considerable number of people in the country familiar with Chinese methods of administration.

Perhaps one of the reasons for the survival of Nangnang even after the other colonies had been abandoned was that it enjoyed the best communications with China, both by land and by sea. Nangnang was thus the center of Chinese culture and influence in Korea at this time. To it came Chinese administrators, merchants, and even scholars and intellectuals, and through it the political, economic and cultural power of China was implanted in Korea.

The county-and-prefecture bureaucratic administration of China in Ancient Choson, which was still at the relatively primitive tribal stage of development, proved a highly effective method of exploitation. Many clan patriarchs were metamorphosed into Chinese petty officials, and thus became supporters of the regime. Leaders of the (Korean) Han tribes of the south were also offered posts or bribes, and many of them accepted, thus weakening the resistance of their people to Chinese rule.

But emigration to areas not under Chinese rule continued, and outlying areas where Chinese authority was weak were frequently attacked and the Chinese officials killed or driven away. This resistance, in turn, led to very strict regulations for the protection of Chinese lives and property. Ancient sources, which mention "eight prohibitions" (laws) as constituting the legal system of the kingdom of Ancient Choson, also mention "sixty prohibitions" as being observed under Chinese rule, an indication of the increase of legal complexities, and probably of Chinese efforts to control the local population.

One of the chief aims of the Chinese government of Nangnang appears to have been economic exploitation. Fish, salt, iron, timber and farm products were exacted from the Koreans for local use or for shipment to China. Forced labor, often used by Chinese governments, was imposed on the Koreans, one ancient record telling of a labor force of 1,500 men drafted to cut timber in the Han region south of the colony. Chinese merchants also went south, and we hear of iron being supplied from Pyon-han, one of the divisions of the Han tribes. Salt and iron had long been government monopolies in China, and these commodities were so regarded in Nangnang.

The Chinese officials in Nangnang appear to have lived a comfortable, even luxurious life. They brought with them all the customs and techniques of ancient Chinese culture and created, in effect, a miniature Chinese society on the far fringe of the empire. This can be seen especially in the tombs they built. Many of these are to be found in the neighborhood of the city of P'yongyang, which some scholars claim was the capital of the colony. Personal ornaments of gold and silver filigree and exquisite lacquerware were buried in the tombs, either of wood or brick. Objects of this sort from the Han dynasty period are extremely rare even in China itself, and the materials from the Nangnang tombs are thus of great value to students of ancient China.

Chinese culture and social institutions appear to have had little impact on the general population of Korea at this time. But technology was another matter, and the metal-working techniques of the Chinese spread rapidly throughout the peninsula. This had the effect of strengthening the tribal communities outside the area of Chinese domination. This was especially true in the north, where tribal leagues like that of Ancient Choson were well established. The Han tribes of the south seem to have lagged behind somewhat, and the formation of tribal leagues was still in its early stages there. Nevertheless, copper swords, iron implements and Chinese coins have been found as far south as the Kimhae district near the southeast coast, indicating the nationwide dissemination of Chinese metal culture.

Stimulated by the Chinese example and strengthened by the new technology, the tribal communities bordering the Chinese colonies began to develop into integrated political units.

II. Puyo

The group of tribes known collectively as Puyo first appears in historical records living on the vast fertile plains along the Sungari River in northern Manchuria. Nothing is known of its origins, although Chinese records mention a foundation myth which indicates that the Puyo people came from even farther north. By the first century A.D. Puyo had become a considerable tribal power, ranking with the Koguryo tribes to the south of it.

Unlike some of the other tribal groups on the frontier, Puyo appears to have sought friendly relations with the Chinese Han dynasty as a means of self-preservation. Puyo had the Hsien-pei tribes to its north, and Koguryo to the south, with both of whom it was in chronic contention. Support from the powerful Chinese helped to fend off its rivals and at the same time was insurance against Chinese attack. According to Chinese records, the Puyo leader used the Chinese title of king when he dispatched an envoy to the Chinese court in 49 A.D. Use of this title implied that the leader placed himself in a position of subordination to the Chinese emperor. The Puyo policy of conciliation led another leader to visit the court of the Later Han in person, and another took as his wife the eldest daughter of the Kung-sun family at the time when the Kung-sun had taken control of Liaotung.

This policy enabled Puyo to survive for a time, but after the fall of the Chinese Han conflicting groups grew so numerous that it was impossible to conciliate them all. The Chinese state of Wei attacked Koguryo in 244 A.D. but was persuaded by Puyo to make an alliance when offered supplies for its troops. In 285 the Hsien-pei tribes of the north attacked Puyo and were only beaten off with the help of the Chinese Chin state. But it was unable to repel the Hsien-pei when they again attacked in 346 A.D. and carried off 50,000 prisoners, including the Puyo leader. This was really the end of Puyo as an independent power. When the Hsien-pei later declined it became dependent on Koguryo, whose power was then growing. Finally, in 494 A.D., all the leading families of Puyo migrated voluntarily to Koguryo territory and put themselves under the rule and protection of the Koguryo leaders. Thus, after a relatively brief period as a powerful tribal league, Puyo was absorbed by the kingdom of Koguryo and ceased to exist.

Like that of Ancient Choson, the basic unit of the Puyo tribal league was the clan. Clans were grouped into tribes of varying size and power, and ultimately, under the stimulus of metal culture and pressure from the Chinese and from neighboring groups, into a tribal league.

But there is an interesting difference. Whereas Ancient Choson and the other tribal groupings of the Korean peninsula were mostly dependent on agriculture, the Puyo people appear to have been engaged to a considerable extent in stock-raising, indicating a relationship with the nomadic tribes of north and central Asia. One indication of this dependence on animals is the titles of tribal leaders. The common designation for a tribal leader was *ka*. Each individual leader had a distinguishing suffix. Some of the common ones were *ma* ("horse") *ka, u* ("cow") *ka, cho* ("pig") *ka,* and *ku* ("dog") *ka.* The names of the animals which were vital to the tribes' survival were thus embodied in the titles of their leaders.

One of these tribal leaders took the title of king, as previously mentioned. But this title seems to have been used only out of deference to the Chinese. For domestic purposes the title had no special significance, and the person so designated had no administrative organization and no power over his fellow tribal leaders.

While the tribal leaders controlled matters of concern to the tribal league as a whole, such as war, migration, and so on, the everyday life of the people was controlled by the patriarchs of the clans composing each tribe. Their power appears to have been absolute, the clan members under them being little better than slaves.

And indeed, slavery was a Puyo institution. Most of the slaves, as in other tribal communities, were either prisoners of war or criminals. While the number of slaves in Puyo at any given time is unknown, it must have been considerable. When a clan patriarch or other important person died, it was customary to execute his slaves, presumably so that they could continue to serve him in the spirit world. As many as a hundred slaves are recorded to have been executed at one time, indicating that slaves must have formed a fairly high proportion of the population.

Crime and punishment were much the same as in other tribal groups. Murderers were put to death and their families enslaved. Adulterers both male and female, and also jealous women, were executed and their bodies left unburied on mountainsides. Thieves, when apprehended, had to pay their victims twelve times the value of the things they stole. These legal customs show the growth in Puyo of the institutions of private property, slavery, and patriarchal rule. There is also evidence that polygamy was practiced. A significant difference from the other tribal groups of Korea was the practice of a younger brother marrying his deceased elder brother's wife, perhaps a survival from primitive times.

We have already noted that the Puyo people depended to some extent on stock-raising and may have been related to the stock-raising nomads of north Asia. Agriculture, however, was also firmly established among them, as we can see from the fact that, like most of the people of East Asia, they had an annual harvest festival. This took place during the first month of the lunar year. Besides ceremonies of thanksgiving to the gods for the harvest, there was much singing and dancing, which continued for several days. Prisoners were granted amnesty at this time, and criminals were sentenced.

Questions concerning the community as a whole, such as war and peace, were decided by a general council of the tribes. In reaching their decisions, the Puyo people often sought the guidance of spirits. Sometimes they would sacrifice a cow or a bull and examine the body. The state of the hooves especially was held to be an omen.

Puyo thus managed to reach the tribal league stage of development as its neighbors of Ancient Choson and Koguryo had done, but was absorbed by Koguryo before it was able to develop into a kingdom.

III. Koguryo

The Koguryo tribes lived in the mountain valleys forming the Tongga River basin to the north of the middle course of the Yalu River. This was one of the principal routes by which bronze and later iron culture entered the peninsula, so that the Koguryo tribes were among the first to practice metal working. Their country was rough and mountainous, with little land suitable for agriculture. They had to eke out what few crops they could grow by hunting, and probably by some judicious banditry. In any case, they soon gained a reputation as skilled horsemen and courageous fighters.

During most of their existence, the Koguryo tribes were in more or less continuous contact with Han dynasty China, and most of this contact was hostile. As early as 128 B.C. a Chinese colony called Ch'anghae had to be abandoned because of Koguryo invasions. Similar events occurred at later times, as we shall see. It is most noteworthy that the Chinese were never able to subdue or conquer Koguryo, as they did Ancient Choson.

The legendary founder of Koguryo was believed to be a man named Chumong, said to have been the leader of one of the Puyo tribes which came south in ancient times. The origins of Koguryo are thus closely connected in legend with Puyo, perhaps as a consequence of Koguryo's absorption of Puyo in historical times, as has been previously pointed out. Also mentioned in connection with Koguryo's origins are the tribes of Ye and Maek, believed to have been the builders of many of the dolmens in Koguryo territory. They were probably the more prominent of the tribes that formed the Koguryo league.

Surrounded by Puyo in the north, Ilou in the northeast, and the Chinese colonies in the west, the Koguryo tribes often had to struggle for existence. Short of vital foodstuffs in their own territory, Koguryo developed warfare as a way of life, becoming at least partly dependent on conquest for daily necessities. This led, as noted above, to frequent clashes with the Chinese colonies that had been established after the conquest of Ancient Choson. One of the three colonies that the Chinese were forced to abandon, Hyont'o, collapsed in 75 B.C. as a result of Koguryo pressure.

When the usurper Wang Mang came to power in China at the close of the Former Han dynasty in 8 A.D., he asked the help of Koguryo in subduing the perpetually troublesome Hsiung-nu. Koguryo not only refused this request, but took hostile action against the Chinese. This occurred during the period (53–146? A.D.) traditionally designated as the reign of T'aejo (a title, not a name), who is recorded as the sixth king of Koguryo, when the tribal league was beginning to emerge as a kingdom, with a fully organized government.

Five core tribes dominated the Koguryo tribal league: Kyeru, Sono, Cholno, Sunno and Kwanno. In the early period of its existence, the ruler of the league was usually the head of the Sono tribe, but later, as it grew more powerful, the Kyeru tribe succeeded in placing its heads in the top position. This appears to have happened during the transitional period, the reign of T'aejo already mentioned.

Some of the titles of tribe leaders and leaders of the tribal league have been recorded. As in Puyo, the syllable *ka* suffixed to a name designated the head of a tribe. All the patriarchs of a tribe which had contributed a league leader in the past, and also those of the tribe of the wife of the contemporary leader were entitled to call themselves *Koch'u-ka*. The league leader and the heads of powerful tribes had three sorts of *kasin* ("family vassal") called *Saja, Choui* and *Sonin*. Clan patriarchs of the ordinary sort were called *Sang-ka*. These various designations would seem to indicate the development of a rudimentary sort of administrative organization.

As the tribal league developed into a kingdom, a kind of central official hierarchy began to appear, a group of officials with specialized functions directly under the league leader. The titles *P'aeja, Taero, Chubu* and *Udae,* designating these officials, are evidence of this. The highest post in this hierarchy was *Tae* ("great") *daero,* comparable in some ways to the modern prime minister. This post appears at first to have been elective, although what the voting qualifications were is not clear. Subsequently, power struggles often broke out among the tribes over the post.

The preoccupation of the Koguryo tribes with war and conquest is reflected in their social structure. League leader, tribal leaders and clan patriarchs functioned like a military chain of command, with the clan forming the basic military unit. We hear of patriarchs with as many as 10,000 men under their command, with subordinates called *haho.* Military training was more or less constant for all the men of each clan. Menial tasks were left to large numbers of slaves, mostly prisoners of war or criminals. Criminals were judged by a council of clan patriarchs and either executed or enslaved.

Off the battlefield, the life of the aristocracy was luxurious. They dressed in silks imported from China and wore ornaments of gold and silver. Warriors wore feathers in their hats. At death, an aristocrat was buried under a huge mound of earth or a stone pyramid, together with many of his personal possessions.

While Koguryo society was thoroughly patriarchal by historical times, marriage customs retained vestiges of an earlier matriarchal or at any rate matrilocal type of society. Marriages were, of course, arranged by the families of the bride and groom. After the wedding, the bride would remain with her family and the groom would visit her each

night, after securing her parents' consent. Only after the
wife had produced a son and the son had grown to maturity
did she leave her family and join her husband's clan.

Like the Puyo tribes, the Koguryo tribes celebrated an
annual harvest festival. It was called *tongmaeng* and was
celebrated in October. The people of each tribe gathered
for music and dancing and for religious ceremonies. The
tribes worshipped a legendary progenitor of the Koguryo
people called Tongmyong. Interestingly enough, they are
also said to have worshipped the male organ, which they
called *Susin*.

Each clan and tribe, of course, had its own founder and
ancestors to worship, and various family shrines were
established for these rites. As the tribal league developed
into a kingdom with a hereditary monarch, the worship of
a national founder also developed, complete with a national
shrine.

The culture and customs of Puyo and Koguryo appear to
have been quite similar. According to the Chinese writers
who are our chief source of information for this early
period, however, their temperament, character and out-
look were quite different.

IV.   The Tribes of the East and South

The power of Koguryo did not extend as far as the east
coast during the period of the tribal leagues. The inhabitants of this area, however, roughly the modern provinces
of Hamgyong and Kangwon, strongly resembled the
Koguryo tribes in language, food, dwellings, clothing,
manners and customs.

Two tribes dominated the area. To the north, around the
plain of Hamhung lived the Okcho tribe. Further to the
south, in the vicinity of the present city of Wonsan and
Anbyon county the Tong-Ye tribe was found. Evidence for
the close relationship between these tribes and the Koguryo

tribes is strong. Textiles produced by the Okcho, for instance, were called *Maek-p'o* (*Maek* textiles), recalling the name of the Maek tribe which was one of the early Koguryo groups. Similarly, *Tong-Ye* simply means "Eastern Ye," recalling the name of the other early Koguryo tribe. It seems fairly certain, then, that these two tribes were offshoots of the early Koguryo group.

Social development in these tribes lagged behind that of Koguryo. Clans retained a large degree of their independence and exclusiveness, and persons encroaching on the territory of rival clans were enslaved and their families made to pay compensation in cows and horses. The concept of private property was as yet undeveloped, and money was unknown. There was tribal law of a rudimentary sort, and murderers were executed. Patriarchs in these tribes sometimes had Chinese rank-titles, derived possibly from the *kun-hyon* (county and prefecture) system of the Chinese colony to the west.

Living near the ocean, these tribes practiced a mixed economy of fishing and farming. Okcho, whose territory was relatively fertile, had a more highly developed argiculture than Tong-Ye, which inhabited a more mountainous area and thus was more dependent on fishing. The horse had been domesticated, but these tribes did not use cavalry in warfare as did Koguryo. A certain amount of trade was carried on in hemp cloth, fish, salt, and seaweed from Okcho and in sealskins and birch bows from Tong-Ye, which also bred a type of small horse called *Kwahama*.

The marriage and funeral customs of Okcho differed considerably from those of Koguryo. The parents of a son would adopt a girl of about ten and bring her up in their house until she was old enough to be married. But after the marriage she was sent to her parents, and the groom had to pay a bride-price to get her back. This custom persisted until recent times.

When a man died, his body was placed in a temporary grave and left there until the flesh had completely disappeared. Then the bones were dug up and buried in a wooden box which also contained the bones of other members of the family.

Mostly isolated from the cultural developments in the west and north, these tribes remained on a rather primitive level until they were absorbed by the kingdoms which developed from the old tribal leagues. While the ultimate fate of Tong-Ye is vague, Okcho submitted to Koguryo during the second half of the first century A.D. The tribes retained many primitive customs longer than their more developed neighbors, and there is no record of a money economy ever having developed.

The tribes south of the Han River were the last in Korea to be affected by the metal culture spreading from the continent. Bronze and iron began appearing in the south during the fourth and third centuries B.C. Perhaps owing to the late date, there are no distinct bronze and iron ages in this area, the two metals being found side by side. It was also during this period that the modified southern style of dolmen was used. Tribal communities were formed as a result of this stimulus, but never developed into strong tribal leagues.

At the time when Wiman seized control of Ancient Choson during the second century B.C., the area south of the Han was known simply as the Chin State. The most powerful of its tribes, though its name is not recorded, inhabited an area called Mokchi-guk or Wolchi-guk. Little is known about it except that from time to time it received large influxes of people from the north. It has been explained that when Wiman usurped the throne of King Chun, the King fled south and called himself King Han. It is also recorded that a tribe of some two thousand households left Ancient Choson for Chin after some difficulty with Ugo,

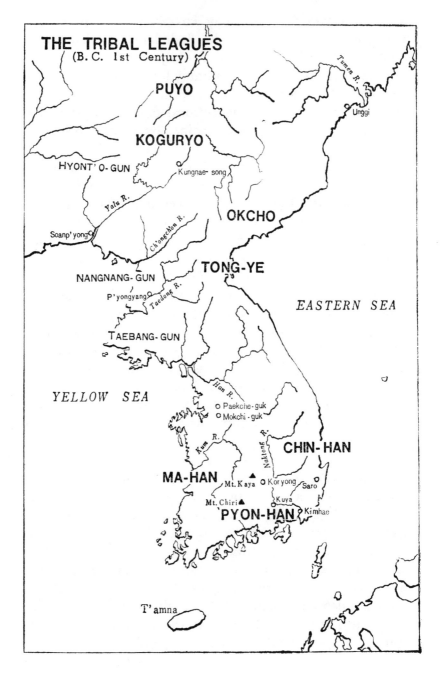

THE TRIBAL LEAGUES
(B.C. 1st Century)

PUYO

KOGURYO

HYONT'O-GUN

Kungnae-song

Yalu R.

Ch'ongchon R.

OKCHO

Soanp'yong

TONG-YE

NANGNANG-GUN

P'yongyang

Taedong R.

TAEBANG-GUN

EASTERN SEA

YELLOW SEA

Han R.

Paekche-guk

Mokchi-guk

Kum R.

Naktong R.

CHIN-HAN

MA-HAN

Mt. Kaya

Koryong

Saro

Mt. Chiri

Kuya

Kimhae

PYON-HAN

T'amna

Tumen R.

Unggi

Wiman's grandson. And after Ancient Choson was conquered and colonized by Han China, not a few people fled south to escape Chinese rule.

The chieftains of the southern tribes appear to have been very active in importing and adopting the bronze and iron cultures of the north as a means of consolidating and extending their power. Roughly from the fourth or third century B.C. to the third century A.D., the tribal powers gradually grew in power and eventually formed tribal leagues, though very weak ones. These were traditionally called by Koreans the Sam Han ("three Hans"): Ma-han, Chin-han and Pyon-han.

Ma-han held the territory south of the Han River and along the west coast. Chin-han was along the eastern Naktong River and Pyon-han along the western Naktong. Information concerning numbers and sizes of tribes is somewhat vague and difficult to interpret, but rough estimates of comparative sizes can be formed. Ma-han is said to have consisted of some fifty tribes, Chin-han of twelve and Pyon-han of twelve. The largest tribe in Ma-han is recorded as having consisted of about 100,000 households and the smallest of several thousand. In both Chin-han and Pyon-han the largest tribes had about four or five thousand households and the smallest some six or seven hundred.

While details of their development are not known, these three tribal leagues were defintely in existence by the third century A.D. When the Chinese state of Wei attempted to invade the Samhan territory after a successful attack upon Koguryo and Tong-Ye, Ma-han dared to attack Taebanggun, a dependency of the Nangnang colony then controlled by Wei. Although the attack failed, it shows that Ma-han was strong enough to compete with the Chinese colonies. Later in the third century, moreover, both Ma-han and Chin-han made direct contact with Chin, which had supplanted Wei, and opened trade relations.

The most powerful of the Pyon-han tribes were the six inhabiting the Kaya area west of the Naktong River. This area is isolated from the rest of the peninsula by Mt. Chiri in the east and Mt. Kaya in the north. These tribes appear to have been formed between the first and third centuries and to have developed into a tribal league after the third century. The Kuya tribe, which lived in the Kimhae district on the lower Naktong eventually came to be called Kumgwan-Kaya or Pon-Kaya ("Main Kaya"), which seems to indicate that it was the most powerful of the six. A rival for this position was the tribe living in the Koryong district on the middle Naktong, which was called Tae-Kaya ("Great Kaya"). These two tribes, then, were in all probability the basis for the organization of the six Kaya tribes into a tribal league.

In a shell mound which archeologists have excavated in Kimhae, the Pon-Kaya territory, looms, glass, stoneware, daggers, and Chinese coins minted in the reign of the u-surper Wang Mang (14 A.D.) have been found. The mound also yielded carbonized rice grains and bones of wild pigs, deer, cattle, horses, otters, and turtles, as well as the oyster and other shells of which it is composed. The daggers are fairly numerous and are all made of iron, indicating the widespread use of this metal. The nature and date of these relics (third century or thereabouts) indicate that the Sam-han area lagged considerably behind the tribal leagues of the north, although metal culture finally did become widespread, and that the southern tribes had developed rice as a staple crop. The information that Pyon-han sup-plied iron to the Chinese colonies of Nangnang and Tae-bang, and also to Tong-Ye and to Japan, indicates that iron was locally produced.

The lateness of the Kaya league's formation prevented it from developing into a true state. In the middle of the sixth century it was completely overrun and absorbed by the rapidly expanding Silla kingdom.

The formation of the Sam Han tribal leagues seems to have owed a good deal to refugees from the more highly developed north, and there is evidence that the leaders of tribal leagues were occasionally northerners. A Korean legend has it that one of the Puyo tribes fled from Koguryo and settled in the Han River basin. This may have been the Paekche tribe, whose leader the legend identifies as one Onjo. It was this tribe that succeeded in unifying all the tribes of Ma-han to form the ancient kingdom of Paekche.

Among the Chin-han tribes, the most powerful was Saro. Its territory was centered around the present city of Kyong-ju. Its leaders were members of the Kim and Pak families, the Paks being eastern and northern refugees. Uniting with the Sok family, this group of clans headed a tribal league along the southeast coast. The Kims regularly provided the leaders of the league, with the support of six family groups whose names have survived: Kumyang, Saryang, Ponp'i, Muryang, Hanjo and Suppi. Examination of the appellations of leaders at different times shows the change from clans to tribes and eventually to a kingdom. At first the leader was called *kosogan*, meaning "head," then *ch'ach'a-ung*, meaning "shaman," then *isagum*, meaning "successor," and finally *maripkan*, which has the full sense of English *king*. This last development did not take place until the fourth century, much later than parallel developments in the north.

Because the development of tribal communities came later in the south than in the north, and because these communities skipped the bronze age, going directly from stone to iron, they retained many characteristics of the earlier clan stage of development.

Unlike most primitive communities, the Sam Han tribes had seperate officials for religious purposes, the leader or chieftain having secular powers only. Priests called *ch'on'gun* presided over religious rites in *sodo,* sacred areas usually consisting of groves of trees. Each *sodo* was marked by a bell and a drum hung on a big pole, signifying the presence of the gods and showing the boundaries of holy ground. These *sodo* offered fugitives from justice the right of sanctuary, like the churches of medieval Europe. The *ch'on'gun* acted as the representative of the tribe to the gods.

Communal projects such as the construction of fortresses were carried out by the forced labor of the young men of the tribe. Slavery existed pretty much as it did in the north, the slaves being prisoners of war or criminals. Slaves had their hair cut short to differentiate them from freemen. Records mention that among these slaves were numbers of Chinese from the northern colonies who had been caught cutting trees in Chin-han territory.

Rice culture was well established, and silk textiles were produced. Iron was locally mined, smelted, and fashioned into tools and weapons. Iron tools aided in the construction of embankments and reservoirs, necessary for rice farming, and iron weapons stimulated the formation of tribes and tribal leagues, which had lagged behind the north as we have noted.

Customs and manners were more or less uniform throughout Sam Han territory, although the southern part was somewhat more primitive than the north. Chinese observers of the time, applying the standards of their more sophisticated civilization, found the Sam Han people lacking in discipline and morality, and were shocked at the notion of whole families living together in one-room houses of wood or clay, regardless of age and sex. The cave-house of primitive times had by now given way to a sort of log cabin.

The ruling class probably had somewhat more elaborate houses. We know that they dressed in silk, wore leather shoes, and had necklaces and earrings of precious stones. Commoners wore clothes of hemp cloth and straw shoes.

The characteristic Korean topknot had appeared, and our sources also mention the custom of tatooing.

Sam Han burials did not use the *kwak,* the covered coffin of the north. It was customary to bury cows and horses alive with their owner when he died. In the Pyon-han area birds' wings were buried with the body to enable the soul to fly up to heaven, indicating a belief in an afterlife.

There were several religious festivals connected with agriculture. The two most important came in May, before sowing began, and in October, after the harvest, to pray for a rich harvest and to express gratitude for a year of plenty. The people sang and danced, and drank heartily. In the rural areas of Korea these festivals still survive as *suri-ttok* ("Bread of May 5") and *kosa-ttok* ("Bread for Prayer"). Their dates, like those of their ancient prototypes, are, of course, determined by the lunar calendar.

PART TWO

The Ancient Period (I)

Chapter 4

The Formation of the Ancient Kingdoms

Before beginning our discussion of the ancient kingdoms, it is necessary to insert here a note concerning names and dates. The Chinese historians and later the Korean historians, who followed their example, dated events by the reigns of kings or emperors, so that the exact date of the king in question must be established before the date of any given event can be established. Many of the dates given here, particularly the earlier ones, are traditional dates as given in ancient Chinese and native sources, and must be regarded as only approximate.

Following the Chinese practice, the Koreans gave their kings descriptive titles after their deaths. It is by these titles that the kings are known to history, and not by their personal names. Thus, for example, the title T'aejo was applied to one of the early Koguryo kings. It was also the title of the first Koryo king and of the first Yi dynasty king. It is simply the Korean pronunciation of the Chinese expression *T'ai-tsu,* meaning "grand progenitor." We shall use these reign titles in referring to kings in this work, but the reader must bear in mind that the kings were not generally known or addressed by these titles during their lifetimes.

Koguryo was the first of the tribal leagues to mature into a kingdom. It conquered the neighboring tribes one after another, assuming control of Okcho and Tong-Ye on the east coast and absorbing Puyo. The Chinese colony of

41

Hyont'o was overrun, and in 121 there was even an attack on the Liaotung peninsula. By the end of the second century Koguryo was firmly established.

The rising power of Koguryo brought it into repeated clashes with the Chinese colony of Nangnang. The passing of the Chinese Han dynasty had left this colony in a precarious position, and changes of rule were frequent. The Kung-sun family tried to establish a local dynasty, and extended their power southward, establishing the colony of Taebang. They were succeeded by the Chinese state of Wei during the Three Kingdoms period. Both ruling powers collided repeatedly with Koguryo. In 242 King Tongch'on of Koguryo attacked the districts of Soanp'yong and Kuryon-song near the mouth of the Yalu. Two years later, Wei sent a force of 20,000 infantry and cavalry against Koguryo, and, overwhelming the courageous defenders, took the Koguryo capital of Hwando-song, which the Chinese called T'ung-kou. King Tongch'on was forced to flee to the Okcho area, but was able to return and retake his capital the following year. In 313, taking advantage of the weakness of the Chin state, which had supplanted Wei, King Mich'on succeeded in conquering the Chinese colony of Nangnang and its southern extension, Taebang, ending four centuries of Chinese rule in Korea.

But Koguryo now found itself beset on all sides. The state of Chin, which had managed briefly to reunify China, was invaded by barbarian tribes from the north, and its rulers driven as far south as the Yangtze valley, beginning a period known in Chinese history as the Sixteen Kingdoms. Meanwhile, a tribal league in the Ma-han territory south of the Han River had developed into the Paekche kingdom. Koguryo now faced the Earlier Yen state founded by the Hsien-pei barbarians in the northwest, and the new Paekche kingdom in the south.

The Earlier Yen state invaded Koguryo and took its

capital in 342, the twelfth year of King Kogugwon. The Queen and Queen Mother were captured, together with the royal treasury, containing ritual objects handed down from the royal ancestors. More than 50,000 people were captured and taken away to China. In 371 it was the turn of Paekche, which also defeated the Koguryo forces. King Kogugwon was killed during a battle at P'yongyang. In spite of these defeats, Koguryo survived, and was able to regain enough strength to resist pressure from China during the reign of King Sosurim (371–384).

The details of the founding of the Paekche kingdom are not known. We do know that the name *Paekche* was that of a northern tribe which migrated south, probably one of the Puyo tribes. It settled first in Mich'uhol (now Inch'on) and then expanded to Wire, near modern Seoul, dominating all the tribes of the ancient Mokchi-guk area. Finally its power was extended south to the present Kwangju area, by which time it had become a strong tribal league, ruling the Ma-han tribes. It seems likely that the conflicts between the Chinese state of Wei and the southern Han tribes may have had the effect of forcing these tribes into a closer unity during the third century, and Paekche took advantage of the situation to establish its leadership. In any case, by the reign of King Koi (234–285) Paekche emerged as a fully developed kingdom on a par with Koguryo.

The rise of Paekche coincided with the fall to Koguryo of the Chinese colonies of Nangnang and Taebang. The two kingdoms thus faced each other across a common frontier, and the result was war. Under the strong leadership of King Kunch'ogo (346–374) Paekche first established control over the entire Ma-han area and then marched north to attack Koguryo. As we have already seen, P'yongyang was attacked in 371 by Kunch'ogo, at the head of 30,000 troops, and King Kogugwon of Koguryo was killed. Paekche thus extended its power north of the Han River into the present Hwanghae Province. King Kunch'ogo completed the foundation of the Paekche kingdom by securing trade relations with Japan and with the Eastern Chin dynasty which at that time ruled south China.

About the middle of the fourth century, the tribe of Saro, living in the area of the present city of Kyongju, became the founder of the ancient kingdom of Silla. It will be recalled that it was at about this time that the title of the tribal leader was changed to *maripkan*, which has the full meaning of "king." King Naemul (356–401) was the first to receive this appellation, and his reign may be taken as a convenient starting point for the Silla kingdom. Previous to this time the leadership had rotated among the Pak, Sok and Kim families, but after King Naemul it became hereditary in the Kim family, further evidence that the old tribal league had become a kingdom.

A Chinese source adds corroborative evidence. During his reign, Naemul-maripkan sent envoys to the Chinese state of Earlier Ch'in, as did Koguryo. Chinese envoys visited Saro in return, and one of them reported to his sovereign Fu Chien that Saro was no longer the Saro of former times, for it had progressed as rapidly as the Chinese dynasties had changed. Thus even in the eyes of the sophisticated Chinese the Koreans had developed a society and a government worthy of respect.

But Saro was still not strong enough to compete with the Kaya tribal league to the southwest or the rising Paekche kingdom to the west. It therefore attempted to make common cause with Koguryo, and we hear of important personages being sent there as hostages. This alliance proved successful for a time. In 400, for example, Kwang-gaet'o-wang, the king of Koguryo, sent an army to Saro which defeated and drove out an invading army from Japan.

During the fifth century the royal authority was consolidated and there was much cultural progress. Many dolmens remain from this time, and vast quantities of bronzeware have been unearthed, showing the rapid expansion of metal use. Early in the sixth century, during the reign of Chijung-wang(500-513), the kingdom expanded northwest of the Naktong and to Usan-guk (now Ullung-do), a solitary island in the Eastern Sea. It was during the reign of Chijung that Saro adopted the name Silla for the kingdom, and it was also at this time that the royal title *maripkan* was replaced by the Chinese word for king, *wang*. During the reign of Pophung-wang, the successor of Chijung-wang, Silla emerged as a full-fledged kingdom.

In 370 the Earlier Yen state of north China, which had been contending with Koguryo in the Liaotung and Liao-si areas, roughly the Liao River basin and the Liaotung peninsula in Manchuria, was conquered and destroyed by another group which set up the state of Ch'ien Ch'in. King Sosurim of Koguryo (who also now used the Chinese title *wang*) sought friendly ties with Earlier Ch'in and supported the spread of Buddhism, newly adopted in north China, in his kingdom. He also established a *T'aehak* ("Highest School of Learning") on the Chinese model, to train future government officials, and promulgated various laws and decrees aimed at securing and centralizing the royal authority.

Kwanggaet'o-wang (391–412) entered into close relations with Silla, and launched a military expedition to expand his territory, which opened the golden age of Koguryo. How successful he was is shown by the posthumous title by which he is known to history, for Kwanggaet'o-wang means "the king who expanded the country's territory." He was the first to adopt the Chinese custom of naming his reign-period. The Chinese were in the habit not only of giving posthumous titles to their emperors, but

THE EARLY THREE KINGDOMS
(5th Century)

KOGURYO

Liao R.

Liaotung-song

Ansi-song

Yalu R.

Kungnae-song (Hwando-song)

Soanp'yong

Ch'ongch'on R.

Maullyong

Hwangch'oryong

EASTERN SEA

Taedong R.

P'yongyang

Han-song

Mt. Pukhan

Mich'uhol

Han R.

Usan

YELLOW SEA

Ungjin

Kwansan-song

Sabi

Kum R.

SILLA

Naktong R.

Kumsong (Kyongju)

Ch'angnyong

PAEKCHE

KAYA

T'amna

also of naming the period during which a monarch reigned. Kwanggaet'o's reign-period was named *Yongnak,* meaning "eternal happiness," and Kwanggaet'o-wang was thus also remembered by the pleasant title of Yongnak Tae-wang, the Great King of Eternal Happiness.

After a long struggle, Kwanggaet'o-wang extended the power of Koguryo into the Liaotung area, defeating the Hsiao Sin in the northeast and taking a number of fortresses and towns in the process. He also sent troops to Silla, as noted above, inflicting a disastrous defeat on the invading Japanese in an engagement on the Naktong. His monument still stands at Kungnae-song on the upper Yalu, the old Koguryo capital, recording that during his reign he conquered sixty-four fortresses and 1,400 towns.

His successor Changsu-wang ("Long-lived King," 413–491) presided over the greatest expansion of power that Koguryo had yet seen. In 427 he moved the capital from Kungnae-song in the mountainous upper Yalu region down to P'yongyang on the Taedong River, a region of fertile plains. He established diplomatic relations with both of the regimes then ruling China, which was split into what Chinese historians called the *Nan Pei Ch'ao,* the Northern and Southern Dynasties. The transfer of the capital was an expression of his southward expansion policy.

This policy, of course, meant an attack upon Paekche. Aside from the obvious advantages a victory would bring, King Changsu was anxious to avenge the death of his ancestor King Kogugwon, who, it will be remembered, had been killed during an invasion by Paekche in 371. Alarmed by Koguryo's threatening attitude, Paekche concluded an alliance with Silla in 433, and, when invasion seemed imminent, King Kaero of Paekche dispatched a special envoy to the northern Chinese state of Wei to ask for help.

But these efforts proved vain. In 475, the sixty-third

year of King Changsu's reign, Hansan, the capital of Paekche, fell to the Koguryo troops and King Kaero was killed. Paekche was forced to move its capital far to the south, to Ungjin (modern Kongju, South Ch'ungch'ong Province). Koguryo now ruled the entire northern half of the Korean peninsula, the Liaotung peninsula, and a considerable portion of Manchuria.

Ungjin remained the capital of Paekche for sixty-three years. It had virtues as a military strong point, being located in a mountainous area, but was too remote and difficult of access to be an effective administrative center. When the nation had somewhat recovered from its defeat, Song-wang (523–553) removed the capital to Sabi (modern Puyo) and also attempted to change the country's name to Nam-Puyo ("South Puyo"), although this did not last long. The new capital had two great advantages. First, it controlled the broad, fertile southwestern plain, thus giving the government easy access to the farmland which was then the principal form of wealth. Second, it was located on the broad, navigable Kum River, giving the country direct access to China by sea.

Song-wang reorganized both central and local administrations, established ties with China and Japan, and encouraged the spread of Buddhism. The Liang dynasty in south China in particular was influential in disseminating Chinese culture in Paekche. In turn, Chinese culture and the Buddhist religion were exported to Japan through the Paekche kingdom, which appears to have had particularly close ties with the island kingdom at this time. Paekche craftsmen of many kinds went to Japan to teach their skills to the Japanese. Korea, and Paekche in particular at this time, thus served as a bridge over which Chinese culture and Buddhism traveled from China to Japan.

While Paekche was convalescing, the power and prosperity of Silla developed rapidly. In 520 Pophung-wang

(514–539) instituted a major legal reform. Buddhism was officially recognized in 527, and in 536 the king changed the name of his reign-period to Konwon. This last was a Chinese custom by which ancient monarchs marked major changes or reforms in their governments. The most important external development during this reign was the annexation of the territory of Pon-Kaya, the most powerful of the Kaya tribes in the Naktong River basin. The conquest of the other Kaya tribes would soon follow.

The growing power of the two neighboring kingdoms led inevitably to conflict. They were briefly allied in an attack upon Koguryo in which Song-wang of Paekche was able to regain some of the former Paekche territory on the Han River in 551. But Chinhung-wang of Silla (540–575) took advantage of the situation to occupy the upper Han area. Plagued by civil war, Koguryo was unable to resist this combined attack.

With Koguryo temporarily impotent, Silla could safely turn upon its former ally. Two years later Chinhung-wang's armies occupied the lower Han region which Paekche had regained. Enraged by this treachery, Song-wang personally led his troops into Silla. Battle was joined at Kwansan-song (now Okch'on) and the result was utter defeat for Paekche. Song-wang was killed and his army routed. Chinhung-wang then turned south, conquering the Tae-Kaya tribe on the middle Naktong and extending Silla control over the whole Kaya territory soon thereafter. With his southern borders secured, he then turned north, sending his armies up the east coast all the way to modern Hamgyong Province, the old Tong-Ye territory ruled by Koguryo. Monuments commemorating these campaigns have been found at Ch'angnyong in the south, erected in 562, on Mt. Pukhan in the Seoul area erected six years later, and at Hwangch'oryong and Maullyong in Hamgyong Province, marking the incursion into Koguryo.

This territorial expansion placed the economically important Han and Naktong River basins under Silla control and also brought Silla finally into direct contact with China by way of the Han and the Yellow Sea. Possession of the Han also separated Paekche from Koguryo, and a strong army was stationed there. When Koguryo sent a general named Ondal to try to regain this territory at the beginning of the reign of King Yongyang (590–618) the result was a fresh defeat. The power of Silla was now unchallenged in the peninsula.

The formation of the three ancient Korean kingdoms brought a measure of unity and cultural development to the tribes of the peninsula. It also brought large-scale military conflict and the political maneuvering and treachery that went with it. Hereditary monarchies were established and government was centralized. Chinese influence began to permeate the country, as seen especially in the organization of government, and the Buddhist religion in its Chinese form became widespread. Social classes appeared, with an aristocracy at the top among whom ancient Korean culture now began to bloom.

Chapter 5

The Society and Culture of the Three Kingdoms

I. Social Structure and Government

The establishment of the ancient states meant the imposition from above of the Chinese bureaucratic system of government upon the clan and tribal society of Korea, which was basically aristocratic. Thus, while in theory anyone who could demonstrate his competence was admissible to the ranks of government officials under the Chinese system, in Korea only aristocrats were eligible in practice. Clan patriarchs and tribal leaders were given new titles and installed in the various ministries and boards of government, but the change was superficial and real power remained dependent upon ownership of land and family background rather than upon rank in the government. The real change was in the unification of this aristocracy, with the royal family at its head.

Ownership of land was regularized by royal grants to high officials, though much of this land must have been already in the hands of those who now officially received it. Along with the land went frequent gifts of slaves, whose numbers had increased because of the constant fighting during the Three Kingdoms period. Slaves were used as household servants and also to clear uncultivated land. The majority of free farmers were subject to taxes in kind and forced labor.

The king also headed the military organization, with

aristocrats in the positions of staff and general officers. The young men of the aristocracy devoted themselves almost exclusively to military training during this time of frequent conflict, another significant difference from Chinese practice.

The introduction and rapid spread of Buddhism brought new significance and depth to Korean religious thought. The primitive shamanism of earlier times did not disappear, but it was now relegated mostly to the lower classes of society, while the new religion was patronized by the government and enthusiastically taken up by the aristocracy.

These innovations in government and religion required skill and learning, and this meant again importations from China. Contacts with Chinese states in the past had required the ability to speak and read the Chinese language, which now became a part of upper-class education. In particular, the Confucian system of ethics and government embodied in the so-called Confucian classics, which had had so great an impact on Chinese society and government now began to have a similar effect upon Korea.

With these characteristics in common, Koguryo, Paekche and Silla each built a social tradition of its own.

The organization of a regular administrative system governing through laws and decrees began in Koguryo during the reign of King Sosurim (371–384). The full development of the system is believed to have taken place after the capital was transferred to P'yongyang. There were at first twelve grades of officials, though this number was later increased. The duties of these officials were not at first specialized. The bureaucratic system thus formed completed the subjugation of clan and tribal leaders to the monarchy by making them part of it, and by the imposition of taxes, mostly in the form of grain and textiles.

The Koguryo administration was divided into two major

sections, *hyong* ("elder brother") and *saja* ("messenger"). The *hyong* section took over the powers formerly exercised by the various tribal leaders, and each clan head was given an official post. The *saja* section was concerned specifically with communications and with tax collecting. Its members were mostly of somewhat lower rank. There were eventually fourteen principal posts in the government, each with its own rank and title. It will be noted in the list that follows that several of these titles suffix either *hyong* or *saja,* indicating the section to which the official belonged.

1. *Taedaero*
2. *T'aedaehyong*
3. *Ulchol* or *Chubu*
4. *Taebusaja*
5. *Chouidut'aehyong*
6. *Taesaja*
7. *Taehyongga*
8. *Palwisaja*
9. *Sangwisaja*
10. *Sohyong*
11. *Chehyong*
12. *Kwajol*
13. *Pujol*
14. *Sonin*

Little is known of how this system of graded officialdom affected social status. It would appear, however, that the first five grades disposed of all important affairs of state. The *Taedaero,* the highest ranking official, was not appointed by the king like the others, but was elected by his fellow officials every three years, and was prohibited from succeeding himself. This seems to be a survival of the election system known to have existed in tribal communities.

The nation was divided into five administrative districts. Each of them was governed by a military official called *Yoksal* and a civil official called *Ch'oryogunji.* Under them were the commanders of *song* (fortresses), which had been the bases of tribal power and had now become local military and administrative headquarters. These *song* were now charged with collecting taxes and with the general administration of their areas, as well as being military headquarters. Each was the post of a military unit, more or less independent of the others but under the direct control of the king.

When the capital was moved to P'yongyang, a further elaboration of this system was made. To the five districts were added three regional capitals. In addition to P'yong-yang, Kungnae-song, the former capital, and Hansong (now Chaeryong) were made centers of civil and military administration.

The system of land ownership was to some extent regularized under the new royal authority. In theory, all land belonged to the King, who parcelled it out to his officials in proportion to their rank and merit. Certain lands were, of course, reserved for the royal family. Two kinds of land-grant were made to officials and local leaders: *sajon* was a permanent grant which became the hereditary property of the family of the official to whom it was given; *sigup* was the assignment of the tax income of a given tract of land to an official for his lifetime, after which it reverted once more to royal ownership. These awards could become the usual perquisites of office or could be special awards for particularly meritorious service to the state, either civil or military.

This system fostered the growth of large private estates. Slaves captured in war were used to clear uncultivated land, and the aristocratic landowners sometimes also expanded their holdings by appropriating land abandoned by independent farmers who had fled their farms because of crushing tax burdens and too frequent corvée labor.

Little is known about the legal system of Koguryo except that it was probably much influenced by the Chinese Wei state which was Koguryo's neighbor, and by the Chin state which succeeded Wei. Some information is available on taxes, however. The basic levy was a kind of head-tax. Each adult male was obliged to pay either five *p'il* (rolls) of cloth or five *sok* (one sok is about five bushels) of grain yearly. Landless men paid a small amount of cloth every years. For other tax purposes, the people were divided into three groups, according to income.

The state depended heavily upon forced military duty and corvée, or forced labor. All males above the age of fifteen were liable to corvée, and were employed to build walls, fortresses, and the like.

To provide some measure of relief to the farmers who bore this heavy burden of taxation and corvée, the government instituted the practice of *Chindaebop,* a form of government loan. When farmers ran short of grain in the spring they were given loans from government stock, which were repayable in autumn after the harvest. Property such as land, houses, cows, horses and slaves was freely bought and sold.

The formation of the Paekche kingdom was somewhat different from that of Koguryo. The Ma-han tribes of southwestern Korea did not form a tribal league until one of the Puyo tribes of the north settled among them. This tribe soon dominated the local people, leadership became hereditary, and Paekche emerged as a kingdom after only a comparatively short period as a tribal league. For this reason, the Paekche government showed very few survivals from tribal rule. The rulers did not impose themselves on the other tribes entirely by force, and the names of eight great families which supported the monarchy have been recorded: Sa, Hae, Yon, Hyop, Chin, Kuk, Mok and Paek.

Almost from the beginning civil and military affairs were controlled by different officials, as in Chinese governments. There were sixteen official grades. Officials of the first grade, six in number, formed a kind of cabinet, each one being in charge of one of the six ministries: Imperial Household, Finance, Rituals, Royal Guard, Justice and Defense.

This again is markedly similar to Chinese practice.

The sixteen grades were divided into three groups and distinguished from each other by the colors of their clothes. Officials of the six highest grades wore purple dress, those of the next five scarlet, and those of the lowest five blue. The ranks and titles of these sixteen grades were as follows:

FIRST GROUP (purple)	SECOND GROUP (scarlet)	THIRD GROUP (blue)
1. *Chwap'yong*	7. *Changdok*	12. *Mundok*
2. *Talsol*	8. *Sidok*	13. *Mudok*
3. *Unsol*	9. *Kodok*	14. *Chwagun*
4. *Toksol*	10. *Kyedok*	15. *Chinmu*
5. *Hansol*	11. *Taedok*	16. *Kugu*
6. *Nasol*		

Despite many resemblances to the Chinese system of government, which can hardly have been accidental, this was basically an aristocratic system. The holders of the various offices were not chosen competitively, but on the basis of their position in society, so that the organization of government simply made official the existence of different social classes.

The government offices staffed by these officials had specialized functions, and were divided into *naegwan* ("internal offices," concerned with the royal court) and *oegwan* ("external offices," concerned with general administrative affairs). There were twenty-two such offices. The officials in charge of them were changed every three years, an apparent survival of the election of clan patriarchs, used at this time to insure that all of the aristocracy would have a measure of political power at one time or another, thus preventing the dominance of any single group or revolts by those who felt they had been excluded from the government.

Like Koguryo, Paekche was divided into five administrative districts corresponding to the five directions of Chinese tradition: east, west, south, north and center. The capital city was correspondingly divided. The boundaries of these districts or *pang* were arbitrarily determined, with no regard for tribe or clan territory. Each pang was ruled by a civilian governor appointed by the central government. Under each of these *Pangyong,* were ten *kun.* In addition to its civil administration, each kun had three military officials of the fourth grade, *Toksol,* in charge of 700 to 1,200 soldiers for local defense.

We have few details about the landholding system of Paekche, but it appears to have been similar to those of Koguryo and Silla. Farmers paid taxes in silk and hemp cloth and in grain, and were subject to military duty and corvée labor. As in the other kingdoms, prisoners of war were enslaved.

Silla was the last of the three states to develop a royal government, emerging as a kingdom during the reigns of Chijung-maripkan and Pophung-wang in the sixth century. It was during this time that the name Saro, a word of purely Korean origin, was replaced by Silla, a name derived from a Chinese expression. Also at this time the title *maripkan,* meaning literally "great chieftain," was replaced by the Chinese title *wang,* "king." Pophung-wang was the first to bear this title. During his reign a government administration was created, various laws were promulgated, and the grades and distinctive dress of officials were decreed. Military and civil administration were separated and the *Sangdaedung* or prime minister was first appointed by the king. By the end of the sixth century the Silla kingdom had reached the level of development of the other two.

The seventeen grades of officials who constituted the national government appeared shortly after the reign of King Pophung, but the ranking of district officials was not completed until after the unification of the three kingdoms under Silla. The bureaucratic organization was based on the strict and detailed social class system prevalent in Silla. Like the other two kingdoms, Silla thus adopted certain aspects of the Chinese system of government, but preserved the aristocratic basis of its society, restricting positions of authority to the upper classes.

Silla had evolved a unique status system called *Kolp'um* ("Bone Ranks"). Social status was determined by heredity and strongly influenced the kinship and marriage systems. Government positions, occupations, and social life were all governed by *Kolp'um*. At the top of society were two classes called *Songgol* ("Sacred Bone") and *Chin'gol*("True Bone"). These were made up exclusively of the royal family. Below them were six classes called *Tup'um*, designated only by numbers, which made up the rest of society, the sixth *Tup'um* being the highest social class and the first the lowest.

The distinction between the royal classes, *Songgol* and *Chin'gol,*appears to have become blurred with the passage of time. Originally, it seems, the kings, who were always of the Kim clan, had married only women of the Pak clan. The children of these marriages and their families constituted the Songgol class. In later times, however, this connection with the Pak clan ceased, and royalty had a wider choice of marriage partners. The descendants of these later marriages made up the Chin'gol class. The King's father and brothers, the Queen's husband when she was the reigning monarch, and the fathers of the King's mother and the King's wife bore the honorary title *Kalmun-wang*.

The high offices of government were monopolized by royalty and aristocracy, and there were strict rules regarding promotion. The first five grades were restricted to the royal clan. Grades six through nine were reserved for men of the sixth social class, the highest after royalty, which was also known as *Tuknan* ("Difficult to Attain"). Men of the fifth social class could get as high as the tenth and eleventh grade, and the remaining grades were occupied by the fourth class. People below the fourth class were evidently regarded as commoners and did not participate in government at all. The seventeen grades were divided into four groups corresponding to the social classes permitted to occupy them, each group having a distinctive color of clothing. They were as follows:

First Group (purple)	Second Group (scarlet)	Third Group (blue)	Fourth Group (yellow)
1. *Ibolch'an*	6. *Ach'an*	10. *Taenama*	12. *Taesa*
2. *Ich'an*	7. *Ilgilch'an*	11. *Nama*	13. *Saji*
3. *Chapch'an*	8. *Sach'an*		14. *Kilsa*
4. *P'ajinch'an*	9. *Kuppolch'an*		15. *Taeo*
5. *Taeach'an*			16. *Soo*
			17. *Chowi*

The original intention of the system seems to have been that each post should be occupied by one man only. But the restrictions on promotion and the increasing demand for the power and prestige of government posts led in time to an expansion in the grades below the first five. Thus the sixth grade (the highest open to non-royal aristocrats) came eventually to include four different posts, while the tenth and eleventh each had seven.

The government of Silla was thus a more or less exact reflection of its traditional social structure. Chinese methods of organization and administration were adopted, but not slavishly or mechanically, the Silla rulers adapting their model to fit their own circumstances and customs. In addition to the strongly aristocratic bent of Silla government, the old tribal conference was also retained. Important matters were decided at a meeting of all the important men of the ruling class, called *Hwabaek*. The decisions of this conference had to be unanimous, just as those of the clan and tribal conferences had been. The *Hwabaek* had four special meeting places in Kumsong (now Kyongju), the capital, which indicates that its meetings must have been fairly regular.

Government offices with specialized functions began to appear during the first half of the sixth century, and military and civil administrations were separated. The various departments of government eventually numbered seven, including those concerned with revenue, rituals, and personnel. During Queen Chindok's reign (647–653) a general reorganization was instituted. *Chipsabu,* the Executive Office, became the highest organ of government, *Ch'angbu* was entrusted with the management of tax grain, and *Ibangbu* was created to draft laws and regulations. (The syllable *-bu* in Korean denotes a division or department of government, and is used at the present time to designate the various ministries.) A legal system thus emerged to replace government by custom or by the whim of the ruler.

Local administration during the Three Kingdoms period seems to have been mostly in the hands of the military. The largest administrative unit, called *chu,* was ruled by a *Kunju* ("Military Commander") whose subordinates were *Songju* ("Fortress Commander"). Military units called *tang* constituted the royal bodyguard and a special unit called *chong* defended the capital. As Silla's wars expanded its territory, *chong* units were dispatched to newly established *chu.*

The core of the military organization was an institution peculiar to Silla called *Hwarang* ("Flower Knights"). This was evidently a survival of the youth bands of tribal times, and served as a sort of military academy. Its members were young men of aristocratic birth who dedicated themselves to preparing to serve the state in war. In addition to their practical training they visited famous mountains (doubtless in connection with the belief in the spirits of such places) and engaged in ritual songs and dances whose purpose was to pray for the welfare of the nation.

Most of the great military leaders of Silla had been members of *Hwarang*. Prominent among them was Kim Yu-sin, the military leader who was chiefly responsible for the victories that led to the unification of the peninsula under Silla. Another was Kim Ch'un-ch'u, later King Muyol, whose political leadership both before and after he succeeded to the throne was also extremely important in the unification.

The ideology which underlay this society was a combination of the traditional way of life of the tribal communities with the new Chinese imports of Buddhism and Confucianism. Quite often Buddhist monks were instructors of the Hwarang. The monk Won'gwang Popsa, in fact, was the author of the famous *Sesok Ogye,* or Five Commandments, which became the basic rule of life for the Hwarang. These were: 1) to serve the King with loyalty; 2) to serve one's parents with filial piety; 3) to be faithful to one's friends; 4) not to retreat in battle; and 5) not to kill indiscriminately. It is obvious that Won'gwang had in mind both the Buddhist injunctions against taking life and the Confucian virtues of loyalty, filial piety, and faithfulness.

Many tales of heroism of the Hwarang survive, including those of Sa Ta-ham, Kim Yu-sin and Kwanch'ang. In the early eighth century Kim Tae-mun wrote a book called *Hwarang segi*(The Records of Hwarang), which set forth the lives of some two hundred Hwarang. This was presumably the source of the Hwarang tales that are still known, although, unfortunately, the book itself has not survived.

Land was theoretically royal property, and was held by

aristocrats at royal pleasure only. Vast tracts did in fact remain in the hands of the royal family, but inevitably, land being the chief source of wealth, much of it was really in private hands. Grants were made to deserving civil and military officials, some of them (*sajon*) entailing permanent, hereditary possession. *Sigup* grants, on the other hand, were made only for the lifetime of the receiver or during his tenure of office. When the leader of the Pon-Kaya tribe came to do obeisance to the King, for example, he was granted the Pon-Kaya territory as *sigup*, thus acknowledging his subordination to the King. The official encouragement of Buddhism had stimulated the building of temples, which soon became great landowners through the gifts of pious, royal and aristocratic patrons.

Little information has survived concerning the lives of the farmers who worked this land, but what we do have would seem to indicate that they were permanently attached to their farms, so that when the land changed hands the farmers and their families came under the control of the new owner and paid a proportion of their crops to him. This was something of a problem because, as more and more land passed into private hands, the taxes which the farmers paid passed into private hands also, depriving the government of part of its revenue. The heavy taxes demanded by the government, in addition to corvée labor, and the exactions of private owners seem sometimes to have driven farmers to abandon their lands in despair.

II. Culture and the Arts

In considering the intellectual activities of this period, certain facts must be borne in mind. Most importantly, when Korea came into contact with Chinese culture no writing system had yet been devised for the Korean language. Consequently, all literary works during the ancient period and down to the fifteenth century, with certain exceptions, were written in the Chinese language. When we speak of literary or historical works, therefore, it must be understood that, unless otherwise noted, these works were written in Chinese, by means of the Chinese ideographs.

Chinese culture being much more highly developed than Korean at this time, not only the Chinese language but also Chinese institutions and ideas came to dominate Korea. The most significant fact is not that Korea adopted Chinese culture in such massive doses but that she managed to retain her own distinctive individuality and to adapt Chinese culture to her own purposes while many other peoples who came under Chinese influence were completely absorbed into the body of Chinese culture and their own cultures ceased to exist.

Koguryo had the earliest contact with China and was the first of the ancient kingdoms to adopt Chinese culture. It will be recalled that a school called *T'aehak* ("Great Learning"—the word itself is Chinese) was established by King Sosurim in 372 A.D. This school taught the Chinese language and the Confucian classics and was intended mainly to train prospective government officials, as were the Chinese institutions upon which it was modeled. Private schools called *kyongdang* soon followed in which the youth of the aristocracy studied Chinese and archery, an important military skill. Chinese dictionaries began to appear. The Confucian social philosophy was generally adopted, although, as we have seen, it was not allowed to affect the prerogatives of the ruling aristocratic class.

One important custom which was adopted from China was the compiling of historical records. The scholars of ancient China kept careful records of the reign of each emperor or king, and when there was a change of dynasty or one state was absorbed by another, an official history of the dynasty or state would be compiled. As soon as Koguryo scholars were sufficiently familiar with the Chinese language and writing system, the history of Koguryo was recorded in a work called *yugi*. It is said to have consisted of one hundred volumes, although the exact meaning of the term "volume" is not clear, since this work has not survived. It was probably compiled during the reign of King Sosurim in the late fourth century. It is also recorded that a condensation of it was made in the year 600 by Yi Mun-jin.

One important historical record has survived from early Koguryo times. In 314 a stone monument in honor of King Kwanggaet'o was erected at the early Koguryo capital of Kungnae-song (Chinese T'ung-kou) on the northern side of the upper Yalu. This monument, which is still extant, contains an inscription of 1,800 characters in the so-called "seal writing," a style of character used for carving the personal stone or wooden seals which the Chinese and people within the sphere of Chinese influence used, and still use, in lieu of written signatures. It is not only valuable historical evidence but also much admired by modern connoisseurs of the great art of calligraphy.

The first record of Buddhist influence in Koguryo states that a monk named Shun Tao brought a Buddhist image and Buddhist scriptures from the Chinese state of Earlier Ch'in. It should be pointed out that this was not the rather austere Hinayana (or more accurately and more politely Theravadin) form of Buddhism which still dominates much of southeast Asia, but the popular Mahayana form in which Buddhism spread from India to China. Mahayana Buddhism did not require that the individual work out his own salvation, as did Theravadin. It had evolved the doctrine of Bodhisattvas, persons who had achieved Buddhahood but who voluntarily abstained from passing into the state of Nirvana in order to help suffering humanity

11. *Stone Monument of King Kwanggaet'o:* North P'yongan Province. H. about 6.4m. Koguryo dynasty, 5th century.

12. *Vessel in the Form of a Warrior on Horseback:* Gray stoneware. Excavated from the Golden Bell Tomb, Kyongju. H. 23.8cm, L. 29.2cm. Old Silla dynasty, 5th–6th century. National Museum of Korea.

13. *Overall View of the Tomb of the General:* Possibly Tomb of King Kwanggaet'o. Chian Prefecture, Manchuria. L. about 33m, H. about 13m.

14. *Details of Murals, Twin Pillar Tomb:* Painting on plaster. South P'yongan Province. Koguryo dynasty, 5th–6th century.

15. *Interior of the Twin Pillar Tomb:* South P'yongan Province. Koguryo dynasty, 5th-6th century.

17. Pagoda, Chongnim-sa: Puyo, South Ch'ungch'ong Province. H. 8.7m. Paekche dynasty, 6th-7th century.

16. Sakyamuni: Gilt bronze. H. 17cm. Koguryo dynasty, 539? National Museum of Korea.

18. Pagoda, Punhwang-sa: Kyongju. H. 8.4m. Old Silla dynasty 7th century.

19. Ch'omsongdae (Stone Observatory): Granite. Inwang-dong, Kyongju, North Kyongsang Province. H. 9.29m. Old Silla dynasty, 7th century.

20. Tiles: (a) Lotus flower in relief. Red paste. From P'yongyang area. Koguryo, 5th-7th century.
(b) Landscape in relief. Gray paste. From Puyo area. Paekche, 7th century.
(c) Lotus flower in relief. Decorative disk of semi-circular tile. Gray earthenware. From Kyongju area. Old Silla, 5th-6th century.

21. Kaya Ceramics: Excavated from Koryong, South Kyongsang Province. Kaya, 6th-7th century, Koryong County Seat.

to achieve enlightenment. (The word *Buddha* itself is not a name but an epithet, meaning "the enlightened one.")

Mahayana thus offered not only escape from the wheel of existence to those who achieved enlightenment but also help and protection in this world. It also offered protection to the King and the nation. For these reasons, it was immediately popular and received official recognition and support. Two years after the appearance of Shun Tao, another monk, A Tao, came from Earlier Ch'in. King Sosurim had two temples, Ch'omun-sa and Ibullan-sa, built for the two monks. As Buddhism spread among the people it combined with and absorbed many popular beliefs, as this hospitable and undogmatic religion had so often done in other times and places. Buddhism was appealed to for protection from illness, for cure or healing, to ward off personal calamities, and in times of peril to the state.

Koguryo art and architecture are mainly known through the tombs of kings and aristocrats, many of which still exist. The tombs are of two types. One is a kind of step-pyramid of stone blocks, similar to the early Egyptian pyramids, while the other consists of a large earth mound. In both kinds of tomb, the corpse was placed in a walled and sometimes pillared chamber, often decorated with murals and sometimes also containing ritual objects and personal possessions of the deceased.

The murals in these tombs are valuable evidence of the manners, customs and dress of Koguryo times, as well as exhibiting a high degree of artistic skill. The figures on the walls of the Twin Pillar Tomb and the Tomb of the Dancers (these are modern designations, not the original names) are especially important in this respect. Each of the four walls of the Great Tomb is decorated with a mythical beast representing one of the four directions—the blue dragon of the east, the white tiger of the west, the red phoenix of the south and the tortoise and snake of the north. These are painted in vivid colors in a masterly, swirling style of graceful curves forming an intricate design. All of these tomb paintings display a bold, vigorous style, quite sophisticated but quite different from the calm serenity usually associated with Chinese art. They are evidence of the distinctive culture that was developing in Koguryo, despite the heavy Chinese influence. Together with surviving Koguryo rooftiles and the stone monument mentioned earlier, they confirm the impression given by other sources of a vigorous, aggressive, outgoing people.

Buddhism strongly influenced the art of Koguryo. There are records of many Buddha images, paintings, and stupas or pagodas in a style derived from that of the Chinese Northern Wei state, but unfortunately very few of these have come down to us. A terra-cotta figurine and a small gilt-bronze standing Buddha have been unearthed near P'yongyang. It is also recorded that monks and artists from Koguryo travelled to Japan in considerable numbers and were instrumental in the introduction of Buddhism there. The name of one of these is also recorded, one Tamjing, who painted a mural for the Horyuji temple in Japan.

None of the poetry or music of Koguryo times survives, although the records state that the Koguryo people, like Koreans of all ages, enjoyed singing and dancing. It is known that a musician named Wang San-ak devised the six-stringed *Hyonhakkum* or *Komun'go* by adapting a seven-stringed musical instrument from the Chin state in China. He is also said to have written one hundred musical compositions, although what they were like is unknown.

Paekche was not far behind Koguryo in adopting Chinese culture. By the time of King Kunch'ogo (346–375) a scholar named Ko Hung had written a historical work in Chinese called *Sogi*. Several other histories of Paekche followed, including *Paekche-gi* (Records of Paekche), *Paekche pon'gi*(History of Paekche)and *Paekche sinch'an*(New History of Paekche). Contacts with Japan were frequent, and a scholar named Wang In introduced the Confucian *Analects* and the *Thousand Character Classic* to the Japanese.

Buddhism came to Paekche only twelve years after its introduction into Koguryo. In 384 a monk named Maranant'a arrived from the Eastern Chin state of south China. As in Koguryo, Buddhism was warmly welcomed because of its offer of protection to the state. Other monks from China followed, and King Ch'imyu ordered a temple built on Mt. Namhan for ten monks. From the late fourth century onward, Buddhism spread rapidly throughout the kingdom.

Paekche continued to be active in the importation and adaptation of Chinese culture. Even during the chronic conflicts with Koguryo, cultural ties were maintained, and relations were established with several of the Chinese states known as the Northern and Southern Dynasties. The southern states of Sung, Ch'i, Liang and Chin in particular are known to have had relations with Paekche, and it is recorded that in 541 scholars, artisans and painters from Liang were sent there upon Paekche request. According to Chinese records, the Paekche aristocracy soon became well versed in the Confucian classics and Chinese historical writings, and also in the philosophical theory of *yin* and *yang*, in Chinese medical practice and in divination. Paekche also had close relations with Japan, and transmitted a good deal of her newly acquired Chinese culture to that country. Several works of art still extant in Japan were produced by Paekche artists.

Many earth-mound tombs near the modern cities of Kwangju, Kongju and Puyo, each a Paekche capital at one time or another, have been excavated, but unfortunately most of them were the victims of tomb-robbers. A few small objects have been recovered. The tombs carried on the

Koguryo custom of mural decoration, and those at Kongju on the upper Kum River show strong Koguryo influence. But the cloud and lotus designs and the Four Spirits mural on the ceiling of a tomb found at Nungsal-li near Puyo show a new departure, and are more characteristic of Paekche art as we know it.

Koguryo art had been bold and vigorous, perhaps reflecting the Koguryo connection with the nomads of central Asia. Paekche art, on the other hand, had an elegance and refinement closer to the ideals of Chinese art. This may be seen in the image of Miruk (Maitreya, the Buddha of the future) now preserved in the Toksu palace museum in Seoul, and in the Maae-sokpul, a relief of Buddha carved on a cliff near Sosan, north Ch'ungch'ong Province. Mention should also be made of Crown Prince Ajwa, famous for his artistic skill, who went to Japan in the early seventh century and painted a portrait of Prince Shotoku which was widely admired.

Paekche buildings, like those of the other kingdoms, were mostly made of wood and so have not survived. Several stone pagodas, customarily erected on temple grounds to house the relics of famous monks and other sacred objects, are still extant and give us a notion of Paekche architecture. Notable are those at Chongnim temple in Puyo, at Miruk temple in Iksan, and the Wanggungp'yong pagoda also at Iksan. The Miruk temple pagoda is of particular interest because it shows the transition from wood to stone. The structure, though built of stone, shows a technique obviously more appropriate to the use of wood. Stamped or incised roof-tiles and bricks from Paekche also show the refined elegance which characterized its art.

Silla was the last of the three kingdoms to adopt Chinese culture, and also preserved tribal customs and ideas longer than the others. Confucianism became important socially, and the Confucian virtues were inculcated, but it had little influence on the institutions of government during the Three Kingdoms period. But the influence of Chinese culture on the intellectual life of the country was all-pervasive. The Chinese language and writing system spread rapidly after its introduction. In 545 a scholar named Koch'ilbu compiled a history of Silla in Chinese at the order of King Chinhung, from which it can be deduced that Chinese history and literature were fairly well known by that time.

Silla was also the last to adopt Buddhism. It is first recorded with the entry of the monk A Tao (who had helped introduce it to Koguryo) into the county of Ilson (now Sonsan), during the reign of Nulchi-maripkan (417–457). But Buddhism did not at first receive the kind of official recognition that it had had in the other kingdoms, and when finally King Pophung attempted to establish it under royal sponsorship he at first met strong resistance. The people of Silla were apparently much more conservative than those of the other kingdoms, and it was not until after the martyrdom of the monk Ich'adon in 528 that King Pophung succeeded in persuading the aristocracy to accept it. After this time, however, it spread rapidly, and many temples and pagodas were built. The government dispatched monks to each of the administrative districts to supervise religious administration, and many monks went to China to study, bringing back not only Buddhist documents and ideas but also elements of Chinese culture, including architecture, sculpture, and other arts.

By the time Mahayana Buddhism reached China, it had already split into several different sects, which were hence generally known by their Sanskrit names. They were also given Chinese names, however, and eventually Korean names and then Japanese names, which makes the matter of nomenclature somewhat confusing. We shall generally give here the Korean name with the Sanskrit name in parentheses. Since Buddhism is not an exclusivist or dogmatic religion like Christianity or Islam, these different sects managed to coexist fairly amicably most of the time, and it had become the custom by the time they were introduced into Korea for a really learned monk to be versed in the doctrines of all the important ones.

Some of the names of monks who introduced new sects and founded temples have been recorded. We read of Won'gwang, well versed in the doctrines of the principal sects, and of Chajang, who brought Buddhist scriptures from China and founded T'ongdo temple. It was Chajang also who introduced the Kyeyul (Vinaya) sect. Uisang studied under the Chinese monk Chih Yen and returned to found Pusok temple and to introduce the Haedong Hwaom (Avatamsaka Sutra) sect. (*Haedong* was a Chinese designation for Korea.) And, although he did not study in China, Wonhyo wrote many commentaries on Buddhist scripture which contributed to the spread of Buddhism in Korea.

Several famous temples were built around the royal capital, Kyongju. Among these were Punhwang-sa (*sa* means "temple" in Korean), Sach'onwang-sa, and Hwang-yong-sa, the Temple of the Royal Dragon. A huge wooden pagoda was set up at Hwangyong-sa, but was destroyed during the Mongol invasions in the Koryo period. The many-storied stone pagoda of Punhwang-sa still stands. It was constructed in a curious manner, of stones cut into the shape of bricks, hence its nickname, "mock-brick pagoda." Also preserved are the sculptured figures of Kumgang Yoksa ("Vajra Deva," the four Deva kings of Indian legend who guard the portals of many Buddhist temples throughout East Asia), from the same temple.

Among other Silla works of art still extant is Ch'om-songdae, the stone observatory built during the reign of Queen Sondok (632–646), the first such building in the Orient, famous for its elegant lines. A gilt bronze Maitreya of the Silla period is more forceful and impressive than the Paekche image mentioned earlier. Several roof-tiles with a lotus-petal design are about all that remain of the palaces and temples. All of these objects combine a graceful elegance with force and vigor that testify to the skill and taste of Silla artists. It has been conjectured that the pagodas and perhaps the tiles were in part the work of monks. A painter named Solgo is mentioned in the records, but no Silla paintings survive.

Much of our knowledge of Silla arts and crafts comes from the excavations of tombs, presumably of royalty, dating from the fifth and sixth centuries. Several of these huge earth mounds have been investigated, and have yielded gold crowns, bracelets, earrings, belts, pendants, glass vessels, bronzeware, and many superb pieces of lacquer. All of these show artistic skill and taste of a high order, and testify to the luxurious life of the upper classes. Three tombs in the Kyongju area contained particularly rich finds and are named after objects discovered in them: the Gold Crown Tomb, the Lucky Phoenix Tomb and the Golden Bell Tomb.

No Silla music has survived, but we have some information about it. It appears to have been strongly influenced by the music of Koguryo. The ancient records state that a musician named Okpogo brought to Silla the compositions of the Koguryo musician Wang San-ak, and added some thirty compositions of his own. When Silla conquered the Kaya tribes, a Kaya musician named Uruk introduced to Silla musicians an instrument which was accordingly named the *Kayagum*. This is similar to the name of a Korean instrument still used to play traditional Korean music, the *kayagum*, although whether it was the same instrument is doubtful. Twenty kinds of musical instrument are mentioned, including wind, string and percussion instruments.

In the matter of literature we are more fortunate. A system called *Idu* was invented to record Silla songs and poems, the first attempt to devise a writing system for the Korean language. Clumsy but adequate, it consisted of employing Chinese characters as phonetic symbols. It was mainly used to record the lyrics of songs, many of which have come down to us intact. These were called *Hyangga* or "Native Songs," and most of them were composed by Hwarang and by monks.

PART THREE

The Ancient Period (II)

Chapter 6

The Unification of
the Three Kingdoms by Silla

For a full understanding of the events we are now to discuss, we must once again turn briefly to the political history of China. During most of the Three Kingdoms period in Korea, China had been politically divided and torn by chronic internal conflict, states and dynasties appearing and disappearing with confusing rapidity. The Korean kingdoms were thus free of the sort of political pressure and expansionism which had existed while China was united under the Han dynasty. Toward the end of the sixth century, however, in 589, China was once again united by the Sui dynasty, and though this dynasty lasted only about thirty years, it was succeeded by the T'ang dynasty, which lasted for some three hundred years, during which the Chinese imperial government first consolidated its power and then expanded its political influence and control and its cultural influence. As we shall see, the T'ang dynasty played a formidable part in the course of Silla history.

In the later part of the sixth century, Silla power was on the rise, whereas the other two kingdoms had grown weaker. The balance of power was thus upset and the relations of the three kingdoms changed. Whereas formerly an alliance between Silla and Paekche had been able to keep Koguryo in check, now only an alliance between Paekche and Koguryo could successfully oppose the rising power of Silla, which by now had occupied the former Koguryo territory on the Han River and driven a wedge between it and Paekche.

Unable to conquer its two rivals by its own unaided strength, Silla might have been content with the status quo. But now China was united under the Sui, and Silla promptly sought an alliance with her newly powerful neighbor. The stage was set for conflict, which was not long in coming. Realizing that a Sui attack was imminent, Koguryo mounted an attack across the Liao River in 598 to secure strategic bases for its defense. As expected, Sui forces which the records put at some 300,000 men attacked in the same year. But the Koguryo strategy proved to have been successful, and the attack was beaten off. Bad weather and disease added to the Sui army's troubles, and finally the invasion had to be abandoned and the troops withdrawn.

This was not the end of the matter, however. When the Sui Emperor Yang Ti succeeded his father Wen Ti, he was determined to clear his borders of all states that might pose a threat to Chinese power, and to avenge his father's defeat. After successful campaigns against the nomadic tribes of the west and north, he turned his attention to Koguryo. A great army was mobilized. Chinese sources, which are not always reliable as to figures, say that the invasion force numbered 1,130,000 troops, and its marching column stretched 1,000 *li* (about 240 miles). In addition, a navy took part in the invasion which must also have been large, although no figures are given. In the year 612 this immense force advanced upon Koguryo.

The Koguryo army was fully prepared, and had worked out a highly effective plan of defense. Under general Ulchi Mun-dok, the Chinese forces were checked in the Liaotung peninsula, Koguryo's first line of defense, and held there for several months. Impatient at the delay, Emperor Yang Ti ordered generals Yu Wen-shu and Yu Chung-wen to lead a detachment of 300,000 (again the figure seems suspect) in a surprise attack on P'yongyang. This tactic proved unsuccessful. Unable to take the city, cut off from their base, and with supplies running low, the Sui troops attempted to retreat.

This was what Koguryo general Ulchi Mun-dok was waiting for. He had astutely recognized the possibility of just such an attack, and laid his plans accordingly. The Sui force was ambushed at the Salsu (now Ch'ongch'on River) and suffered a disastrous defeat. Only 2,700 of the 300,000 men are said to have escaped. The tenacious courage of the Koguryo soldiers, combined with the military brilliance of Ulchi Mun-dok, proved unbeatable.

The defeat at Salsu was a mortal blow to Sui morale. Emperor Yang Ti was obliged to order a retreat. In subsequent years, he mounted several other attacks against Koguryo, but with no success. Indeed, these military failures played a large part in the fall of the Sui dynasty in 618.

The T'ang dynasty which succeeded Sui also entertained ambitions of conquering Koguryo. Aware of this, Koguryo constructed elaborate fortifications along the Liao River, said by ancient historians to be 1,000 *li* long. (This expression, "1,000 *li*," frequently used by Chinese historians, does not generally represent an actual measurement, but simply means that the thing in question was impressively long.) Construction took ten years, and was completed in 631.

But now Koguryo began to be plagued by dissension within the ruling class, the chronic complaint of Oriental monarchies. Eventually Yon Kae-so-mun, who had been in charge of constructing the fortifications, emerged as the victor in the factional struggle in 642. He had himself appointed *Taemangniji,* a kind of military dictator who replaced the *Taedaero,* or Prime Minister in wartime, completely dominating the government and even King Yongyu. He correctly interpreted the international political situation and attempted to avert the danger to his country by replacing Silla as the ally of T'ang China. He also concluded an alliance with Paekche and demanded the return of the Han River territories which Silla had taken from Koguryo, and even attacked Silla. When the T'ang dynasty came to the aid of its ally and peremptorily demanded that Koguryo withdraw from Silla, Yon Kae-so-mun refused with equal brusqueness. There were several exchanges of this kind, which finally provided the T'ang rulers with an excuse for attacking Koguryo.

In 644 an army recorded as 200,000 strong set off for the Liaotung peninsula while a naval force of 43,000 men in 500 ships sailed for P'yongyang. Emperor T'ai-tsung put general Li Shih-chi in command of the 60,000-man attack force, while Chiang Liang commanded the navy.

Again the fortified Liao River line held. There was fierce fighting at several points along this line, especially at Ansi-song fortress, where the siege lasted for sixty days. And again ultimate victory went to Koguryo. This time an unusually harsh winter aggravated the blow to Chinese morale. Defeated, cold and hungry, the T'ang troops began to retreat. News of the military reverses reached the naval force before it went into action, and it too withdrew. Like the Sui invasion a generation earlier, the T'ang attempt to eliminate Koguryo had been a complete failure. Three further attempts under T'ai-tsung in 647, 648 and 655 proved equally unavailing.

Finding it impossible to eliminate the Koguryo power on their northeastern border by direct attack, the T'ang rulers turned to an alliance with Silla in order to attack from the south, and this proved successful, although with a different outcome from what a victory in the north would have brought.

While Koguryo was thus occupied in defending itself, Silla took advantage of the situation to increase its own

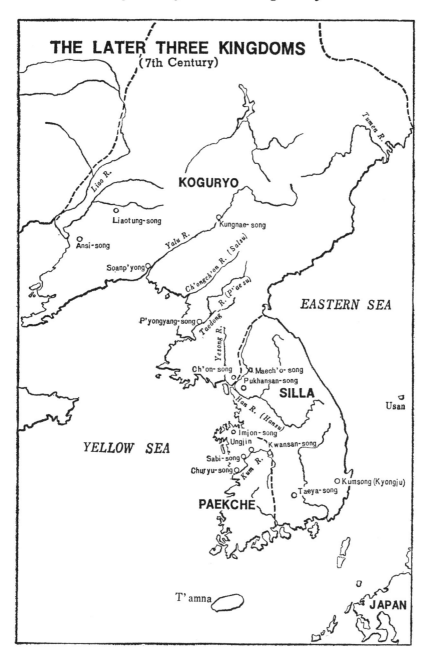

THE LATER THREE KINGDOMS
(7th Century)

KOGURYO

Liaotung-song

Ansi-song

Soanp'yong

Kungnae-song

Liao R.

Yalu R.

Ch'ongch'on R. (Salsu)

Tumen R.

P'yongyang-song

Taedong R. (P'aesu)

Yesong R.

EASTERN SEA

Ch'on-song

Maech'o-song

Pukhansan-song

SILLA

Usan

Han R. (Hansu)

Imjon-song

YELLOW SEA

Ungjin

Kwansan-song

Sabi-song

Churyu-song

Kum R.

Kumsong (Kyongju)

Taeya-song

PAEKCHE

T'amna

JAPAN

power in preparation for the conquest of the whole peninsula. This inevitably brought it into conflict with Paekche,
which attempted to forestall Silla expansionism by taking
some forty forts along the border, including Taeya-song
fortress at modern Hapch'on in 642, and by attempting to
block Silla relations with T'ang China.

But Silla proved too strong for Paekche, and indeed was
more powerful than at any previous time in its history. This
was partly due to the appearance during the seventh
century of many able and energetic political and military
leaders. Especially notable among them were the statesman
Kim Ch'un-ch'u and general Kim Yu-sin, a product of
Hwarang training.

Kim Ch'un-ch'u was a member of the royal family, and
thus automatically in a position of power. He had a distinguished career as a diplomat, and played a vital part in
Silla's ultimate domination of the whole of Korea. When
Paekche attacked in 642, he went to Koguryo in an attempt
to secure military aid. But Koguryo, then ruled by the
dictator Yon Kae-so-mun was naturally opposed to supporting an ally of China, and refused. In 647 Kim Ch'unch'u went to Japan, where he managed to improve relations somewhat. Silla had been more or less at odds with
Japan ever since the conquest of the Kaya tribes had pretty
much eliminated Japanese influence on the peninsula.
But his most important achievement was the establishment
of friendly relations with T'ang China. He personally
visited China twice, and finally negotiated an agreement
which was nothing less than a T'ang military commitment
to aid Silla in the conquest of Paekche and Koguryo.

When Queen Chindok died in 654, Kim Ch'un-ch'u
became king, and is known in Korean history as King
T'aejong Muyol. He continued the close association with
China and planned the conquest of the peninsula. His
strategy was to attack the weaker Paekche first, and then to

subdue Koguryo with Chinese aid. This policy fitted well with the T'ang ambition to eliminate Koguryo. T'ang military leaders had by now concluded that the only way to do this was by means of an attack from the south, in alliance with Silla, which would involve an attack on Paekche.

King Mu of Paekche had needlessly wasted the country's military power in the earlier attacks on Silla, and had moreover strained his economic resources by extensive building projects. The Paekche ruling class appear to have been rather dissolute and oppressive, which further weakened the kingdom's powers of resistance.

King Uija, who succeeded King Mu in 641, concluded an alliance with Koguryo and once more attacked Silla, taking several forts on the northwest border. The T'ang government strongly remonstrated with Paekche for this, and demanded that it return all Silla territory and prisoners. But King Uija, confident of the support not only of Koguryo but also of Japan, with which he had made a treaty, launched another invasion in 655, taking some thirty Silla border forts. He then relapsed into an idle and dissolute life, and national defense was neglected. Although a few patriotic officials warned him of the dangers he was thus incurring, he refused to listen.

In 660 the allied forces of Silla and T'ang launched an all-out attack on Paekche. A Silla army of 50,000 under Kim Yu-sin crossed the hills at T'anhyon and reached the Hwangsan plain where the Paekche army was encamped under general Kyebaek. These troops were pushed back and their lines broken. The Silla troops advanced to lay siege to Sabi-song, the fortress which guarded Sabi, the capital. Meanwhile, a T'ang force of 130,000 under general Su Ting-fang attacked Sabi from the north after landing at the mouth of the Kum River.

Attacked from all sides and with his own troops defeated,

King Uija fled to Ungjin (modern Kongju), and when Sabi fell and all possibility of resistance vanished, Paekche surrendered to the Chinese on July 18, 660.

T'ang intentions toward Korea were made plain in the aftermath of the war. The King and his family and many civil and military officials were sent as captives to China. Administrative offices were set up at Ungjin, Mahan, Tongmyong, Kumnyon, and Togan, staffed with Chinese officials. General Su Ting-fang returned to China with the prisoners, leaving behind a force of 10,000 men under general Liu Jen-yuan, who was made military governor of the Paekche territory. The T'ang rulers plainly intended to incorporate all conquered Korean territory into the Chinese Empire.

Koguryo was now ripe for conquest. The fall of Paekche had placed it in a strategically dangerous situation and the years of war with China had exhausted its resources. In addition to this, the kingdom was rent by internal power struggles. When the strong military dictator Yon Kae-so-mun died in 666, his brother Yon Chong-t'o and his sons Namsaeng, Namgon and Namsan all became contenders for his position. Namsaeng was driven into exile and surrendered himself to the Chinese at Kungnae-song. Yon Chong-t'o, also defeated, went over to Silla, surrendering a number of fortresses and troops which were under his control.

The Silla and T'ang forces which had destroyed Paekche advanced upon Koguryo in 661, and laid siege to P'yong-yang. There was fierce fighting, and the Koguryo troops under Yon Kae-so-mun were able to drive the invaders back. In 667, however, after Yon Kae-so-mun's death and the dissension which followed, the outcome was different. Large Chinese forces led by generals Li Shih-chi and Hsueh Jen-kwei attacked by land and sea, while Silla launched a coordinated attack from the south under general Kim

In-mun, the king's brother.

Again the Koguryo soldiers proved themselves formidable warriors, and the invaders had to pay a heavy price for their gains. But ultimately the Koguryo troops were overwhelmed, and King Pojang, seeing that the situation was hopeless, surrendered together with the leaders of his government in September, 668. General Li took with him to China some 200,000 prisoners, including the King and the high officials.

The Koguryo territory was treated just as that of Paekche had been. The country was divided into administrative districts and Chinese officials were put in charge of them, with general Hsueh Jen-kwei as military governor. Some Koreans occupied subordinate positions. The two conquered kingdoms were treated as Chinese provinces and Silla's part in their conquest was ignored.

The T'ang policy toward the Korean peninsula was thus much the same as that toward other peoples bordering China. Conquest was to be followed, if possible, by assimilation. Doubtless the Chinese assumed that, once the Paekche and Koguryo territories had been fully pacified and Chinese power firmly established there, Silla would be the next to fall to Chinese arms. Silla was compelled to acquiesce in this policy at least until after the fall of Koguryo because she dared not challenge the military power of China. Once that was complete, however, and the bulk of the Chinese forces was withdrawn, the situation developed differently from Chinese expectations.

Actually resistance to T'ang domination began in Paekche even before the fall of Koguryo. A rebel army said to number 30,000 under Hukch'i Sangji seized Imjon-song fortress near modern Taehung and won many victories, capturing about 200 forts. Meanwhile, another army under Poksin, a member of the Paekche royal family, and a monk named Toch'im took Churyu fortress and besieged Sabi, the capital. Twenty thousand Silla and Chinese troops were cut off and surrounded and reinforcements had to be sent from China, while King Muyol of Silla personally led a relieving force. The rebels retreated to their stronghold of Imjon, but were far from defeated. The second of the two rebel armies then marched out of Churyu and attacked Ungjin, and this time they made their intentions clear by declaring Prince P'ung, who had recently returned from Japan, King of Paekche.

But there was dissension among the leaders of the rebellion. Poksin killed Toch'im, and was in turn assassinated by Prince P'ung. Silla and T'ang forces seized the opportunity and took Churyu fortress in 663. The rebels at Imjonsong held out for a little longer, but were defeated after their leader Chisusin fled to Koguryo. In a conciliatory gesture, the T'ang authorities abolished all but one of the administrative units they had set up and made Prince Yung, a son of King Uija, titular head of their government in Paekche.

By the time Koguryo had fallen it became clear that Silla would have to fight the Chinese to maintain her independence. The T'ang authorities set up puppet regimes under members of the old royal families of Paekche and Koguryo and encouraged them in hostility to Silla. Former Silla territory in Koguryo was not returned, and Silla was compelled to repair Chinese ships damaged in an abortive invasion of Japan.

Silla commenced active resistance to Chinese domination soon after the fall of Koguryo, at first by supporting rebellions in Chinese-controlled territory. In 670 a rebel army under Kommojam appeared and seized Kungmosong fortress. A Koguryo prince named Ansung was declared King and the rebels moved south and made contact with Silla forces, which gave both direct and indirect support, on at least one occasion sending troops to the rescue of a rebel force which was in danger of defeat.

In 671 Silla began her own military operations against Chinese rule. Paekche territory was invaded, and Sabi, the former capital and now Chinese administrative head-quarters, was taken. All the territory of former Paekche was now in Silla hands, and Silla administrative organs were set up. Emperor Kao-tsung of China attempted to counter this by ordering, in the high-handed manner of Chinese monarchs, that King Munmu be replaced by his brother Kim In-mun, who had led the victorious Silla armies in Koguryo. To make sure he would be obeyed, he also dis-patched troops in 674.

It was now the turn of Silla to face a Chinese invasion, and she faced it superbly. Decisive victories were won at Maech'o-song fortress near Yangju and at Ch'on-song for-tress at the mouth of the Yesong River on the west coast. The Chinese were driven out of their headquarters at P'yongyang and fled all the way to the Liaotung penin-sula before setting up a new administrative base. Silla now controlled most of the Korean peninsula.

Emperor Kao-tsung persisted in political maneuvers aimed at Silla, though large military forces were not again employed. In 677 he appointed Pojang, the former Kogu-ryo king, military governor of the Liaotung district and Yung, a Paekche prince, military governor of Ungjin, one of the former Paekche capitals, evidently in the hope that they might be able to muster enough strength to take these territories from Silla. This attempt was a failure, and Silla remained in effective control of most of the peninsula. The Chinese, however, persisted in claiming the former Paekche and Koguryo territories until 735, when they at last formally acknowledged that all the territory south of the P'aesu(Taedong River) belonged to the independent king-dom of Silla.

The territory north of the Taedong, which now is an

integral part of Korea, remained under Chinese control. The inhabitants of the former Koguryo kingdom, in addition to Koreans, had been a mixture of various Tungusic tribes, known by different names at different times. We hear of Suksin in the fourth century B. C., of Ilou in the third century A. D., Wuchi in the sixth century and Malgal in the seventh. In later centuries the kindred Juchen or Jurched tribes founded the semi-barbarian state of Chin or Kin at the breakup of the Sung dynasty in China. They ranged widely in Manchuria and thus some of them had come under the rule of the Koguryo kingdom, whose boundaries stretched far to the north and west of the modern Korean frontiers.

When Koguryo fell, the Chinese armies took many thousands of Koguryo captives to Yingchow (now Chaoyang) and set up there a base from which to control the eastern tribes. When a wave of resistance to Chinese domination swept the Korean peninsula, it naturally affected these people, especially the Malgal and Khitan tribes. Finally in 696 a Khitan chieftain named Li Chinchung led his people in revolt. At the same time, Taejoyong, a former Koguryo general, formed an army of Koguryo and Malgal people, and led a migration out of Chinesecontrolled territory. They settled eventually near Kirin in northern Manchuria, and there founded a state which was at first called Chin, but in 713 renamed Parhae (P'ohai in Chinese). Parhae soon gained control of most of the former Koguryo territory. Though it was made up, as we have seen, of a mixture of tribes, the ruling class of Parhae was mostly Koguryo (i.e. Korean) people. Parhae declared itself the successor of Koguryo, and sometimes called itself Koryo-guk (Koryo country).

The appearance of Parhae was naturally not welcomed either by T'ang China or by Silla, which proceeded to build a long wall along its northern border. In 733 Silla again concluded an alliance with China and attacked Parhae, but without success. Later the Chinese accepted the existence of Parhae as they had that of Silla, and regular relations began. Parhae also established trade and cultural

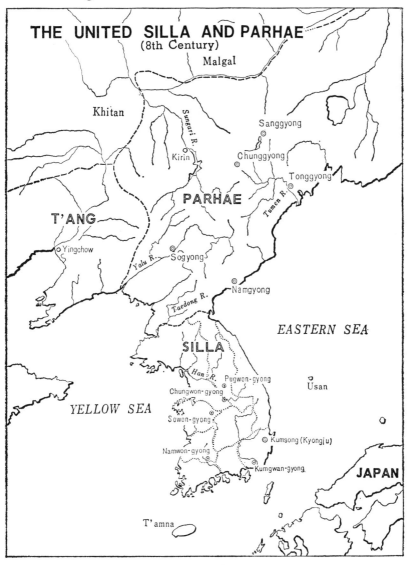

THE UNITED SILLA AND PARHAE
(8th Century)

relations with the nomadic tribes of the north and with Japan.

Parhae prosperity reached its height during the first half of the ninth century, in the reign of King Son. At that time, Parhae territory extended from the Sungari and Amur Rivers in northern Manchuria all the way down to the northern provinces of modern Korea. Its capital was Tonggyong, in the Kirin area where the state had original-ly been founded.

Like other states, near China, Parhae adopted the Chinese form of government, with six ministries, five boards, and nine courts. The country was divided into provinces and sub-provinces, and there were five sub-capitals. The capital was laid out in a gridiron pattern in imitation of Changan, the T'ang capital. There was an outer wall around the city and an inner wall around the royal palace compound and a central road leading from the south to the north gate of the city. The ruins of the walls and palaces still stand as a monument to Parhae culture.

Tiles with lotus designs, the *ondol* heating system, and stone tombs all show strong resemblances to Koguryo arts. Buddhist images and stone lanterns indicate the predomi-nance of Buddhism. The stone lantern of Namdae-myo is especially famous for its beauty.

As might be expected, there are indications of strong cultural influence from China, and finds of Japanese coins indicate at least trade relations with that country. By the later eighth century Chinese chroniclers were referring to Parhae as Haedong Songguk, the prosperous country of the East. Through tribute-trade with China it imported silk and books. It also imported silk thread and silk floss from Japan, and exported animal hides, ginseng and honey.

Parhae was a victim of the political confusion and violence which accompanied the fall of the T'ang dynasty. In 926 the Khitan, who later came to dominate much of

Manchuria and north China, conquered Parhae. Many of the ruling class, who were mostly Koreans, came south and joined the newly founded Koryo dynasty, which replaced Silla at this time.

While the Manchurian portion of the Parhae lands were lost, the part south of the Yalu-Tumen boundary remained Korean, and **Parhae** has always been considered a Korean state. Silla ruled all the rest of the peninsula, and its culture supplanted the fundamentally similar cultures of the other two kingdoms, though local variations remained, and still remain. The three segments became one people and one culture. Buddhism remained the dominant religion, which also had a unifying effect. The foundation was laid for the rapid development of Korean culture which was to follow.

Chapter 7

The Political and Social
Structure of United Silla

The great expansion of Silla territory necessitated adjustment and refinement of the government organizations. While Silla was not in control of the northern areas along the Yalu and Tumen Rivers, it did control all the territory south of the Taedong River. Most of the area north of that line is in any case mountainous and thinly populated.

First of all, a change occurred in the royal marriage customs. It will be recalled that members of the royal clan were given the social rank of *Songgol* ("Sacred Bone"), and that this was later changed to *Chin'gol*("True Bone"). This change came about at the time of the unification, and may be explained as follows. It had formerly been the custom for the Silla kings to marry only members of the Pak clan, possibly because the royal (Kim) clan and the Pak clan had held dominant positions during the tribal period. At the time of the unification, however, the kings began to deviate from this custom, and the royal clan was renamed Chin'gol to indicate the change. King Muyol's mother had come from the Kim clan (another Kim, not the royal one. There were—and are—several different Kim clans in Korea) and King Muyol himself married a younger sister of general Kim Yu-sin. Also at this time the kings began to receive Chinese-style posthumous titles rather than the Buddhist titles that had formerly been given them.

The *Kolp'um* or Bone Rank system was regularized and strictly enforced. As we have noted in an earlier chapter, positions in government were closely related to social status, certain grades in the bureaucracy being restricted to certain social classes. The old system of decision-making by a conference of clan leaders was now abolished, and the organs of government acquired specialized functions. It is necessary to emphasize here that these developments took place after the unification, not before.

Of the specialized ministries and offices which now began to be set up the most important was the *Chipsabu,* or executive office, whose head had duties and powers resembling those of a modern prime minister. *Ibangbu,* the justice ministry, is recorded to have promulgated some sixty pieces of legislation during the reign of King Muyol. One of the most interesting developments was the establishment of the *Sajongbu,* or board of censors, whose duties were to detect and expose all instances of corruption or maladministration in the government.

In the next reign, that of King Munmu, the justice ministry was enlarged and divided into two sections, designated left and right in Chinese fashion. As new provinces and subdivisions (called respectively *chu* and *kun*) were established, local boards of censors were set up to keep watch over the newly appointed officials. Thus, in the period following the unification, a fully developed bureaucratic government on the Chinese model but modified by the strongly aristocratic nature of Silla society had appeared. The names of the various government offices and their functions were as follows:

Chipsabu, Executive	*Sajongbu,* Board of Censors
Chobu, Revenue	*Wihwabu,* Personnel
Yebu, Rituals	*Sarokkwan,* Paymaster General
Pyongbu, Military	*Yejakpu,* Public Works
Ch'angbu, Supply	*Yonggaekpu,* Foreign Relations
Sungbu, Horses	*Ibangbu,* Justice
Sonbu, Marine	

Special administrative offices were set up from time to time, whenever a city wall or a Buddhist temple was to be built. Construction increased greatly after unification, and Kyongju, the capital, was crowded with palaces and temples. The records speak of 170,000 houses in Kyongju, and it was proudly noted that not one of them had a thatched roof, all of the citizens being sufficiently affluent to afford tile.

The imposition of this Chinese bureaucratic type of government upon a strongly aristocratic society was not without its difficulties and was never complete. The main reason for this is that, while the Chinese type of government was authoritarian, it was also equalitarian, at any rate in theory. It tended, when fully applied, to strengthen the power of the monarch and his government at the expense of the aristocracy, and to place qualified persons in positions of power regardless of social status. In Silla the positions of real political power were reserved for the Chin'gol, the royal clan, which naturally increased in numbers and collateral branches as time passed. The development of an efficient bureaucracy was thus considerably impeded.

Even though they had a monopoly of power, the aristocrats resisted any attempt at really effective application of Chinese political theory. The matter of local government is a case in point. The country was divided into nine provinces, or *chu*, each of which was subdivided into *kun* and *hyon*. King Kyongdok, who reigned from 742 to 765, attempted to set up a Chinese type of administration in the provinces, with officials appointed and controlled by the central government. The aristocrats, especially the Chin'gol, viewed this as a danger to their power and position, which was mainly based upon ownership of land and control of local affairs. The following King, Hyegong (765–780), was compelled to nullify Kyongdok's action and to restore the old names of the provinces, which had been changed to symbolize the new type of administration.

The division of the country into *chu, kun* and *hyon* and the establishment of provincial capitals began during the reign of King Chijung (500–513). As the nation expanded through conquest, new provincial governments were set up. By the reign of King Sinmun (681–691) the system was complete.

The location and organization of the new provinces were at first based mainly upon military considerations, as these areas were mostly conquered territory on the frontiers of the other two kingdoms. Provincial governors were called *Kunju,* a military title, during the period of conflict that preceded unification. This was changed during the reign of King Munmu (661–680) to *Ch'onggwan,* a civilian title, and finally to *Todok,* or provincial governor-general, when the conquests were complete and it was no longer necessary to use the provincial capitals as military bases.

The location of Kyongju in the southeastern part of the peninsula was rather an awkward one for governing the expanded kingdom. At one time it was suggested that the capital be moved west to Taegu, which was more centrally located, but royalty and aristocracy had such strong traditional connections with Kyongju that this suggestion was dropped. Instead, a system of sub-capitals was resorted to. There were five of these, the cities of Kumgwan (now Kimhae), Namwon, Sowon (now Ch'ongju), Chungwon (now Ch'ungju) and Pugwon (now Wonju). Officials from the capital were sent to govern these places and to check the power of local landowners. Mayors called *Sasin* or *Sadaedung* governed these cities, while kun and hyon were governed by T'aesu ("Great Defender") and Hyollyong ("Hyon Chief"). Like the central bureaucracy, the occupants of these posts were drawn only from certain social classes, the higher posts going to the higher classes. The

Todok or Governor-General, a quasi-military official, for example, had to be no higher than the second or lower than the ninth grade. A special eleven-grade ranking system was set up for these local officials which was correlated with the seventeen-grade system of the capital.

Paekche and Koguryo aristocrats were provided for in the reorganized government if and when they voluntarily gave themselves up to Silla. They were given rank and posts corresponding to those they had had in their old kingdoms, or (as in the case of Paekche) one rank below their former positions. This was not simply a gesture of kindness to defeated enemies. It brought the majority of the ruling classes of the former kingdoms firmly under Silla control, and thus deprived any rebellions that might have taken place of most of their leadership.

In addition to the regular local administrative units, special areas called *hyang, so* and *pugok* were organized. These were populated mostly by people called *yemin* ("subordinate people"), who were actually prisoners of war employed by the government on large-scale projects requiring heavy labor. Sometimes such a community could earn promotion to the status of a regular hyon by meritorious service.

The lowest-ranking officials in local administrations, and hence those who did most of the actual work of government, were chosen from the wealthy or powerful among the local populations, another practice designed to bind all natural leaders of society to Silla allegiance.

The expanded kingdom required an expanded military organization, both to police the conquered populations and to resist foreign incursions. The T'ang armies had withdrawn and Silla was recognized by the Chinese court as a legitimate government, but the threat from China was nevertheless still very real.

The Silla army had originally consisted of two large units,

taedang stationed near the capital and *chong* in the countryside, in addition to the royal bodyguard. The wars and the consequent increase of territory necessitated the expansion of these forces, and eventually there were nine units now called *Ku-sodang* at the capital and one *chong* in each province except for Hanju, which had two.

Six of the nine capital units were made up of recruits from the conquered areas of Paekche and Koguryo and a Tungusic tribe called Malgal which had been under Koguryo rule. This is still another instance of the Silla efforts to unite the whole peninsula in loyalty to its rule. Each *sodang* was distinguished by a two-colored uniform collar, much in the manner of modern army shoulder-patches, and it seems clear that this was part of an effort to encourage *esprit de corps*. The pride of the conquered peoples was thus appeased and rebellious elements simultaneously checked.

The Silla attempts to reform the bureaucracy in conformity with Chinese practice were paralleled by equally futile attempts to reform the landholding system. Beginning in 689 a system called *Kwallyo-jon* ("Office Land System") was instituted under which government officials received the incomes of designated farming areas but did not directly control the land or people of these areas. This was essentially the Chinese system. It lasted only about seventy years, having been completely abolished by 757 and replaced by the old *Nogup* system under which government grants of land were permanent and hereditary. The aristocrats thus once more asserted their power and independence of authority and preserved their private estates, which were the bases of that power.

Another attempt to apply Chinese ideas was the system known as *Chongjon-je* ("Adult Male Land"). Under this system, the amount of land each farming family occupied was determined by the number of adult males between twenty and sixty years of age in the family. Ideally, the land was to be redistributed at regular intervals to take account of changing family composition. The system had the dual merit of providing adequate land for each farming family and giving the government accurate information for its tax rolls. Buildings, trees and livestock were also taken into account in distributing land and levying taxes, which, it should be remembered, were mostly paid in agricultural produce rather than in cash. The system was first instituted in 722, and its details may be studied in Silla tax documents still preserved in the Shosoin temple in Japan.

The aristocrats did not find it necessary to ask for the repeal of this system. It was frustrated by the simple expedient of buying up or otherwise transferring farm freeholds to the private estates, where the taxes paid by farmers went to the aristocratic landholder rather than to the government treasury. This was easy to do, since the government officials were themselves all landed aristocrats. It caused considerable difficulty for the government, whose income steadily shrank as the great estates grew in size. Buddhist temples added to the problem by acquiring large areas of tax-free farmland for themselves.

As Silla prosperity increased in the period of peace that followed unification, both domestic and foreign trade likewise increased. As early as the end of the fifth century we find mention of a market in Kyongju, and by the reign of King Hyoso (692–701), four markets were operating there under government control. They existed ostensibly to supply the needs of the royal clan and the government, but soon began selling to the general population as well.

Foreign trade was closely tied to official foreign relations. It was the custom whenever a diplomatic mission was sent abroad to send with it a quantity of gifts for the monarch being visited. He in his turn would send back gifts with the mission when it returned. Private individuals began sending along trade goods with these missions and this eventually became an officially accepted practice.

The bulk of foreign trade was with China, as there were frequent exchanges of embassies with the T'ang government. It was mostly in luxury items such as gold, silver and silk, Silla ginseng and Chinese tea. Silla monks studying in China also took a hand in it, though their imports were cultural rather than commercial, consisting mainly of books. There was also some trade with Japan, and Japanese imports far exceeded exports, one of the many indications of Japan's cultural debt to Korea.

The reason for all this subterfuge in the matter of trade was the disdain for merchants both in Korean tradition and in Confucian doctrine. Buying and selling were classified as non-productive activities in the Confucian texts, and merchants, even though they might become rich, had a lower status than farmers in the social scale. Governments only grudgingly recognized the need for trade, and it was seldom given official encouragement or seriously considered as a source of revenue. Money-lending was subject to a similar prejudice.

From early times peddlers had supplied the needs of farming villages, forming markets called *hyangsi*. They could be set up anywhere, whenever there was a need for them, and consisted of simple, portable stalls. Eventually each district came to have regular market days, and the custom persists to this day. Transactions in the Silla markets were mostly barter rather than cash, the local housewives exchanging rice for the various articles they bought.

The manufactured articles used by the aristocracy and royalty were produced by the low-class people in the special villages (*hyang*, *so* and *pugok*) mentioned earlier. A government office was in charge of each handicraft, and each area, *so* especially, specialized in one product—a sort of primitive factory system. The workers were virtually government slaves. There are practically no articles of perishable materials extant from this period, but the stone structures and sculptures, some jewelry and numerous ceramic items give some idea of the high development of arts and crafts during the United Silla period.

The documents preserved in the Shosoin temple in Japan give us considerable information about village life. They were evidently compiled in 755, and concern the subcapital of Sowon and four neighboring villages. The number of inhabitants, houses, livestock, and the number and variety of trees, as well as the amount of land belonging to each individual, are set down in minute detail. These censuses were taken every three years, and were the basis not only of tax assessments but also of the imposition of corvée labor and military service. Families were placed in nine categories according to the number of men between twenty and sixty, who were liable to corvée and military duty. All males were classified in six categories, according to age, in order to keep regular records of the numbers available for corvée and the army.

The villages were ruled by officials called *ch'onju,* usually prominent local people, appointed by the government. They were given the use of certain tracts of land in return for their services. Some of the land belonged to the government, and the rest was distributed among the farmers, as previously explained, unless the village was part of a private estate.

The failure of the Chinese system of stipends, by which officials received their income from the taxes on certain tracts of land but did not own or control the land itself, meant that the village heads were no longer part of the bureaucracy. They became increasingly independent during the closing years of Silla, and were probably a factor in the fall of the dynasty.

Chapter 8

United Silla Culture

Once its conquests had been consolidated, its borders settled, and its government adapted to meet its new circumstances, Silla entered a great period of peace, prosperity, and cultural development. This was also the period of greatest Chinese influence upon Korea, for the T'ang dynasty now also entered upon its greatest days. Indeed, it may be said that it was the T'ang dynasty that set a permanent mark of Chinese influence, not only upon Korea, but also upon all the lands and peoples bordering China.

Buddhism was the predominant religion. It had flourished exceedingly since the days of the Three Kingdoms, and now temples were built on a grand scale. Particularly notable were Sach'onwang-sa, Pongdok-sa and Pulguk-sa in the Kyongju area. In other parts of the kingdom, Pusok-sa rose in Yongju, T'ongdo-sa in Yangsan, Pomo-sa in Tongnae, Haein-sa in Hapch'on, Hwaom-sa in Kurye, and Popchu-sa in Poun. Many of these temples still exist today, and although most of the wooden buildings have been destroyed and rebuilt several times, the stone pagodas and the stone, iron and bronze images still remain from Silla times.

One of the great stimuli of Buddhist development was the travel of numerous Korean monks to China for study. Some even went as far as India, to visit the scenes of Buddhism's founding, and to obtain scriptures. The monks

Chajang, Uisang, Wonch'uk and Hyech'o were especially outstanding. Wonch'uk remained in China all his life, translating Buddhist scriptures from Sanskrit into Chinese, writing commentaries, and contributing much to Chinese Buddhism. Hyech'o went to India by sea upon completion of his studies in China and made a tour of Buddhist shrines and temples, returning to China by way of Central Asia. He wrote a book based on his travels, a fragment of which was recently discovered in China. It contains priceless information about India and the countries on China's western border and their relationships during the T'ang dynasty.

Another consequence of this cultural contact was the increasing introduction of the numerous Buddhist sects, some of which we have discussed in our consideration of Three Kingdoms Buddhism. In the closing years of the Three Kingdoms, Podok had already introduced the Yolban (Nirvana Sutra) sect into Koguryo, and Chajang had introduced the Kyeyul (Vinaya) sect into Silla. After the unification Uisang established the Hwaom (Avatamsaka Sutra), Wonhyo the Popsong (Dharmata) and Chinp'yo the Popsang (Dharmalakshana) sect. These together constituted the *Ogyo* ("Five Doctrinal Sects"). They were grouped together because they all laid special emphasis upon scripture, their differences consisting in which particular parts of the vast Buddhist scriptures they most venerated.

The Hwaom and Popsong sects were the most influential of the five, Hwaom being particularly popular among the aristocrats. It spread throughout the country from its center at Pusok-sa. Popsong was based upon the ideas of Wonhyo, who had tried to harmonize the doctrines of all the principal sects. This was embodied in his book *Sipmun hwajong-non* (Treatise on the Harmonious Understanding of the Ten Doctrines), from which his posthumous title, Hwajong Kuksa, was derived. Since this was a distinctively

Korean sect, it came to be called Haedong-jong, the Sect of Haedong, i.e. of Korea.

Since they laid emphasis on the study of the scriptures, the Five Sects appealed particularly to the aristocracy, since only they had the means and opportunity to obtain education. Among the masses, however, there now appeared a new sect called Chongt'o-gyo ("Pure Land"), which made no such demands. It was an elaboration of the Mahayana doctrine of the Bodhisattvas, which we have previously discussed, and taught that one could obtain salvation (enter the "Pure Land")simply by praying to the Bodhisattvas. It thus had great popular appeal, and soon spread throughout the kingdom. In this it was greatly helped by Wonhyo, who abandoned his earlier doctrinal beliefs to spread the new sect, devoting all the latter part of his life to preaching and teaching it. Chongt'o-gyo soon became the largest of the sects in Korea.

During the latter part of the Silla period there appeared in Korea what was perhaps the most influential sect in all Buddhist history. This was called Ch'an in Chinese and Son in Korean, but is most familiar to the western world under its Japanese name, Zen. The word means "meditation," and that is what it emphasized. It taught that the state of true enlightenment was to be attained, not by study of the scriptures nor yet by prayer to the Bodhisattvas, but by meditation, a concentrating of the mind upon the central truths of existence, to the exclusion of all physical perceptions, until, in a flash of intuition, one reached the state of enlightenment in which one was aware of the true nature of reality and passed beyond the eternal cycle of rebirth and suffering which Buddhism regarded as the nature of earthly existence.

The Son sect first appeared in Silla with the return of the monk Pomnang from China in the middle of the seventh century. It was popularized by Sinhaeng in the latter part of the eighth century and by Toui at the beginning of the ninth, by which time it was firmly established and in lively competition with the Five Sects. It was eventually divided into nine branches known as *Kusan,* or the Nine Mountains, each with its own central temple, generally on a mountain, which accounts for the name. It became particularly popular among the rich and powerful local families who began to emerge during the period of unrest that led to the fall of the Silla dynasty.

The imposition of Chinese-style bureaucratic government involved the setting up of numerous educational institutions, for in Chinese practice a man's qualifications for office were determined by his learning. Chiefly this consisted of knowledge of the so-called Confucian classics. These had a place in Chinese education similar to that occupied until comparatively recent times by the Greek and Roman classics in European education. From this time on they came to occupy a similar place in Korea. In order to understand Korean education, therefore, it will be necessary to discuss them briefly.

Confucius himself, according to tradition, always disclaimed any originality for his ideas. Like many another reformer, he claimed rather to be restoring the ideas and practices of the past in their pristine purity. The books referred to as the classics he claimed to have edited from old documents. The list varied at different times in Chinese history, but generally included these five: the *Shih ching* or Classic of Songs, a collection of ancient poetry; the *Shu ching,* or Classic of Documents, a collection of historical records and speeches dating to very ancient times (it should be remembered that the traditional dates for Confucius' life are 551–479 B. C.), many of which are now considered to be spurious; the *I ching,* or Classic of Changes, a book on the ancient art of divination using the eight trigrams and sixty-four hexagrams, patterns of solid or broken lines (four of them can be seen on the modern Korean flag); the *Ch'un ch'iu,* or Spring and Autumn Annals, a terse chronicle of events in the state of Lu (Confucius' native place) between 722 and 481 B. C.; and the *Li chi,* or Record of Rituals, a miscellaneous compilation dealing with rituals, which were very important in Confucian thought.

There were several other books of almost equal importance, and commentaries on the classics reached vast proportions. Two books were considered as being on almost the same level as the classics, and were especially important in Korea: the *Lun yu,* or Analects, a collection of Confucius' sayings supposedly compiled by his students; and the *Hsiao ching,* or Classic of Filial Piety, which inculcated the virtue most highly prized in Confucian thought.

It has become fairly clear by now that the attribution of much of this material to Confucius, either as author or as editor, is mistaken. Most of it is compilations of varying date, and many of the documents can be shown to have been written after Confucius' death. But it should be borne in mind that the attribution of a work to a great thinker in order to confer authority upon it was not felt to be wrong in ancient China.

Education, for the Chinese and also for the Koreans from Silla times onward, consisted mostly in the study of these books. Furthermore, education meant preparation for an official career, the theory being that a thorough grounding in the classics would implant in the student's mind those virtues necessary to a ruler. The Chinese schools were theoretically open to anyone who could pay the fees, but the Korean schools which now began to appear were open only to aristocrats. When we mention "schools" in what follows, it must be understood that, unless otherwise noted, we means schools for training officials.

The first such school was established in 682, and was called *Kukhak,* or National School. It was renamed *T'aehak-*

kam, Great Learning Institute, about the middle of the eighth century. The teachers were *Paksa* ("Learned Men," a word used in modern times to designate the holder of a Ph. D.). It was open to sons of aristocratic families between the ages of fifteen and thirty. The course lasted for nine years and ended, as in China, with examinations which determined the candidates' eligibility for office.

These examinations ranked the candidates in three grades. Those who were well versed in either the *Spring and Autumn Annals* or the *Record of Rituals,* and who understood both the *Analects* and the *Classic of Filial Piety* constituted the highest grade. Those who had mastered the *Record of Rituals,* the *Analects* and the *Filial Piety* occupied the middle grade, and those who knew only the *Record of Rituals* and *Filial Piety* were in the lowest grade.

While this training and examination system was limited to the aristocracy, it was still in conflict with traditional Silla social custom, which placed great stress on differences of rank within the upper class. As we have seen, the result was that the higher government positions were reserved to the royal clan, thus defeating the purpose of the examination system, which was to staff the government exclusively on the basis of merit.

The adoption of Chinese government and educational institutions (in highly modified form, to be sure) stimulated the growth of Confucian scholarship among the upper classes. Aristocratic young gentlemen now joined the monks in journeys to China for study, and eminent Korean scholars began to appear, most notably Kangsu and Sol Ch'ong. Kangsu was particularly admired for his ability in drafting government documents and diplomatic notes, a difficult and intricate art of great importance in the Chinese type of government, while Sol Ch'ong was best known for his broad scholarship in Chinese literature and history. He was the son of Wonhyo, the great Buddhist

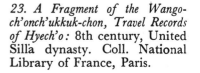

24. *General View of Sokkuram Grotto:* Near Kyongju, North Kyongsang Province. United Silla dynasty, 8th century.

25. *Entrance, Sokkuram Grotto and Four Deva Kings:* Granite. Buddha, H. 3.26m, throne, H. 1.59m. Deva Kings, H. 1.93m.

26. *Main Entrance, Pulguk-sa:* Near Kyongju, North Kyongsang Province. United Silla dynasty, 8th century.

27. *Sokka Pagoda (Sakyamuni Stupa):* Granite. H. 7.38m. United Silla dynasty, mid 8th century. Pulguk-sa, Kyongju.

28. *Bhaisajyaguru (Yaksa Yorae):* Gilt bronze. H. 38.1cm. United Silla dynasty, 8th-9th century. National Museum of Korea.

29, 30. Pongdok-sa Bell and Detail:
Bronze, with long inscription with
date 771 A.D. H. 3.33m, D. 2.27m.
United Silla dynasty, 8th century.
Kyongju Branch of the National
Museum of Korea.

31. Memorial Stele of King Muyol: Granite. H. 1.94m. United Silla dynasty,
7th century. Tomb of King Muyol, Kyongju.

scholar, and it was he who adapted *Idu,* the system of using Chinese characters phonetically to record Korean songs and poems, to the writing of Korean prose. He did this by rearranging the characters which carried the basic meanings to conform with Korean sentence structure and then adding the Idu characters to indicate the inflectional endings, a vital part of the Korean language but largely absent in Chinese. In this way he not only wrote original works but also made Chinese literature more accessible to Korean readers by providing a method which amounted, in effect, to translation into the Korean language. He is said to have been the author of many works, but his *Kye-hwa-wang* is the only one which has survived.

It will have become apparent that history was highly important in Chinese learning. Historical works bulk large in the Confucian classics, and histories of states, reigns and dynasties were regularly compiled by Chinese historians. This now began to be done for Silla, particularly by the eminent scholar Kim Tae-mun, during the early eighth century. It is recorded that he wrote *Kosung-jon* (Tales of the Great Monks), *Kyerim chapchon* (Tales of Silla, Kyerim being another name of Silla), and *Hwarang segi* (The Records of Hwarang). These books were used as source material by the Koryo historian Kim Pu-sik, who is said to have compiled his *Samguk sagi* (History of the Three Kingdoms) in 1145. Unfortunately, however, none of these Silla works has survived.

Distinguished scholars continued to appear and to obtain their education in China during the closing years of the Silla dynasty. Kim Un-gyong, Kim Ka-gi and Ch'oe Ch'i-won are representative figures. Ch'oe Ch'i-won is most notable for having passed the Chinese government examinations and having obtained a government post in China, a very rare accomplishment for a foreigner. On his return to Korea he was appointed *Hallim haksa,* the scholar-official who drafted royal proclamations and decrees, a very high post. But perhaps his greatest contribution from our point of view was his composition of *Kyewon p'ilgyong,* a collection in twenty volumes of the essays he wrote during his stay in China. This precious work is still in existence, the oldest surviving document of the Silla period. Several of Ch'oe Ch'i-won's poems have also survived.

There was some development of the natural sciences, chiefly as a consequence of Chinese influence. Astrological beliefs, which were closely connected with agriculture, led to the development of astronomy, and the most notable of the few surviving Silla buildings is a stone observatory, which has already been described. A government office of astronomy was instituted, which conducted research and training programs. This in turn led to the study of mathematics, for which government officials were also appointed. An office was also set up to encourage the study and practice of Chinese methods in medicine, but this was somewhat impeded by the tenacity of folk and religious beliefs.

Geomancy, which still has a certain importance today, was imported from China during the closing years of Silla by the monk Toson. Its Korean name was *P'ungsujiri-sol,* the Theory of Water, Wind and Earth. Under this system, every landscape was described by two of four attributes, depending upon its conformation: *swoe* (decay), *wang* (prosperity), *sun* (right) and *yok* (wrong). These qualities were held to influence the destinies of persons residing in places which possessed them. Thus areas possessing the qualities of *wang* and *sun* were chosen for the sites of houses and important buildings, and also for graves, while those exhibiting *swoe* and *yok* were chosen for temples, in order to avert calamity. During the Koryo period geomancy was often used in political maneuvering.

With the introduction of Chinese writing and later of the Idu system of writing the Korean language, many myths and legends from oral tradition were recorded during the Silla period, some of which found their places in the *Samguk sagi* and *Samguk yusa* (Memorabilia of the Three Kingdoms). Most of them were related to religion, especially Buddhism, but many were purely secular. Among these, some of which are still known and loved in Korea, are the love story of Hodong, Prince of Koguryo; the fine story of Ondal, son-in-law of King P'yongwon of Koguryo; the heroic tales of the Hwarang of Silla; the tragedy of Tomi; the love-affairs of Sol; and the story of Master Paekkyol.

Hyangga, the special Silla poetic form, developed a rich lyricism. Among the most admired poems were Wonhyo's "Hwaom-ga," Hwarang Tugogok's "Mo chukchirang-ga," monk Wolmyong's "Tosol-ga" and "Che mangmae-ga," and monk Ch'ungdam's "Anmin-ga." Most of the poets were either monks or Hwarang. Their poems mainly concerned patriotism, Buddhism, and praise of the illustrious dead.

Toward the close of the ninth century Taegu Hwasang and Wihong gathered a large number of these hyangga into an anthology called *Samdaemok,* but unfortunately it has not survived. Only twenty-five hyangga poems, included in the texts of the *Samguk yusa* and *Kyunyo-jon* exist today. These survivors provided models for later Korean poetry, and are also extremely important for the study of the ancient Korean language.

Some of the greatest achievements of Silla were in the plastic arts. What remains to us is mostly work in such durable materials as stone and metal, so that we have little idea of Silla painting or architecture, but there is enough to indicate the high sophistication and skill of Silla artists. Most of what has come down to us is Buddhist religious art, including stone pagodas, Buddha images and bas-reliefs, and temple bells.

Perhaps the highest achievement of Silla art still extant is Sokkuram, a grotto shrine on the summit of Mt. T'oham near Pulguk-sa in the Kyongju area. Construction was begun at the suggestion of prime minister Kim Tae-song in 751, during the reign of King Kyongdok, and was finished during the following reign.

Unlike similar north Chinese shrines, which were usually carved out of the living rock, Sokkuram is an artificial grotto. It consists of an anteroom and a large domed chamber constructed of granite blocks so skilfully fitted that the dome has remained intact for twelve centuries without admitting enough moisture to seriously damage the sculptures within. This was accomplished by covering the finished dome with earth, which also gives the shrine the appearance of being a natural part of the landscape.

Except for the great central image, the decoration of the grotto is all in stone relief. On the walls on either side of the entrance are the four Deva Kings, guardians of most Buddhist temples in Korea. The passage widens slightly, and four other relief figures are seen, two on either side, just before the doorway of the central chamber. Surrounding the central figure on the walls of the main chamber are carved stone panels depicting bodhisattvas and arhats, slim, graceful figures, including the eleven-headed Kwanum (the Chinese Kwan-yin and Japanese Kannon), a bodhisattva who became the symbol of compassion and the center of a popular cult.

The round, domed chamber is dominated by the figure of the Buddha in the center, carved from a massive block of white granite almost ten feet high, but in no way bulky or awkward. The pedestal is carved in the form of a lotus, an ancient Indian symbol. Buddha sits in the familiar cross-legged posture, his right hand pointing downward in a gesture symbolic of calling the earth to witness the truth of his teaching. His robe is so delicately carved that it seems about to flutter in the breeze, and the whole figure is graceful and well proportioned. This is the mature perfection of Silla art.

Nearby is Pulguk-sa, the Temple of the Buddha Land, which was begun in the same year as Sokkuram. Its wooden buildings were burned during the Japanese invasions at the end of the sixteenth century and subsequently rebuilt, but the stone portions of the original temple remain. Two flights of stone steps ascend the raised earth platform on which the main buildings are situated, symbolizing the passage from the world of illusion to enlightenment. They are flanked at the top by two stone pagodas, Sokka Pagoda, strong and simple, Tabo Pagoda, complex and intricately carved. A comparable pair of pagodas from the Silla period is found at Hwaom-sa in South Cholla Province.

Several bronze temple bells of the Silla period are also still extant. They differ from western bells in that they do not flare at the mouth and were not sounded by a clapper from inside, but by a wooden post suspended horizontally by two chains or ropes next to the bell. The most famous of these is the great bell of Pongdok-sa, now preserved at the Kyongju museum. Over ten feet tall and about seven feet in diameter, it is the largest of the surviving Silla bells. Graceful reliefs decorate its sides, divine beings flying through swirling clouds within the floral borders at top and bottom. It was cast during the second half of the eighth century.

A similar bell, smaller but older and not less beautiful, is found at Sangwon-sa in Kangwon Province. Records tell of a huge bell, four times the size of the Pongdok-sa one, at Hwangyong-sa, a temple which was destroyed during the Mongol invasions in the Koryo period.

Many other Silla works of art, too numerous to describe here in detail, are still extant. Of particular interest are the base and capital (the inscribed stone slab has been destroyed) of the memorial stele found at the tomb of King Muyol near Kyongju. The base is a stone tortoise, while the capital is a lively and life-like dragon, if such an epithet may be applied to a mythical beast. There are also stone slabs carved with the twelve animals of the Chinese zodiac which were erected at royal tombs, stone lanterns which decorated temple grounds, and stamped or incised tiles and bricks.

We learn from ancient records that painting and calligraphy flourished during the Silla period, but no examples have survived. Kim Saeng, Yo Kug-il and Ch'oe Ch'i-won (whom we have met before in another connection) are mentioned as masters of calligraphy.

Music flourished also, and a special government office was in charge of music to accompany court rituals. Such stringed instruments as the *Komun'go* and *Kayagum,* still in use today, were used, in addition to lutes and flutes. Okpogo and his disciple Kwigum are mentioned as distinguished composers.

Chapter 9

The Fall of Silla

Silla reached a peak of power and prosperity about the middle of the eighth century, during the reign of King Kyongdok. Thereafter it steadily declined until its fall in 935. This decline was attributable to several factors. In the first place, the contradiction between the Chinese system of administration and the essentially aristocratic nature of Korean society led to feuds within the ruling class and outbreaks of violence which weakened the power of the central government. This enabled the merchants, who had always been discriminated against by the government, to expand their activities and eventually to acquire such wealth and power that they were virtually independent of government control. It also enabled the great landowners to set up what became in time small independent states, with their own armies and governments, feuding among themselves and so oppressing the people that a number of peasant revolts resulted. We shall examine each of these factors in turn.

The royal clan had by now grown large enough to contain several collateral branches, and these were the immediate cause of political conflict. Two in particular concern us here. Down to the middle of the eighth century, the Kings of Silla had been direct descendants of King Muyol, the ruler under whom Silla had unified the peninsula. But a rival branch of the clan which traced its descent to King Naemul (356–401) arose during the reign

111

of King Hyegong, who succeeded King Kyongdok in 765, and eventually managed to seize control of the throne.

In 768 a group of conservative aristocrats, fearful of the threat to their power posed by the Chinese style of government which had been adopted, rose in revolt. They were joined by many others, and the revolt took several years to quell. A similar revolt broke out in 780, this time with much more serious consequences. King Hyegong was assassinated and Kim Yang-sang, a member of the Naemul branch, seized the throne. He is known by his posthumous title, Sondok. He ruled only four years, and was succeeded by King Wonsong, another descendant of Naemul.

The lines were thus clearly drawn between the descendants of Muyol, who stood for the adoption of Chinese administrative methods, a strong central government, and subordination of the aristocracy, and the descendants of Naemul, who stood for the power and privileges of the aristocratic class. Kim Hon-ch'ang, pretender to the throne in the Muyol line, led an unsuccessful revolt in 822, and his son, Kim Pom-mun, led another in 825. While these revolts did not topple the Naemul clan, they were sufficiently successful in the countryside. Kim Hon-ch'ang, who at the time of the revolt was governor of Ungch'on Province, set up an independent government and managed to defy the central authority until he was killed in battle.

The conflicts thus initiated by the split within the royal clan settled into a chronic state of civil war which lasted for the next 150 years, until the end of the dynasty. Twenty kings succeeded each other during this period, most of them seizing the throne by violence and losing it the same way. Often they conspired with the rising merchants such as Chang Po-go, whom we shall meet again, who aided King Hungdok and later, in 836, helped to place King Sinmu on the throne.

As a result of all this, the power of the central government was almost completely destroyed. The capital aristocracy and the provincial magnates did pretty much as they pleased, expanding their holdings, ruthlessly exploiting the people and feuding with each other. The country was sinking rapidly into a state of political and social chaos.

While the conservative factions in the Chin'gol, the royal clan, were struggling for power and against the establishment of truly Confucian institutions and practices, a countervailing pressure arose in the ranks immediately below them. It will be recalled that positions of political power were reserved to Chin'gol in the Silla government. This had not been especially resented under the comparatively liberal regimes of King Muyol and his descendants, but when the conservatives came to power the non-Chin'gol aristocrats began to feel keenly their exclusion from effective participation in government, and even to challenge the Bone Rank system itself. The situation was exacerbated by the fact that the conservatives often punished their opponents by excluding them from Chin'gol rank, thus providing the lower aristocrats with allies and further weakening the class system. All this contributed significantly to the political upheavals of the time.

Revolt against the Silla class system was further strengthened by men who had been educated in China. They had acquired there the equalitarian ideas of the Confucian political philosophy, which stressed the selection of government officials on the basis of merit alone, regardless of social class or royal affiliation. Many of them had been encouraged to go to China in order to remove them from the political scene, in the hope that they would not return or would lose their influence through long absence. This policy boomeranged, however, and a powerful group of

Confucian scholars ranged itself against the conservative Chin'gol who held the throne.

Prominent among these scholars were the men whose eminence and achievements made them known to history as the Three Ch'oes: Ch'oe Ch'i-won (whom we have met before), Ch'oe Sin-ji and Ch'oe Sung-u. Their fates were significant of the temper of the times. Ch'oe Ch'i-won, as we have seen, obtained a high government post upon his return from China, but when his advanced Confucian ideas proved unacceptable to the Chin'gol rulers he abandoned it to spend the remainder of his life in scholarly seclusion. Both Ch'oe Sin-ji and Ch'oe Sung-u were involved so deeply in reform movements that they were ultimately forced to flee, Ch'oe Sung-u to the evanescent state of Later Paekche which appeared during the breakup of the dynasty and Ch'oe Sin-ji to Koryo, which ultimately replaced Silla as the ruler of Korea.

As government control of the population declined, a class of rich merchants appeared. Trade generally had been despised in Silla society, which in this followed the Confucian doctrine that trade was non-productive and that a healthy national economy must be based primarily on agriculture. Merchants had been strictly controlled and foreign trade almost monopolized by the government. But now that the ruling class was absorbed in factional strife the merchants began to trade freely with foreign countries.

This trade was primarily with China and Japan. The art of shipbuilding was very advanced in Korea, so much so that Japanese travelling to China often made use of Silla ships in preference to their own, and this gave the merchants a distinct advantage. Silla quarters began to appear in numerous Chinesec coastal ities, where the agents of these merchants lived, each with its own self-governing body which mediated between the merchants and negotiated on their behalf with the Chinese. The permanent nature of these settlements is indicated by the fact that numerous Buddhist temples were set up for their exclusive use. While trade with Japan was not so extensive, there is at least one recorded instance of several dozen ships visiting there at one time, an expedition said to have been enormously profitable.

The position and influence of the merchants are well illustrated by the career of one of the most powerful of them, Chang Po-go. He went to China in his youth and served for a time as a soldier. Then he entered trade, in which his astuteness soon made him wealthy. In 828 he established his headquarters on the island of Ch'onghae, now known as Wando, one of the numerous islands off the southern coast of South Cholla Province.

The Yellow Sea at this time was infested with Chinese pirates, who frequently plundered Korean coastal towns and carried off the inhabitants to sell as slaves. The weak, strife-torn Silla government of the ninth century was unable to control this menace, so Chang Po-go set about doing it himself. He recruited his own private army and navy, a force that is said to have grown to 10,000 men, and policed the Yellow Sea and the Korea and Cheju Straits so effectively that Chinese pirates no longer dared to operate there, and Chang Po-go had a virtual monopoly on Korean foreign trade. He was known as King of the Yellow Sea. King Hungdok could only acquiesce, despite the fact that Chang was usurping powers that properly belonged to duly appointed government officials of the ruling class.

This great acquisition of power inevitably led Chang Po-go to take a hand in politics. He helped to place King Sinmu on the throne in 839, placing the royal government under obligation to him. But finally he overreached himself. He began to entertain dreams of entering upon a political career himself, and tried to compel King Munsong to take his daughter as his queen. This was too much for the capital aristocrats. Chang Po-go was assassinated in 846, and his stronghold on Ch'onghae fell. This did not break the power of the other merchants, however, and it was partly owing to their support that the new Koryo dynasty was able to take control of the country.

Parallel to the rise of the merchants was the growth of the great private estates in the provinces, which was also due to the weakening of government control. There were three sorts of these estates. First, there were aristocrats who were excluded from the government. They often left Kyongju to concentrate on the management and expansion of their holdings. Second, there were the village headmen, who now began to exercise control and even to assert ownership of the areas under their administration. Third, the Buddhist temples and monasteries, which had original-ly acquired land and the farmers who went with it from the government or as donations from the pious rich, now began to expand aggressively.

All these landholders expanded their property by buying it from destitute farmers at bargain rates or simply seizing it by force. This meant that tax revenue disappeared from the government treasury, thus further weakening it in a vicious circle. The great estates became virtually independent kingdoms, each with its own fortifications, troops, tax and corvée systems, and rudimentary organs of governments, similar to the estates of feudal Europe.

The lot of the farmer had hardly been enviable when he was under the control of the central government. He was taxed in kind, forced to contribute corvée labor, and pressed into military service. But his life under the great landlords was far harsher. His land was seized, his forced labor was increased, and he was allowed to keep only enough of what he produced to sustain life. When disease or poor harvests struck, he was helpless. Many farmers abandoned their land in despair and turned bandit, ravaging the countryside and increasing the social chaos of the times.

Conditions became so bad in the late ninth century that mass uprisings of farmers began to occur. These began at Pugwon (now Wonju) in 889 and soon spread all over the country, one of them, known as the "Red Trousers" from the distinctive clothing the rebels adopted, even threatening to capture Kyongju.

These were not revolutions in the modern sense. The outraged farmers had no ideology to back their protests, and no program of political reform. They were simply reacting to the intolerable conditions in which they lived, and even when they had a limited success were unable to establish viable governments which would accomplish their simple aims. Thus though they contributed to the fall of the Silla dynasty, their influence upon the formation of the new government was negligible.

Out of this chaos certain shrewd, ambitious men began inevitably to emerge as leaders. They rose to the command of insurgent farmer bands or headed leagues of landowners for mutual protection, and sometimes both. During the early tenth century three of these leaders managed to establish governments, one of which ultimately prevailed over the others.

The rebel leader Kungye was the son of an aristocratic family. Banished from court in his youth, he at first took refuge in a small Buddhist temple, but soon left it to join the rebel army of Yanggil at Pugwon. Yanggil put him in command of a body of troops, and he proceeded to occupy the district of Ch'orwon and parts of Kyonggi, Kangwon and Hwanghae Provinces. Insurgent farmers, monks and local landlords submitted to him, and many joined his forces. In 897 he killed his master Yanggil and assumed leadership of the revolt in his own right, and in 901 he organized a government at Songak (present Kaesong) and proclaimed the Kingdom of Later Koguryo. The name was subsequently changed and the capital moved. Ultimately it was called T'aebong, with its capital at Ch'orwon, and controlled all the territory north of Sangju and Kongju.

Kungye attempted to organize his government in the same manner as that of Silla, and tried to impose the same kind of ranking system. But this sort of thing was not in tune with the times and he was ultimately driven from power.

At about the same time another rebel leader named Kyonhwon appeared at Mujinju, now Kwangju, in South Cholla Province. He was the son of a farmer and had become a professional soldier in his youth. He rose to the command of the army unit stationed on the southwest coast. In 892 he appeared at the head of an insurgent farmer band which occupied Mujinju. By 900 he had captured Wansanju (modern Chonju) and felt himself powerful enough to proclaim a kingdom which he called Later Paekche. Once he even attacked Kyongju, killing King Kyongae and carrying off numerous craftsmen and some aristocrats as prisoners.

But Kyonhwon, like Kungye, lacked the political astuteness to found a viable state. As a product of the lower classes, he set himself against the Silla aristocracy and royalty, but when he came to power he practiced the same abuses they did. Moreover, he neglected seeking alliance with the provincial landlords, whose wealth and power made them an essential element in any government at that time. Later Paekche was short-lived.

The last of the three, Wang Kon, was a native of Kaesong. He came of a merchant family which had grown wealthy on the China trade. By the time of the revolts they had risen to control the Kaesong area and parts of Hwanghae Province, Kanghwa Island, and the area of the lower Han River. When Kungye's troops reached this area, Wang Kon joined the rebellion. Kungye recognized his ability and put him in command of a large body of troops, with which he soon subdued most of the west coast. When Kungye set up his government, Wang Kon was made *Sijung,* first minister. Wang Kon repaid this favor by overthrowing Kungye in 918 and founding the Koryo dynasty, with the capital at his native town, Kaesong.

Silla's doom was now sealed. No help could be expected from China, since the T'ang dynasty had fallen in 907 and China, like Korea, was rent by internal conflict. The new kingdoms of Koryo in the north and Later Paekche in the southwest alike menaced the ancient kingdom. Another turning point in Korean history was at hand.

PART FOUR

The Medieval Period

Chapter 10

The Founding of Koryo

Wang Kon's regime succeeded largely because he sought and received the support of the landlords and merchants whose power and wealth had grown as the Silla government grew weaker. This policy succeeded the more easily because Wang Kon belonged to this class himself and so its members trusted him. With their assistance he consolidated and expanded his power.

Wang Kon's opportunity came with the conflict between the shrunken Silla kingdom and the rebel Kyonhwon's Later Paekche. Kyonhwon had already sacked Kyongju in 920, assassinating King Kyongae and placing King Kyongsun on the throne. After the invading troops withdrew, King Kyongsun, fearful of further aggression and powerless to repel it, called on Wang Kon for help.

He was more than happy to comply. Troops were promptly dispatched and a fierce engagement followed at Kongsan, northeast of modern Taegu, in which the Later Paekche army, though not completely defeated, was at any rate repelled. Wang Kon paid a courteous visit to Kyongju to pay his respects to King Kyongsun and to assure the people of Silla of his good intentions. In 934 he personally led his forces in an invasion of Later Paekche, fighting a battle at Unju (modern Hongsong) and taking about thirty fortresses along the northern border.

In addition to these setbacks, Later Paekche now began to be plagued by an internal power struggle. To explain

this, we must point out that in East Asian monarchies the
throne did not go automatically to the King's eldest son,
but could be bequeathed by him to any heir whom he
cared to designate. Kyonhwon had designated his fourth
son, Kumgang, as Crown Prince. Resentful and ambitious,
his eldest son Sin'gom assembled a following, seized the
throne, banished his father to a monastery, and murdered
Kumgang. Three months later Kyonhwon escaped and
went over to Wang Kon, who welcomed him warmly.

Meanwhile King Kyongsun and the Silla aristocracy
were facing the bleak realities of their situation. Beset on
every hand, without allies, and powerless to defend themselves, they made a rare and difficult decision. The power
of Wang Kon was growing daily, and the days of Later
Paekche, and of Silla itself, were plainly numbered. Together with all the leading government officials, King
Kyongsun surrendered himself and his country to Wang
Kon in 935. Perhaps this goes against the patriotic tradition of fighting to the last, but compared to the scenes of
chaos, slaughter and flight which have marked the collapse
of other monarchies, the end of Silla has a certain dignity.
It had lasted, according to the traditional dates, which
may not be accurate, for 992 years.

In 936 Wang Kon (whom we must now call King T'aejo,
the posthumous title by which he is known to history)
attacked and easily subdued Later Paekche, and Korea was
once again united. The provincial magnates who were the
basis of the new dynasty's power were duly rewarded with
posts in the bureaucracy, and the work of reorganizing the
country and bringing it gradually under central control
was begun.

King T'aejo was at first wisely content to leave the
provincial magnates undisturbed, granting them official
titles but not interfering with their power or wealth. He
thus secured their allegiance and soothed their pride. In

time many of them occupied high posts in the government. Thus the danger of local rebellions which had so plagued Silla was averted.

The King was particularly careful to placate the Silla aristocracy. He gave former King Kyongsun the highest post in his government, superior even to the Crown Prince, and made him governor of Kyongju, whose revenues were set aside for his use. He also took a woman of the Silla royal clan as his wife, thus somewhat legitimizing his rule.

In order to avert the peasant revolts which had played a large part in the fall of Silla, taxes on farmers were drastically reduced, and farmers were made immune from taxation for a period of three years. This had the added advantage of stimulating agricultural production.

King T'aejo was an ardent Buddhist and a believer in geomancy, both of which thus came to play a prominent part in Koryo government and society. The post of *Kuksa* ("National Teacher") was established and filled by prominent monks. Numerous temples were founded and Buddhist religious festivals were dutifully supported and observed by the government. The political testament which King T'aejo left for the guidance of his descendants, known as the "Ten Rules," clearly shows the influence of these beliefs. This document opens with a declaration that the Koryo dynasty owes its supremacy to its Buddhist piety and to the goemantically fortunate location of Kaesong, its capital. Buddhist monasteries, therefore, must not be interfered with in any way, but the King adds that they should not be allowed to proliferate unduly. In like manner, Buddhist festivals are to be duly observed but should not become over-frequent. The city of P'yongyang, also occupying a geomantically favorable site, is to be honored, whereas the territory south of Ch'aryong and the Kum River is an area of evil fortune, and people dwelling there must not be selected as government officials. The throne

must always be occupied by legitimate descendants of the
founding monarch, and usurpation is to be guarded against.
The manners and customs of the barbarian Khitan must
not be allowed to influence the people.

All this is not to be taken as blind superstition or simple
piety. It is clear, for example, that while King T'aejo was
a pious Buddhist, he had no intention of allowing the
monks to control the government, and instructed his sons
to keep them in bounds. In like manner, he asserts the
geomantic virtues of Kaesong because it is the capital, and
of P'yongyang because he felt it to be a strategic area
worthy of attention for quite practical reasons. It would
not be fair to call him cynical, but pious though he was,
he was also a shrewd and astute politician, quite capable
of taking advantage of popular beliefs for the benefit of
the dynasty he had founded.

Foreign relations were conditioned, as always, by the
political situation in China. At this time, China was under-
going one of those periods of division usually consequent
upon the fall of a dynasty. T'ang had collapsed in 907, and
China entered the period called by Chinese historians the
Five Dynasties and Ten Kingdoms. It was not as long nor
as chaotic as the period following the fall of the Han dynasty, but a new factor had entered the political picture. The
nomadic Khitan tribe, the same people King T'aejo
mentioned in his will, had appeared along the upper Liao
River. They grew rapidly in power, dominating most of
Manchuria and Mongolia, and quickly assimilating
Chinese culture and technology. In 916 their leaders began
to call themselves emperors in Chinese style. They engulfed
the Korean state of Parhae in 926, and began encroaching
on north China. In 946 a regular Chinese-style state was
founded, with the dynastic name of Liao.

As we have seen, many of the Parhae aristocracy, who
were of Korean race and culture, fled to Koryo after the

Khitan conquest, where they were welcomed and assimilated into the ruling class. This conquest also brought Khitan power close to the Koryo frontier. In 922 the Khitan attempted to open diplomatic relations, sending envoys and a present of camels, but this was firmly repulsed and preparations for military defense were intensified.

As yet, however, the Khitan posed no real threat to Koryo. China was occupied with her own internal troubles, and thus incapable of causing trouble to the new dynasty. King T'aejo was therefore able to consolidate his rule and organize his government free of foreign interference. The fall of Parhae also made it possible to initiate plans for the conquest of the old Koguryo territory within the peninsula.

The city of P'yongyang was one of the means to this end. Situated on the Taedong River, which had been the northern boundary of the Silla kingdom, it was strategically important both for the protection of the frontier and as a base for territorial expansion. The city had declined after the fall of Koguryo, and its population was small and its buildings and fortifications dilapidated. This King T'aejo proceeded to rectify. In 918 he stationed a large military force there under his cousin, general Wang Sing-nyom. In 922 he began the repopulation of the city, encouraging people from the south to settle there. Branches of the central government offices were set up, schools were established, and the fortifications were rebuilt. P'yongyang soon became the second city of the kingdom, politically, culturally and militarily.

Military forces were also sent to the northeast under general Yu Kum-p'il. By the middle of the tenth century Koryo territory extended up to the Ch'ongch'on River on the west and Anbyon and Yonghung to the northeast on a line about halfway between the old Taedong River frontier and the modern boundaries. The Koryo dynasty was now firmly established at home and pushing northward toward the natural frontier of the Yalu and the Tumen.

In the early days of his rule King T'aejo had adopted the policy of encouraging members of his family to marry the daughters of the provincial landlords in order to bind them more closely to the throne, and married several of them himself, multiple marriage for royalty being then customary. This was moderately successful at the outset but led to serious complications later. Several factions were formed among the King's numerous in-laws, each supporting one of his sons. Conflict over the succession began immediately upon King T'aejo's death.

There were three factions in contention: that of Pak Sur-hui, which supported Mu, the King's eldest son; that of Wang Sing-nyom, supporting Yo, a son by another wife; and that of Wang Kyu, supporting Kwangjuwon-gun, King T'aejo's son by his sixteenth wife. Wang Kyu was the grandfather-in-law of Kwangjuwon-gun and the father of Mu's wife.

In accordance with King T'aejo's w,ill Prince Mu duly succeeded to the throne and was given the posthumous title Hyejong. But he ruled for only two years and was succeeded at his death by Prince Yo, whom we know as King Chongjong. This King managed to eliminate the factions of Pak Sur-hui and Wang Kyu with the help of his supporter Wang Sing-nyom. But the factions of royal relatives continued to form and plots and intrigues were a constant danger. King Chongjong then proposed moving the capital to P'yongyang, ostensibly because its situation promised a more favorable destiny according to geomancy. The real reason, of course, was to remove the court from the factional infighting in Kaesong. But before this plan could be carried out the King's protector Wang Sing-nyom mysteriously perished, and Chongjong soon followed him. The causes of the deaths of Kings Hyejong and Chongjong are not recorded, but, given the circumstances, they are not hard to guess.

These dynastic disputes were making stable and continuous government impossible. King Kwangjong, who succeeded Chongjong in 949, solved the problem after a fashion by ruthlessly eliminating all opposition. Royal relatives, families that had aided in the founding of the dynasty, and all others who showed the least inclination to raise up rivals to the King were slaughtered without discrimination, until King Kwangjong attained complete and unopposed dominance of government and society.

King Kwangjong, once he was free to do so, then turned his attention to the reorganization of the government, with special attention to measures which would reduce the power of the aristocracy in favor of the monarchy. In 956 he promulgated a law which freed large numbers of people who had been unlawfully enslaved. This had the double merit of weakening the aristocrats and at the same time increasing revenues by adding the freed slaves to the tax rolls.

The manumission of slaves was only a prelude to full-scale reorganization of the government along Chinese lines. This went considerably further than it had during the Silla period, although, as in Silla, the aristocrats retained their monopoly of important posts. An examination system for appointing officials was set up in 958 which was apparently a good bit more liberal than the Silla system had been, and was aimed partly at displacing the great landlords from positions of power. Officials were carefully distinguished from one another, in Chinese fashion, by the style and color of their clothing. There were four ranks in the bureaucracy, the highest wearing purple, the second red, the third scarlet and the lowest green. The establishment of a centralized bureaucratic government was completed during the reign of King Songjong (981–997).

It is significant that one of the most influential men in the work of reorganization was Ch'oe Sung-no, an eminent Confucian scholar. He drew up a plan in twenty-eight articles which was adopted by the King.

Local administration underwent similar changes. Here the most remarkable change was the substitution of officials appointed by the King and sent out from the capital for the local landlords who had previously regarded these posts as their perquisites. The central government now had full control of the provinces and no longer needed to fear local officials' acting in their own private interest and defying or evading government orders.

An important practice adopted under Songjong was that of buying up grain at harvest-time and releasing it to the market when it grew scarce, thus at the same time insuring a constant food supply and stabilizing prices. Iron coins began to be minted at this time, indicating the growth of a money economy.

The centralized bureaucracy thus established was reformed somewhat and fully consolidated during the reign of King Munjong (1046–1083), the high point of Koryo society and culture. The central organs of government now consisted of three boards, under which there were six ministries. The first of the three boards, the Royal Secretariat, conferred directly with the King and drafted orders and decrees. The second, the Royal Chancellery, then reviewed these and put them into final form. The third, the Secretariat of State Affairs, then executed the laws by referring them to the appropriate ministries. These were the ministries of Personnel, War, Revenue, Rites, Justice and Public Works, of which the ministries of Personnel and War were considered the most important. At the top of the pyramid was a Privy Council, which had general authority over all organs of government but usually concerned itself only with particularly important matters, which were discussed and decided on by the Council meeting jointly with the Three Boards.

Other organs of government included a financial secretariat and the Board of Censors, a watchdog organization which had the power not only of exposing maladministration and corruption but also of dismissing the culprits. It was not subject to any other authority, but reported directly to the King.

A military secretariat administered the armed forces, which were divided into two armies of three divisions each (the size of these is not clear). Military officers had considerable influence during the early days of the dynasty, but with the coming of peace and the reorganization of the government they found themselves completely subordinated to the civilian officials. This tendency to "despise the sword and respect the pen" was a cause of revolts among military officers in later years.

As we have seen, local administration was regularized and brought under the authority of the central government. This was a long and complicated process, but by the reign of King Hyonjong (1009–1031) it had been completed, and there were no further major changes. The country was divided into provinces, counties, prefectures and sub-prefectures, with the appropriate officials for each. In addition there were two special military districts called *kye*, to the northeast and northwest, located in areas of strategic importance in case of invasion.

To supervise local administration and ensure central control, two subordinate capitals were established, one at P'yongyang and the other at Kyongju. The latter was subsequently moved to Hanyang (modern Seoul). Officials of the central government were given concurrent appointments in the provinces in a supervisory capacity. In addition, the leading citizens of each district were compelled to send their sons to Kaesong for certain periods, a method of insuring their loyalty, or at any rate their passivity.

At the lowest level, villages continued to be ruled by village headmen as before, though of course they were incorporated into the bureaucracy. Special villages of people of the lowest class, government slaves really, who labored to provide the daily needs of court and government, became administrative units.

A system of post roads was built for speedy communication of government orders and for the movement of military forces in time of war. It also facilitated the transportation of tax grain to the capital and made government supervision easier and more effective.

The examinations by which officials were chosen were of three kinds. The highest concerned Chinese literature generally, the second the Confucian classics, and the third scientific and technical subjects. All candidates for higher posts had to pass one of the first two, the first leading to the highest posts, while the third selected various specialists such as doctors and astronomers who were attached to certain government offices. In conformity with the Confucian idea that the pursuit of literature and scholarship fits men for government, each civil official had to write a poem every month and present it to the King. No examinations were given for military posts until somewhat later than the establishment of the civil examinations, when a parallel system was set up.

The examination system as originally devised in China had been intended to bring men of intelligence and ability into the government, regardless of social origin. But the persistence of a class-conscious aristocracy during the Koryo dynasty vitiated this purpose in important ways. While the old Bone Rank system of Silla had disappeared in the confusion and violence attending the dynasty's fall a new aristocracy soon formed among the supporters of King T'aejo and the great landowners and society again came to be divided into graded classes.

The aristocratic principle in government was preserved in various ways. In the first place, sons of bureaucrats above the fifth grade were exempted from examinations, thus ensuring that no member of the upper classes could be excluded from the government. In the second place, the schools which prepared candidates for the examinations were so organized as to favor the aristocrats. Schools which prepared students for the higher examinations were restricted to students from the first five grades, corresponding to the upper classes of society, while only the scientific and technical schools were open to the lower orders.

Within these rather stringent limits, the system of education worked fairly well. A school was set up in Kaesong quite early in the dynasty, and in later years schools were established in each province and teachers were appointed to them by the government. Libraries were maintained at Kaesong and P'yongyang.

The system of land ownership was a matter of constant contention between government and aristocracy and underwent many changes. In theory all land belonged to the government and could be redistributed whenever this was felt necessary. In fact the aristocrats managed for the most part to hold on to their private estates and often to enlarge them.

During the early years, before Koryo had extended its rule over the whole peninsula, King T'aejo had used grants of land to secure allies. After the wars, he granted land as rewards to those who had been of particular service to him in establishing the dynasty. This led in time to the growth of a group of families of great wealth and power. These families were behind the dynastic struggles that broke out at T'aejo's death and were not ended until King Kwang-jong broke their power and undertook a reform of the landholding system.

Landholding was now made dependent upon government rank, the amount of land each official could hold being legally stipulated. Military officials, interestingly enough, were at first given larger grants than their civil counterparts, possibly because of the Khitan invasions. With various changes, this system persisted for some time, and gradually the civil officials began to receive better treatment than the military. There were major reforms in 1034 and again in 1076, in which the discriminatory treatment of the military was a little improved and sinecure officials were excluded from the land grants.

Because these lands could only be held during an official's tenure of office, problems arose in the cases of the families of officials who died early and the sinecure officials who were excluded. In 1049 permanent, hereditary grants again began to be made. Grants were also made to the widows, parents, and brotherless unmarried daughters of officials on the officials' deaths, but these were not hereditary. Land was also granted, for political reasons, to tribal chieftains in the north and to the local aristocracy of Cheju Island. Land granted to the lower-level district officials was hereditary, but the land granted to soldiers was not, although a son could retain possession of his father's land if he in turn became a soldier. Lands were also granted to schools for their maintenance and to Buddhist temples.

Taxes were generally collected in kind from farmers, mostly in grain. Farmers living on government land or on non-hereditary grants paid a tax of one fourth of their harvest, while those on private estates usually paid the landlord one half. The efforts of the government to keep as much land as possible out of private hands was directly related to its finances, since the more private land there was the smaller the government's revenues became. Tax rates could be adjusted to take into account the quality of the land being taxed and the quality of the harvest, but taxes were generally levied without regard to the welfare of the taxpayers.

The Koryo government encouraged the bringing of waste land under cultivation, and farmers who did so were immune from taxes for a year or two. Tax grain was collected in government storehouses at various points throughout the nation and transported to the capital by land or sea. In addition to the regular tax on crops, special taxes called tribute were also levied. There was an annual tribute to be paid in textiles, generally hemp cloth and a special tribute consisting of local specialties.

The most difficult burdens the farmers had to bear were corvée labor and military services. All men between sixteen and sixty years of age were required to perform these services. They were employed on all sorts of public works, which was not so bad as military service. Military service was permanent. When a man reached twenty years of age he was enrolled in the district military unit. The only way to avoid this was to make regular contributions to the military. Some farmers were fortunate enough to become military officers, but they were very few. As in the previous dynasty, the burdens which the farmer had to bear sometimes became so intolerable that he left his land in despair.

Below the farmers, at the very bottom of society, was a class called *ch'onmin* ("mean" people). Most of them were slaves, either government or private and their status was hereditary. Another group of similar status, though not called by the same name, were the artisans who lived in special areas and engaged in mining or porcelain-making and other crafts for the government. Actors, butchers and weavers of willow baskets were also in the lowest class. They did not appear on the tax rolls and so were immune from taxation and government services.

Koryo had been established by military force and there

were clashes with the tribes on the northern border almost from the first. This meant that military affairs were of great importance and the armed forces were constantly being strengthened and expanded.

The military forces had two main divisions: the Two Armies and Six Divisions stationed in the capital and the various district units. The capital troops, who were the military elite, were charged with defending the capital, policing the city, and guarding the palace. There were about 45,000 officers and men from all classes above farmers, divided into units called *yong* of 1,000 men each. Each man was given a grant of land and two men to farm it.

The district units made up the national defense, and had to be prepared for instant mobilization at any time. They also included a labor corps whose members were classified as soldiers but did not receive land grants.

Chapter **11**

Koryo Repels the Khitan

At roughly the same time as the rise of the Koryo dynasty, the Khitan tribes to the north and west began to confederate and expand. In 916 a chieftain known from Chinese records as Yeh-lu A-pao-chi declared himself emperor of Khitan and led the tribes in numerous invasions. In 926 the kingdom of Parhae was conquered, as we have already noted. A puppet state called Eastern Khitan was at first set up, but this was soon annexed to the growing Khitan state. Basing themselves at Liao-yang near modern Mukden on the Liao River, they prepared to invade the Jurched territory to the north of the peninsula and then Korea itself.

As early as the reign of T'aejo the Khitan monarch had sent envoys and gifts of camels, with the intention of setting up diplomatic relations. But the Koryo government, well aware of the fate of Parhae and suspicious of Khitan intentions, repulsed the offer and raised an army of 300,000 in preparation for an expected invasion.

In 983 and 985 the Khitan attacked the Jurched tribes and occupied the middle course of the Yalu River and the Tongga River basin. A third attack was launched in 989, and three fortified strong points were erected along the north bank of the Yalu. At the same time, Koryo troops erected fortifications along the south bank of the Yalu, so that the two states confronted each other at the river line.

Meanwhile, the political confusion and fragmentation

of China was ending with the rise of the Sung dynasty. By
the time of the events we are here describing most of south
China had been unified, and the Sung were moving to
recapture the sixteen border prefectures in the Peking area.
In 985 envoys were dispatched to the Koryo court asking
military aid in this endeavor. The kingdom was not in a
position to respond to this request due to the military
threat to its own northern border, but diplomatic contact
with the Chinese Empire continued.

The Khitan state, feeling that any alliance between the
Koryo kingdom and China was a threat to its safety, first
countered by again proposing friendly relations with
Koryo. When this offer was ignored and Koryo contacts
with the Sung dynasty continued, the Khitan decided that
their only alternative was to invade and conquer the Koryo
kingdom. In October of 993 a Khitan army under Hsiao
Sun-ning said to have numbered 800,000 attacked the
Koryo border from the northwest.

But the Koreans had known of the invasion plan for
two months. The armies were fully mobilized and divided
into three army groups. Headquarters were established at
modern Anju and advanced units crossed the Ch'ongch'on
River, while King Songjong himself came west to P'yongyang to direct operations. The opposing armies met at
Pongsan-gun, and the Khitan were able to advance as far
as the Ch'ongch'on. Their advance was considerably
hampered, however, and they decided that total conquest
would be too costly. Instead, they asked for a negotiated
peace. They asked that Koryo surrender former Parhae
territory to Khitan, that it cease relations with Sung China,
and that it accept tributary status under the Khitan ruler.

These proposals were the subject of hot debate in the
Koryo court. Many of the officials were in favor of accept-
ing them in order to prevent further Khitan incursions.
But general So Hui, commander of one of the three armies,

and other military men disagreed. When a Khitan attack upon Anju, launched mainly to hasten negotiations, proved a failure, So Hui volunteered to negotiate directly with the Khitan commander, and the court gave its permission.

In the negotiations So Hui pointed out to Hsiao Sun-ning that Khitan claims to Parhae territory were ill-founded, since the Koryo dynasty was clearly the successor of the Koguryo kingdom. He went further, and in a veiled threat pointed out that the Liaotung peninsula itself was former Koguryo territory, and hence the Khitan base at Liao-yang properly belonged to Koryo. He added that friendly relations between Khitan and Koryo had been hampered in the past by the Jurched tribes which inhabited the area between the two countries, but as soon as these tribes were driven out of Koryo territory diplomatic ties would certainly be established.

The key factor in these negotiations, as both parties knew, was the Khitan confrontation with Sung China. The Sung, as we have seen, were pushing northward to regain Chinese territory under Khitan control, and were friendly to the Koryo kingdom. Not having achieved the easy conquest of Korea which they had expected, the Khitan faced the alternatives of either withdrawing from Korea or fighting a two-front war. For these reasons Hsiao Sun-ning acknowledged the force of So Hui's arguments, and the Khitan forces were withdrawn without having achieved any substantial results.

Diplomatic relations between Koryo and Khitan opened in 994, and contacts with Sung China were temporarily suspended. This gave the Koryo rulers the opportunity to drive out the Jurched tribes in the northwest, which they promptly did. Koryo power now extended all along the banks of the Yalu, where numerous fortifications were erected in expectation of fresh Khitan incursions. This done, relations with the Sung court were resumed in defiance of Khitan displeasure.

Fresh dynastic disputes now arose in Kaesong. In 1009 King Mokchong, aware of a plot of Kim Ch'i-yang and his group to depose him, appointed a relative named Sun, the son of his uncle Uk and the widow of King Kyongjong, as Crown Prince, and summoned Kang Cho, the military administrator of the northwest district, to come to his protection. But Kang Cho proved to be somewhat more ambitious than the King had expected. After duly eliminating the Kim Ch'i-yang clique, he proceeded to have King Mokchong assassinated, and Prince Sun ascended the throne (posthumous title Hyonjong) to preside over a government under Kang Cho's control.

Everything now favored a Khitan invasion. Kang Cho's absence from his post had weakened the defenses in the vital northwestern area. The Jurched tribes, still not fully subdued, were quite willing to make common cause with the Khitan, who were at the peak of their power. The Khitan were now a fully organized Chinese-style state, and since 946 had adopted the dynastic title Liao.

In 1010 the Liao king led 400,000 troops to the Koryo border on the excuse of punishing the murderer of King Mokchong. Kang Cho, having had himself promoted to supreme military command, awaited them at T'ongju, modern Sonch'on. The first attack was beaten off, thanks largely to the excellent tactics of general Yang Kyu, but Kang Cho waxed over-confident, and a second attack defeated the Koryo forces. Kang Cho was captured and executed.

The Liao troops now easily pierced the fortifications along the Yalu and marched south to besiege P'yongyang. The city did not fall, but the news of Kang Cho's defeat threw the court into a panic, and many were in favor of immediate and unconditional surrender. The King, however, listened to the advice of general Kang Kam-ch'an, who proposed that the court take refuge in Naju and that the remaining Koryo forces reorganize and counterattack when the force of the Liao drive was spent.

This plan was adopted, but at high cost. The invaders took Kaesong and sacked it thoroughly, raping and killing and destroying many precious monuments and documents. When the Liao army began to withdraw, general Yang Kyu attacked as planned, inflicting casualties said to have been as high as twenty or thirty thousand. But when King Hyonjong attempted to sue for peace the Liao king demanded that he come in person and do obeisance, formally acknowledging Koryo vassalage to the Liao state.

There was no further immediate conflict, but the intolerable demands of the Liao dynasty continued. In addition to having the King do formal obeisance, it now further required that certain strategic border areas be ceded to it. The Koryo court, as expected, stubbornly refused, and the stage was set for a final showdown.

At this critical moment a *coup d'état* by Koryo military officers occurred, and Kim Hun and Ch'oe Chil assumed control of the government in 1014. Discontent had long been festering among military officers, who received less compensation than their civilian counterparts. When wartime expenses strained the national treasury and it became difficult to pay government stipends, the granting of land to soldiers was suspended, and this was the last straw. Two of the leading civil officials were beheaded, and military officers henceforth took precedence over civilians.

Meanwhile Liao forces had built a fortified bridge across the Yalu in preparation for occupying the northern districts which they had demanded. In December of 1018 the Liao general Hsiao Pai-ya led an army of 100,000 across the frontier.

This time Liao confidence was misplaced. General Kang

Kam-ch'an, seconded by Kang Min-ch'om, awaited the invading forces at Anju with an army that outnumbered it two to one. When the Liao army crossed the Yalu it was ambushed by general Kang Kam-ch'an's troops and badly mauled. Those who escaped this engagement were then harassed by general Kang Min-ch'om, and their retreat cut off.

Unable to return to its base and under constant attack by Koryo troops, the Liao army could only gamble on marching south and taking the capital. But here it encountered the astute defenses which Kang Kam-ch'an had set up before his departure. The city could not be taken, and the only hope was to find some means of withdrawal. When the army had managed to get as far back as Kuju, Kang Kam-ch'an and Kim Chong-hyon launched a concerted attack upon it which resulted in total victory for the Koryo forces. Only a few thousand of the 100,000 Liao troops survived to return home in 1019. This was the final result of thirty years of war.

It was now clear that neither side could achieve total victory. Eventually diplomatic relations were begun, envoys were exchanged, and the Liao state ceased to be a military threat to the Koryo kingdom.

Nevertheless, the fall of Kaesong had brought home vividly to the Koryo rulers the necessity of national defense. The Jurched tribes were still a problem and there was no assurance that the peace with Liao would endure. Accordingly, an outer wall was begun around the capital at the instance of Kang Kam-ch'an, and finished in 1029. Subsequently work was begun on the defenses of the northern border, and by 1044 a stone wall streched all the way from the mouth of the Yalu on the west coast to Kwangp'o on the east coast.

The social and cultural ravages of war were also attended to. In 1023 the government again began to buy up rice stocks to hold in reserve for times of scarcity. Land grants were made to the childless widows of soldiers. The government examination system was liberalized so as to permit the candidacy of the provincial gentry.

The Liao forces that took Kaesong had destroyed not only the national shrine and the royal palace but also the library, and many rare and valuable records were lost. King Hyonjong therefore ordered Ch'oe Hang and others to compile historical records of the seven reigns from that of the founder T'aejo down the end of King Mokchong's reign in 1013. Also at this time the carving of wooden blocks for printing the complete Buddhist scriptures, the *Tripitaka,* which had been undertaken in the pious hope of securing the protection of Buddhist deities for the kingdom, was completed.

Chapter 12

The Culture of the Early Koryo Period

The Khitan invasions were followed by a long peace. The damage inflicted by the wars was repaired, political stability was achieved, and agriculture expanded. This prosperity and stability were the basis for the great age of Koryo civilization.

The constant inflow of tax goods made Kaesong not only the political and cultural center but also the central exchange market. Many government-patronized markets and shops sprang up in Kaesong, and there were numerous provincial markets. But merchants still suffered from the Confucian prejudice against them, and there was no real effort by the government either to foster trade or to use it as a source of revenue.

Foreign trade was extensive, but was limited largely to luxury goods. As in the previous era, it flourished largely under the guise of "tribute," the goods to be sold or exchanged being sent with diplomatic missions more or less disguised as presents exchanged between monarchs. It was accepted practice by the late eleventh century to allow private merchants to send trade goods in addition to the official presents.

The Koryo kingdom traded with China, Japan, the Khitan, Liao state, and the Jurched tribes. Even Arab ships are known to have called at Koryo ports, but the most important trade was, of course, with China. Silk textiles, porcelain, books, drugs, musical instruments and stationery

144

were the main imports. Porcelain and books from China had important influences on the development of the famous Koryo celadons and on printing from wood blocks, but for the most part this was a luxury trade, without importance for the kingdom as a whole. Exports to China included gold, silver, copper, ginseng, pine-nuts, hides, and such manufactured goods as silk cloth, hemp cloth, paper, metalwares, knives, and stationery. Korean ginseng, pine-nuts and stationery were most highly favored by the Chinese. There was some trade with the Liao state, although both sides were, understandably, extremely cautious. The Arab merchants brought in mercury, aromatics, dyestuffs, copper and drugs, which they traded mainly for silk and gold.

Both domestic and foreign trade were mainly carried on through barter, rice and textiles being the primary media of exchange. We hear of coins being minted in 996, but it was only in the second half of the eleventh century that a mint was established as a regular part of the government. By 1097 coins of the Chinese type were circulating freely. We hear also of large, heavy silver coins, weighing as much as 600 grams, being used by the aristocracy.

But the growth of a money economy was slow and limited. While it came to prevail to some extent among the upper classes and in foreign trade, barter continued to be used by the bulk of the population for most everyday transactions despite official encouragement of the use of coins.

As we have already pointed out, the Bone Rank system which had distinguished the Silla aristocracy had disappeared by the time the Koryo dynasty was founded. In its place there appeared a new upper class, composed of the expanding royal clan, families which had been raised to affluence for their help in founding the new dynasty, and the powerful local magnates who had appeared toward the close of the Silla dynasty. This class was designated individually and collectively by the Korean term *yangban*, meaning civil and military officials, which will accordingly henceforth be used in referring to them in this work.

Aristocratic wealth, as before, was based on land. We have noted previously the government's efforts at land reform on the Chinese model as a means of checking the power of the upper class. But these efforts were for the most part futile. As the number and variety of land grants and distributions increased, it was not difficult for the officials to add gradually to their holdings, not only through official grants but also by clearing waste land and by purchase. Government office was monopolized by this class by means of the discriminatory education system previously discussed.

A new element in the accumulation of official wealth was the practice of usury. Despite the Confucian disapproval of it, revenues from yangban estates were frequently lent at interest, and even the government participated. Ostensibly such loans were made for the purpose of raising money to support scholars, for poor relief, for the celebration of Buddhist festivals, and for the support of monks.

Buddhism was the dominant religion among the officials, many of whom, including members of the royal clan, became monks. There thus grew up a monkish aristocracy parallel to that which dominated secular life. Since Buddhism was felt to be not only the refuge and salvation of the individual but also the protector of the state, the leaders of the monks became men of great influence and power, and the temples grew wealthy. All this, plus the monks' immunity from taxation and military duty, made a religious career attractive not only to the pious but also to the ambitious.

The monks were organized in a hierarchy similar to that of the government, with schools, examinations, grades and titles. At the top were *Wangsa,* the royal tutor, and *Kuksa,* or national teacher, an honorary title. The monasteries, with wide lands in their possession, engaged in money-lending, brewing, livestock breeding and commerce, and thus played an important part in the economy.

Buddhist thought did not at first develop in any significant way. The split between the Five Sects and the Son (Zen) sect continued, but there was little that was new until a monk named Uich'on gave Korean Buddhism a new direction.

Uich'on was the son of King Munjong and the brother of King Sonjong, and thus automatically in a position of power. He became a monk at the age of eleven, and was later sent to China for study. When he returned he brought with him the doctrines of the T'ien T'ai sect (Korean pronunciation Ch'ont'ae). Unlike most of the other sects, this one was of purely Chinese origin, and was another attempt to harmonize the various conflicting Buddhist doctrines which had grown up over the centuries. It proved to be very stimulating to Korean Buddhism, especially since it attempted to harmonize the two chief sects in the nation. It will be recalled that the Five Sects emphasized study of the scriptures, while the Son sect emphasized meditation alone as a means of salvation. The new sect taught that pious scholarship and meditation were equally valid methods and that there was no essential conflict between them.

The introduction of T'ien T'ai stimulated considerable activity among the hitherto rather stagnant older sects. The nine branches of the old Son sect were brought to-gether and reorganized into a new grouping and body of doctrine known thereafter as Chogye. The Five Sects were also aroused, although they remained substantially as before, and T'ien T'ai became firmly established, so that we may now speak of three main divisions of Korean

Buddhism: the Five Sects (Ogyo), Chogye and T'ien T'ai (Ch'ont'ae).

Uich'on brought with him from China some 3,000 volumes concerning the doctrines he taught. These were added to the already extensive collection kept under government auspices at Hungwang temple in Kaesong. A special government body was in charge of collecting and publishing Buddhist works, and had already published the *Tripitaka*, the complete Buddhist canon, printing some 6,000 volumes from carved wooden blocks.

The work took sixty years. It was a great stimulus to the development of the art of printing in Korea, and led eventually to the invention of movable type, more than two centuries before its appearance in Europe. The hand-carved wooden blocks, one for each page of a book, were kept in Puin temple in Taegu. Unfortunately, this temple was destroyed during the Mongol invasions, and the blocks with them. The books printed from them have also vanished completely.

Buddhism dominated the various annual festivals patronized by the state. Of these, the two most important were the Lantern Festival held in February (later in January) and the Harvest Festival in November (October in P'yong-yang). The first of these was a purely Buddhist affair involving processions in the evening with lighted lanterns, singing and dancing, and prayers for the welfare of the state. Similar celebrations can be seen today on the traditional date of Buddha's birth. The second appears to have been much older, perhaps related to the ancient harvest festivals of the tribal leagues before the introduction of Buddhism. It was held under Buddhist auspices, of course, but its rituals were quite complicated and involved practices unrelated to Buddhist doctrine. Perhaps the most interesting aspect of the Harvest Festival was that it had become a time not only for national celebrations but also for the envoys of foreign countries to arrive for the purpose of international trade.

While Buddhism ministered to the people's spiritual needs, Confucianism continued to be the dominant influence in social ethics, education and government. We have already mentioned the schools set up by the government to train future officials. A new development in the eleventh century was the appearance of private schools for the same purpose, which soon became more popular than the government schools. This movement was led by Ch'oe Ch'ung, an eminent scholar who had occupied posts at the head of the government. When he retired in 1055 at the age of 74, he founded a school and began accepting yangban students. The fame of this school spread rapidly, and the students developed a lifelong affection and admiration for their great teacher. Graduates found it easy to secure government posts, and retained their group identity in the public mind, being called minister Ch'oe's students during his lifetime, and then Munhon's disciples, after his posthumous title.

Many distinguished scholars followed Ch'oe Ch'ung's example, and eventually there were twelve such private schools. Their graduates far surpassed those of the government schools in their ability to pass examinations and secure posts, and the "Students of the Twelve" soon dominated the bureaucracy.

In response to this situation, the government schools were reorganized. A publication center was added to the highest government school at Kaesong, the curriculum was overhauled, and government schools were established throughout the country. In the process of this reorganization, military subjects were dropped, an omission not without future significance. During the late eleventh and early twelfth centuries these schools produced many eminent scholars and men of letters, in addition to furnishing the government with officials.

But the omission of military training from these schools, and the general downgrading of military men at this time were the cause of future trouble. The military men would not for long submit to this sort of treatment, and political turmoil followed.

Chapter 13

Internal Dissensions and Military Government

We have had occasion previously to mention a group of tribes called Jurched or Juchen inhabiting southern Manchuria and the Korean border area. They made occasional raids on Koryo territory, and sometimes a chieftain would make submission to the court, mainly for the sake of the presents he received. They constituted a continuous problem. The Koryo policy was to overpower them by force when possible, and when not possible to entice them into submission with promises of gifts and honorary government posts. This policy was only moderately successful, and the northern fortifications had to be constantly maintained.

In the second half of the eleventh century one of the Jurched tribes, the Wananpu Jurched, began to dominate the others. It conquered several of them under a leader named Ukkonae, moving steadily southward, which brought it into contact with the Khitan state of Liao. Ukkonae was succeeded by his son Ying-ko, who sent envoys to the Koryo court on four occasions. Ying-ko's son Uyasok took the Chinese name Wu Yu-tzu (always a portentous move on the part of a barbarian leader), and attacked the Koryo kingdom in 1104, reaching as far as the outskirts of Chongp'yong (now Chongju).

The court dispatched troops under Im Kan to drive out the invaders, but they were defeated. Another force under Yun Kwan had no better success, although Yun Kwan

151

did manage a temporary peace agreement. Awakened to the seriousness of the threat by these reverses, the court decided upon a radical reorganization of the armed forces. A sort of mass conscription was instituted. All petty officials, both civil and military, and all merchants (a significant inclusion) formed the cavalry. The bulk of the army, the farmers as usual, formed the infantry. There was even a third unit composed of Buddhist monks, which perhaps testifies to how gravely the situation was regarded.

By these means an army of 170,000 was raised and organized, and in 1107, it set out for the north under the command of Yun Kwan, seconded by O Yon-ch'ong. The Jurched forces were routed at Chongp'yong and the Koryo forces pursued the retreating enemy by land and sea, killing 9,000 of them, taking 5,000 prisoners, and destroying 130 villages.

The territory thus retaken was in the mountainous northeast coast area, and was difficult to defend. Yun Kwan ordered the construction of nine fortresses at strategic points, and encouraged people from the south to come and settle there to ensure future Koryo control. In April of 1108 he returned in triumph to Kaesong.

But the matter was not settled. Stung by their defeat, the Jurched made repeated attacks upon the northeast. Lines of communication between it and the capital were long and difficult, so that the court could not react with sufficient speed to these attacks. Chronic, indecisive conflict was exhausting both sides. Finally Wu Yu-tzu made the cession of the fortified northeast territory the price of peace. Faced with a continued drain on its already strained resources if the conflict continued, the Koryo court complied, but stipulated that Wu Yu-tzu must do obeisance at Kaesong and declare himself henceforth the vassal of the Koryo kingdom. The Jurched thus ultimately acquired the territory which the Koryo kingdom had spent so much blood and treasure to retain.

The Jurched now turned against the Khitan monarchy of Liao, whose fortunes were declining at this time. Wu Yu-tzu's brother A-ku-ta, who succeeded him, conquered much of the Liao territory along the Yalu, and in 1115 declared himself founder and emperor of the Chin dynasty. He attacked Liao repeatedly and successfully. By 1117, when he seized the important city of Pao-chou on the lower Yalu, he controlled most of southern Manchuria.

Confident of his power, the Chin monarch now showed a somewhat different attitude toward the Koryo kingdom. He sent an envoy to the Koryo court with a proposal for a treaty of peace and alliance which included the haughty demand that the Koryo King declare himself the "younger brother" of the Chin Emperor. The Chin dynasty needed such an alliance to secure its flank before an all-out attack on Liao.

The Koryo rulers could not, of course, submit to this insolent demand, and they were moreover suspicious of Chin intentions toward themselves. They also did not wish to become entangled in the three-cornered power struggle that was brewing among the new Chin empire, the Liao state and Sung China. Instead they severed relations with Chin and began anxiously to strengthen the border defenses.

Koryo relations with the Sung dynasty had always been cordial and of mutual benefit, the Koryo kingdom supplying military pressure which kept Liao in check and receiving in return valuable cultural and technological knowledge from the highly developed culture of Sung China. Normal diplomatic relations had been suspended during the forty-year period after Koryo made peace with Liao, but trade continued and relations were ultimately restored.

Sensing an opportunity to eliminate their old enemy Liao, the Chinese now asked the Koryo rulers to mediate an alliance between themselves and the new Chin empire.

Knowing from experience that the Chin rulers were unlikely to honor such a treaty once their objectives had been gained, the Koryo court refused and endeavored to maintain neutrality. The Sung dynasty thereupon made direct overtures to the Chin, who were, of course, amenable, and a military alliance was concluded. The doom of Liao was sealed.

The Sung rulers had to pay dearly for their folly. The Liao dynasty fell easily to the coordinated attacks of the two allies, and was fully conquered by 1125. The Chin forces immediately turned upon their erstwhile allies and invaded China. In 1126 Kaifeng, the Chinese capital, had fallen, the Emperor and Crown Prince were captives, and the remnants of the Sung court and military forces had been forced to flee all the way to Hangchow, south of the Yangtze River. The Chin empire now included the entire northern half of China.

Koryo relations with what must now be called the Southern Sung dynasty were restored after the fighting ended, and the Chinese requested Koryo help in rescuing the Emperor and Crown Prince. But the Koryo rulers had to tread with extreme caution with the Chin empire so near by and grown to such immense power and size. Some Koryo officials argued that loyalty to an old ally demanded that the Sung request be granted, but others, notably Kim Pu-sik, pointed out that such a course would be extremely reckless and would endanger the kingdom. This view prevailed, and while contacts with the Southern Sung were not broken off, the Koryo court continued a policy of cautious neutrality.

While the international situation was being thus ominously transformed, serious factional strife was again developing in the Koryo government. It will be recalled that similar struggles involving the royal in-laws had occurred in the tenth century. They were quelled by King Kwangjong, but their underlying cause remained, and in the early twelfth century the families of royal consorts (and there could be several at the same time) again began to dominate the court.

Already in the late eleventh century Kim Un-bu, a yangban from Ansan, had managed to get his three daughters installed at court, and as a result enjoyed fifty years of wealth and power. He was succeeded by Yi Cha-yon, who also had three daughters who found royal favor, and the Yi family dominated the court for the next eighty years. Their power reached a peak under Yi Cha-gyom, son of Yi Cha-yon, whose second daughter married King Yejong and whose third and fourth daughters married King Injong, binding the Yi family ever more closely to the throne.

Injong had obtained the throne largely thanks to the help of Yi Cha-gyom, who exercised decisive influence over him from the first. He occupied several important government posts concurrently, accumulated wealth and land, and rivaled the King himself in affluence and power. The high posts which he did not occupy himself were distributed among his family, and opposition was ruthlessly put down. No one in the court, not even members of the royal family, could stand against him.

Naturally all this made him enemies, and even Injong turned against him. In 1126 a secret cabal was formed by the King and a group of his advisors hostile to Yi Cha-gyom with the purpose of eliminating him. It was a failure. Yi Cha-gyom led a band of soldiers to the palace, set fire to it, captured and beheaded his enemies, and incarcerated the King and attempted to poison him. It was even rumored that he intended to usurp the throne.

This event occurred in the same year as the Chin conquest of north China. As might have been expected, the Chin rulers again demanded that the Koryo dynasty acknowledge Chin suzerainty. Many of the Koryo officials stubbornly held out against such humiliation, but Yi Cha-gyom saw the inevitability of Chin dominance, and an envoy was dispatched in the same year. While this showed his political realism, it also weakened his position at court. He was ultimately overthrown and banished, as was his henchman Ch'ok Chun-gyong.

The factional struggle now developed into a regional one as well. The group which vanquished Yi Cha-gyom were mostly from P'yongyang, which the Koryo monarchs had designated the West Capital and had carefully fostered from the first. It was held by geomancers to be on a highly favorable site, and it had its own bureaucracy, which acted as a counterweight to the officials in Kaesong and gave the King some freedom of maneuver among the various factions.

The fall of Yi Cha-gyom meant increased power and influence for the P'yongyang officials. A monk named Myoch'ong decided that he could turn this situation to his own advantage. Basing his arguments on geomancy, he told the King that the beneficent forces of the site of Kaesong were now exhausted, but that if the royal capital were moved to P'yongyang the power of the Koryo kingdom would grow and prosper until all foreign countries sent tribute and the proud Chin dynasty would voluntarily surrender. Beguiled by these flattering prognostications, the King ordered a palace built at Imwon, near P'yong-yang, and stayed there frequently.

Myoch'ong reasoned, probably correctly, that if he could get the capital moved to P'yongyang he would receive large rewards for having helped, in a sense, to refound the dynasty. But he tried to go too far, too fast. Seeing that the King did not immediately transfer the capital, he now advised him to declare himself emperor (i.e. independent of any other nation) and attack the Chin empire, hoping by this appeal to patriotic motives to advance himself. But this was unwise and even dangerous advice, as the Kaesong officials were quick to point out. Their leader, Kim Pu-sik, went so far as to demand that Myoch'ong and his followers be beheaded for treason.

Finding his attempts at intrigue unsuccessful, Myoch'ong resorted to outright rebellion. Together with Yu Am and Cho Kwang, he raised an army and proclaimed a new kingdom called Taewi in 1135. Troops were dispatched to several of the provinces, and the rebels set up headquarters at P'yongyang.

The revolt was short-lived. Kim Pu-sik, Myoch'ong's arch-enemy, was commanded by the court to put down the rebels. After capturing and beheading some of Myoch'ong's confederates in Kaesong, he marched on P'yongyang, defeating all the forces that opposed him on the way. There Cho Kwang, belatedly realizing the hopelessness of the situation, treacherously beheaded Myoch'ong and Yu Am in an attempt to buy pardon. When this failed he tried to continue resistance, but P'yongyang fell in February of 1136 and Cho Kwang perished in the flames.

Military officials continued to suffer the high-handed dominance of the civilian bureaucracy. There had already been one military rebellion about a century earlier, during King Hyonjong's reign, but this had been ephemeral. It was during the reign of Uijong (1146–1170) that military pride and ambition, so long thwarted by the civilian government, fueled a revolt of truly serious proportions.

King Uijong, it would appear, did not possess the virtues of a ruler. His reign was marked by scenes of debauchery and idleness, and in this he was encouraged by the civil officials around him. Military men were treated as little better than servants, sometimes with outright contempt. It is even recorded that younger civilians were disrespectful of elderly military men, a scandalous thing in a society supposedly governed by Confucianism, which lays heavy emphasis on respect for the aged. The stage was set for rebellion.

The military officials made their plans, and bided their time. Their opportunity came in the year 1170, in August. King Uijong was traveling from Kaesong to the Pohyon-won monastery nearby. On the way, he paused to witness a sort of game or contest between a military man and a civilian. When the military man was defeated, all the civil officials in the King's party burst out laughing at him, and went unrebuked.

General Chong Chung-bu, with Yi Ui-bang and Yi Ko had been seeking just such an opportunity. Their action was swift and terrible. When the royal party reached Pohyonwon the soldiers escorting it turned upon it and slaughtered it to a man, killing even eunuchs and petty clerks, until only the King was left. The palace was immediately attacked and every bureaucrat who had the misfortune to be there perished. The King was deposed and banished to Koje Island and the Crown Prince was similarly imprisoned on Chindo Island. The King's younger brother, Prince Ho (posthumous title Myongjong), was placed upon the throne in 1171, and for the next twenty-six years presided helplessly over a series of bloody coup and counter-coup.

Chong Chung-bu and his followers confiscated all the property of the court and the officials and even of some of the monasteries, and divided it among themselves. Military men were placed in all important government posts, and the rule of the military grew even more arbitrary and oppressive than that of their predecessors had been.

In 1173 Kim Po-dang, military commander of the northeast district, raised an army in support of the banished King and the civilians. But this was easily defeated, and merely led to a fresh round of executions, in which Uijong himself perished, together with scores of civil officials who had thus far managed to survive. Not only the central government at Kaesong but also all provincial and local administrations were now staffed by military men. When the governor of P'yongyang attempted a revolt in 1174, he was easily brushed aside.

The generals were not long in falling out among themselves. In the very first year of their reign Yi Ko perished at the hands of Yi Ui-bang, who was in turn murdered by Chong Kyun, the son of Chong Chung-bu, leader of the revolt. Chong Chung-bu managed to retain his primacy for some years, and had himself appointed prime minister. But he was overthrown and killed by general Kyong Tae-sung in 1179. General Kyong, taking note of the fate of his predecessors, was accompanied at all times by a bodyguard of a hundred soldiers. But ironically he perished of disease within four years, and was replaced by general Yi Ui-min, who proved to be even worse than Chong Chung-bu. He managed to stay in power for thirteen years, only to be overthrown in 1196 by general Ch'oe Ch'ung-hon and his brother, who managed at last to bring a measure of stability to the bloody chaos which the rule of the generals had become.

The confusion and violence resulting from the power struggles among the generals was compounded by a series of peasant uprisings. The extravagance of King Uijong and his court had seriously depleted the national treasury. This led to the raising of the already crushing burden of taxation to intolerable heights. Farmers and ch'onmin (mainly government slaves) were in extreme distress, and the confusion attendant upon the rule of the generals encouraged them to seek redress in violence.

Even during the reign of King Uijong there had been local uprisings here and there, but after the coup of 1176 they became nationwide. The first really serious one occurred at the village of Myonghakso, near Kongju in Ch'ungch'ong Province. This was a ch'onmin village engaged in government manufacturing. The people rose in January, 1176, under the leadership of Mangi and Mangsoi. By September they had occupied the cities of Kongju and Yesan. Troops were sent to suppress them, and the government, in a conciliatory gesture, promised to raise the status of Myonghakso to that of a regular prefecture, thus automatically promoting the people in social rank.

But the people were not satisfied with this, and the revolt continued to spread, overrunning most of Ch'ungch'ong Province and spilling over into Kyonggi Province by the following year. It even threatened the capital before Mangi was finally captured and the rebels dispersed.

Meanwhile, a peasant uprising swept P'yongan Province in the northwest in 1177, which took two years to suppress. In 1182 soldiers made common cause with government slaves engaged in shipbuilding at Chonju. They seized the city and controlled it for more than a month before government troops finally defeated them.

These early uprisings had been inchoate gestures of despair rather than planned and organized rebellions. They had no clear political programs or objectives, and their leaders were unable to cope with disciplined government troops. But in later years they began to take on a more threatening tone. The most serious ones broke out in north and south Kyongsang Provinces, in the southeastern quarter of the nation. More than twenty thousand men, under the leadership of Kim Sa-mi and Hyosim, seized control over the whole area during the 1190s. Troops sent against them suffered a series of bitter defeats, and several commanders, fearful of the punishment their failures might incur, either secretly joined the rebels or committed suicide. Kim Sa-mi was finally captured and killed in February 1194, and in April about 7,000 of the farmers fell during an engagement at Miryang. In December Hyosim was at last caught, putting an end to a rebellion that had lasted for a year and a half.

Having killed and supplanted Yi Ui-min, general Ch'oe Ch'ung-hon now proceeded ruthlessly to eliminate all possible rivals. He replaced all court officials with loyal henchmen, and banished from the palace all monks who were of royal blood and thus might become centers of disaffection. High-ranking officials, generals, and even leading Buddhist priests were banished and the government was under his complete control by 1197. He even deposed and replaced the King whenever it suited his purpose, and after King Myongjong there were five significantly brief reigns during his years of power. He allowed nothing to stand in the way of his drive for absolute power. When his own brother attempted to gain influence by marrying his daughter to a Crown Prince, he was promptly executed.

Ch'oe Ch'ung-hon dealt with the peasant uprisings by a combination of military force and conciliation. Rebels who surrendered might have their districts promoted in social and administrative status, while those who persisted were not only suppressed by force but degraded. It was at this time, for example, that Kyongju, the old Silla capital, ceased to be a sub-capital because of a revolt there. This policy was on the whole successful, and social stability gradually was restored.

The regime of Ch'oe Ch'ung-hon and his descendants lasted for about sixty years, during which the administrative structure of the Koryo government was completely and radically transformed. One of his first steps was to set up an elite corps of 3,000 soldiers to be his personal bodyguard and to police all government offices. This force was under his personal control, and thus ensured not only the safety but also the obedience of all government officials under him. To support these men and insure their loyalty, the income of vast farmlands worked by slaves was assigned to them.

An attempt on his life in 1209 prompted Ch'oe to set up a new government organ called *Kyojong togam,* which he headed personally. Its main function at first was simply to detect and expose plots against the Ch'oe regime. But gradually it began to absorb other functions, until it became the real leading organ of government. Since it reported to Ch'oe Ch'ung-hon, and subsequently to his descendants, rather than to the King, it constituted an important innovation in the Koryo government. The King now became a mere figurehead with no real powers while the Ch'oes governed through the new administrative structure they had superimposed on the old form of government.

Ch'oe Ch'ung-hon was succeeded by his son, Ch'oe U, who not only completed his father's reorganization of the government, but also made a series of shrewd moves aimed at soothing the pride of those his father had injured and so forestalling plots and rebellions. Land and slaves confiscated by Ch'oe Ch'ung-hon were returned to their former owners, while a large amount of the elder Ch'oe's wealth was presented to the King. Most importantly, the Confucian scholars and civil officials who had survived the pogroms of the revolt of the generals were invited to participate once again in government and given important posts, thus removing the most likely source of disaffection.

But these officials were not placed on the boards and ministries which had governed the kingdom in former years. Rather, they were placed in the personal organizations through which the Ch'oe regime maintained control of affairs. They were given official residences which were always strongly guarded by soldiers, probably not so much to protect them as to see that they behaved themselves. These arrangements were all completed by 1225.

The military was reorganized in similar fashion. Special units were created to patrol the countryside for bandits and for night patrol in the capital. The old military organization, which had been under the control of the King and his officials, disappeared or became merely ceremonial or honorary.

Ch'oe control of the government was now complete, and it was lasting. A kind of hereditary dictatorship had been set up, completely displacing the traditional organs of Koryo government.

But the Ch'oes were no more able than the Koryo Kings had been to find solutions to the chronic discontent of peasants and slaves. In 1198 a plot was uncovered among private and government slaves in Kaesong to murder the government officials and, significantly, to burn the government records which, among other things, noted the social status of all persons, including slaves. It will be recalled that slave status, like other ranks, was permanent and hereditary. The destruction of these records would thus have allowed the slaves to escape their lowly status. The revolts were growing ominously more specific and intelligent in their aims. The discovery of this plot led to the arrest and execution by drowning of over one hundred persons.

In 1199 the peasants of the Kangnung area rose in revolt and took the cities of Samch'ok and Ulchin. They were joined by the farmers of Kyongju, still smarting over the demotion of their city from subsidiary capital. After a time they were persuaded to surrender by government offers of pardon and a rise in social status. In 1200 slave risings in numerous areas killed thousands of petty local officials, especially around Miryang, where the houses of many officials were looted and burned. They were later joined by farmers who had risen at Mt. Unmun. In 1202 there was a mutiny within the army itself when a unit composed of farmers revolted, demanding among other things the rehabilitation of Kyongju. This last was really serious, and was only with difficulty defeated by government troops.

Although they had managed to take over the apparatus of government and to secure, for the most part, the loyalty of the upper classes, the Ch'oe rulers could find no solution to the major problem which plagued all the East Asian dynasties in greater or less degree: the chronic exploitation of the peasants (and, in Korea, of slaves) and the consequent uprisings whenever a loosening of government control offered the slightest opportunity of success. And as these revolts continued, they grew more specific in their aims and more sophisticated in their methods, so that they were more and more difficult to suppress.

Chapter **14**

Koryo and the Mongols

While the Ch'oe family was consolidating its rule of the Koryo kingdom, new troubles for Korea, and indeed for all East Asia, were brewing in the steppes of central Asia. Between the Altai Mountains to the west and Manchuria to the east and centered roughly around Lake Baikal to the north, in the area that now bears their name lived a group of nomadic tribes known to history as the Mongols. They began to be a factor in Asian affairs toward the close of the twelfth century, when a man named Temujin led his tribe in conquering most of the others and creating a unified state. It was ruled by a conference of clan and tribal leaders who chose the leader, or khan. This conference, called the Kuriltai, duly elected Temujin in 1202, and under the familiar title of Chinggis Khan he proceeded to spread the Mongol power far and wide.

Though primitive in their government and culture, the Mongols were the most skillful and effective cavalrymen that Asia had yet seen, and few armies of the time could stand against them. Within a comparatively short time their empire extended from China all the way to Europe. Only Southeast Asia and Japan remained unconquered.

Having unified the Mongols and made them into an effective fighting force, Chinggis Khan turned his attention to the Jurched state of Chin which, it will be recalled, then ruled Manchuria and most of China north of the Yangtze River. Chinggis Khan first led his armies against the Chin

165

state in 1211. By 1215 the Chin capital of Yen-ching (modern Peking) had fallen and the Mongols were in control of all the territory north of the Yellow River.

The repercussions of this event were rapid and serious. Some of the Khitan tribes, whose Liao dynasty the Jurched had conquered, attempted to refound their kingdom on the Liaotung peninsula when Chin fell. This was quickly and easily crushed by the Mongols, and the Khitan fled across the Yalu River into Korea, pillaging and burning as they went, and reaching all the way to P'yongyang before they could be stopped. A second invasion of Khitan refugees occurred in 1218. This resulted in the first contacts between the Mongols and the Koryo kingdom, when a Korean contingent was sent at Mongol request to help stamp out the Khitan tribes once and for all.

The Mongols demanded an immense tribute from the Koryo kingdom for having driven out the Khitan. This, of course, the Koryo rulers were far from willing to pay, but the threat of a Mongol invasion made the situation an extremely awkward one. At this critical juncture, a Mongol envoy returning home from Korea was killed near the Yalu River by an unidentified man. The Mongols had the excuse they needed and invasion was inevitable.

Ogodei Khan, who had succeeded Chinggis Khan in 1227, set out in 1231 to crush the last remnants of the Chin state. At the same time, he sent an army under general Sartai to invade the Koryo kingdom. The border city of Uiju was quickly taken, and the Mongols marched south. Ch'oe U hastily organized the defenses and called up all available troops. Engagements were fought at Kusong and Anju, and the Koryo forces had some scattered successes, but in spite of these the Mongols pressed steadily southward. Kaesong was invested and some Mongol troops got as far as Ch'ungju. Ch'oe U had no choice but to sue for peace before the whole kingdom was destroyed.

The Mongol peace terms included a tribute so immense as to be absurd. They demanded 10,000 otter skins, 20,000 horses, 10,000 bolts of silk, clothing for 1,000,000 soldiers, and numerous children and artisans to be taken as slaves. To see that these terms were kept and the war was not renewed, the Mongols sent seventy-two officials to be stationed in the principal cities.

Though Ch'oe U and his government were forced to accept this humiliating peace, they did not give up hope of resistance. In June of 1232, when Mongol supervision had been somewhat relaxed, the entire court and government were removed to Kanghwa Island at the mouth of the Han River on the west coast. Most of the population of Kaesong was forced to move with them. The island's coasts were fortified with a double wall, and all available ships were commandeered for the transportation of supplies from the mainland. The native population was evacuated and ordered to seek refuge in the mountains or on other islands.

As a result of these activities general Sartai's forces returned in December, guided this time by a traitor from P'yongyang named Hong Pog-won. Kaesong was quickly taken and the Mongols occupied all of the kingdom north of the Han River. It was only saved from further conquest by the leading monk Kim Yun-hu, a skilful archer, who shot and killed general Sartai. Thrown into confusion by the death of their leader, the Mongol troops retreated and ultimately withdrew from the peninsula.

The stubborn Korean resistance drew repeated Mongolian invasions during the next thirty years. The troops that arrived in 1235 got all the way to Kyongju, and were only withdrawn upon a Koryo promise to become the vassal of the Mongol emperor. Some years of peace followed, but Korean resistance continued and there were four seperate attacks between 1253 and 1257 before it finally ceased. The Cholla Provinces, the nation's richest agricultural area, were taken, and destruction was widespread. It was at this time that the nine-storied pagoda at Hwang-yong-sa was destroyed and the thousands of wood blocks for printing the Buddhist *Tripitaka* kept at Puin-sa, were burned. All the major cities were sacked, with great slaughter and indescriminate destruction of temples and palaces, and many precious works of art and historical documents vanished.

During all these invasions the court on Kanghwa Island continued to live as if it were back in Kaesong in peacetime. Government officials continued to collect taxes wherever they could, and the supply ships regularly plied between the island and the mainland, bringing back all that the court required, regardless of the miseries of the people. Naturally there was a good deal of disaffection among the populace, but the only worry of the court seemed to be that the Mongols might take to the sea and cut off the supply ships.

The main political question at court was, of course, policy toward the Mongols. Ch'oe Ui, the fourth of the Ch'oe dictators, held out for continued resistance, as his family had always done. But the King, who had now gathered a considerable number of supporters, had always objected to the removal to Kanghwa and was now ready to face the inevitable. In 1258 Ch'oe Ui was assassinated, bringing sixty years of Ch'oe rule to an end. The King once more assumed personal control of the government, and the way was open for peace negotiations.

In March of 1259 Crown Prince Chon was sent to the Mongol court as a sign of submission. The fortifications on Kanghwa Island were destroyed in accordance with Mongol demands. When King Kojong died in June of that year, Prince Chon returned to assume the throne (posthumous title Wonjong) and was obliged in his turn to send his eldest son to the Mongols.

But there was still a group of diehard military officers who could not accept submission to the Mongols. Led by one Im Yon, they assassinated Kim Chun, the man who had killed Ch'oe Ui, eliminated the peace party and seized power. In June of 1269 King Wonjong was deposed and replaced by his younger brother Ch'ang.

But this coup was foredoomed to failure. Mongol strength was too great, and there were too many Koryo officials who realized that resistance was futile. King Wonjong was restored in 1270 and in that same year, after thirty-nine years of exile, the court returned to Kaesong. Mongol dominance was now complete, at any rate in the north. A Mongol army garrisoned P'yongyang, and Mongol troops guarded other strategic points in the northern half of the country, securing the flank of the main army which was then pushing into China.

Matters were somewhat different in the south, where stubborn resistance to foreign rule continued for a further four years. The special military units which had guarded Kanghwa refused to obey the royal orders to disband when the court moved back to Kaesong. Instead, they rebuilt the fortifications and declared one of the King's relatives ruler. Later, finding Kanghwa inconveniently close to Kaesong, they removed to Chindo Island off the southwest coast of Cholla Province, bringing with them all the people of Kanghwa and all the goods and supplies they could transport.

From this base they began to stir up anti-Mongol feeling among the southern peasants, and issued a manifesto proclaiming themselves the legitimate rulers of the country. Thousands flocked to join them, and soon they had control of all the southern coast. The transport of tax grain from the rich Cholla farmlands to Kaesong was blocked, cutting off a major source of government revenue.

But Chindo fell to a combined Koryo-Mongol force in

1271, and many of the leaders of the resistance were captured. The remnant of the insurgents retreated to Cheju, the southernmost of the Korean islands. There, finally, lacking supplies and equipment, they were defeated by a Mongol force in 1273 and all effective resistance to the Mongols was at last ended. But Korean hatred of foreign rule, which had appeared as early as Silla times, had again been demonstrated, and not for the last time.

While these events were taking place in Korea the Mongol invasion of China went steadily forward. Much of the northern area had been conquered by 1271, in which year the Mongol rulers assumed the Chinese dynastic title Yuan, by which they are known in Chinese histories. They established their capital at Peking, where a regular Chinese-style government gradually appeared. The conquest of China was complete by 1279, and Khubilai, the grandson of Chinggis Khan, could style himself the Son of Heaven.

The Mongol policy in Korea was to subordinate the court and government completely to the Yuan Emperor and use it as a tool to govern the country. This was accomplished in various ways. In the first place, there was the matter of names and titles, always important under autocratic regimes and particularly so in China and Korea. Koryo officials in the past had generally had titles roughly corresponding to those of their counterparts in the Chinese Imperial government. At Mongol insistence these were all changed in such a manner as to indicate that Koryo officials were lower in rank than Mongols or Chinese.

Then there was the matter of posthumous royal titles. Koryo kings had often had the ending *jo* (progenitor) or *jong* (ancestor) in their titles. These were actually the Korean pronunciations of the corresponding Chinese words, as we have previously pointed out, and were adopted in imitation of Chinese posthumous titles of emperors. This was now forbidden as implying equality between Koryo kings and Yuan emperors. Instead, the six Koryo kings beginning with Ch'ungyol all had the prefix *ch'ung* (loyal) in their titles to indicate their subordination to the Yuan Emperor. Even the forms of address used when speaking to royalty were altered to somewhat less respectful terms than formerly.

One of the most effective methods of keeping the Koryo court under Mongol control was the system of royal marriages. Once Mongol domination was established, the Koryo Crown Prince was regularly sent to the Yuan court at Peking, where he lived until the death of the reigning king and where he was obliged to marry a Mongol princess. In a few generations the Koryo royal family was so thoroughly Mongolized that the Yuan Emperors had little to fear from that quarter.

In addition to the overall reorganization of the government, the Mongols installed a special organization called the Office for the Conquest of the East, which was to oversee the coming invasion of Japan. The invasion failed, as we shall see, but the office remained as a convenient means of checking any independent tendencies in the Koryo court. The northern areas of Korea remained under direct Mongol rule, as did Cheju Island.

During the period of Mongol dominance the Korean people suffered a twofold exploitation. In the first place, there were the expenses of the Koryo court, with the frequent and costly comings and goings between Kaesong and Peking necessitated by the royal marriages to Mongol princesses, and all the other expenses of the regular government. On top of this there was the immense annual tribute which the Koryo government had to pay to the Yuan court. Gold, silver, ginseng and hawks were the principal items. Indeed so popular was falconry among the Mongols that special officials were stationed in Korea for the collection of hawks. But there was human tribute too. Every year numbers of artisans, eunuchs and women departed for Peking to supply the various needs and desires of the Mongols.

The heaviest burdens the people had to bear resulted from the Mongol invasions of Japan. Soon after the Koryo court had submitted, the Mongols had called upon the Japanese rulers to submit themselves as vassals to the Yuan Emperor. This the Japanese refused to do. Caught in the middle, the Koryo court urged the Japanese to submit, while at the same time trying to persuade the Mongols of the extreme difficulty of launching an invasion from Korea. Unfortunately for Korea, both the Japanese and the Mongols remained impervious to persuasion.

Preparations for the invasion proceeded accordingly. Some 35,000 Korean workmen were compelled to build a fleet of about nine hundred ships. In 1274 this fleet set out from Masan carrying 20,000 Mongol and Chinese and 5,000 Korean troops, bound for Hakata, an important harbor in northern Kyushu.

The invasion proved a disaster. The troops could make little progress against the tough Japanese resistance, and were soon compelled to re-embark to prevent their ships from being broken up on the shore by an approaching storm. This storm, when it arrived, proved so severe that many of the ships were lost, and the survivors found their numbers so depleted that they could not risk continuing the invasion. They limped back to Korea decimated and empty-handed.

Undismayed, the Emperor Khubilai ordered the mounting of another invasion, despite Koryo protests that Korean resources were already so strained that another expedition would ruin the country. Another fleet of about 900 ships was built and provisioned with huge quantities of Korean rice. Ten thousand Mongol, Chinese and Korean troops went aboard and the expedition sailed in 1281.

It proved a repetition of the first. Again the Japanese could not be pushed back, and again a great storm scattered the ships and destroyed many of them, compelling the invaders to return. The immense labor required of the Koryo kingdom to furnish these expeditions, and the exactions for supplies reduced it to the brink of utter ruin.

The policy of compelling the Koryo kings to marry Mongol princesses led inevitably to dissension within the Koryo court and thus served the Mongol purpose of keeping the Korean rulers weak. When King Ch'ungyol's Mongol queen died in 1297, for example, the Crown Prince returned from Peking and had large numbers of the court women and eunuchs executed because he blamed them for his mother's death. When he came to the throne in 1309 he dismissed most of the officials appointed by his father and tried to check the power of the eunuchs and the aristocrats.

King Ch'ungson (his posthumous title) had a concubine named Cho. His Mongol queen became jealous of this woman, and made a slanderous report to Peking. Seeing an opportunity to get rid of an independent-minded ruler, the Yuan Emperor summoned the royal couple to his court to go into the matter more thoroughly. His final decision was to restore King Ch'ungyol (who had evidently retired or been deposed and was still living) to the Koryo throne and make King Ch'ungson the ruler of Shen-yang, which consisted of parts of southern Manchuria and the Liaotung peninsula.

This setting up of a Koryo monarch in non-Koryo territory had the desired effect of creating rival factions in the Koryo court. Since no King could rule the two territories simultaneously, and since the Yuan emperors could enthrone or depose them at will, Koryo Kings and their heirs were frequently at odds with each other. On the death of King Ch'ungyol, King Ch'ungson occupied the Koryo throne briefly, passing on Shen-yang to the son of his brother Ko. He then abdicated in favor of his son, Prince Kangnung, who became King Ch'ungsuk. When he later fell from favor in Peking, King Ch'ungsuk took the opportunity to get rid of his father's followers, who constituted the Shen-yang faction.

When King Ch'ungsuk's Mongol queen died of illness in 1319, the Shen-yang faction retaliated by spreading a report that she had been murdered, which got King Ch'ungsuk in trouble with the Yuan court. They continued their efforts to place Prince Ko on the throne even into the next reign, and went so far as to raise an armed revolt, which was suppressed. With all this factional pulling and hauling going on, and with the Mongols in their very midst as queens, there was little chance for the Koryo rulers to organize any effective opposition to their Mongol overlords.

The lot of the farmers under the Mongols was more miserable than it had ever been. Large numbers of them abandoned the land and became brigands, while others turned to the trade of butcher, the most despised occupation in Korea. But most of them, unable to pay the exorbitant taxes, became the tenants of private estates, or even the slaves of the landowners, whose wealth and power grew rapidly, especially if they cooperated with the Mongols. The movement of land and tenants into private hands became so widespread that government revenues shrank to almost nothing and the great landowners became virtually independent of the court.

There were a few spasmodic efforts at reform and fiscal sanity. King Ch'ungson, for example, tried to stop the flow of land into private hands and to regain some of the authority of the court. He had some success for a time, but the landowners he was attempting to check had Mongol backing, and his efforts came to nothing. Even one of the

Mongol officials attempted at one time to bring some sense and efficiency into the chaos of the Koryo economy, though no doubt with different motives from those of Korean reformers, but he too was powerless against the aristocrats and their Mongol backers. The Mongol dominance thus encouraged and accelerated adverse tendencies in the Koryo society and economy, and the kingdom began to slide into complete disintegration.

The Mongol invasions led indirectly to one of the great achievements of Koryo culture. It has been noted already that the carved wooden blocks for printing the Buddhist *Tripitaka* which had been kept at Puin-sa were destroyed during the conflict. While the court was at Kanghwa Island, as a work of pious patriotism to secure the Buddha's protection against the Mongols, this immense collection was prepared anew. The work began in 1237 and took sixteen years. When it was finished, the Korean people had given the world one of the great treasures of Buddhist culture— the whole of the basic Buddhist canon permanently preserved and readily reproducible. The 86,600 large wooden printing blocks can still be seen today at Haein-sa, an important temple near the modern city of Taegu.

After the return of the court to Kaesong, Mongol customs and culture had considerable influence on the upper classes. Mongol words entered the language and Mongol dress and hair styles became fashionable. Early marriage, so prominent a feature of Korean society in later days, became widespread as a means of preventing young girls from being taken off to China as part of the annual tribute.

Most of these young girls became either concubines or slaves of the Yuan Emperor or the Mongol aristocrats. For the most part, their lot was unenviable, but occasionally one was lucky. A case in point is the daughter of one Ki Cha-o, a farmer from Haengju. Shipped off to Peking in one of the annual tribute groups, she was lucky enough to be chosen for the Emperor's court. The Emperor made her his concubine, and liked her so much that eventually she was promoted to the official status of second wife, inferior only to the Empress herself. This meant that her offspring were legitimized, and when the Emperor died it was her son who succeeded to the throne. The simple farmer Ki Cha-o found himself the grandfather of an Emperor and reveled in wealth and idleness for the rest of his days.

If the Mongols had one redeeming virtue, it was their practicality. Though primitive and cruel, they were quick to see the usefulness of any idea or practice they encountered, and had none of the xenophobic distrust of foreign ways which characterized the Chinese. Having little material or intellectual culture of their own, they rapidly absorbed whatever they met with during their conquests. More specifically, many important aspects of Moslem culture reached East Asia after the Mongol conquest of Persia brought them into contact with the Arabs, including astrology, mathematics, medicine, artistic techniques and calendar reform. Korea benefited from these contacts to a modest extent, and Arab traders occasionally came to buy and sell.

Three other innovations appeared in China under the Mongols which were to have important effects upon Korea as well. These were the cultivation of cotton and the manufacture of cotton cloth, the use of gunpowder, and the neo-Confucian philosophy of Chu Hsi, which had so profound an influence on the Yi dynasty which replaced Koryo at the close of the fourteenth century.

Chapter 15

The Fall of Koryo

The vassal status which had been forced upon the Koryo kingdom by the Mongols and the close connections between the two courts meant that political events in China now had greater influence than ever before upon Korea. To these we must now once more briefly turn our attention.

After a period of prosperity and power the Mongol rulers began to be plagued by a series of internal struggles for the throne. Emperors appeared and disappeared every few years as one group or another seized power, and Mongol control of the native Chinese, who had never really accepted them, began to weaken. These difficulties were compounded by frequent famines in north China, often accompanied by disastrous flooding of the Yellow River, aptly known as China's Sorrow. From the middle of the fourteenth century on the Mongol power rapidly declined.

The Chinese were quick to grasp this opportunity to throw off foreign rule. From the 1340s on, rebellions broke out all over the country. The Mongols had plainly lost the Mandate of Heaven, as the Chinese put it, and their replacement by a new dynasty was only a matter of time.

But China was not again to undergo an extended period of division, with various rival states controlling different parts of the country. Most of the uprisings were short-lived, although they tried to legitimize themselves in

177

various ways. Some set up rulers whom they claimed were descendants of the Sung dynasty and thus legitimate heirs to the throne seized by the Mongols. Others, appealing to popular religious beliefs, claimed to be incarnations of Maitreya, the Buddha of the future. Secret societies appeared in connection with the rebellions, notably the White Lotus society.

One of these self-styled Sung states in northwest China had a direct effect upon Korea. Its power was based upon a secret society called the Red Turbans, a particularly aggressive group. When they pushed their way into southern Manchuria and occupied the Liaotung peninsula in 1359, they were met and defeated by a Mongol army, and about 40,000 of them fled into the Koryo kingdom. They had occupied four northwestern prefectures and taken P'yongyang before a Koryo army was able to defeat and drive them out.

They returned again in 1361, this time 100,000 strong. All the northern part of the kingdom fell to them, and Kaesong was in danger, so that the court was forced to flee to Andong in the south. Kaesong fell soon after. The court, however, regrouped its forces in the south and counter-attacked. The Red Turbans suffered a disastrous defeat and were slaughtered in such numbers that they were permanently eliminated as a threat to Korea.

Meanwhile, the fate of China was being decided in the south. A young commoner named Chu Yuan-chang, from the Huai River area northwest of Nanking, had joined a rebel band in 1352. His ability and ambition soon made him its leader, and in 1356 it seized Nanking. Chu Yuan-chang spent the next ten years gradually extending his power and organizing his forces until he was in control of most of China south of the Yangtze River.

He was now ready to face the faltering power of the Mongols. In 1368 a great attack was launched which swept all before it. Before the year was out Peking had fallen and Chu Yuan-chang proclaimed himself the first Emperor of the Ming dynasty, which was to rule China for the next three hundred years. Mopping-up operations continued for the next decade or so, and by 1382 the Ming dynasty ruled all of China proper.

Free at last from Mongol domination, the Koryo kingdom began efforts to reform its government and arrest the decline into which it had fallen. King Kongmin, who came to the throne in 1351 during the revolts in China, first set about removing the pro-Mongol aristocrats whom the Yuan rulers had placed in influential positions. The supervisory organ which the Mongols had imposed upon the government was disbanded and the northwestern territories which the Mongols had retained under their direct rule were brought back under Koryo sovereignty. Military officers who had been appointed by the Mongols were removed from their positions and the army reorganized under the direct control of the court. The old royal names and titles which the Mongols had replaced with humiliatingly subordinate ones were restored.

But though the Mongol power was shattered, the Koryo kingdom still faced external and internal problems that were nearly insuperable. When the Red Turbans had been driven off at heavy cost in lives and resources, the rulers faced an increasing problem of Japanese piracy. The rulers of Japan at this time, the Ashikaga Shoguns, were only in nominal control of most of the country. Many of the people of northern Kyushu and the islands off its coast had taken to piracy, and regularly plundered the coasts of China and Korea, where they were known by the contemptuous name of *Woegu,* dwarfs.

The raids of these pirates increased in seriousness during King Kongmin's reign. They no longer confined themselves to attacking coastal towns, but would march overland or sail up rivers to attack large cities such as Kongju and Chonju. When they took a town they would utterly destroy it and kill everyone who did not manage to escape. Farmland was left fallow in many coastal areas and the transportation of tax grain to the capital was interfered with. At one point the pirates even dared to attack Kanghwa Island, and the court seriously considered transferring the capital to a safer place.

The kingdom managed to survive the pirate raids and eventually they died down, but meanwhile very serious internal difficulties had developed. While most of the people had opposed the Mongols and were glad of their defeat, there was a class of large landowners and military officials who had benefited from the Mongol presence. These now formed a faction opposed to King Kongmin's reforms.

Though driven out of China, the Mongols were still a power in Manchuria, and still capable of taking a hand in Koryo affairs. Through Ch'oe Yu, who had fled the Koryo court to escape punishment for a crime, they got in touch with the pro-Mongol faction at Kaesong and a plot was formed. Kim Yong was to lead an attack on Hungwang-sa monastery, where the King was staying for safety, assassinate him and place Prince Tokhung, younger brother of King Ch'ungsuk, on the throne.

This plot was a failure, and though he managed to kill Hong On-bak, a leading minister, Kim Yong was killed and his followers dispersed. The Mongol ruler (who still called himself emperor, though he no longer had an empire) then sent orders for the change of kingship just as in the old days, at the same time giving Ch'oe Yu the leading government post. When this brought no response, Ch'oe Yu led 10,000 troops across the Yalu in an attempt to restore Mongol hegemony by force. They were soundly defeated by Koryo defenders and the Mongol ruler, seeing the folly of further attempts to dominate Koryo, reopened peaceful relations and sent Ch'oe Yu in chains to Kaesong, where he was executed.

A second internal problem which the kingdom faced after regaining its independence was the perpetually troublesome one of private landholdings. The various factions which had succeeded each other in power during the period preceding Mongol domination had always enriched themselves and secured the support of their followers by expropriations and grants of land, so much so that the system of using temporary grants of land to pay official salaries had broken down. After the revolt of the military officials fraudulent documents, foreclosures and simple force were often resorted to build up estates.

The coming of the Mongols did not end these practices, but simply eliminated most of the civil officials in favor of military men patronized by the Mongols and the royal family. By the end of the Mongol period the vast majority of agricultural land had passed into great estates called *nongjang*, worked by tenant farmers and slaves. Even during the period when the court had been on Kanghwa various schemes of land reform had been tried, but they all had the fatal flaw which plagued all such efforts: the government could not exist without the support of the great landowners, many of whom were the very officials who were supposed to put the land reforms into practice.

Thus when King Kongmin attempted to institute his reforms he faced an almost impossible situation. On the one hand, the nongjang had become so extensive that the government was without economic foundations. On the other hand, the recent incursions of the Red Turbans and the Japanese pirates had given the military a position of dominance, and military men were not notably partial to Chinese-style civilian rule. If he was to succeed at all he had to find some means of subordinating both of these groups.

A bold and ingenious expedient was tried. In 1365 the King selected an obscure monk named P'yonjo (he later changed his name to Sin Ton) who had no connection with either of the dominant groups. He first raised the monk to *Kuksa,* the highest clerical post, and then invested him with temporal power and instructed him to carry out the program of reform.

Sin Ton set about it vigorously. The high-ranking officials who opposed the King's program were eliminated. Decrees went out returning land and slaves illegally appropriated to their original owners. Other slaves whose status was vague were raised to the rank of commoners. Songgyun'gwan, the center of Confucian training, was reorganized. The examination system for choosing government officials was reformed and enforced. A thoroughgoing reestablishment of royal authority and enlightened bureaucratic government was under way.

But Sin Ton inevitably fell foul of the entrenched landlords whose power and wealth he threatened. He was accused of using his position to further his private fortune, and of immorality. His status as a monk laid him open to charges that he was wasting state funds on Buddhist ceremonies. His opponents managed to raise such an outcry against him that in 1371 he had to be banished on a trumped-up charge of plotting to assassinate the King. Once out of the way, he was quietly done away with.

The fall of Sin Ton was a fatal blow to King Kongmin's hopes. He was forced to compromise with the landlords and all his brave plans for a vigorous centralized state came to nothing. In despair, he abandoned all further attempts at reform and gave himself up to luxury and idleness.

But the entrenched bureaucracy which represented the landlords' interests could not forgive him. Fearful of further attempts at reform, a group led by Yi In-im had the King assassinated and placed his son Prince U, a child of ten, on the throne. Rumors that the boy was not a legitimate heir but the son of King Kongmin by one of Sin Ton's concubines further damaged the royal prestige and enhanced the power of the landlord group over the throne.

But a new force was emerging in society that was ultimately to transform the kingdom. While King Kongmin and Sin Ton had been unable to open the top posts to talent, the lower offices were increasingly occupied by Confucian scholar-officials, the products of the Confucian schools and the examination system. This was not in itself remarkable and might have had little effect but for the transformation of Confucianism itself that was going on at the time.

In the late twelfth century in China, in the period immediately preceding the Mongol conquest, there had flourished a great Confucian scholar named Chu Hsi. His historical works and commentaries on the Confucian classics had made Confucianism a systematized philosophy of government, with, for the first time, a fully worked out metaphysical base. This version of Confucianism spread throughout China and became orthodox doctrine everywhere. It sharpened and revitalized Confucian thought, giving it clear and definite aims and ideals.

Chu Hsi's neo-Confucianism inspired the scholar-officials of late Koryo times with reforming zeal. In the government and society of which they were a part they saw violations of Confucian principles on every hand. Land properly belonging to the state was in the hands of private individuals. The leading offices of government, which, for the good of the nation ought to be filled by those best qualified, were awarded on the basis of wealth and position alone. Above all, the state was dominated by a religion which in many ways ran contrary to the Confucian principles of social relations.

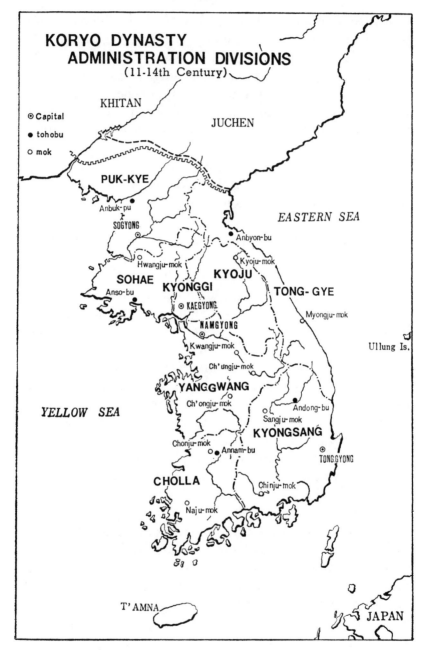

KORYO DYNASTY
ADMINISTRATION DIVISIONS
(11-14th Century)

KHITAN

JUCHEN

⊙ Capital
● tohobu
○ mok

PUK-KYE

Anbuk-pu

SOGYONG

EASTERN SEA

Anbyon-bu

Hwangju-mok

Kyoju-mok

KYOJU

SOHAE   KYONGGI

Anso-bu

TONG-GYE

⊙ KAEGYONG

Myongju-mok

NAMGYONG

Kwangju-mok

Ch'ungju-mok

YANGGWANG

Ch'ongju-mok

Andong-bu

Sangju-mok

KYONGSANG

Chonju-mok

Annam-bu

YELLOW SEA

Ullung Is.

TONGGYONG

CHOLLA

Chinju-mok

Naju-mok

T'AMNA

JAPAN

We have had frequent occasion previously to point out the dominant position of Buddhism in the Koryo kingdom. During most of its history Buddhism and Confucianism had been felt to be more or less complementary, and there had been little conflict between them. But Chu Hsi drew the lines more sharply, and the scholar-officials began to look with jaundiced eyes upon the great expenses incurred by the state in sponsoring Buddhist festivals, the wealth and power of the monasteries, the many men withdrawn from a productive life and service to the state, and the violation of family and social relationships, the heart of Confucian social philosophy, involved in renouncing family ties to become monks. Many advocated that state expenditures on temples and monuments should cease. Some even took the extreme position that all monasteries and temples should be confiscated and their land nationalized, while the monks should be returned to secular life to supply the need for farm labor and troops, and that in future it should be illegal to become a monk.

Had this new movement appeared in stable and prosperous times, it might have led to little more than minor reforms within the government, with perhaps a few restrictions on Buddhism. But the times were disturbed, the government was almost bankrupt, and the factions were clamorous. When a capable leader appeared in whom the scholar-officials could have faith, the stage was set for sweeping changes.

Yi Song-gye came of a family which had supplied military leaders to the area of modern Hamgyong Province in the northeast for four generations. His ancestors had fought the Mongols at various times, and he himself had a distinguished military career. He had suppressed two local rebellions in the royal service, and had been prominent in driving out the Red Turbans. His forces played an important part in the suppression of the pro-Mongol rebellion of Ch'oe Yu. In 1370 he led an expedition across the Yalu to mop up the remnants of this rebellion and to secure a Koryo foothold in the old Koguryo territories on the Liaotung peninsula, a policy that was ultimately abandoned.

With these successes behind him, he turned his attention to the Japanese pirates, whose depredations were becoming intolerable. It was no longer a matter of hit-and-run raids. In many areas the pirates had established permanent bases on the Korean coast, and as has been mentioned, at one time even invaded Kanghwa Island and threatened Kaesong. General Yi repelled pirate attacks in his own northeastern area and then fought a series of engagements over the next several years that reduced their power and kept them more or less at bay.

Yi Song-gye's rise to eminence coincided with the factional struggles at court which led to the assassination of King Kongmin in 1374. King Kongmin, it will be recalled, had wished to reform the administration and to eliminate Mongol influence. The group which opposed him was, of course, primarily interested in protecting the privileges of its members, but important aspects of foreign policy were also involved. The conservative group also wished to renew ties with the Mongols, who by now had for the most part been driven back to their old territories in Central Asia, while King Kongmin and the more enlightened officials wished to establish ties with the new Ming dynasty in China.

When King Kongmin was assassinated and replaced by King U (it is perhaps significant that this king has no posthumous title) envoys were dispatched to the Mongol court. In an effort to forestall Chinese displeasure, however, a messenger was also sent to the Ming court to ask the Emperor to choose a posthumous title for King Kongmin, an act symbolizing the Koryo kingdom's "younger brother" status in relation to the Chinese Empire.

But the Ming rulers were suspicious about King Kong-min's sudden and unexplained death and doubtful of King U's legitimacy. The choice of a posthumous title was delayed, heavy tribute in horses and precious metals was demanded, and the Koryo court was asked to send an official of senior status as ambassador. When the Koryo court temporized, saying that everyone was so occupied with repelling the Japanese pirates that no high official could be spared, Ming suspicions increased.

The Mongols, on the other hand, immediately recognized the legitimacy of King U's accession, and asked that the Koryo court send troops to attack a Ming fortress, plainly intending to use the Koryo kingdom to reestablish themselves in China. Even the pro-Mongol faction was not willing to go this far, however, and the kingdom remained in a state of uneasy neutrality between the two hostile powers.

The Ming court finally recognized King U's legitimacy in 1385, but continued to make threatening gestures. In 1388 the former Mongol fortress of Ch'ollyong on the northern Koryo border area was occupied by Ming forces. General Ch'oe Yong, the highest of the military officials, thereupon consulted Yi Song-gye about the situation, and they agreed that the pro-Mongol faction would have to be overthrown in order to relieve this menacing Ming pressure. Yi In-im and his group were accordingly removed, and Ch'oe Yong took personal control of the government.

But the Ming forces continued to occupy Ch'ollyong and the territory north of it, and this the court found unacceptable. Even the pro-Ming officials grew fearful of this encroachment on Koryo territory, and the feeling grew that preventive measures must be taken. Ch'oe Yong decided that a military expedition must be sent, and placed Yi Song-gye in command.

General Yi obeyed, but he had grave misgivings. Having closely observed the fall of the Mongols, he was well aware of the great power of the Ming, and doubted whether a kingdom as small and weak as his could have any success against them. In addition, the Japanese pirates were sure to take advantage of the withdrawal of a large body of troops to renew their depredations. Finally, the expedition had been ordered to set out during the rainy season of early summer, which general Yi, an experienced commander, knew would be sure to hamper his operations seriously.

By the time general Yi and his army reached Wihwa Island in the Yalu River and were ready to cross into Ming-held territory the heavy rains had set in. Desertions and disease were decimating the troops. The general was now certain that the expedition was doomed to failure, and sent a request to Kaesong that it be withdrawn. Neither Ch'oe Yong nor King U would countenance such a move, but ordered general Yi to proceed against the Ming forces.

Yi Song-gye was now placed in the same position, roughly, as Caesar at the Rubicon. Pressing the attack against China meant not only certain defeat for his country but also personal disgrace and probably death. But if he took any other action he would be in a state of rebellion against his king and government. In that rainy summer of 1388 on the banks of the Yalu, the fateful decision was made which doomed the Koryo dynasty and altered the course of Korean history. He marched back to Kaesong at the head of his troops, overpowered what defenders there were, deposed King U, and took charge of the government.

Although the power of the Koryo kings was thus reduced to virtually nothing, Yi Song-gye was too astute a statesman to terminate the dynasty at once and make himself King, for such an action would have made too many enemies and he needed to consolidate his position first. King U's son Ch'ang was elevated to the throne and the outward forms of Koryo government were carefully observed while Yi Song-gye set about a thorough-going reform from within.

The most pressing problem to be settled was the matter of land reform. As we have seen, more and more land had been taken over by the great landlords in late Koryo times, reducing government revenue until the government could not even pay its own officials adequately. The landlords held the real power in the country, which led to disunity and strife. Yi Song-gye clearly saw that if he was to continue in power he would have to break the power of the landlords and create a strong central government with himself at its head.

In this endeavor he shrewdly enlisted the support of the Confucian scholar-officials who occupied most of the lower grades of the bureaucracy. They had long been resentful of the inadequate compensation they were given, and hopeful of reforms along the lines of Chu Hsi's neo-Confucianism. They readily gave their support to Yi Song-gye, who thus showed himself to be a wise statesman capable of bold decisions and quick action but cautious enough never to act rashly or without due deliberation. His regime was to be no mere military dictatorship but a truly reformed, viable government.

A program of land reform was duly drawn up by the scholar Cho Chun. As might have been expected, it followed fairly closely the traditional Chinese system which had been instituted before with varying degrees of success. All land was to be nationalized and redistributed, most grants being temporary, for the support of government officials. The great estates were to be broken up and the bulk of their land returned to the government tax rolls to provide revenues. As Yi Song-gye eliminated his rivals with the help of the army and the scholar-officials, this plan was gradually put into practice.

Two years after his seizure of power Yi Song-gye was ready for the next decisive steps in his progress toward complete control of the country. It will be recalled that the deposed King U had been rumored not to be the legitimate son of King Kongmin, but a son by a mistress of Sin Ton. The same was true of his son, King Ch'ang, who had replaced him. On these grounds King Ch'ang was deposed and Wang Yo, a descendant of King Sinjong, ascended the throne.

This was not a mere gesture of propriety but part of a careful plan. When, as expected, conservative officials loyal to Kings U and Ch'ang opposed the move, Yi Song-gye took the opportunity to remove them from office, thus destroying the last vestiges of conservative power in the government. Now free to act more boldly than before, he made the dramatic gesture of burning the old land registers which were the legal basis of the landlords' power.

In the next year, 1391, Yi Song-gye completely reorganized the military forces and had himself appointed commander-in-chief. Officers loyal to him occupied all the higher posts. He was now able to proceed unopposed with the land reform program. All civil and military officials were assigned tracts of land for their support, while coastal lands, islands and newly reclaimed land were reserved for the support of the army. Slaves, artisans, tradesmen and, significantly, Buddhist monks were specifically excluded from the list of those eligible for land grants.

Many of these grants were of course permanent and hereditary, but the new regulations contained significant innovations. In the first place, owners of large estates were now made liable to the land tax just as independent farmers were, so that their growth could not again sap the government finances. Secondly, rents were carefully controlled, landlords being allowed to charge their tenants no more than one tenth of their crops as rent. Thirdly, landlords were forbidden to dispossess tenants without sufficient cause, and tenants were forbidden to sell or otherwise dispose of their rights of tenancy without permission. Government revenues were thus secured, unwarranted exploitation of farmers was prevented, and the firm attachment of farmers to the land aided social stability.

With the power of the old landlords defeated and their estates broken up, and with the firm support both of the army and of the scholar-officials who now held most government offices, Yi Song-gye was ready to take the final momentous steps in the founding of a new dynasty.

Chapter **16**

The Culture of
the Later Koryo Period

Buddhism remained the dominant religious and intellectual influence during the later years of the Koryo dynasty, and underwent little significant development. The Son (Zen) sects maintained their dominance, and there were continued efforts to harmonize the various doctrines under the influence of the T'ien T'ai sect which had been imported from China. In this the monk Chinul was particularly active. Though he was nominally a member of the Chogye-jong, the revitalized Son sect, he taught that salvation could come both through meditation leading to sudden enlightenment, the basic Son teaching, or through earnest study and meditation on the scriptures, the teaching of the earlier introduced Five Sects.

Two other monks of the Chogye sect, T'aego and Naong, were also influential during this period. Both went to China for study, and Naong was taught by an Indian monk while there. T'aego brought back a new Son sect, the Imje-jong, and also developed it into a major force. Naong was most notable for the men whom he trained, one of whom, Muhak, was a friend and mentor of Yi Song-gye, the founder of the Yi dynasty.

The most notable event in the intellectual history of later Koryo times was the introduction of the Chinese thinker Chu Hsi's reinterpretation of Confucianism. Besides revitalizing Confucian thought itself, it brought about organized opposition to Buddhism. It is particularly

192

32. *Taegak Kuksa:* Uich'on (1055–1101), the fourth son of King Munjong, Koryo dynasty. The founder of Ch'ont'ae Sect.

33. *Illustrated Sutra:* Woodblock printing on paper. Koryo dynasty, 11th century. Coll. Judge Kim Wan-sop, Seoul.

34. Miruk (Maitreya) and Lantern: Stone. Kwanch'ok-sa, near Nonsan, South Ch'ungch'ong Province. Maitreya, H. about 18.3m. Lantern, about 6.1m. Koryo dynasty, late 10th century.

35. Pagoda, Wolchong-sa: Mt. Odae, P'yongwon-gun, Kangwon Province. H. about 14.6m. Koryo dynasty, 11th century.

36, 37. Tripitaka Koreana Storage Building and Tripitaka Koreana Wood Block, Haein-sa: Hapch'on, North Kyongsang Province. (Below) Constructed in the 19th year of King Songjong's reign, 1488. (Above) One of the wood blocks for printing the complete Buddhist scriptures, completed in 1251.

38. Muryangsujon, Pusok-sa: Yongju-gun, North Kyongsang Province. Koryo dynasty (rebuilt about 1350).

40. *Water Dropper:* Celadon glaze; modelled and underglaze iron decoration. H. 10.2cm. Koryo dynasty, early 12th century. Coll. Chon Hyong-p'il.

39. *Wine Pot with Cover and Bowl:* Celadon glaze; reticulated, modelled, and incised decoration. Pot, H. 17.8cm, D. at base 10.5cm. Bowl, H. 8.9cm, D. at top 18.3cm. Koryo dynasty, 12th century. National Museum of Korea.

41. *Details from Mural, Bodhisattva and Deva King:* Painting on wood. Pusok-sa, Yongju-gun, North Kyongsang Province. H. about 1.8m. Koryo dynasty, 14th century.

significant that this neo-Confucianism was mainly identified with the supporters of Yi Song-gye, while Buddhism
had greatest influence on the Koryo royal family and the
old landlord aristocracy.

Confucianism, of course, had long been an influence
upon Koryo life as part of the predominant Chinese influence. When Chu Hsi's ideas appeared at the close of
the Sung dynasty and became the generally accepted form
of Confucianism under the Mongols, it was naturally
accepted by the Koreans as well. Both King Ch'ungyol
(1274–1308) and King Ch'ungson (1308–1313) encouraged
the importation of neo-Confucian writings, and King
Ch'ungyol founded a national academy which taught the
new doctrine, set up a Confucian shrine at the capital, and
founded scholarships for the encouragement of Confucian
studies.

King Ch'ungson was in contact with many eminent
Chinese scholars while living in Peking as Crown Prince,
and when he returned home to ascend the throne he
brought some four thousand books with him. After his
abdication he retired to Peking for a life of study, and
summoned the Koryo scholar Yi Che-hyon to visit him
and to discuss the neo-Confucian philosophy with Chinese
scholars there. His successor King Ch'ungsuk was also an
enthusiastic neo-Confucian, and imported still more books.
In this way Chu Hsi's interpretation of Confucian thought
became dominant among the Koryo bureaucrats.

This change in Confucian thought was of no particular
importance during the Mongol period because the scholars
were unable to put their ideas into practice so long as their
government was denied freedom of action. But during
King Kongmin's reign, when the Mongols had been driven
out of China and so ceased to rule Korea, the scholar-
officials who had been trained in Chu Hsi-ism became a
major force in the government and, as we have seen, were

among the most important groups supporting Yi Song-gye.

Chu Hsi-ism was not a break with the past in the sense that any of the basic Confucian principles were denied. The importance of social and personal relationships was emphasized as before, and the virtues of loyalty and filial piety remained paramount. What Chu Hsi did was to provide the simple, practical ethical concepts of Confucius with a metaphysical backing that amounted almost to a religion. The Confucian virtues and relationships were now seen not merely as being good for pragmatic reasons, because they worked, but as manifestations of the nature of the universe itself. To live by the Confucian social and political standards was to live in harmony with the cosmos and to iolate them was to go against nature itself and thus sure to cause misfortune. The changeless hierarchical society governed by a bureaucracy with a monarch at the top which Confucius had envisioned as his ideal thus came to be seen as ordained by the very nature of reality, and Confucianism gained a greater intellectual and emotional force than it had ever had before. Innovations in government and the violation of the relationships as set down by Confucius now became not only foolish and impractical but sinful.

Confucius was at one with Plato in the belief that the ideal state is that which is ruled by the wise and virtuous. Wisdom and virtue were to be acquired by education, which meant in practice by the study of the Confucian classics and their commentaries, especially those of Chu Hsi. Such study would lead to the acquisition of the four basic virtues of love, uprightness, propriety and wisdom which made a man fit to be a ruler. The greatest of these was uprightness, which would manifest itself in the results of the official's administration. Even natural catastrophes could be attributed to the ruler's lack of virtue.

The Koryo scholar-officials did not at first attack Buddhist doctrine directly, but generally confined themselves to criticism of the corruption of the monks and of the unseemly wealth of the monasteries, which led to meddling in government matters by persons not properly trained. As their conflict with the landed aristocrats sharpened, however, they began to attack the religion itself as anti-social, and to advocate the suppression or at any rate the strict curtailment of its institutions.

The establishment of the new dynasty placed many of the Confucian officials in a dilemma and ultimately they split into two groups. Confucianism makes no provision for such an event, and enjoins complete loyalty to the monarch at all times. The Chinese had developed the concept of the Mandate of Heaven, which was seen as having been withdrawn from a ruler when times grew evil. But aristocratic-minded Korea did not accept this idea. When the Koryo dynasty was at length ended, some of the officials felt themselves in duty bound to stand by it, while others were flexible enough to see that it was no longer capable of ruling and supported Yi Song-gye.

One of the important aspects of Confucianism was its emphasis on history. The events and thinkers of the past were thought to be the source of wisdom and virtue and the compilation of histories was therefore a virtuous act. Many historical works appeared during the Koryo dynasty, but unfortunately most of them were destroyed during the Mongol invasions. Of those which survive, the most important are *Samguk sagi* (History of the Three Kingdoms) and *Samguk yusa* (Memorabilia of the Three Kingdoms).

Samguk sagi was compiled by the Confucian scholar Kim Pu-sik in 1145, following the model of Chinese histories. The author was able to draw upon ancient chronicles and sources no longer extant, and on the whole seems to have written objectively, though he was inclined to put a Confucian interpretation upon events. He placed the Korean Three Kingdoms on an equal footing with the Chinese Three Kingdoms that were roughly contemporary with them, and referred to them as "we," an instance of Korean nationalistic feeling.

About a century after the compilation of *Samguk sagi*, during the reign of King Ch'ungyol, the Buddhist monk Iryon compiled the *Samguk yusa*. This is rather more anecdotal than Kim Pu-sik's scholarly work, and contains many folk tales and other materials presumably from oral tradition that help to give a clearer idea of life in the ancient period than the bare outline of political events. It was written from a Buddhist point of view and intended to inspire a spirit of patriotism and resistance in the people, who were then suffering from the Mongol invasions.

Most of the other historical works of the time have perished. We find references in extant records to various national chronicles and histories of successive reigns made in compliance with the Confucian injunction that records must be kept, but the only one that has survived is *Che-wang un'gi*, a book of poems eulogizing various Chinese Emperors and Korean Kings. In addition, some parts of *Haedong kosung-jon* (Lives and Works of the Great Korean Monks) have survived.

The spread of Buddhism and Confucianism, both of which were dependent upon written records, stimulated the development of printing. We have already described the immense work of printing the Buddhist *Tripitaka*, which involved the carving of 86,600 wood blocks to print 6,780 volumes. Other books were published by this method, and a government printing office was set up. Some time before 1234 (the exact date is not known) movable metal type was invented in Korea, over two centuries before Gutenberg. The metal used is not known, but there are indications that it may have been copper. By 1392, at the close of the Koryo dynasty, a government office had been created for this type of printing also, and printing techniques continued to improve during the Yi dynasty.

Toward the close of the dynasty, during King Kongmin's reign, an envoy named Mun Ik-chom returned from China, bringing with him the first cotton seeds ever seen in Korea. He had his father-in-law plant and cultivate them and soon cotton cloth began to be made. Hemp for the common people and silk for the upper classes had been the only textiles hitherto available in Korea, and cotton soon became very popular, since it was superior to hemp in many ways and could be cultivated and manufactured at relatively low cost.

Another technological innovation of the period was gunpowder. It had long been known to the Chinese but was just beginning to be applied to weapons of war. Ch'oe Mu-son made a special visit to China in order to learn how to manufacture it, and in 1377 King U authorized its production under government auspices. Weapons were then developed which played a conspicuous part in repelling the Japanese pirates who were plaguing the nation at that time.

Literature during the Koryo period was mainly connected with Confucianism. In the earlier part of the dynasty the main emphasis had been on brief, impromptu lyric poems in Chinese fashion. But during the period of military dictatorship prior to the coming of the Mongols, extended narratives began to be written. This was partly the result of the fact that most of the Confucian scholars had been excluded from the government by the military rulers and were living in retirement. To beguile the tedium of their exile they often gave literary form to the myths and legends of their people. Most of these works appeared during the late twelfth and early thirteenth centuries, and were published in collections. Yi Il-lo, Yi Kyu-bo, and Ch'oe Cha were outstanding writers of narratives during this period. Though he wrote during the early fourteenth century, Yi Che-hyon's works belong to the same genre.

During the Mongol period the scholars reacted to alien domination by producing works inspiring patriotism and resistance. Typical of these was Yi Kyu-bo's *King Tong-myong*, a long epic which emphasized national pride in Korean culture and tradition. It had somewhat the same spirit and purpose as the histories that were being produced at the same time. Poetry, of course, continued to be popular among the aristocrats, a narrative form called *Kyonggi-che'ga* making its appearance under the dictators.

The tradition of popular folk-songs continued as in Silla, and many of these songs, now known as *changga* or *kayo* have come down to us. These songs were, of course, in the Korean language. It is important to remember that most of what we speak of here as literature was written in Chinese, not in Korean, which had only the rather clumsy *Idu* system, of which we have spoken before, as a means of writing. Just as education for the medieval scholar of the West consisted mainly of training in the Latin language and literature, so education for the Koryo scholar consisted mainly in mastering the Chinese language and the literature and the philosophy of China.

In the plastic arts we find a division which corresponds interestingly to the ideological division of society: architecture and sculpture were mainly of Buddhist inspiration, while painting and calligraphy were associated with Confucianism.

In Koryo times as in Silla wood was the main building material and so, unfortunately, little is left of most of the great Koryo temples and palaces except their cornerstones and stone steps. A few wooden buildings do survive. The Muryangsujon and Chosadang halls of Pusok-sa in Yongju were built about the middle of Koryo times, as was the main hall of Sudok-sa in Toksan. These show a skilful adaptation of Chinese styles, dignified yet graceful.

The Buddhist images produced during the Koryo dynasty show somewhat of a decline from Silla sculpture, perhaps reflecting the fact that, although Buddhism was the dominant religion throughout the period, intellectuals and artists were drawn away from it by the attractions of Confucian studies. The colossal stone Maitreya at Unjin in Nonsan, while it blends well with its surroundings and is impressive by its very size, is rather coarse and clumsy. The wooden image of Amitabha at Pusok-sa, on the other hand, shows excellent skill.

The stone pagodas usually erected in temple courtyards at first continued the Silla styles, but eventually evolved into something distinctively Koryo. Many of these can still be seen, notably the nine-tiered octagonal pagoda at Wol-chong-sa on Mt. Odae, Hyonhwa-sa pagoda in Kaep'ung, the ten-tiered Kyongch'on-sa pagoda now on the grounds of Kyongbok palace in Seoul, and the Chongdu-sa pagoda now at the national museum, also in Seoul. Smaller stone stupas and large temple bells of Koryo times have also been preserved.

But the glory of Koryo art was its ceramics. The variety of pottery known as celadon was imported from the Sung dynasty early in the period, and the Koryo potters soon made this technique their own and began producing original works which even today are unsurpassed in design and execution. The earlier examples are undecorated pieces with a pale green glaze which is inimitable today. Later pieces have incised and inlaid decorations or designs of great delicacy. The Chinese themselves, the master potters of Asia, regarded the Koryo celadons as without peer. Many of them have been preserved and can be seen in the Toksu museum in Seoul.

Painting in Koryo as in later times was intimately connected with the great art of calligraphy, something which has no parallel in the West. It was the natural outgrowth of the variety and complication of the Chinese ideographs, which in the western sense are drawn rather than written. Skill in calligraphy was an essential part of a scholar's equipment, and it naturally followed that painting became closely associated with Confucianism. The Sung dynasty saw one of the greatest flowerings of painting in China, which furnished the chief inspiration of Koryo painters. Many of them studied in China and at least one, Yi Yong became so skilful that he was asked by the Sung Emperor Hui-tsung to paint a picture, which he did to the Emperor's complete satisfaction.

The Koryo government maintained a school of painting in conjunction with the school for training officials, which produced many fine artists. The ideal was to attain mastery of all three of the related arts: poetry, calligraphy and painting. The Confucian scholar Yi Che-hyon is said to have achieved this ideal. King Kongmin, the last of the really effective Koryo rulers, was a fine painter, and a hunting scene which is still preserved is ascribed to his hand. Calligraphy also had many illustrious practitioners, although unfortunately most of their work has perished, except for a few inscriptions on stone monuments.

Native music was enriched by T'ang court music which had been prominent in Silla times and then took from the Sung dynasty a kind of court music called *A-ak,* for the performance of which many musical instruments were imported from China. A kind of popular musical dance-drama called *kamuguk* developed during Koryo times and became extremely popular. Some of the *kamuguk* were still being performed in comparatively recent times.

PART FIVE

The Modern Period (I)

Chapter **17**

The Foundation of the Yi Dynasty and Growth of the Yangban Bureaucratic State

After his seizure of power in 1388 Yi Song-gye waited four years before actually proclaiming the foundation of a new dynasty. During this time, although the outward forms of Koryo government were carefully observed and King Kongyang remained upon the throne, a thorough-going reorganization of the government took place, directed by the Confucian scholar-officials whose support Yi Song-gye had wisely sought. Most of the Koryo nobility were killed or banished and land was redistributed, as previously noted. When all serious opposition had been vanquished and the reorganization had progressed to a point where all positions of power were occupied by Yi's Confucian supporters, he was ready to make his move.

But even now he did not crudely ascend the throne by right of conquest. Instead, in a careful attempt to give the new dynasty every appearance of legitimacy, the Supreme Council, the highest organ in the Koryo government, formally declared in 1392 that the Koryo dynasty had come to an end and that Yi Song-gye was the rightful King. Like the founder of the Koryo dynasty, he was given the posthumous title T'aejo (grand progenitor) by which he is known to history.

One of the first orders of business was, of course, to eliminate the old royal family to prevent rebels from rallying around it. The former King was banished to Wonju and most of his more prominent relatives were executed. To

203

soothe those who were offended by this, and also in line with his policy of always observing the proprieties when possible, King T'aejo had the tombs of the founder of the Koryo dynasty and seven of his more prominent successors removed to Majon in Kyonggi Province and sent the few surviving members of the royal family there to tend them as Confucian filial piety required.

More sweeping reforms were now in order. The military was reorganized and a royal bodyguard put at its head. The Supreme Council, which had been so cooperative, was left undisturbed for the time being, but the King's brother Yi Hwa was placed in real control of all government affairs, both civil and military. The more prominent of those who had stood by the King during his rebellion in 1388 were raised to the special status of Merit Subjects and given grants of land and slaves, while supporters of lesser status were proportionately rewarded. Both the bureaucracy and the aristocracy were now firmly bound in loyalty to the new dynasty.

In foreign policy King T'aejo followed the practice of his predecessors by attaching himself to the paramount power in China. As soon as he felt himself secure in the kingship he sent an envoy to the Ming court with the polite request that the Emperor choose a new name for the kingdom. A choice was offered between Choson, the name, it will be recalled, of the earliest of the Korean states, and Hwaryong, the name of the new King's birthplace. The Emperor chose Choson, saying that it was both a beautiful name and one hallowed by history.

It is indeed a beautiful name, and perhaps a brief explanation is needed here. Choson (the Korean pro-nunciation of the Chinese phrase *Chao-hsien*) may be roughly translated "morning freshness" or "morning calm." Korea thus acquired the epithet by which it is still known today, the Land of the Morning Calm.

But the Chinese were not wholly favorable to the new ruler because of friction over the amount of tribute to be paid and over Korean reluctance to repatriate the numerous Chinese residing in the kingdom. In consequence, the Emperor did not at first grant King T'aejo the golden seal which was regularly given to tributary kings for use in dealing with the Imperial court and to establish their legitimacy in Chinese eyes. King T'aejo was thus unable to use the title of king when dealing with the Ming court, and had to be content for the time being to be called simply the man in charge of Koryo.

With these initial steps completed, King T'aejo was ready in 1395 to transfer the capital from Kaesong to the city of Hanyang, modern Seoul, where, with brief interruptions, it has remained ever since. This step had more than merely symbolic significance. Kaesong had been associated in the public mind with the Koryo dynasty for almost five hundred years, and was saturated with the traditions of the old aristocracy, which had always been opposed to a strong central government.

As soon as the transfer was complete the King set about beautifying the new capital. New palaces were erected, ancestral shrines were set up in accordance with Confucian practice and the various organs of government were newly housed. By 1397 the Yi dynasty was fully established both internally and externally as the legitimate ruler of a sovereign state.

As government reforms began to take effect and the neo-Confucian scholar-officials began to exercise their power more freely, not only government but also society was increasingly dominated by Chu Hsi's doctrines. Specifically, his book on family propriety, which set down in detail the modes of conduct for each family member toward the others, was much studied, and became the norm for all proper yangban behavior.

In government administration, the scholar-officials strove to put into practice the Confucian ideal of benevolent paternalism, although they were also careful to protect their own interests and those of their class. As time passed they became increasingly powerful until eventually they were the actual makers and executors of policy and were able to check the power of the King himself.

The closing years of King T'aejo's reign were marred by fratricidal strife among his numerous sons for the succession. Prince Pang-sok had been appointed Crown Prince, much to the displeasure of his half-brother Pang-won, an able, intelligent man who had been of great service to his father in founding the dynasty. In the summer of 1398 Pang-won's men assassinated Prince Pang-sok, together with another brother, Pang-bon, and their supporters, including Nam Un and Chong To-jon, one of the King's early supporters who had been given the rank of Merit Subject. When King T'aejo abdicated that September, Pang-won, rather than admit his guilt by ascending the throne himself, managed to secure the throne for yet another brother, Pang-gwa, who was duly crowned and is known under the posthumous title Chongjong.

King Chongjong attempted to escape from the influence of his ambitious brother and to remove himself from the bloody strife among the princes by transferring the capital back to Kaesong. He was encouraged in this by geomancers, who said that some natural disaster had occurred in Seoul during T'aejo's reign, and that it was thus an unlucky place.

He was unsuccessful. Pang-won removed the last of the obstacles between himself and the throne after fierce fights between his personal retainers and those of the last surviving prince, Pang-gan. There were several bloody clashes in the streets of Kaesong, but Pang-won ultimately secured his brother's banishment. He then further showed

his shrewdness by having himself made Crown Prince
rather than proceeding to depose the King.

This fighting had been made possible partly by the
assignment of large bodyguards to each member of the
royal family in the early days when its power was not yet
secure. Pang-won, although he had used this means to
achieve power himself, was wise enough to see that the
continued existence of what amounted to private armies
would lead to further conflicts that would weaken the
dynasty. In 1400, when all serious rivals had been eliminated, private bodyguards were decreed illegal and all
fighting men brought under the control of the government.

In the same year, 1400, Pang-won felt secure enough to
persuade his brother to abdicate and at last achieved his
goal. His posthumous title is T'aejong. During the eighteen
years of his reign he dedicated himself chiefly to completing
the reform of the administration begun by his father. A
clear division was made between civil and military functions, so that no official could combine the two. Many of
the old Koryo government organs were abolished or made
merely nominal or honorary. The consultative body of the
old aristocrats, which had represented their power as against
that of the King, was disbanded. The Supreme Council,
which had been generally left undisturbed because it had
authorized King T'aejo's accession, was renamed and
reorganized. A royal secretariat was set up to draft laws
and decrees and the Board of Censors was reestablished to
keep watch over the bureaucrats. The six ministries usual
in Chinese-style governments were reestablished.

The main point of these endeavors was to get rid of the
organizations through which the Koryo dictators had
governed, and by means of which many bureaucrats had
exercised almost independent power, and restore a strictly
centralized bureaucracy in which royal authority was
paramount.

Both criminal and civil law were also reformed. King T'aejong decreed an end to excessive litigation and established new organs to administer criminal law. One rather charming touch was the setting up outside the palace gate of a large drum. Anyone with a grievance which he felt could not be redressed through the regular courts could come and beat upon this drum, whereupon the King would hear his case in person. It was also to be used to warn the court of plots and rebellions. A special organization was also set up to guard against rebellion and put in control of the Royal Guard Corps.

In October of 1404, as soon as he felt secure in his power, King T'aejong moved the capital back to Seoul. This time the change was permanent, and Seoul remained the political and cultural center of the kingdom throughout the Yi dynasty.

With the accession of King T'aejong's son and successor Sejong (1418–1450) the Yi dynasty acquired its greatest monarch and entered its greatest period of cultural creativity. King Sejong was a firm believer in the Confucian doctrine that cultivation of the literary arts is the path to individual virtue and hence to virtuous government. One of his earliest acts was to reestablish the *Chiphyonjon,* which was modeled on a Chinese institution going back to T'ang dynasty times. It had been set up by the Koryo court but had been much neglected. It now became not only a center of learning but eventually a center of power.

The Chiphyonjon was a kind of royal research institute. It conducted political studies, wrote and compiled commentaries on the Confucian classics, issued monographs on geography and medicine, compiled the official histories of the kingdom, sponsored open lectures attended by the King and his court, and furnished tutors for the Crown Prince. Perhaps its finest achievement, inspired by King Sejong, was the invention of the Korean alphabet, known as

Han'gul. This is the only known alphabet still in use which was deliberately contrived. For the first time in their history the Korean people had a convenient, efficient system of writing their language phonetically. While the prestige of Chinese was too great and the borrowings from Chinese into Korean were too many to allow Han'gul to replace the Chinese ideograms completely, it was now possible to represent Korean inflections and to write native Korean words in conjunction with Chinese ones, so that literary works in the Korean language could easily be written. The Korean people regard the invention of Han'gul as being of such great importance that even now it is honored with a national holiday, perhaps the only holiday in the world in honor of an alphabet.

The Chiphyonjon started with a staff of ten, later expanded to twenty. Appointment to it was one of the highest honors the court could bestow. In addition to its other functions, it trained many aspiring officials, and its members were often given long leaves from their regular duties to conduct research. It gained an important influence over policy-making, both through direct intervention and through the officials which it trained. Sejong also established in conjunction with it a school for the children of the royal family in which Confucian works on filial piety were stressed.

Neo-Confucianism soon spread from the court and government into the daily lives of the people. The rituals for coming-of-age, marriage, funerals and ancestor worship, which had all been more or less Buddhist in the past, were now held in accordance with Confucian precepts, and family relationships, as we have already seen, were governed by Chu Hsi's book on the subject. This collision of Confucianism with Buddhism set off an important social and cultural change.

It will be recalled that even in late Koryo times many

Confucian officials had objected to Buddhism on various grounds. They were now in the ascendant, and the ancient religion suffered accordingly. No longer regarded as the protector of the state, it was no longer subsidized by the court. Excluded from eligibility to receive land grants, the temples and monasteries declined in wealth. Temple lands were taxed, and in addition any person wishing to become a monk had to pay a special tax. The number of temples and monks and the number of slaves held by them were strictly limited, and much temple land was expropriated by the government and redistributed. The days of Buddhist dominance in government and society were over for good.

But this is not to say that Buddhism became a completely negligible factor in Yi dynasty society. The bonds of tradition, together with more tangible links with the past, were too strong for that. Many of the leading monks, for example, came of yangban families, and were thus in a position to mitigate, if not to prevent, official strictures on their religion. Time-honored Buddhist ceremonies continued to be held at court, and in times of natural disaster the temples were resorted to not only by royalty but by the people generally. Moreover, King Sejong became openly favorable to Buddhism in his old age, and the protesting Chiphyonjon scholars were compelled to put up with the erection of a small temple within the palace compound, and even to compile copies of the Buddhist scriptures. While Buddhism had permanently lost its dominant position, life in court and countryside retained a Buddhist flavor and the monks and temples continued to play a modest but pervasive part in society, as they still do today.

It was also during the reign of King Sejong that the northern territories of the kingdom were finally made secure. These territories had been under the direct control of the Mongols during their rule. When the Mongols were driven out and the Ming dynasty was established in China, a sort of power vacuum was created in Manchuria and northern Korea. The area was still occupied by the nomadic Jurched tribes, who made frequent and troublesome border raids and had to be alternately subdued by force and bought off with bribes and honorary titles. Some attempts were also made, in Roman fashion, to bring them over to the Korean side as troops.

Although the Ming dynasty held firm control of China proper, its power did not yet extend very far into Manchuria. Chinese troops garrisoned the frontier area, but this was remote from the Korean borders along the Yalu and Tumen Rivers and the Yi rulers had to face the task of subduing the nomads and integrating the northern area into the kingdom alone.

All of the first four Yi Kings had to concern themselves with this matter. The northeast, along the coastal area near the Tumen, had already been pacified to a degree by King T'aejo in his soldiering days, before he became King. After his accession he both conducted diplomatic relations with the nomads and had certain key points fortified. Attempts were made to set up regular local governments in some of the northern areas, but nomad attacks remained troublesome. King T'aejong had to move some of the new administrative units back out of danger.

Under King Sejong a vigorous, systematic policy was instituted to establish control once and for all over these northern areas, which the Koreans had always thought of as properly belonging to them, and which reached to the natural boundaries of the country. In the northeast, which was the more easily controlled, six cities at key points were fortified and permanently garrisoned. Between 1434 and 1444 there was a regular movement of population into this area, encouraged by the government, until the border along the Tumen River was fully secured.

The Yalu River boundary in the northwest, easily accessible to the nomads from the Liaotung peninsula and Manchuria, was more troublesome. The area near the mouth of the Yalu had been pacified under King T'aejong, but the nomads roamed unchecked in much of the region. In 1433 King Sejong sent a military expedition to subdue the Uryangha tribes. This was done and a fortress built at Chajang-ni, soon followed by the establishment of a local administration. Nomad attacks continued, however, and in 1437 a second expedition under Yi Ch'on had to be sent. This resulted in a second administrative unit along the Yalu, duly fortified and garrisoned. Two others followed in 1443 and 1444, completing the occupation of the northern territory. The six garrison cities of the northeast and the four garrison counties of the northwest linked up to form a continuous chain of strong points, under whose protection the northern territory, lost since Koguryo times, was finally and fully integrated into the Korean kingdom.

King Sejong suffered from frequent illnesses in the later years of his reign. Anxious about the future of the dynasty and the stability of the government, he made arrangements for the Crown Prince, who later became King Munjong, to take over as acting ruler in 1445, five years before Sejong's death. While this was a logical move, it increased the influence of the royal tutors to a considerable degree, and in turn of the scholar-officials in general.

King Munjong duly ascended the throne in 1450, but died only two years later, at the age of thirty-nine. His son, whose posthumous title is Tanjong, was only twelve, too young to rule, and a council of regency had to be established, giving the Confucian officials complete control of the government. This created a precarious situation because King Sejong had had a large family and several of his sons, the boy-King's uncles, were able and ambitious men who now saw a chance to seize the throne.

The eldest and also the most intelligent and the most ruthless of the uncles was Prince Suyang. He laid his schemes carefully, accumulated influential supporters, and assembled a body of armed men. In 1453, when Tanjong had been on the throne for less than a year, he struck. The regents were all murdered and Prince Anp'yong, another son of Sejong, was banished to an island, where he was later compelled to drink poison. Prince Suyang took over all the important posts of government and became ruler in all but name. In 1455, having eliminated all opposition at court, he deposed the boy-King and ascended the throne. His posthumous title is Sejo.

One of King Sejo's first official acts was to abolish the State Council, a move which put the Six Ministries directly under the King and so weakened the authority of the higher bureaucrats and tightened the King's personal control of the government. The Chiphyonjon scholars who had been raised to eminence by King Sejong reacted to the usurpation and the invasion of what they considered their proper authority by plotting to restore the deposed Tanjong. Two years after the usurpation, however, they were detected. Five of the six leaders of the plot were executed, while the other committed suicide. Over seventy of their followers were also put to death.

The deposed King was now degraded in rank and banished to Yongwol. When Sejong's sixth son Prince Kumsong led another unsuccessful rebellion, King Sejo at last decided that his rule could not be secure as long as Tanjong lived. Both the deposed boy-King and Prince Kumsong were compelled to take poison and there were no further serious threats to Sejo's power. King Tanjong was only seventeen when he died.

The usurpation split and weakened the Confucian officials. Trained to respect the principle of legitimacy, many of them felt that they could not properly support Sejo and withdrew from the government. Others, as at the founding of the dynasty, were able to interpret the Confucian teaching somewhat more flexibly, with profit both to themselves and to King Sejo. They were enriched and given influential positions.

But though Sejo was now secure in court and government, he experienced trouble in the northern areas, relatively recently subdued and always sensitive to any weakening of central control. The problem was compounded by the difficulties of communication over the rugged mountain country that lay between Seoul and the northern border. Especially the area along the middle course of the Yalu, where the river sweeps out in a sharp curve to form a salient surrounded on three sides by foreign territory, was difficult to control. Three of the four garrisons of the northwest had been abandoned during Tanjong's brief reign, and under Sejo the last of them was relinquished.

In the northeast Sejo's usurpation brought outright rebellion. Yi Ching-ok, military commander in Hamgyong Province, formed an alliance with the Jurched tribesmen when Sejo attempted to replace him with a man he deemed more trustworthy. The Jurched element in the revolt is plain from the fact that Yi Ching-ok took the grandiloquent title of Emperor of Great Chin, recalling the Chin state of the Jurched tribes which had been destroyed by the Mongols. Though his revolt was soon crushed, it showed clearly the attitude of many of the military men toward King Sejo. A second revolt, led by Yi Si-ae, though it too was easily put down, was significant because it was aimed not at the usurper particularly but at what was considered excessive interference by the central government in local affairs.

This was the direct result of King Sejo's attempt to keep the country under his control by sending out governors and magistrates from Seoul rather than choosing them from among the local population. Yi Si-ae had been governor of Hoeryong in Hamgyong Province in the northeast. When the new officials from Seoul attempted to assume their posts he raised an army, killed the military governor and the magistrate of Kilchu, and demanded that all local officials be chosen from local populations. He gained wide sympathy, especially in the area around the city of Hamhung, and his movement was joined by many local officials in danger of being displaced.

Government troops were eventually dispatched and inflicted a series of disastrous defeats. Yi Si-ae fled to his home in Kilchu and tried to get in touch with the Jurched tribes on the border, but was caught and beheaded before he could do so.

King Sejo was not the kind of man to be intimidated by this sort of thing. Immediately after the rebellion had been quelled he ordered the replacement of every single official in Hamgyong Province and the abolition of all local consultative bodies, the strongholds of local power. From then on all local administration throughout the country was firmly under the thumb of the Seoul government.

Although Sejo abolished the Chiphyonjon, he could not very well abandon Confucian methods of organization and administration, and in fact he encouraged them, but with a clear change of emphasis. Most of his reforms, while they contributed to strengthening the government and abided by Confucian precepts, were aimed at increasing the personal power of the King, rather than that of the officials. A good instance of this, and also perhaps his most revolutionary reform, was the new landholding system which he instituted. Land was now to be held by officials only while they were in office, and was to be supervised by and pay taxes to a special government office under the King's control and not directly by the officials themselves.

This had a double effect. In the first place, since only officials in office could hold land, those who had disapproved of Sejo's usurpation and been dismissed or resigned automatically lost their incomes and were rendered powerless. In the second place, since they could not control their lands directly, the officials became dependent on the King's favor for the payment of their salaries and so were unlikely to take any independent action which might displease him. To remain within the yangban class and retain their wealth, it became necessary for each yangban family to have at least one member in office and the whole of the aristocracy was thus brought under royal control.

One important subject to which all the early Yi kings turned their attention was the codification of the law. This had never been done before, and was felt necessary for the orderly operation of government. An attempt had been made during the Koryo dynasty by the scholar Chong Mong-ju, who just before the end of the dynasty completed a compilation modeled on Yuan (Mongol) and Ming dynasty Chinese codes. The change of dynasty necessitated changes, however, and a new code was made by Chong To-jon in 1395. But this was only a single scholar's work and could not cover the entire field. What was needed was a complete law code based on thorough research and taking into account the changes made by the new dynasty.

In 1397 King T'aejo gave orders that all the laws and decrees from the time of King U in the late Koryo dynasty down to his own time be collected and published. This was duly completed, after which a regular office was set up for the compilation and publication of laws. The code was revised and published anew in two parts. It was known as the *Six Codes,* corresponding to the six ministries of the government. Copies were sent to all government officials throughout the country, who now for the first time had a comprehensive code of law, conveniently organized, on which to base their work.

In several ways, however, the *Six Codes* proved unsatisfactory. Many of the old decrees proved inapplicable because of changed political circumstances, and many laws made at different times contradicted each other. Also, with the passage of time, new laws not included in the codes had been made. This being the case, King Sejong established an institute in 1424 to revise them. The revision was now accompanied by another volume, *Records of Precedents*. Still a third revision appeared some years later, but, it, too, was found unsatisfactory.

A new method was then resorted to. Instead of seperate codes for different reigns the laws were treated as a whole, classified according to subject, reconciled with each other, and finally published during Sejo's reign. This active and dominant King, as might be expected, took particular interest in the law code and personally revised the manuscript. Other changes became necessary, however, and the complete code of law, known as the *Kyongguk taejon* was finally promulgated in January of 1470, the second year of King Songjong's reign. It was to be the basis of all Korean law for the next several hundred years.

The *Kyongguk taejon,* like its predecessors, consists of six codes corresponding to the six ministries of the government: Personnel, Revenue, Rites, War, Justice and Public Works. The Personnel section deals with appointments and evaluation of officials; Revenue with the census, landholding and taxation; Rites with religious ceremonies, education and the examination system; War with military organization and administration; Justice with criminal law and laws relating to slaves; and Public Works with engineering, building and repair and laws relating to artisans. It is an extremely valuable document, not only for the study of Korean law but also for what it reveals about the structure of Yi dynasty society.

Korean foreign relations were conditioned, as always by the situation in China. As already explained, the Mongols had been driven out and the Ming dynasty founded in 1368. The Mongols retreated northward through Manchuria, pursued by Chinese troops, who established garrisons and outposts at strategic points to prevent their return. One of these was as far north as the Sungari River in northern Manchuria.

But this advance did not go unchecked. The Jurched people of Manchuria liked the Chinese no better than the Mongols, and their resistance was sometimes effective. And the Koryo kingdom, which had taken advantage of the situation to regain its northern territories, objected so violently to the establishment of a Chinese fort on its territory that the Ming rulers were obliged to withdraw and content themselves with fortifying the Liaotung peninsula.

This left most of Manchuria to the Jurched tribes, but obviously no Chinese ruler could tolerate hostile nomads on his borders. A gradual process consisting of military force alternating with conciliation extended Ming control over most of Manchuria. Jurched chiefs who were willing to cooperate were appointed magistrates in their areas, and more and more of them were absorbed into the Ming government in this way.

The new Ming rulers attempted to enforce the Confucian strictures on trade. This had been rather lax during the Sung dynasty and the Mongol Yuan dynasty, and considerable private international trade had developed. The new rulers decreed that exchanges of goods between China and other countries would be limited to official tribute and gifts only. Immediately upon the founding of the dynasty, the first Ming Emperor T'ai-tsu had sent envoys to the courts of all the countries surrounding China announcing his accession as the legitimate ruler of China and demanding tribute.

What this meant in practice was that the rulers of the peripheral states were given a monopoly on their countries' trade with China in return for their submission. Trade goods moved only in authorized tribute ships and had to be accompanied by appropriately respectful messages to the Emperor dated by the Emperor's rule-period. Each of the countries was assigned a single port of entry, Ningpo for Japan, Ch'uan-chow for the Ryukyu Islands and Kwang-chow for Annam, Siam and other southeast Asian countries. Until the second half of the sixteenth century, when the system was altered, Chinese ships were forbidden to go abroad.

Japan at this time was under the rule of the Ashikaga Shoguns. At the time of the founding of the Yi dynasty a civil war was going on, ostensibly over the succession to the throne, from which Yoshimitsu, the third Ashikaga Shogun, emerged victorious. His direct rule, however, was pretty much limited to the Kyoto area, most of the country at this time being controlled by the great landlords, who were virtually independent of the central government. This was especially true on the island of Kyushu, which was both remote from the Japanese capital at Kyoto and within easy reach of China and Korea by sea.

We have had occasion before to mention the Japanese pirates who raided the coasts of both China and Korea all through the period we are discussing. Despite the best efforts of both countries, they could not be suppressed. The only effective alternative was to find some way to induce the Kyushu landlords to control the pirates in their home bases, on Kyushu and the small islands off its coast. It was with this in mind that the first Ming Emperor, in the demand for tribute and submission which he sent to the Shogun, made suppression of the pirates a condition for Ming recognition of the Shogun as ruler of Japan and for tribute trade with China.

The Ashikaga Shogun Yoshimitsu saw in this a golden opportunity. Trade with China could be highly profitable. If he could induce the Kyushu lords to suppress the pirates in return for being allowed to trade through him with China, he would be able at the same time to enrich himself and to extend direct Ashikaga control into Kyushu, which would strengthen him importantly in ruling the country as a whole. He sent off a message in suitably humble terms, promising loyalty and tribute to the Ming Emperor, and was promptly rewarded with the patent and seal of a vassal king. Matters worked out as he had planned, and his authority was recognized throughout Japan. When he sent tribute ships to China he always included a captured pirate chief as earnest of his efforts to suppress the pirates as ordered.

T'ai-tsu, the first Ming Emperor, had made very stringent laws concerning the tribute, and the various nations participating in it were allowed to send ships only once every three years. Under the Emperor Ch'eng-tsu in the early fifteenth century, however, these regulations were relaxed and trade with Japan expanded considerably. Chinese ships now began to visit Japan and the Ryukyus for trading purposes. The laws were revised so that private trade became legal in practice, although the legal fiction of tribute was maintained. The lords of western Japan, in collaboration with the merchants, grew wealthy.

But in the second half of the fifteenth century the Ming government again restricted trade. As a result, the pirates resumed their old ways. When civil war again broke out in Japan they were completely out of control, while the country was thrown into chaos.

Like the other nations bordering on China, Korea received a demand for submission and tribute from the Ming Emperor soon after the new dynasty was founded. This, it will be recalled, was during King Kongmin's reign.

When King Kongmin was assassinated and King U enthroned, the Koryo court sent an envoy to China offering submission and asking the Emperor to choose a posthumous title for King Kongmin and recognize King U. This the emperor at first refused to do, remarking that the Koryo court was trying to use him to legitimize a usurper and justify the crime of regicide. Later, however, when the annual tribute of horses was received from Korea, he relented and sent the royal patent and golden seal which symbolized Chinese recognition of King U as the legitimate ruler of Korea, and Korea's vassal status.

One of the first actions of T'aejo after becoming King was to send an envoy to the Ming court asking recognition of his rule and the choice of a name for the state. He was well aware that he would be unable to rule Korea undisturbed without Ming support or at least toleration. Though the Emperor did choose the name Choson, as previously noted, and offered no active opposition to the new regime, he refused to grant the royal seal and patent. The matter dragged on for years. Numerous envoys were exchanged, and on one occasion the Emperor protested that the language of the request was not sufficiently respectful and demanded that the man who drafted it be sent to him in chains for punishment. It was not until King T'aejong's reign that the royal patent and the golden seal, together with a posthumous title for the late King, were finally received.

The main reason for this Chinese intransigence was Korea's reluctance to repatriate large numbers of Manchurians who had migrated to the kingdom from the Liaotung peninsula to escape the conflicts resulting from Ming expansion into the area. The Chinese needed all the manpower they could get to hold the territory and to expand their control into the rest of Manchuria. Moreover, they regarded these people as a potential threat, and seemed to fear that Korea might help them resist the Chinese advance. Demands for their return accompanied the first Ming contacts during King U's reign, and for a time during the reign of T'aejo relations were completely severed and tribute missions blocked. The rupture ended only when T'aejo sent about four hundred Manchurians to China as a gesture of good faith.

When a succession dispute erupted into civil war on the death of the first Ming Emperor, large numbers of Manchurians again entered Korea, where they were welcomed and given land in the southern provinces. Many of them were actually Koreans. The Chinese tried to prevent this migration as far as they were able, and renewed demands for repatriation of the refugees. But Korea, while being careful to offer no direct opposition to China, took advantage of the temporary Ming weakness to restore her northern territories, which were fully occupied during Sejong's reign, and was not sorry to see the Chinese hold on the Liaotung peninsula weakened. Conciliatory gestures were made from time to time so as to avoid actual hostilities but in general the Koreans managed to absorb the Liaotung refugees and make themselves secure in the north.

These events clearly show that the vassal status which Korea had accepted as a condition for peace and trade with China was only nominal. In addition to accepting refugees and fortifying the northern borders, the Yi government established trade relations with many of the Manchurian nomads, trading precious metals, textiles, tools and staples for fur and hides. Nomad chiefs who were willing to acknowledge Korean rule were given official posts, and thus a kind of buffer zone was established between the Kingdom of Choson and Ming China. The Ming rulers issued strong protests at these activities, but little came of them. Moreover, Korea, like other "vassal" states, gradually increased its private trade with China despite official prohibitions.

The official tribute missions were seldom profitable because of the large quantities of horses and precious metals demanded by China. It was not until 1429 that the Chinese allowed the substitution of textiles for gold and silver.

The regular tribute missions had originally been limited by the first Ming Emperor, T'ai-tsu, to one every three years. In later reigns, however, these were increased on various pretexts until there came to be three each year, on the occasions of New Year's Day, the Ming Emperor's birthday, and the Crown Prince's birthday. Another mission became customary at the Winter solstice. In addition, special missions went on special occasions such as the death or the accession of an Emperor and ceremonies in honor of the Ming royal ancestors. Trade became fairly extensive in this way, Korea exporting horses, ginseng, hides and textiles and importing silk, porcelain, chemicals and books. The Ming court occasionally demanded virgins and eunuchs, and the visits of Ming envoys to the Yi court were often burdensome, both because of the excessive demands they always made and because of the great expense involved in entertaining them.

While the tribute trade was on the whole profitable to the yangban class, it was a burden to the mass of the people, who after all had to supply the goods sent to China. Moreover, when the Yi rulers wished to avoid the sending of gold they closed down mines in an effort to convince the Chinese that their supplies were exhausted, causing economic dislocations. The luxury goods imported from China impeded the development of domestic industries and the Chinese demands for virgins and eunuchs created social evils and social unrest. Perhaps the only advantage to the general population was the continuing influence of the highly developed Chinese civilization.

Contacts with Japan, as has been explained, were for a long time complicated by the raids of Japanese pirates based on Kyushu and the minor islands, especially Tsu-shima northwest of Kyushu in the Korea Strait. Korea resisted these incursions as best it could and sent envoys to the Ashikaga Shogun's court demanding that they be controlled. When the Shoguns had gained sufficient power, they did so, at least in part, and trade between Japan and Korea developed in consequence. The profits to be made in this way influenced the aristocratic landlords of western Japan and the islands (called *daimyo* in Japanese) to help suppress the pirates and join in the trade. Koreans captured by the pirates were returned and a period of relative peace and commercial relations began.

It now became customary for the Japanese, when sending tribute ships to China, to send a corresponding mission to Korea at the same time. The Shoguns regularly sent envoys to the Yi court in the name of the Japanese Emperor and Korean envoys were sent to Japan. Significantly, most of the trade was monopolized by the daimyo of Tsushima, whose strategic position in the Korea Strait made it possible for him to control the pirates. Tsushima itself had been a major pirate base.

In addition, Korea made direct contact with pirate leaders, applying to them the same policy that had been used with the nomadic tribes of the north. Pirate chiefs who submitted were given official posts and trading privileges, and their piratical raids were thus converted into peaceful commerce. This policy was partially successful, but was hindered by the Yi dynasty attitude toward foreign trade in general.

The Yi dynasty shared with the Chinese government the Confucian distaste for commerce, and attempted to limit it. During King T'aejong's reign in the early fifteenth century foreign ships were restricted to the two ports of Pusanp'o at Tongnae and Naeip'o at Ungch'on on the southern coast. Japanese captains were required to carry special passports endorsed by their respective daimyo, and their numbers were strictly limited. This policy caused considerable dissatisfaction among the Japanese, and former pirates who found such limited trade unprofitable seldom hesitated to return to their old ways, despite their daimyos' prohibitions. In 1419 a major military expedition had to be launched against Tsushima, where the pirates suffered a stinging defeat. It is interesting that this expedition was commanded by King T'aejong, who, though he had abdicated in favor of Sejong the previous year, still had a considerable voice in the government and interested himself particularly in the suppression of the pirates.

With the pirates' striking power temporarily in a-beyance, an appeasement policy was tried. An additional port, Ulsan, was opened to them and regular traders were allowed to set up permanent offices at each of the three ports of entry. Ships came in such numbers that King Sejong finally had to limit them to fifty each year. In the Kyehae Treaty concluded with the daimyo of Tsushima in 1443 he also limited the amount of rice to be given to each ship to two hundred *sok* (about a thousand bushels). Exceptions were made for ships sent by the Japanese court and for others sent to Korea on special missions from time to time. The treaty was a precedent for the regularization of trade with Japan in general.

Regular procedures were established for handling this trade. When a Japanese ship landed at one of the three designated ports, the passport and seal which it was required to carry were first checked. The merchant was then allowed to land his goods and transport them to the capital for presentation to the King. The commonest Japanese trade goods were sulphur, medicinal herbs, silver, copper, lead, chemicals, dyestuffs and aromatics. They usually took back with them to Japan cotton and hemp cloth, ginseng, animal hides, embroidered cushions, porcelain and books. It is noteworthy that the Japanese also frequently asked for Buddhist scriptures and temple bells and sometimes requested the loan of architects skilled in the building and maintenance of Buddhist temples, all indications that Japan was still deriving much of its culture from Korea.

The fiction of "tribute" and "exchange of gifts" was maintained throughout most of the fifteenth century, but covert private trade between Korea and Japan increased to such an extent that stringent restrictions were felt necessary toward its close. This brought indignant complaints from the Tsushima daimyo, who had become dependent on Korean imports, and violent protests from the Japanese traders stationed in the treaty ports, developing into armed uprisings which had to be suppressed by force. As a result, the ports were closed and trade between the two countries suspended.

The Tsushima daimyo begged King Chungjong to resume trade, and in 1512 it was resumed, but on a strictly limited basis. Only twenty-five ships were to be allowed to visit Korea yearly, and there were to be no exceptions for ships on special missions. One of the treaty ports and two of the permanent Japanese trade missions remained closed. These limitations, however, did not apply to vessels sent by the Shogun, which continued their regular visits until the middle of the sixteenth century. However, Korea sent no regular diplomatic missions to Japan after the middle of the fifteenth century.

Besides relations with China and Japan, Korea was also in contact with other countries during the late Koryo and early Yi periods. One of the most important of these was the chain of islands known today as the Ryukyus (Liu-ch'iu in Chinese), which were dominated during most periods either by China or Japan, but at this time were more or less independent. The islanders derived a certain amount of profit by opening their ports to ships engaged in trade with southeast Asia. The first Ryukyu envoy arrived in Korea during the late Koryo period, and thereafter tribute goods began to arrive. On some occasions Koreans who had been taken captive by the Japanese pirates would be repatriated in Ryukyuan ships.

After the founding of the Yi dynasty relations with the Ryukyus became even closer, so much so that Koreans who had been shipwrecked in the islands or left there by pirates were allowed to stay, a relaxation of the prohibition on overseas travel. A Ryukyu tribute ship arrived regularly each year, and Ryukyu officials were given honorary posts and hospitably treated. The tribute goods they brought usually included rare woods, aromatics, sugar and water buffalo horn, all southeast Asian products and therefore very rare in Korea.

Some exchanges, though none of major importance, are recorded between Korea and Siam and Java, countries which the Koreans knew as belonging to the group known vaguely as the "southern barbarians." A ship from Siam is recorded to have brought a cargo of aromatics, while one from Java carried such exotic items as peacocks, pepper, perfume and Indian textiles.

Korean foreign relations during the early Yi dynasty may be summarized as a vassal relation with China and relations on an equal basis with other nations. The relations with other nations were almost exclusively for trading purposes under the cover of tribute and gifts, since the Confucian-oriented government did not approve of private trade. These relations were complicated from time to time by the chronic outbreaks of the Japanese pirates.

The Yi rulers not only tried to prevent private trade, but disliked the idea of their subjects going abroad for any reason, fearing that they might become corrupted or betray the nation. This policy did not, of course, apply to

China, and indeed it was a reflection of the xenophobic arrogance of the Chinese, who considered their nation the fountainhead of all culture and wisdom and regarded all peoples outside their cultural orbit as inferior and destined to be ruled by them.

Chapter 18

Social, Political and Economic Structure of the Yangban Bureaucratic State

The Yi dynasty left the Koryo institutions of government more or less intact during its early years, but, as we have seen, once it was well established extensive reorganization was undertaken. The system adopted corresponded in its broad outlines to that of China, but was not merely a slavish imitation. It had, for example, to maintain a balance of power between the royal court and the yangban bureaucrats, a problem which did not generally arise in China. The Korean rulers were clearly aware of the need for adaptation of Chinese ideas to fit their own circumstances, and King Sejong himself remarked that the political organization of his kingdom was not and could not be a blind imitation of Chinese ways. The political system which prevailed throughout the Yi dynasty was completed in all its essential features by the reorganization carried out during King T'aejong's reign (1400–1418) and the codification of the laws, which was finally completed in 1470.

The major organs of government were the State Council, the Six Ministries and the Royal Secretariat. The State Council supervised all government affairs, which were administered mostly by the Six Ministries. They were the Ministries of Personnel, Revenue, Rites, War, Justice and Public Works. The Royal Secretariat was in charge of drafting orders and decrees, and consisted of six secretaries, one for each ministry. The Six Ministries at first came

229

under the authority of the State Council, but later were placed directly under the King's control, the State Council being relegated to a purely advisory role.

There were also two censorate offices, one Office of Inspector-General and the other Office of Censor-General, to scrutinize the actions of government officials, to watch over the royal court and to advise the King. These offices functioned with freedom and boldness and in time developed into extremely powerful organs of the central government. As the power of the censorate increased, they occasionally became involved in conflicts between the court and the bureaucracy.

In addition, there was the prestigeous Office of Special Counselors, whose assigned duty was to advise the King on the Confucian classics and the other literary matters. As the members of this Office frequently served as lecturers before the Royal Lecture sessions, this Office also functioned as a censorate. Thus, these three offices, the Office of Inspector-General, the Office of Censor-General and the Office of Special Counselors, were together known as the three censorates.

The administration of the Royal Guards gradually evolved into an agency directly under the King, concerned with the gravest of criminal offenses. It concerned itself mainly with threats to the dynasty, especially rebellions. It thus overlapped somewhat the functions of the Ministry of Justice, and in fact the responsibilities of these two organizations were not clearly distinguished. There was also a third judicial organ responsible for the security of the capital city.

Since the whole government was based on Confucian concepts, institutions concerned in various ways with Confucian studies played a key role. There was an office charged with the publication of Confucian texts, and the highest institution of learning, Songgyun'gwan, trained candidates for the examinations in the Confucian classics, which led to government posts. There was also an office which drafted messages and statements by the King. Another office drafted diplomatic documents and notes.

After the reorganizations of the early reigns, the government structure here described remained substantially the same throughout the Yi dynasty. There were various minor offices, too numerous to be described here, and there were, of course, changes in detail from time to time, but on the whole the Yi government maintained a remarkable consistency.

For administrative purposes the country was divided into the eight provinces which still exist today, although the further division of some of them into northern and southern sections was not carried out until later. Each province had a supervisor who combined the duties of administrator, censor, and military governor. Under him were the district magistrates, who had similar multiple functions. According to government regulations, they had seven duties: promotion of agriculture, personal security of the people (i.e. crime prevention), promotion of education, collection of taxes and tribute and management of corvée labor, judgement of civil suits, and prevention of corrupt practices among subordinates. The district magistrate was mayor, police chief, judge and tax collector all in one.

The central government maintained strict control over these officials. Provincial supervisors and district magistrates were never assigned to their home provinces or districts and their tenure of office was limited. The government was especially careful to see that provincial supervisors served for only one year in a given province. This was especially important because the supervisor also commanded the troops stationed in his province.

The district magistrates were also frequently rotated, and for this reason had to depend heavily upon the petty

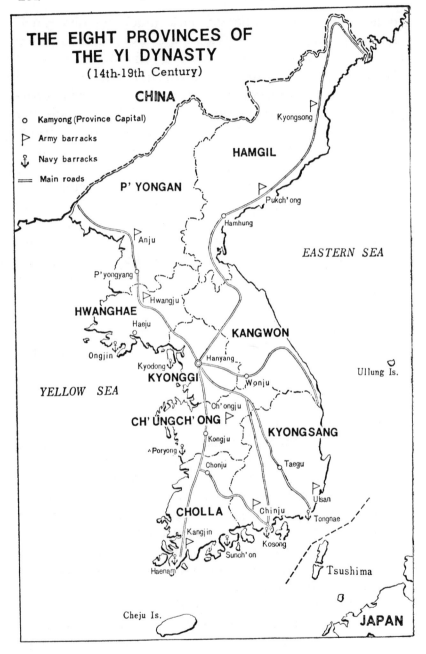

THE EIGHT PROVINCES OF
THE YI DYNASTY
(14th-19th Century)

CHINA

o Kamyong (Province Capital)
▷ Army barracks
⚓ Navy barracks
═ Main roads

CHINA

Kyongsong

HAMGIL

P' YONGAN

Pukch' ong

Anju

Hamhung

EASTERN SEA

P'yongyang

Hwangju

HWANGHAE

Haeju

KANGWON

Ongjin

Hanyang

Kyodong

KYONGGI

Wonju

Ullung Is.

YELLOW SEA

Ch'ongju

CH' UNGCH' ONG

KYONGSANG

Kongju

Poryong

Chonju

Taegu

Chinju

Ulsan

CHOLLA

Tongnae

Kangjin

Kosong

Sunoh'on

Haenam

Tsushima

Cheju Is.

JAPAN

officials under them, who were chosen from the local population and thus had good knowledge of the local situation, which the magistrate needed for the effective discharge of his duties. These local officials were grouped into six departments corresponding to the Six Ministries of the national government. The magistrate's most important duties, so far as the central government was concerned, were the collection of taxes and tribute and the management of corvée labor.

Aside from the petty officials on their own staffs, the magistrates governed through a council of local yangban. This institution had become a means of local self-government during the Koryo dynasty and was at first abolished under the Yi as leading to separatism. Later however, recognizing its value, the government adapted it to the new system of local government in order to keep the magistrate in touch with local sentiment so as to detect grievances early and prevent disaffection. The district council, however, did not have a direct voice in government, acting in a purely advisory capacity.

Central control was further strengthened through a liaison system. One member of the district council and one member of the magistrate's staff were regularly sent to reside in Seoul to manage relations between the national and district governments, facilitating the delivery of messages and taxes. In addition, another member of the magistrate's staff was sent to reside with the provincial supervisor. In this way every member of the yangban class was either absorbed into or controlled by the government and every possible precaution was taken against local uprisings, which had so often plagued Korea in the past.

King T'aejo, whose position as a military commander had helped him in the founding of the dynasty, paid particular attention to the organization of the armed forces after assuming the throne, and so did his descendants. The centralization of military command was a key factor in consolidating the new government's control of the country. One important step taken after the dynastic squabbles which followed King T'aejo's death, it will be recalled, was to abolish the private armies by means of which the various contenders for the throne had fought each other.

By the time of King Sejo the army had been brought fully under royal control, and was organized into five garrisons. The old military command, which had been more or less independent under the Koryo dynasty, still existed, but became purely honorary. The five garrisons corresponded to the five divisions of Seoul, middle, left, right, front and rear, and were assigned to the five military districts of the nation. Each garrison was in turn subdivided into five. The units composing these garrisons corresponded roughly to modern army corps, division, battalion, platoon and squad.

Each province had a military headquarters where army and navy commanders were stationed. The number of these varied according to local circumstances and the military importance of the province. Kyonggi and Kangwon Provinces, for example, located in the central part of the nation and remote from the frontiers, each had only one military commander for both land and sea forces. Kyongsang and Cholla Provinces, on the other hand since they were located on the south coast within reach of Japanese pirates, each had two navy commanders. Fortified cities were established at strategic points and troops assigned to them.

Three kinds of soldiers formed these military units. First, there were the bodyguards, who were assigned to protect the King, the royal family, high officials and their families, and the families of Merit Subjects. These troops had mostly a police function and were not of much use in time of war. Next there was the military elite, crack units specially selected and trained, and assigned to the defense of the capital and the important northern frontier. It was composed mostly of men of the yangban class.

The third group, the majority of the troops, was composed of commoners who were regularly conscripted for military service. This was imposed upon all able-bodied men between the ages of sixteen and sixty. Commoners who wished to escape conscription could do so by payment of a special tax, and in fact most of the expenses of the military were defrayed in this manner. This was systematized during Sejo's reign, when it was decreed that each man on active duty must be supported by two men exempted from conscription.

This system did not work very well. In the first place, the number of men paying the expenses of a conscript varied, depending upon which branch of the service he was in. In the second place, confusion soon arose over the number of men in a household who were actually exempted and so liable to the tax. Frequently the burden became so heavy that men would choose to serve in the armed forces rather than pay it, and military revenues shrank. The Ministry of War attempted to correct this situation by conscripting only a set number of men and imposing a tax to be paid in textiles on the rest. But there was widespread corruption among local conscription officials and many farmers managed to evade both the tax and military service. By the reign of King Songjong (1469–1494) the army consisted mostly of yangban and commoners who had voluntarily chosen a military career.

District garrisons were mostly made up of commoners, yangban soldiers serving mostly in the elite units in the capital. The petty officials who served on the staffs of district magistrates were exempt from military service, as were the ch'onmin, the lowest social class. Both of these, however, could be mobilized in grave national emergencies such as invasions.

The close identification between the aristocratic class and government which resulted from the requirement that only officials could own land is seen in the very name of the class. Civil officials were called *munban* and military officials *muban,* the ending—*ban* signifying "class." *Yangban* simply means "both classes," but because of the structure of Yi dynasty society it also has the meaning "Literati." To be an official in those times one had to be a literatus, and vice versa.

The official system constituted a hierarchy whose structure was strictly observed. There were nine grades, corresponding to the importance of the posts held. Each of these grades was divided into upper and lower, and these divisions were in turn subdivided into two, so that there were four ranks within each grade, making a total of thirty-six ranks of officials. Promotion from one rank to another was possible but strictly limited. This was especially true of the upper first of the third grade and above, the group which occupied the most important posts. Promotion into this group was extremely rare and difficult; consequently, the group remained relatively small, a self-perpetuating ruling class.

The next lower group consisted of officials from the sixth up to the third grade. Promotion from the lowest three grades into this second group was somewhat easier. District magistrates were chosen from the three middle grades, and indeed service as a district magistrate was a prerequisite for promotion to the higher grades.

It became a common practice for officials of the highest ranks to hold several posts concurrently, which contributed to the further centralization of power and made possible fairly close coordination among the various branches of government.

Generally speaking, civil officials were held superior to

military, in accordance with the spirit of Confucianism, which "honored the pen and despised the sword." High civil officials often had concurrent military posts, and it was quite common for district magistrates to be also in command of the military units in their districts. The distinction between civil and military officials thus became somewhat blurred in time, an undesirable situation in time of war. According to records of the early Yi dynasty, there were 4,820 civil and military posts in the government, of which 820 were civilian. Military officials thus greatly outnumbered civilians, but the civilians occupied all the positions of power and monopolized the making of policy.

A certain amount of influence on policy was allowed to officials of lower rank through the custom of presenting memorials to the throne. This came to be used especially by Confucian scholars, who were always anxious to ensure that the government respect the principles of neo-Confucianism. In addition, when decisions of real importance to the nation were to be made, the King might consult all his officials and ask for their opinions. Even the commoners might ask for redress of grievances or reveal dangers to the kingdom by use of the *Sinmun'go* drum outside the palace established by King T'aejong. But while lower officials and commoners could by these means go over the heads of high officials and appeal directly to the King, they did not in practice exert much influence on policy, and the state remained authoritarian and aristocratic to the end of the dynasty.

Men to fill government posts were recruited through the national examination system, which we have had occasion to mention several times before. In the Yi dynasty it was administered with considerably more rigor and regularity than had previously been the case, but it is important to remember that positions of power continued to be reserved to the yangban. Examinations were in

three categories, civil, military, and miscellaneous, the last
being used to choose technicians, interpreters and so forth.
The most important, of course, was the civil examination.

There were actually two civil examinations, the higher
and the lower. They were given every three years. Candidates for the lower examination first took a test administered in the provinces. If they were successful, they then
proceeded to Seoul, where another test was given. There
were two general subjects, Confucian classics and poetry
and composition. Successful candidates in the first were
given the *saengwon* degree and those in the second *chinsa*.
They were qualified to attend Songgyun'gwan, the national
university.

The higher examination was similarly organized. Preliminaries for this were also held every three years in the
provinces and low-ranking officials were eligible. If successful, they too proceeded to Seoul where thirty-three of
them were selected in the second stage. The third and final
examination was held in the presence of the King. Successful candidates were placed in three grades and were
immediately assigned to posts corresponding to the grades
they achieved. Candidates in the top category were placed
in medium-grade posts if they were new men or promoted
four grades if they were already officials. Because the
higher civil examination qualified the successful candidates
to serve in all important governmental offices, the success
in the examination was by far the most coveted honor.

The military examinations roughly paralleled the civil,
though they were not subdivided into higher and lower.
Two hundred candidates were selected every three years,
and from them the second examination in Seoul chose
twenty-eight, who took the final examination and were
assigned to military posts corresponding to the grades they
achieved. They were examined in archery, spear-handling,
horsemanship, Chinese literature and tactics. It is notable

that qualifications for candidacy in these examinations were much more liberal than for the civil ones, and sons of petty officials and even commoners might be admitted to them if they displayed military skill.

The miscellaneous examinations selected specialists for assignment to the government translation bureau, the office in charge of the calendar, which therefore was concerned with astronomy and also with geomancy and meteorology and the construction of water-clocks, to the office concerned with medicine and the care of the royal family, and to the Ministry of Justice.

In addition to these regular examinations, special ones were held on various occasions such as national holidays, or on the occasion of the King visiting Songgyun'gwan to participate in the semi-annual rites in honor of Confucius. The scholars of Songgyun'gwan predominated in all of these. There was also a simplified form of examination whereby persons of exceptional talent who had not passed the regular examinations for one reason or another might be appointed to civil or military posts, or qualify in the miscellaneous category. Scholars of outstanding accomplishment might occasionally be appointed to government posts by high-ranking officials without examination. Finally, members of families which had rendered outstanding service to the throne were sometimes given appointments.

The educational system, naturally enough, was geared to the examination system. In accordance with the aristocratic principle this was pretty much limited to yangban families, with a few exceptions to be noted later. At the age of seven or eight the yangban boy entered a *sodang* or elementary school, one of which was to be found in every village or city community throughout the country. Here he acquired the rudiments of the Chinese language and began his study of Chinese literature, with emphasis, of course, on Confucian studies.

After eight years, at the age of fifteen or sixteen, the boy, if he lived in Seoul, entered one of the four *haktang* or secondary schools established by the government. If he lived outside Seoul, he entered a *hyanggyo*, corresponding institutions established in each district. The four haktang each admitted two hundred students, while the hyanggyo, which had grown rapidly due to the encouragement of the district magistrates, admitted students in proportion to the size of the district. Graduation from one of these schools entitled the student to sit for the lower civil examination.

The two hundred students (later reduced to one hundred and twenty-six) who annually entered Songgyun'gwan, the national university in Seoul, constituted the elite of the educational system and concerned themselves mainly with preparing for the greater civil examination. They comprised the holders of saengwon and chinsa previously mentioned, graduates of the four haktang, sons of Merit Subjects, and lower officials. The university had two residence halls, a lecture hall, and a shrine where rites were regularly celebrated in honor of Confucius and of eminent Confucian scholars.

Training in technical and scientific subjects and in foreign languages was under the direction of the government offices which had need of such persons. The yangban considered such activities beneath them, and the students, who went on, as we have seen, to occupy technical posts, constituted a sort of middle class or *chungin*, together with the petty government functionaries not included in the nine official grades. Since their posts were hereditary their numbers grew as time passed.

The most pressing economic problem in this as in previous periods was the matter of landholding. There were two reasons for this. In the first place, since time immemorial, there had been conflict between the aristocrats, whose wealth and power depended on ownership of land, and the central government, which derived the majority of its revenues from taxes on this land, which the aristocrats were reluctant to pay and evaded whenever they could. This problem was exacerbated, in the second place, by the Confucian prejudice against commerce and finance, which inhibited the growth of trade and prevented the government from deriving any significant income from this potentially rich source.

At the beginning of the Yi dynasty all land had been nationalized and redistributed, as previously explained. It was later decreed that land should be assigned only to officials during their tenure of office, exceptions being made for the families of officials who died during their tenure. All land privately held was made taxable, moreover, and the amount of rent which landlords could collect from tenants was fixed by law. As a further refinement, all land used to supply the salaries of government officials was located in Kyonggi Province, in which Seoul was located, so that no official could attempt to establish himself as an independent power in an area remote from the capital.

But there were, inevitably, exceptions. The collateral branches of the royal clan, which increased in numbers as time wore on, could not be denied economic support, and they soon accumulated large amounts of hereditary land. Merit Subjects, who had helped the founder establish the dynasty, were awarded hereditary land, and their numbers grew with each political crisis, when the King was compelled to seek and to suitably reward new supporters. And many of these Merit Subjects were, of course, high-ranking officials, the very men who were supposed to enforce the government policy against the accumulation of great estates. Despite all the government's good intentions, a class of rich landlords reappeared and set about expanding its power. Just as during the Koryo dynasty, they enlarged their estates by whatever means came to hand, clearing wasteland, purchasing freeholds and seizing land by force whenever they could get away with it.

The Yi kings were aware of the problem, and various efforts were made to deal with it. King Sejo, that ruthlessly efficient monarch, decreed in 1465 that only officials in office might hold land, and later under King Songjong it was further stipulated that the officials were not to collect the income from the land themselves or otherwise control it, all of this being put into the hands of the government.

Ironically, however, Sejo had been compelled to create quite a number of new Merit Subjects in connection with his usurpation, and these, of course, had to be rewarded with hereditary grants of land. The rules regarding land held by officials were more and more ignored, not surprisingly since many of those who were supposed to enforce the rules were themselves landlords. By the sixteenth century most of Sejo's and Songjong's land tenure reforms were dead letters.

In some other respects the land-tenure system functioned tolerably well. Land was assigned to retired soldiers, to government offices for operating expenses and to schools. The size of Buddhist temple estates, on the other hand, was strictly limited, and much of the land they had accumulated during the Koryo dynasty was expropriated and redistributed. Ch'onmin (the lowest social class, mostly slaves), merchants, artisans, blind fortune-tellers, shamans male and female, kisaeng (female entertainers analogous to Japanese geisha), Buddhist monks and commoners generally were prohibited from owning land.

Tenants on government land paid a tenth of their crops as rent. Private landlords paid a fifteenth of the rent they received from their tenants to the government in taxes. These rates were adjusted to take the variations in harvests into account under King Sejong in 1444. For this purpose careful records were kept of the amount and quality of land each taxpayer owned. This was very difficult under the conditions of the times, however, and considerable confusion resulted. Though a census of landholdings was carried out every twenty years, it was not found possible to record accurately what each holding would produce, and the system of taxing according to the yield of the land was subject to many abuses.

While private estates tended to expand in spite of government efforts to prevent it, the laws regulating the relations between landlords and tenants were effective to a degree, and the farmers were somewhat better off than they had been during the Koryo dynasty. Private landlords collected half of their tenants' crops as rent, as a rule, but could not go beyond this and, as we have seen, had to pay part of this amount in taxes. Farmers were at the same time better treated and more closely bound to the soil than previously. To enhance agricultural production, newly reclaimed wasteland was exempt from taxes for a certain period of time.

The Confucian prejudice against commerce which had such a limiting effect on international trade was also applied to the domestic economy. The government did recognize the need for buying and selling, but only grudgingly. In Seoul, certain merchants dealing in staple commodities were authorized in order to supply the needs of the yangban class. Dealers in silk, cotton and hemp textiles and in paper and fish were officially licensed in return for their support of national festivals and aid in the maintenance of government buildings. There were six main official shops, located on Chong-no (Bell Street, because of the big bell located there), the main street of Seoul.

All shops including the Six Shops were supposed to have monopolies on the goods they dealt in, but inevitably smaller enterprises sprang up, both in Seoul and in the countryside, to supply the needs of commoners. While not encouraged, they were not especially restricted by the government, and were not taxed, since Confucian doctrine did not favor dependence on commerce for revenue. A government office was in charge of price control, weights and measures, buying commodities for government use and the prevention of fraudulent practices.

Outside of Seoul there had long been itinerant peddlers who traveled from town to town bringing daily necessities which the farmers did not produce themselves. Eventually periodic markets developed, usually held every five days, at which farmers could exchange their surplus produce for manufactured goods and marine products. Many of the merchants who operated in these markets were former farmers who had left the land because of the burden of taxation or to escape military service. This, like any movement off the land, was viewed with grave disapproval by the government, and at first attempts were made to abolish the markets altogether. When this did not succeed, they were reluctantly recognized and laws were made regulating them. Each district came to have its own regular market and group of merchants. It was not until late in the Yi dynasty, however, that merchants formed their own guilds and were recognized as a distinct class in society. Even then they continued to be regarded as at best a necessary evil.

International trade has been already dealt with. Suffice it to say here that the official "tribute" trade and the covert private trade which accompanied it were of comparatively minor importance to the economy of the kingdom as a whole, and that the commodities which could be imported or exported were strictly regulated both in kind and quantity. There were regulations against the export of gold, silver, jewels, munitions, iron, certain animal hides, paper and textiles, which pretty well exhausts the list of profitable exports. It is doubtful whether these rules were always observed to the letter.

With such stringent limitations, it is hardly surprising that a money economy was slow in developing. The government made a few attempts at issuing paper currency, but financial principles were poorly understood and the paper money fell so rapidly in value that it soon became worthless. Under King Sejong copper coins were minted but the supply of metal was insufficient and they were discontinued. For all practical purposes early Yi dynasty Korea remained a barter economy, with rice and textiles serving as the principal media of exchange.

The production of manufactured goods was mainly controlled by the government. Special offices existed to supervise the making of all articles deemed needful. The artisans were commoners or slaves maintained by the government for this specific purpose. Records speak of some 2,800 artisans controlled by thirty offices in Seoul producing 129 varieties of goods and 3,500 in the provinces producing twenty-seven varieties. Quantity and quality were prescribed by the appropriate offices and any surplus was subject to a special tax if it were sold. The Seoul artisans produced ceramics, bows and arrows and textiles, while the provincial ones made paper, rush mats, bows and arrows, wooden tools, lacquerware and leather goods. A good deal of what they produced went to China as tribute.

This system severely limited the development of industry and cramped the artisans' creativity. In addition, the regular influx of trade goods from China, especially high-quality silk textiles, inhibited the development of domestic manufactures.

A few trades and industries were allowed to exist outside these government monopolies. Some Buddhist monasteries, for example, manufactured paper and also made noodles. Wickerwork and leather became hereditary trades, as did butchering. Butchers were a distinct class at the very bottom of the social ladder, at least partly a consequence of the Buddhist prohibition against taking life. Farmers, who still had to make most of the things they needed, occasionally produced a few surplus handicraft goods, which they sold in the district markets.

Communication and transportation, as might be expected in such a primarily agrarian economy, were slow to develop. Travel of men and goods was mainly on horseback, in ox-drawn carts and by coastal shipping. What there was of it was mainly for government purposes of various kinds. Most of the roads were little more than footpaths. There was, however, a system of post roads and post stations for travelers on official business. They were identified by copper plaques with pictures of horses engraved on them, the number of horses on the plaque corresponding to the number of mounts to which the official and his party were entitled at each of their stopping-places. There were about five hundred of these stations throughout the country, each with the appropriate officials. A supervisor was appointed for the post stations of each district. High-ranking travelers were accommodated at the headquarters of the district magistrate, while those of lower rank were provided with inns at the more important post-stations. Inns for commoners also existed.

Means of transportation were mainly oriented toward the carrying of tax grain to Seoul. All tax grain went to the capital except that of P'yongan and Hamgyong Provinces in the north, which was used for the reception and entertainment of foreign envoys, mainly Chinese, who usually entered the country through them, and for the support of border troops. Storehouses for this grain were built at strategic points along roads, rivers, and the seacoast as central collecting points. The grain went to Seoul mostly in coastal ships or in river boats, little being sent by cart. The many islands and narrow straits of the south coast often caused shipwrecks, and crews were sometimes suspected of deliberately wrecking ships in order to steal the grain. A system of awards and punishments had to be instituted to insure that the ships reached Seoul safely.

It is time now to examine in detail the social structure which underlay the political and economic systems we have described. As we have had frequent occasion to remark, Korea had a strongly aristocratic society during most of its history. After the founding of the Yi dynasty social classses came to be clearly distinguished and class boundaries strictly enforced. Ostensibly this was in conformity with the Confucian principle that ruled and rulers must always be distinct from one another and that the principle of subordination must apply both to political and social relations. But Korean society went far beyond Confucian injunctions in the rigor of its class structure, which, as we have seen, was rooted in its own distinctive past.

There were, broadly speaking, four classes in Korean society. At the top, of course, were the yangban, the aristocrats who monopolized both political power and wealth. Immediately below them were the *chungin* (middle people), a relatively small class of petty officials. Next came the *sangmin* (common people) who were mostly farmers and formed the bulk of the population. Finally there were the *ch'onmin* (low-born people) who were mostly slaves, but also actors, *mudangs* (female shamans), kisaengs and butchers. Status in all classes was hereditary, and Chu Hsi's assertion that the Confucian social precepts reflected the nature of the universe was interpreted to mean that any attempt to change one's social status was not only a crime against society but also a sin against heaven.

As a consequence of Confucianism and the examination system, the yangban class devoted itself to intellectual pursuits to an extent which must seem strange to the western reader familiar with the disdain for book-learning typical of European aristocracies in the past. Education and success in the examinations were the keys to political power and were thus the main preoccupation of the aristocrats. As we have seen, this meant in practice the study of the Chinese language and literature, with particular emphasis on the Confucian classics and, in the period now under discussion, the commentaries on them and related works by the Chinese scholar Chu Hsi, whose interpretation of Confucian thought and pervasive influence in East Asia might be compared to the work and influence of Saint Thomas Aquinas in medieval Europe.

The yangban were also the landlord class, and here we find the contradiction which troubled not only Korea but also China and other East Asian states throughout much of their history. In their capacity as officials it was the duty of the yangban to see to it that the central government was strong and efficient, and in their capacity as Confucian scholars they were supposed to insist that all government action be based upon virtue as Confucius defined it. But in their capacity as landlords, obligations of family and clan impelled them to increase their holdings by whatever means they could, and this was possible, as a rule, only by evading the laws which they themselves had made or assented to and led also to practices which in effect robbed the state of part of its revenues.

We have seen how, from the very beginning of the dynasty, the Yi kings made repeated attempts to curb the growth of private estates or *nongjang* by various legal limitations on land tenure and by taxation. King Sejo, it will be recalled, went so far as to rule that only officials in office could hold land, and that they should not be allowed to administer it directly, but receive the income from it through the government. But many exceptions were inevitably made to this law, and the nongjang continued to grow. This conflict of interest continued to the end of the dynasty.

In social relations class distinctions were extremely strict. Yangban could marry only yangban, and any transgression of this rule was severely punished. This did not mean, of course, that irregular unions were altogether disallowed, and concubinage was fairly common. But concubines could not be yangban, and it was a rule that the social status of children was determined by that of their mothers. Children of concubines were thus automatically chungin class and were descriminated against in many ways.

Most yangban tried to live in Seoul whenever possible, and the northern and southern quarters of the city were dominated by them. It was common, however, for a yangban who was out of office to retire to his country estates until fortune favored him again. These nongjang were concentrated mostly in the south, the northern provinces of P'yongan and Hamgyong being mostly mountainous and unsuitable for agriculture.

The chungin class was inferior to the yangban but distinct from the sangmin, or commoners. It consisted largely of minor government officials of various sorts. The technicians, interpreters and so on were of this class, as we have seen, it being considered beneath the dignity of a yangban to engage in such pursuits. Local officials, chosen from the native population, who served on the staffs of district magistrates were also of chungin status. A third component of this class was the children of yangban and concubines discussed above.

Strict limits were set to the posts to which chungin could be promoted. Certain rewards were given for good service and occasionally a chungin might ascend as high as the third grade in the official ranking system, but no higher. There was, of course, a hierarchy within the class, and opportunites for promotion were graded according to the post previously held. Some minor officials serving the government in Seoul, for example, were allowed to take the qualifying examinations for district magistrate.

Children of concubines were excluded from the civil examinations altogether, but might occasionally take the military ones. Some efforts were made to provide minor posts for them, and their status within the chungin class depended upon the power and the concern of their fathers and the social status of their mothers.

No salaries were prescribed for minor officials in the districts, their stipends being set by each district magistrate. This often led to corrupt practices of various kinds, which were facilitated by the fact that the district magistrates were rotated every few years and never assigned to their native places, while the minor officials possessed the advantages of continuity and local knowledge.

Technicians and interpreters usually accompanied diplomatic missions to China, and often took advantage of their positions to indulge in private trade.

The sangmin class included the majority of the population. Most of them were farmers, but merchants and some artisans were also included. The guarantees of land tenure and limitation of rent and taxes had improved their status somewhat since Koryo times, but their lives remained generally austere. A few of them owned their farms outright, but very few. All the rest were tenants, either of private landlords or on government land.

It was this class which supplied the taxes, the labor and the troops which sustained the kingdom. Rents generally were half of each year's crops for private landlords, and somewhat less for government land. Attempts were made from time to time to lower rents, notably under King Sejong, but without a great deal of effect. In addition to rent, the farmers paid an annual "tribute" to the government, consisting usually of manufactured items which were the specialty of each district, or materials available there. Minerals, marine products, furs, timber, fruit, tools, textiles, paper and rush mats were typical forms of tribute. Quotas were set each year and rigorously collected, regardless of poor harvests, natural catastrophes or the like. The tribute was usually even greater in value than the land tax or rent.

In addition to all this, military service and corvée labor were required of all able-bodied male sangmin between sixteen and sixty years of age. The military system has already been discussed, but the details of the corvée system are pertinent here. Legally, each man owed the government six days of labor per year, but in practice much more than that was required, the amount depending simply on the magnitude of the projects undertaken. Maintenance of roads and royal tombs, building levees and making ditches and dams for irrigation purposes, construction of fortifications and mining were all accomplished by corvée labor.

A special group was made up of those who, though officially classified as soldiers, were actually used as servants. They ran errands in government offices both in Seoul and in the provinces, manned ships transporting tax grain, maintained the signal-fires which were a means of military communication, and did the menial labor in post stations. Though they had the legal status of sangmin, they were usually treated and regarded as ch'onmin, the lowest class.

Though forming the bulk of the population and bearing most of the burdens of the state, the sangmin were actually given no opportunities for education or advancement, and were excluded from even the most minor of the government examinations. Like the members of all other classes their status was hereditary, and they were legally bound to the land they tilled.

At the very bottom of the social ladder were the ch'on-min. The majority of them were slaves serving either the government or private individuals, and they were regarded as hardly human and treated accordingly, though government slaves had a somewhat easier time of it than private ones. The government slaves worked mostly in the workshops which supplied court and bureaucracy with various manufactured goods and performed various menial tasks for the officials. Private slaves served as household servants and also frequently tilled the soil, their labor being much less expensive than that of sangmin farmers.

The slaveholding system had certain interesting peculiarities. While slave status was hereditary, it was sometimes possible for a man to be a slave of a given person while his family was not. It was also possible for a slave to be the tenant of someone other than his master, so that there existed a group of indeterminate status, somewhere between sangmin and outright slavery. It was sometimes even possible for a slave to own slaves. Marriage outside the ch'onmin class, however, was impossible, and the children of slave women were classified as slaves no matter what their fathers' status might have been.

There had been a time toward the close of the Koryo dynasty when some mobility had been possible between the two lowest classes, but the Yi rulers instituted a rigid classification. The number of slaves was considerable, and grew rapidly during the fifteenth century. In its early years there were about 200,000 of them out of an estimated total population of two million; by the close of the century there are said to have been 350,000.

In addition to slavery, certain other occupations were regarded as so demeaning as to merit ch'onmin status. These included strolling actors (there were no actresses), mudangs, kisaengs, and butchers. Butchering was the most despised of all occupations, so much so that butchers and their families were often compelled to live in segregated villages.

The basic social unit was, as it had always been, the extended family, but this unit was now constituted and functioned according to the rules and precepts laid down in Chu Hsi's *Code of Family Propriety*. It should be borne in mind in what follows, however, that while the Confucian precepts were quite strictly obeyed by the yangban class, they were rather more loosely observed among commoners and ch'onmin. There was even a saying: "Legal punishment does not apply to yangban and propriety (i.e. observance of the Confucian precepts) does not apply to commoners."

"Four generations under one roof" was the Confucian ideal, and though it was seldom achieved it was actively striven for. The absolute ruler of this group was the eldest male, to whom obedience and deference had to be paid at all times. In accordance with Confucian teaching, filial piety on the part of sons and chastity on the part of wives were the primary virtues, and were inculcated at an early age. Dutiful sons and faithful wives were on occasion publicly praised and rewarded by the government. Undutiful sons might be punished at will by the family patriarch, and the rules of chastity were such that it was felt impious for a widow to remarry, no matter what the circumstances. Children of remarried widows were degraded in social rank.

These extended families were each constituents of a larger unit, the clan. Clans had played a part in Korean society since ancient times, as we have seen. Under the stimulus of the Confucian emphasis on ancestor worship and pride of lineage the yangban clans especially began to try to establish who their ancestors were. By the late sixteenth century most clans had established their pedigrees. Each clan regarded itself as descending from a common ancestor, though in practice this simply meant that clan members all had the same surname.

Each clan had its own rules for the behavior of its members, and regular clan meetings were held. The clan would also gather for coming-of-age ceremonies, weddings and funerals, all of which were now Confucian ceremonies. A common fund was established to help clan members in difficulties or emergencies. Ceremonies were held regularly to honor each man's ancestors for four generations back, and it was also customary to assume any obligations or debts which the four preceding generations had left. Degrees of kinship between clan members were important and carefully calculated by a numbering system and a special nomenclature, extending as far as the eighth degree.

Marriage was strictly exogamous. No two persons with the same surname were allowed to marry, no matter how distant or even nonexistent their relationship might be, nor was marriage across class lines permitted. The legal age for marriage was fifteen for men and fourteen for women, and early marriages were encouraged.

Marriages were arranged by the parents of the bride and groom, little attention being given to the desires of those most directly involved. Especially among the yangban, marriages often amounted to alliances between families or clans. Men could remarry at the death of their wives, and were in fact encouraged to do so, especially if the first marriage had produced no sons. Widows, as we have seen, could not remarry.

Another Confucian custom of considerable importance, especially among the yangban, was that of mourning for a deceased relative. The mourning period for a parent was three years, and that for other relatives varied with the closeness of the relationship. Special clothing was worn during the mourning period and there were frequent commemorative ceremonies. These ceremonies now became strictly Confucian, the Buddhist services for the dead having been banned.

Each family of any standing had its own family shrine, where these and other rites were duly performed. The family head presided over these, and women were excluded from some of them. Proper decorum on these occasions was considered extremely important.

These customs had notable economic consequences. Weddings, funerals and ancestral ceremonies were accompanied by elaborate and expensive feasting and entertainment, so much so that they were a factor in yangban prosperity. They were responsible for the ruin of many of the less affluent yangban in the later years of the dynasty.

Chapter 19

Breakdown of the System and Foreign Invasions

As we have noted in the previous chapter, the land reforms of the early Yi kings did not long survive. Without strong backing from the bureaucrats, it was impossible to enforce the rotating system of landholding, with regular redistribution, envisaged by the reformers. And the bureaucrats were also the landlords. Soon after each reform, ways were found to circumvent it, and the yangban estates, the nongjang, continued to expand. Moreover, as each generation added to the numbers of the royal clan, land had to be provided to support them in fitting style until they came to possess a considerable proportion of the private estates.

The nongjang were not large, continuous tracts of land like the big farms and ranches with which Americans are familiar. Rather, they consisted of numerous, relatively small patches scattered here and there throughout the country. When the land belonging to the yangban Song Sam-mun was confiscated early in King Sejo's reign, for example, he was found to have possessed land in eleven separate places in three provinces. Consequently, the yangban did not manage his land personally, and seldom lived in the countryside if he could manage to reside in Seoul. Management was left mostly to slave overseers, who supervised the work of the tenants and collected the rents. Though tenant farmers remained in the majority, an increasing number of slaves was used to work the nongjang. Members of the royal family, of course, were able to use royal slaves on their estates.

The government had early recognized this problem, and one of the main purposes of confiscating Buddhist temple property had been to reduce the number of slaves. There were also laws limiting the number of slaves who could be owned by a single individual, but these, like the land laws, eventually became ineffective.

Perhaps the most ominous trend in the expansion of the nongjang was the removal from the tax rolls of the tenant farmers on them. Just as during the Koryo dynasty, government revenues shrank as the nongjang grew, and nongjang tenants were also withdrawn from corvée labor and military service. This led many farmers to enter the service of the landlords to escape taxes and corvée. Those who owned their own land were often compelled to sell it, and land was added to the estates in various other ways. Frequently farmers of sangmin status were willing to suffer degradation to the ch'onmin class in order to secure employment on the nongjang, while on the other hand landlords would sometimes forcibly degrade tenants to ch'onmin status, which actually amounted to enslaving them. Clearing waste land for cultivation was one of the chief methods of expanding estates, an activity possible only for the rich because of the large investment of capital and labor required before any tangible result could be achieved. In addition to purchase, confiscation of land for debt and even outright theft were resorted to.

The heart of the matter was that land was the chief source of wealth, and land ownership was most easily secured by means of government posts. The system of using the produce of the land to pay officials proved self-defeating once the government lost control of the expansion of the nongjang. Every yangban family strove to place at least one of its members in the government, from which position he could protect and increase the family holdings. Service to the government or to the nation as a whole became completely subordinate to service to the family group.

The yangban usually maintained at least one principal country residence on one of his properties in which to live upon retirement or in case he lost his post. Such residences, and the land supporting them, were also used at times to provide for poor relations. As time passed, the country residences increased in importance. A symptom of this, to be examined later, was the foundation on many of them of private Confucian academies called *sowon*.

In addition to the regular taxes paid in grain, farmers, as we have seen, were also compelled to pay "tribute," in the form of local specialties and products. The collection of this tribute was subject to increasing confusion and corruption.

Collection of the tribute was the responsibility of the magistrate of each *hyon* or prefecture, the smallest administrative unit in the countryside. It was used to supply the needs of both central and local governments and those of local military garrisons. The amount to be supplied was periodically estimated from information on the productive capacity of each household in a prefecture. But the magistrates often exceeded these estimates and diverted the surplus to their own use, and imposed additional levies of such things as sesame oil, honey, pheasants, chickens, firewood and charcoal. The value of the tribute which an individual household paid often amounted to three or four times that of its land tax. Mining, carried out by corvée labor, was considered a form of tribute, while ship-building and the manufacture of weapons of war by slaves in government yards and workshops was supported by a tribute paid in textiles.

"Presentation gifts" for the use of the royal court in rituals and feasts were also periodically required of local officials, and this burden was added to the tribute already paid by the farmers. Like the other tribute, the amount required was seldom altered or reduced, regardless of the circumstances of the taxpayers, and indeed tended to become larger as the court became more extravagant. This was especially true during the reign of Yonsan'gun.

There were numerous other evils in the tribute system. Many of the items demanded, for example, were not actually the specialties of the region where they were collected, and the people were obliged to purchase them from other places. Moreover, each tribute was required to conform exactly in size and quality to specifications. If it did not, it could be rejected and a replacement demanded, which could be a calamity to a household already strained to the limit by these exactions. Tribute collectors often took advantage of this requirement in order to enlarge the amount of tribute and enrich themselves. And the unreasonable demand for such perishable items as fish, very difficult to preserve and transport, caused great trouble for everybody.

The corruption of the tribute system was increased during the latter part of the fifteenth century by the appearance of a group of petty officials, merchants and high-ranking government slaves who, with the tacit support of the official tribute collectors, contracted to collect the tribute. This meant, of course, that they collected as much in excess of official requirements as they possibly could, and often bribed local officials to allow them to act as intermediaries for the farmers in the officials presentation, in order to cover up their activities. All of this, of course, was patently illegal, but the contractors usually had friends in high places, so that little could be done about it. Another burden was added to the already crushing load carried by the helpless farmers.

Yet another tax resulted from the military and corvée

systems. The original intention of the government, as has been explained, was that each soldier on active duty should be supported by taxes paid by two others who were exempted. As the times were peaceful, soldiers came increasingly to be used in public works, and there was a sort of blending of military and corvée service. Farmers, understandably enough, were very reluctant to serve in either capacity, for their absence from home meant that their crops could not be properly tended and harvested. Always in need of income, the government was willing to commute these services for a tax paid in textiles, which were becoming an important medium of exchange. In addition, provincial officials would often exact bribes from farmers in return for exempting them from duty. The military forces were seriously weakened.

The practice of commuting military service for payment in textiles became so widespread and was subject to so many abuses that the government eventually had to regularize it (the exact date is not known) at two rolls of cloth per year for each able-bodied man in a household. But even though government regulation reduced the tax considerably, it still came to about three times as much as the land tax.

The commutation tax applied not only to farmers obligated to military service but also to district government slaves and petty officials who were subject to corvée labor. Both the military draft and the corvée system were in a state of collapse by the end of the fifteenth century.

As if all this were not enough, still another burden was placed upon the farmers, and in a particularly ironic way. Unless they had unusually large harvests, farmers found themselves in difficulties every spring when stocks of the previous year's rice began to run out. To remedy this problem, district magistrates were instructed to buy up stocks of surplus rice at harvest-time and hold it in government warehouses until spring, when it could be loaned to farmers at need and repaid at the next harvest, without interest. The flaw in the system was that if there were poor harvests in consecutive years, as there were around the turn of the fifteenth and sixteenth centuries, the farmers would be continually in need of loans and at the same time unable to repay them. A shortage of relief rice was the inevitable result.

The district magistrates attempted to solve the problem by charging an interest of ten percent on the relief loans. This went unrecorded in their financial reports, which meant that it was often diverted to their own use. The practice went unchecked until the middle of the sixteenth century, when it was decreed that some of this interest be included in the national revenues. During the difficulties caused by the Japanese and Manchurian invasions it was raised from ten to thirty percent. What had started out as a method of relieving farmers' difficulties had turned into an additional tax upon their incomes.

The yangban bureaucracy which presided over this disintegration of the economy was itself unstable by nature. A major reason for this was the contradiction between the obligation of the officials to put the interests of king and country above their own, and the aristocratic, land-based, clan-centered society of which they were a part. It must have been very difficult for even the most virtuous yangban to resist the temptation to enrich his family by taking advantage of the opportunities which government office offered him to acquire land. The purpose of government itself was thus subverted.

A second factor making for instability was the fact that, while the number of yangban increased, the number of official posts did not. Even the number of successful candidates in the examinations far exceeded the demand for them. This situation gave rise to factionalism, and there was con-

flict between an older conservative group and a young reform group. Especially when the royal authority was weak,
as when a minor child ascended the throne, these conflicts
broke out.

Factional strife occurred the more readily because the
Confucian system made no provision for opposing points
of view, or for compromise. It was assumed that there was
always a single policy that was right, and all others were
wrong. There was thus no way to mediate disputes. The
opposing groups usually accused each other of deviation
from Confucian principles in one way or another, or of
incompetence, though their real motivations were personal
animosity and desire for power. The most minute points
of Confucian doctrine or even etiquette could be the
pretexts for factional attacks.

An important element in the growth of factionalism was
the spread of the *sowon,* private Confucian academies
founded on their estates by the yangban. They were usually
founded on sites associated with famous Confucian scholars
of the past, ostensibly for the purpose of providing for the
education of the local yangban youth, in competition with
local government schools. The first one was established in
1543 by a county magistrate in Kyongsang Province
named Chu Se-bung, in honor of the late Koryo scholar
An Hyang. Some time after its founding this academy was
honored by King Myongjong with a calligraphic signboard
done in the King's own hand, an extraordinary sign of
royal favor. The King also bestowed books, land and slaves
upon the institution and exempted the students from taxes
and military service. Other yangban hastened to follow
this precedent and to secure similar royal favor by whatever
means they could. By the time of King Sonjo's reign
(1567–1608) there were over a hundred, mostly in the
southern provinces.

The significance of the sowon was that they provided

employment for yangban who could find no official posts and at the same time functioned as power bases and training grounds for the factional struggles in Seoul. They served also to organize clan solidarity in a period when central control was weakening. Control of education passed from the government into the hands of the factions. Graduates of the sowon, in addition to their Confucian training, would be already committed to one faction or another before even being appointed to official posts.

The historical cause (or pretext) for factionalism was Sejo's usurpation in 1455. While its violation of Confucian principles had been glossed over at the time, and officials whose consciences would not allow them to serve the new ruler had simply retired, there was a continuing uneasiness about the legitimacy of subsequent rulers in the minds of the scholars. This was especially true of the rising generation of yangban in Kyongsang Province. These young idealists were trained in the tradition of Kil Chae, an official of late Koryo times who had refused to support the new dynasty because he felt that its seizure of power violated Confucian principles. He had retired to his estates in Kyongsang Province at the fall of Koryo and devoted himself to private teaching. It was from sowon imbued with his spirit that the young officials came. They found a leader in Kim Chong-jik, an eminent southern scholar, and grew up believing that Sejo's usurpation had been a crime.

While Sejo was alive, of course, this opposition had no opportunity to develop. But after the brief reign of his son Yejong (1468–1469) he was succeeded by his grandson Songjong, who was only a boy. The young southern scholars managed to secure appointments on the boards of censors, which were supposed to expose corruption and mistakes in the other organs of government. They also gained influence over the young King, and by these means began to express their displeasure with the older officials, many of whom had supported Sejo.

The senior officials were vulnerable in other ways as well. Intellectually, they tended to place emphasis on Chinese literature rather than strictly adhering to the study of the Confucian classics. They were also open, as indeed most yangban were, to charges of having illegally expanded their estates and of having profited from collusion with the tribute contractors. When the young King attained his majority and began to appoint members of the southern faction to important posts, they were in a position to institute thorough-going reforms.

This movement was brought to an abrupt end by the untimely death of King Songjong in 1494 and the accession of Yonsan'gun, perhaps the most execrated monarch Korea ever had. He was wilfull, arbitrary and dissolute, and always resentful of the rebukes and even the suggestions of the censors. When in 1498 it was pointed out to him that an associate of Kim Chong-jik, in compiling an official history, had by implication condemned Sejo's usurpation, he made this the excuse for a general purge. The censors were dismissed from their posts and many were executed. Even the body of the dead Kim Chong-jik was dug up and dishonored.

This did not end feuding at court. Yonsan's extravagant debauchery soon had the court in financial difficulties and relatives of the Prince in official positions tried to remedy them by confiscating the property of the senior officials, who had escaped the purge. The officials naturally objected, and again there were two factions in the government. In 1504 the Prince discovered, through one of the royal relatives, that his mother had been deposed and executed during his childhood, a fact which had hitherto been kept from him. Enraged, he ordered a second purge, much worse than the first. Everyone who had been remotely connected with the death of his mother, including hundreds of senior officials and most of the surviving juniors, was put to death.

During the remaining two years of his reign Yonsan's actions verged on megalomania. He disregarded every principle of Confucian decorum, used Buddhist temples to stable his horses, and drove the scholars from Songgyun'-gwan and used its halls as pleasure houses. Provincial officials were ordered to send young girls from the countryside to populate his already extensive harem. When he received a letter critical of his tyrany written in Han'gul, the alphabet over which King Sejong's scholars had labored to such good effect, he banned the use of Han'gul and ordered the destruction of all documents written in it. Actions like these earned him such hatred that in 1506 the surviving senior officials were able to depose him and raise King Chungjong to the throne. A permanent mark of the detestation in which he was held is the fact that he was never given a posthumous title or called "King" by historians. To this day in Korea he is always separated from the other Korean kings by being designated only as Yonsan'gun (Prince Yonsan).

Under King Chungjong (1506–1544) things were restored more or less to normal and a new reform movement was attempted. Young idealists were once more appointed to the boards of censors and their leader, Cho Kwang-jo, obtained the support of the King. Radical reforms were instituted in every department of government and attempts were even made to make the daily life of the people conform more closely to neo-Confucianism.

By means of a change in the examination system by which candidates for any given post could be recommended by the official already in office and then take only a simple test before the King, Cho Kwang-jo filled the government with his followers. No institution and no senior official was now safe from their attacks. Inevitably, they made power-ful enemies, and their downfall came about through a collision with a custom which, though it violated Confucian precepts, was an intrinsic part of the dynastic system.

When Chungjong had been raised to the throne to replace Yonsan, he had rewarded his seventy-six principal supporters by enrolling them as Merit Subjects, as he was more or less obliged to do. This status carried substantial rewards with it, including large grants of land. When Cho Kwang-jo and his followers proposed that this land be confiscated becuase granting it in this manner was not in accordance with Confucian principles (which was true, of course), the King turned against them and began to listen to their enemies. In 1519 matters came to a head, and there was a purge of Cho and his group, some being merely dismissed from office, some banished, and a con-siderable number executed.

Factional strife continued through the rest of Chung-jong's long reign, centered mostly around the rival claims of his sons by different queens. When he died in 1544 he was succeeded by the son of his second Queen, posthumous title Injong. But Injong reigned for only a year and died mysteriously, to be succeeded by Myongjong, son of the third Queen. His faction promptly turned upon that of Injong's mother and most of them were eliminated in one way or another by the end of 1545, terminating yet another long struggle.

The yangban officials were inevitably involved in this rivalry for the throne, and the nature of the struggle was significant. Little pretense was made any longer that either party was motivated by a desire for reform or by disagree-ment over the interpretation of Confucian principles. With the young idealists eliminated the faction-fights had become naked power struggles, and everyone knew it.

Under King Myongjong factionalism intensified.

Excellence in Confucian scholarship, while it remained a factor in appointments, was now not sufficient to gain power. The support of one faction or another was necessary in order to hold even minor posts and it was impossible for any official, no matter how noble his intentions or great his ability, to remain aloof from the struggle and still retain his position. Land tenure, taxation and the military fell into confusion as the officials concentrated all their attention on displacing their enemies.

One of these disputes, which occurred during King Myongjong's later years, may be taken as typical. As was frequently the case, junior and senior officials were ranged against each other. The seniors in this case were led by Sim Ui-gyom, the Queen's brother, while the juniors followed the able and intelligent scholar Kim Hyo-won. Kim was in charge of personnel administration, and while this was not a particularly high post, being only first of the fifth grade, it carried important powers. Its holder was privileged to recommend his successor and at the same time to veto appointments recommended by other officials. The post was thus the key to control of the bureaucracy. Its special powers had originally been granted in order to prevent favoritism, but it now became the center of the struggle.

When Sim Ui-gyom's younger brother was recommended to succeed Kim Hyo-won, Kim imposed his veto, just as Sim had done to him when Sim held the post. This action began a quarrel which ultimately involved every official in the government. Kim's residence was in the eastern quarter of Seoul, while Sim's was in the west. Accordingly, by about 1575 the two factions were known as Easterners and Westerners, and so they remained for many years. The Easterners generally followed the teaching of Yi Hwang, whereas the Westerners were disciples of Yi I. These two were among the greatest Confucian scholars of the Yi dynasty. The factions endured for so long that even the manners and customs of the two groups differentiated.

The Easterners managed to remain in power for about ten years, but then they split into Northerners and Southerners, ostensibly over the punishment of a Westerner who had been involved in some maneuvering about the appointment of the Crown Prince, but really because two of their own leaders had had a falling out. The Westerners, upon gaining power, abolished the powers of the personnel officer which had started all the trouble, but factionalism only continued and intensified.

While Korea was plagued from within by the dissensions of the yangban, situations were developing in neighboring countries which were to have grave effects upon her. Let us turn first to Japan.

The sixteenth century in Japan was an era of almost continuous civil war. The Ashikaga Shoguns who controlled the government (the Emperor was a mere figurehead) had, as we have seen, little control over the daimyo, the noblemen who held great landed estates. Toward the end of the century this situation began to change. In 1573 the Ashikaga Shogunate was overthrown by a military leader, Oda Nobunaga, who had conquered most of the other contenders for power. He was succeeded in 1590 by one of his followers, Toyotomi Hideyoshi, who succeeded in imposing his rule on the whole country. Japan was now unified under a strong leader.

It was also in the sixteenth century that Japan had her first significant contacts with the West. Portuguese ships began appearing in Japanese waters early in the century, and by 1543 were trading with the daimyo of the western islands. The important factor in this trade was the introduction of firearms. In the chaotic political situation all the daimyo were anxious to increase their military strength, and they quickly saw the advantages of this novel use of gunpowder. They competed eagerly for Portuguese trade, and were willing to grant the Portuguese many privileges, including the introduction of Jesuit missionaries. Catholicism soon became fairly widespread in western Japan, especially in the Nagasaki area, where a daimyo presented a whole village to the Jesuits.

In a relatively short time the Japanese had not only imported large numbers of Portuguese muskets, but had also learned how to manufacture them. Military units armed with muskets became increasingly common, and by the time the country was unified they were an important factor in military strategy.

Hideyoshi, a man of humble birth, took a woman of noble family to wife in order to somewhat legitimize his rule, but did not aspire to the Shogunate, contenting himself with the title of Regent for the Emperor. His rule, as was to be expected, was a military one, but despite his origins he believed in and enforced the strict division of society into classes. He also paid attention to trade, taking over several commercial cities in the west for the government for the sake of the revenues. In 1587, before he returned from subjugating Kyushu, he issued a decree banning Catholicism, not so much from anti-Christian motives, but to take over the Portuguese trade for himself. The ban on Catholicism was not strictly enforced at this time. In this and other ways he weakened the power of the daimyo and built up a strong central government.

Because of the uncontrolled activities of the Japanese pirates all through this period there had been few contacts between the Yi dynasty court and the Japanese government, and after a concerted attack by the pirates on the coast of Cholla Province in 1555, relations had been suspended altogether. As soon as Hideyoshi felt himself firmly in control of Japan, he sent envoys to Korea to reopen relations, but his purpose in doing so was completely unacceptable to Korea.

Hideyoshi was in search of new worlds to conquer. The message which he sent requesting the reopening of relations also contained a demand that Korea give free passage to the army with which he was preparing to invade China. This the Korean government flatly refused, but as a precaution sent two envoys to Japan to try to discover whether Hideyoshi was serious in his intentions. When the envoys returned, however, their reports were completely at variance with each other, and the government chose to believe the one which held that an invasion was unlikely, and no military preparations were made to repel it.

The Korean military forces, as we have seen, were weak at this time. Most farmers bought exemption from service with a tax paid in textiles, and what soldiers there were usually employed on public works and had little real military training. Some active units did exist to guard the northern border and to repel the Japanese pirates, but a full-scale field force did not exist, and training and mobilizing one would have taken years. The Koreans knew the military uses of gunpowder, and had a few firearms, but they did not possess the technique of manufacturing their own muskets and had no ready source of supply. Almost all the troops were armed with swords, bows and arrows and spears.

Despite the Korean refusal of free passage, Hideyoshi did not give up his plan. In the Spring of 1592, having completed his preparations, he dispatched an army of 150,000 to invade Korea.

Taken by surprise, outnumbered, and daunted by the muskets with which the Japanese were equipped, the Pusan garrison was no match for the invaders, and the southern port city quickly fell. Three Japanese columns fanned out from Pusan and marched north. One of them got all the way to Ch'ungju, about halfway to Seoul in the central part of the peninsula, before meeting defending forces under general Sin Ip. These they defeated, and continued their march.

Now thoroughly alarmed, King Sonjo and the court left Seoul for Uiju, while two of the princes were sent to Kangwon and Hamgyong Provinces to raise new armies. Seoul fell within two weeks of the beginning of the invasion, and Japanese contingents promptly set off for P'yongan and Hamgyong Provinces to complete the subjugation of the country. In desperation, the government appealed to China for help.

Meanwhile, Korean naval forces were having rather more success than the army. Under the leadership of Admiral Yi Sun-sin, one of the great heroes of Korean history, they had developed the "turtle ship," probably the first iron-clad in history. This was a galley decked over with iron plates to protect the rowers and armed with a large iron ram in the shape of a turtle's head. These ships were pretty much impervious to any weapons the Japanese could muster, and so sank large numbers of troop and supply ships, seriously hampering Japanese operations in Korea.

China responded to Korea's cry for help by sending troops stationed nearby in Manchuria. They reached P'yongyang, which was in Japanese hands, by July. Much indecisive fighting followed, until the city was taken in January, 1593, and the Chinese army pursued the retreating Japanese as far as Seoul. Here, however, they suffered a serious defeat in the battle of Pyokchegwan and were forced to retreat once more to P'yongyang.

The Japanese were having difficulties of their own, and did not at once pursue the Chinese forces. The Korean general Kwon Yul, besieged in the mountain fortress of Haengju near Seoul, beat off numerous Japanese attacks and inflicted considerable damage, while the troops that had been sent to Hamgyong Province were compelled to return because Admiral Yi Sun-sin repeatedly cut their supply lines and because of cold weather and losses from an epidemic.

The Korean hatred of foreign domination now began to assert itself. Led by Confucian scholars and Buddhist monks, guerilla forces sprang up all over the country, and no Japanese force was safe from their attacks. The list of these patriotic leaders is a long one. Among the most famous were Kwak Chae-u, who defeated enemy troops in Kyongsang Province and took Chinju fortress; Ko Kyong-myong, who led revolts in Cholla Province and died fighting at Kumsan fortress; Cho Hon, who allied himself with the Buddhist leader Yonggyu and drove the enemy out of Ch'ongju, but also died at Kumsan; Kim Ch'on-il, who raised a force in Cholla Province and succeeded in taking Suwon, only about thirty miles south of Seoul, but died in the battle at Chinju; Chong Mun-bu, who rose in Hamgyong Province and was instrumental in the Japanese retreat there; and the aged Buddhist monk Hyujong, who rallied all the monks of P'yongan Province into a fighting force which was of great help to the Chinese troops in taking P'yongyang. There were many more.

Beset by all these difficulties and in addition plagued by increasing desertions from their own ranks, the Japanese agreed to peace negotiations with the Chinese. Japanese forces were withdrawn from the country except for a foothold on the south coast, and the talks began, despite objections from the Korean government that it, and not China, should be a main negotiating power. These talks dragged on for years and were frequently broken off, mainly because neither side would agree to any implication that it had been defeated in any way. In 1597, when it had become clear that no agreement was possible, Hideyoshi launched a second invasion.

This time he was not so successful. The Japanese troops were unable to get beyond the southern provinces, while Yi Sun-sin, who had been reinstated after having been dismissed because of an intrigue by an enemy, once more harassed the Japanese shipping to great effect. On land the opposing armies remained deadlocked until the death of Hideyoshi sent them home for good. One of the casualties of the second invasion was Yi Sun-sin, who was hit by a stray bullet during a battle and killed. The invasions had accomplished nothing except to devastate Korea.

The Japanese left behind them a broken land. Numerous commoners had been carried off as prisoners, never to return, while many of those not captured had fled before the Japanese troops and their farms had been ruined. Thousands had been slaughtered and their property destroyed. The farming communities of Kyongsang Province, where the Japanese had stayed the longest and in the largest numbers, were especially hard hit, and this was one of the richest agricultural areas in the country. Famine and disease spread over the desolated land in the wake of war.

The effects of the war on agriculture were the most serious, and were felt for many years. When the Japanese departed the amount of land under cultivation had been reduced to less than a third of the pre-war amount, and that of Kyongsang, the granary province, to less than a sixth. National revenues shrank in proportion, and the government for a time was reduced almost to impotence. Census and land registers had been destroyed, and it was at first impossible to assess taxes in any systematic way. The lack of grain from Kyongsang placed an almost intolerable burden on the other provinces.

In the economic chaos, many of the yangban in and out of office and collateral branches of the royal family appropriated land to which they had no legal right. Central control disintegrated as the pre-war Western faction split into small groups, so that there was no way to stop this land-grabbing, which was often carried out under the pretense of royal consent.

Another result was disruption of the social system. Many slaves had taken advantage of the war to seize and burn the registers which recorded their social status, and the government was in any case unable to support the number of slaves it had previously. It was in such straits that it was driven to sell posts and titles of nobility to the highest bidder, further disrupting the social structure. The class system was everywhere in confusion.

Cultural losses were also great. When Seoul was taken many palaces and government buildings were destroyed, including the King's main residence, Kyongbok palace. The collection of rare books kept at Hongmun'gwan was reduced to ashes, and other rare and valuable books, including the official records of the reigns of the Yi kings were destroyed. Of the four repositories where these records were kept, only that at Chonju survived. Numerous works of fine art of all kinds perished. There is hardly a building left in Korea today, except those made of stone, which antedates the Hideyoshi invasions.

Another legacy was an undying hatred of the Japanese for this wanton and unprovoked attack, which was handed down from generation to generation, and which proved to be justified in modern times.

The Japanese, on the other hand, benefited considerably. Among the Korean captives they took with them, for example, were expert potters, who contributed significantly to Japanese ceramics. Korean printing types were carried off and imitated in Japan, and the many books stolen by the troops were an aid to Japanese scholarship.

After the death of Hideyoshi there was a brief period of

conflict, from which Tokugawa Ieyasu, who had opposed the invasion and remained at home, emerged victorious. He was the founder of the Tokugawa Shogunate, which was to give Japan a fairly stable government until the middle of the nineteenth century. Peaceful relations with Korea were restored in 1606.

Chinese participation in the war had seriously weakened the Ming dynasty, which was now facing the growing power of the Jurched tribes of Manchuria, henceforth called Manchus, and this situation constituted yet another threat to Korea. We must accordingly now turn our attention to the situation in Manchuria.

Ming control of Manchuria had never been complete, and during the fifteenth century the Chinese were gradually pushed back until their effective rule was limited to the area along the lower Liao River. This process became accelerated in the later sixteenth century when a leader named Nurhachi arose, unified the tribes and adopted the title of King in 1589.

During this same period there were repeated Manchu raids on north Korea, made the more serious by the fact that many Manchus lived on the Korean side of the border. These raids were successfully repulsed, and sometimes Korean troops crossed the Yalu into Manchuria, but the Manchus were not effectively deterred. During the Japanese invasions Nurhachi took advantage of the preoccupation of China and Korea to further enhance his power.

In 1616 Nurhachi proclaimed the state of Later Chin, took the title of Emperor, and began to attack the Chinese borders. The Ming rulers raised troops and sent a request for help to Korea. Though fearful of the effects upon themselves, the Koreans complied with their suzerain's request and sent a contingent of 10,000 troops. Meanwhile, however, Nurhachi had soundly defeated a Chinese force at Saruho. When he encountered the Sino-Korean force, the Korean commander, Kang Hong-nip, immediately surrendered to Nurhachi in order to avoid Manchu retaliation on his own country, and this was temporarily successful.

Back in Seoul factional struggles had broken out once more. Kwanghae-gun, who had succeeded his father King Sonjo in 1608, was deposed in favor of his nephew, who became King Injo in 1623 as the result of a bitter struggle between the Northern faction, which had supported Kwanghae, and the Westerners, who now came to power with the accession of Injo. So bitter was the struggle that Kwanghae-gun was never given a posthumous title because of the hatred of the victorious Westerners.

A more serious result of this dispute was that Yi Kwal, a military leader among the Westerners, feeling that he had not been sufficiently rewarded for his services, raised a military revolt. This came so near to success that for a time Seoul was threatened and King Injo had to flee for safety. By the time it was suppressed the Manchus, always suspicious of Korea's ties with Ming China, had turned definitely hostile and the country, weakened by the rebellion, faced another invasion.

The Manchus found themselves in a situation somewhat resembling that of the Mongols before them. Clearly intending to attack and conquer China, they were extremely sensitive to the threat to their flank posed by a Korea allied with the Ming dynasty. When a Chinese force was stationed on the islet of Kado in the Yellow Sea off the west coast of Korea, their nervousness intensified. And in the revolt of Yi Kwal they found the pretext they were looking for to subdue Korea and secure their flank.

When Yi Kwal's revolt was defeated, he escaped with many of his followers to Manchuria. There he appealed to the Manchus to help him redress the injustice done to Kwanghae-gun by deposing the usurper Injo. The

Manchus could have asked for nothing better. An army of thirty thousand crossed the Yalu in 1627, overran the northern provinces, took P'yongyang in short order, and continued south. Injo and the court fled to Kanghwa Island at the mouth of the Han River, the traditional refuge of kings, where a bitter debate broke out on whether to continue resistance.

The Manchus for their part did not want a protracted campaign in Korea because they wished to save their forces for the invasion of China. Eventually the peace party prevailed, and negotiations were initiated by the Koreans. These resulted in what was called (for face-saving purposes) a "brother" relationship between the two kingdoms rather than outright vassalage, and the Manchus withdrew. But a substantial tribute in warships and grain was imposed upon Korea to support the Manchu attacks on China, and Manchu troops reappeared from time to time on the pretext of subduing the Chinese garrison on Kado.

In 1636 Nurhachi's son Abahai, who had succeeded him, named his dynasty Ch'ing, in Chinese fashion, and sent an envoy to Seoul with the demand that Korea become vassal to the Manchu state of Later Chin forthwith. The Korean court refused, and war broke out once more. Abahai in person led a large army across the Yalu in the same year, which swiftly overran the north and appeared before Seoul. The King took refuge in Namhan-san fortress, while the court fled once more to Kanghwa.

This time the issue was never in doubt. Kanghwa quickly fell, and all the royal court was taken captive. Two weeks later Namhan-san fortress surrendered. King Injo was compelled to go to the Manchu camp on the bank of the Han River, and swear fealty to the Ch'ing state. Korea was to renounce all allegiance to the Ming dynasty and to support the Manchus in their attacks on China. The Crown Prince Sohyon and his brother Pongnim were held at the Manchu court as hostages. Officials who opposed this submission were imprisoned and later executed.

The Manchus soon went on to take Peking, and in due course became the rulers of China. Korea, perforce, supported them, sending help at need, as when the Russian Empire began to exert pressure along the northern border of Manchuria on the Amur River between 1654 and 1658. But with the change of rulers in China went a change of attitude in Korea.

The two princes were eventually sent back to Seoul, but Crown Prince Sohyon died soon after, and **Prince Pongn**im succeeded to the throne as King Hyojong. He never forgot the humiliations he had suffered, and harbored plans to attack the Manchus, although this was impossible. His feelings were shared by most of his countrymen, who had been attacked and devastated again with the memories of the Japanese invasions still fresh in their minds.

The Korean kingdom sent envoys and tribute to the Ch'ing court every year, just as it had to the courts of preceding dynasties, and the Korean literati retained their veneration for Chinese culture. But the manner in which the Manchu ascendancy had been gained rankled for a long time, and the Korean attitude toward the rulers of China would never be the same.

Chapter **20**

Early Yi Dynasty Culture

The greatest cultural achievement of the Yi dynasty, and also perhaps in all Korean history, was the invention of the Korean alphabet, first called *Hunmin chongum* (correct sounds in order to teach the people) and commonly known as *Han'gul*. We have already had occasion to refer to it briefly. It is now time to go into more detail.

Historical accident brought Korea into contact with the highly developed Chinese culture at a time when Korean culture had not yet achieved maturity. As a result, Chinese culture played a dominant part in Korea for many centuries. Since Korea had not yet developed a system of recording its own language, it had to use the Chinese writing system. And since the Korean language is radically different from the Chinese, it was all but impossible to adapt the Chinese writing system to Korean. Literacy perforce involved mastery of the Chinese language, and this condition inhibited the development of a Korean writing system for a long time.

Chinese is what linguists call an "analytical" language. That is to say, it conveys grammatical meaning largely through word order, somewhat in the way that English does. Korean, on the other hand, is a highly inflected language, whose grammatical forms consist mostly of changes in the forms of words themselves, especially of verbs. Chinese, moreover, is not written in an alphabetic script but in a system of ideograms, signs representing ideas

279

rather than sounds. There is a unique ideogram for each Chinese word. For these reasons, the Chinese writing system could not simply be taken over to convey another language as the Roman alphabet was in western Europe. It could be adapted to an inflected language only with the greatest difficulty and never with complete success. When we add to this the great prestige of Chinese culture, and hence of the language in which it was conveyed, it is easy to see why a Korean writing system was so long in developing.

As we have seen, a system called *Idu* was developed in order to record Korean songs and poems, which consisted of Chinese ideograms used phonetically. There was also a system called *Kugyol,* phonetic signs added to Chinese ideograms in order to indicate Korean inflections. Neither of these was wholly satisfactory, however, and both still involved the laborious memorization of thousands of Chinese characters. What was needed was a complete system of setting down on paper the sounds of the Korean language.

Although we do not know what the immediate inspiration for Han'gul was, the idea was certainly not new to the Koreans. Both the Mongols and the Manchus had alphabetic scripts, and Korean Buddhist visitors to China must have seen manuscripts in Sanscrit or Pali, the Indian languages in which the Buddhist scriptures were originally written, both of which were conveyed in phonetic alphabets.

King Sejong, the greatest of the Yi monarchs, and also the wisest and the most humane, wished to give his people an easy and convenient means of communication. Until his time, the necessity for learning a foreign language and the difficulty of mastering the great number of Chinese characters had made education and even literacy the exclusive property of the yangban class and the monks. He therefore ordered the scholars of the Chiphyonjon, a sort of

Royal Academy it will be recalled, to make a study of the matter and devise a phonetic alphabet for the Korean language. A special office was set up for the project, and the scholars made frequent visits to Liaotung to study phonetics with the Chinese linguist Huang Tsan, who was living there in exile at the time.

In December of 1443, the twenty-fifth year of his reign, the scholars presented to King Sejong the final form of Han'gul, consisting of seventeen consonants and eleven vowels. During the next two years various works were translated into Korean and written down in Han'gul as a test of its efficiency in recording the language, including the famous *Yongbi och'on-ga,* songs in praise of the founders of the dynasty. Finally, in 1446, Han'gul was a-dopted as a means of recording Korean by royal decree, and a volume was published explaining its use. In the preface, King Sejong said:

> Because the sounds of our language are different from those of Chinese, and because the Chinese characters are too difficult to use as a means of communication, my people are unable to express themselves in writing. Feeling pity for them, we have invented twenty-eight letters which anyone can easily learn and use for every-day communication.

This was an epoch-making event in Korean history. Not only was it now possible to translate Chinese works into Korean and thus make them available to a much wider public, but native Korean literature, so long confined to folk-songs and poetry, could now be created and preserved. The invention of Han'gul led directly to the birth of a truly Korean literature.

Turning to philosophy, at this time the factional disputes discussed in the previous chapter were reflected in two basic trends of Confucian thought. Generally the younger men, and especially those from Kyongsang Province, were strict followers of Chu Hsi, and held, among other things, that the scholar's attention should be directed mainly at the study of the Confucian classics and Chu Hsi's works, and the principles of human behavior which they taught. Many of the older men, on the other hand, clung to an earlier tradition which was more broadly based, and held that the scholar should aim chiefly at proficiency in Chinese literature and composition, so as to be able to draft the official and diplomatic documents that were so important a part of an official's duties.

One of the most important of Chu Hsi's teachings was that a subject must be loyal to his legitimate sovereign no matter what the circumstances. The younger men who followed this teaching approved the example of Kil Chae, a Koryo official who had retired to private life at the founding of the Yi dynasty rather than serve a man whom he considered to be a usurper. When King Sejo seized the throne many of them reacted in a similar manner, re-signing their posts and retiring to a life of study and teaching rather than serve him. This attitude figured prominently in the factional strife that followed Sejo's death.

The older men who had helped to found the dynasty and their successors who supported Sejo were of a more practical turn of mind. Calling them time-servers or hypocrites is not quite fair, although obviously they derived considerable personal advantage from their actions, and most of them were enrolled as Merit Subjects. It would perhaps be truer to say that they felt that continuity and stability in the government were more important than the purity of their Confucian principles. They had formed the majority of the Chiphyonjon scholars under Sejong, which performed so many valuable tasks. It was they, not the young intransigents from Kyongsang, who completed the codification of the laws. It should also be remembered however, that it is a universal rule in politics for those in office to appeal to reason, moderation and practicality, while those seeking it make accusations of corruption and discrimination and propose radical solutions. While there is no doubt that the senior officials were sincere in their belief that strict Chu Hsi orthodoxy was too theoretical and remote from reality to be practical, and that the juniors were equally sincere in opposing them, power politics was the rule, and if the quarrel over Confucian orthodoxy had not arisen another pretext would have been found.

The Confucian emphasis on history and scholarship led to a great deal of activity in compilation and publishing. The reader should bear in mind, however, that scholarship as we know it today, based upon the assumption that knowledge should be sought for its own sake, as an end in itself, did not exist. In the Confucian frame of reference knowledge was to be sought only when it was felt to be of practical value. This attitude is somewhat obscured by the fact that things which seem scarcely practical to a modern Westerner were felt to be of great importance during the Yi dynasty.

Nowhere is this attitude more clearly demonstrated than in history, the most important subject of study from the Confucian point of view. History was seen as the great teacher, showing the ruler and the officials how best to conduct the affairs of state. It was therefore important both to know about the careers of the rulers of the past and to keep a careful record of contemporary events for the edification of posterity. It is significant that the titles of many of the Yi dynasty records, like their Chinese models, contain the word "mirror," showing how the compilers regarded their work.

A special government office, known as Ch'unch'ugwan

(the House of Spring and Autumn) after the title of the Confucian classic, was entrusted with keeping the records of each succeeding reign. When a king died, these records were edited and copies of the resulting history were deposited in each of the four official depositories at Seoul, Songju, Chonju and Ch'ungju, the idea being that in case of invasion or other grave emergency at least one set of records would survive. This indeed proved the case during the Japanese invasion as we have seen, the Chonju copy being the only one to escape destruction. These compilations began in 1413 during King T'aejong's reign and continued thereafter pretty much without interruption.

By the time of King Sejo these chronicles had become so bulky that he ordered a condensed version to be made which should briefly set forth the virtues and good deeds of each succeeding king. The *Kukcho pogam* (Treasure Mirror of the Dynasty) duly appeared in 1456, and was revised and supplemented in each succeeding reign. These records are of inestimable value in the study of the period.

In 1484, during Songjong's reign a condensed history of the Three Kingdoms and the Koryo dynasty was published under the title *Tongguk t'onggam* (Complete Mirror of the Eastern Country) in order that the virtues and accomplishments of past ages should not be forgotten. This and the Yi dynasty records already discussed frequently furnished texts for the lectures before the King which were a feature of Yi dynasty court life. Here again it must be remembered that the function of these lectures was not merely to convey information. They might more properly be compared to the sermons in modern Protestant churches, the lecturer taking a text from a historical work just as the modern pastor takes one from the Bible, and basing his ethical exhortations upon it.

A larger and more detailed history of the preceding dynasty, the *Koryo-sa* (History of Koryo) had been begun earlier by Chong To-jon during the founder's reign and was completed in 1451 by Kim Chong-so and Chong In-ji. King Munjong had it condensed and published in 1452.

Another subject which was a stimulus to study and writing was the superstition called geomancy. This was not strictly a Confucian idea, being derived rather from the Chinese religion called Taoism, but it had had a strong hold over the minds of Koreans ever since the Silla dynasty and had come to be accepted even by the scholars. In brief, it held that the configuration of any given landscape had an influence upon the fortunes of the people living there. It also held that the fortunes of a given family were in part determined by the location of its ancestors' graves. It followed that close study of terrain was of great importance, and from this superstition the science of geography was born.

The first attempt to make maps based on systematic surveys and measurements of the land, like so many other events of cultural importance, took place during the reign of King Sejong. After a great deal of work the *P'alto Chiri-ji* (Geography of the Eight Provinces) was completed and published in 1432. Only the section of this work dealing with Kyongsang Province survives in its original form, but fortunately the book was rearranged and included in the official record of Sejong's reign, so most of this valuable work has come down to us. King Songjong had it revised and expanded in 1481, when it appeared in fifty-five volumes, and a further revision and expansion, still extant, was ordered by King Chungjong and published in 1530.

One of the most important elements in Confucian thought was the principle called *ye* (*li* in Chinese), an almost untranslatable word which has been variously interpreted to mean "propriety," "ritual," "decorum," and so on. The idea was that decorous conduct of social relations and correct performance of rituals on special occasions had an important bearing upon the prosperity of the state. It was therefore necessary to establish precisely what these forms of behavior should be and record them systematically. Rituals for state occasions were traditionally divided into five categories: those for religious occasions, for coming-of-age ceremonies, for the reception of important visitors, for military occasions and for funerals. During Sejong's reign a work setting forth the details of all these rituals was compiled. It was revised under Songjong and published in 1474 under the title *Kukcho o yeui* (Five Rituals of the Yi Dynasty).

In order to promote Confucian decorum among commoners, a simplified explanation of the traditional Confucian relationships, the *Samgang haengsil*, was compiled. Of the five Confucian relationships, it placed special emphasis on those between ruler and subject, father and son, and husband and wife, with illustrative stories of loyal subjects, filial sons and faithful wives.

All this scholarly activity and the government sponsorship which made possible the publication of its results was a great stimulus to the further development of movable metal type, which had been invented during the Koryo dynasty. Early in the dynasty, in 1403, a government printing office was set up and a standard type-face called Kyemi (after the year-name) was designed. An improved type-face called **Kabin** (again after the year-name) replaced the Kyemi type in 1434. Printing technology continued to improve throughout the period and publication correspondingly expanded.

Intellectual activity was not limited to mere compilation, however. The metaphysical underpinnings which Chu Hsi had provided for the Confucian social ethics stimulated the growth of philosophical speculation, and two schools of thought developed. In order to understand them, we must first turn to Chu Hsi's philosophy itself.

Chu Hsi had developed a philosophy somewhat similar to that of Plato, which held that the universe is constituted of *li* or abstract form (this is a different word from the *li* meaning "decorum") and *ch'i,* matter. One might think of this dualism (although the comparison is not exact in all details) as similar to the concepts of soul and body of Western philosophy and religion. *Li,* however, did not consist of individual souls, but was a group of archetypes, one for each form of existence. In applying this doctrine to practical affairs, Chu Hsi said that the *li* of man's nature is basically good, and that it can be cultivated through education to produce virtuous conduct. This in bare outline was the philosophy on which Korean thinkers speculated.

Most prominent in this school of speculative philosophy were the junior officials from Kyongsang Province whom we have mentioned several times before. They had inherited the tradition of the Koryo scholar Kil Chae, whose leadership had been inherited by Kim Suk-cha and then by Kim's son, Kim Chong-jik, the master of the Yongnam (Kyongsang) school. After the attempt of this group to reform the government along strictly neo-Confucian lines had ended in failure, most of them retired to private life and dedicated their energies to teaching and study. While their freedom from political duties gave them the opportunity to develop a systematic body of thought, their isolation from the harsh realities of practical politics produced a sort of unrealistic idealism, abstract and theoretical.

The outstanding thinker in this tradition, and one of the most famous Confucian scholars in Korean history, was Yi Hwang (1501–1570). He interpreted Chu Hsi's thinking to mean the *li* has primacy over *ch'i, li* being the active principle and *ch'i* the inert matter upon which it works. In applying these concepts to human nature, Yi

Hwang followed Chu Hsi in asserting that the proper cultivation of *li* through education would automatically produce the five Confucian virtues: love, uprightness, propriety, knowledge and reliability.

An opposing school was established by another great scholar, Yi I. This gave primacy to *ch'i*, and held that *li* was simply a principle involved in *ch'i*. One is reminded of the controversy between the realists and nominalists in medieval Europe. Yi I and his followers attached greater importance to practical ethics than to metaphysical theory, and so had a greater appeal to the senior officials. The two schools of philosophy reflected the division between the two main factions in the bureaucracy.

While neo-Confucianism dominated both political and intellectual life, Buddhism rapidly declined, chiefly because of the hostility of the officials. In 1425, under Sejong, all the Buddhist sects were compelled to amalgamate into two, Son (Zen) and Kyo. All but eighteen of the nation's main temples were closed. Independent thought on Buddhist subjects was discouraged by limiting the examinations for the higher posts in the clergy to a few basic scriptures, so that others were neglected. As a further result of this, the two sects officially sanctioned began to lose their distinctiveness. Though prominent monks early in the dynasty, especially Muhak, the friend of T'aejo, had asserted that Buddhism was complementary to Confucianism rather than contrary to it, this argument did not prevail, and the stricter neo-Confucians especially regarded Buddhism as a social evil.

Despite all this, Buddhism continued to have a hold over the royal family, to a greater or less degree depending upon the inclinations of the reigning monarch. Under King Sejo it even experienced a brief revival, possibly because of the King's honest convictions but more likely as one of the effects of that shrewd King's policy of establishing his

42. *Founder of the Yi Dynasty:* Portrait of Yi Song-gye (1335–1408). Coll. Kyonggi-jon, Chonju, North Cholla Province.

43. *Yi Hwang (T'oe-gye):* 1501-1570. Great neo-Confucian scholar.

44. *Yi I (Yulgok):* 1536–1584. Great neo-Confucian scholar.

45. *Yangban at Home—A Game of Chess.*

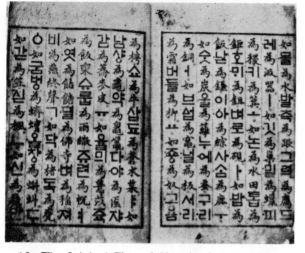

46. *The Original Text of Hunmin chongum, the Korean Alphabet:* Created in 1443 by King Sejong.

47. *Kyemi Type:* The oldest metal type extant today. 1403.

48. *Taedong yojido:* A map of Korea by Kim Chong-ho. 1861.

49. *The Great South Gate, Seoul:* Early Yi dynasty (rebuilt in 1447). One of the oldest wooden structures extant in Seoul.

50. *Turtle Ships:* Battleships invented by Admiral Yi Sŭn-sin prior to the Hideyoshi Invasion.

51. *Sundial:* Made of copper, in the reign of King Sejong.

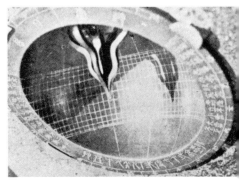

52. *"Mongyu towon-do(Dream of Paradise)"*: An Kyon, 15th century. Horizontal scroll, ink and color on silk. H. 39cm, W. 94cm. Coll. Junkichi Mayuyama.

53. *"Sansu inmul-to (A Man Sitting on a Rock)"*: Kang Hui-an, 1417–64. Album leaf, ink on paper.· H. 26cm, W. 16cm. Early Yi dynasty. National Museum of Korea.

54. *Wine Bottle*: Stamped decoration filled with black and white slip. H. 29.2cm, D. at base 8.25cm. Yi dynasty, early 15th century. National Museum of Korea.

55. *Calligraphy by Kim Chong-hui (Wandang or Ch'usa)*: 1786-1856. Great master.

independence of the bureaucrats. A Buddhist temple in Seoul that had been closed for many years was reopened, and at Sejo's orders the ten-storied stone pagoda that now stands in Pagoda Park was built. A Buddhist publication center was opened and various scriptures were freely published and studied.

At Sejo's death, of course, all this came to an abrupt halt. The old restrictions were once more enforced, and new ones were added. During King Songjong's reign (1469–1494), it was made unlawful to build temples, and the number of monks and nuns was strictly limited. Monks were even solicited to quit their monasteries and return to secular life. Both temples and monks decreased. Prince Yonsan, intemperate in his opposition to Buddhism as in everything else, ordered the closing of the chief temples of both sects, forbade any person to become a monk or nun, and abolished the examination system for Buddhist clergy. By 1566, during Myongjong's reign, the distinction between the two sects had ceased to exist.

One result of these developments was a decline in the social status of monks. Local officials did not scruple to press them into service on public works, though they were legally exempt from corvée, and they were objects of contempt and maltreatment, especially by the yangban youth. There are even recorded instances of monasteries plundered and burned by these youths.

The response of the monks to all this was typically Buddhist. They proclaimed that Buddhism, Confucianism and Taoism were all different aspects of the same truth, an assertion that, from a Buddhist point of view, was quite reasonable. This doctrine was given especial prestige when it was supported by the monk Hyujong, who organized and led an army of monks against the Japanese invaders in 1592.

Moreover, it must not be imagined that Buddhism lost

all its influence over the Korean people. The temples and monasteries remained places of refuge for the helpless and the discouraged. A typical instance is that of the scholar Kim Si-sup, who was so disgusted at the usurpation of Sejo that he threw away his Confucian books and became a monk, wandering over the countryside for some years. Later he was reconciled with Sejo and helped in the translation of Buddhist scriptures. And Yi I, the radical Confucian thinker discussed earlier in this chapter, once entered a Son temple to study, and was generally well-versed in Buddhist teachings.

Besides these intellectual and religious developments, the first two centuries of the Yi dynasty were characterized by important advances in science and technology, especially in the fields of astronomy and meteorology. Two forces stimulated development of these particular fields. In the first place, of course, the kingdom was almost exclusively dependent upon agriculture, and agriculture upon the weather. Knowledge of cycles of rain or drought, and techniques of predicting the weather in order to take appropriate action were therefore important. In addition the Koreans, like farmers in all times and places, saw relationships between the weather and the movements of the heavenly bodies, which stimulated the study of astronomy.

In the second place, Chu Hsi's philosophy, as we have seen, asserted that the social order was a reflection of the cosmic order. This was interpreted to mean, among other things, that natural as well as social calamities resulted from lack of virtue on the part of the rulers. If droughts or floods or storms could be predicted, they might therefore be averted by political reform. A related field was the calendrical system, important not only for fixing the dates of holidays and rituals but also for regulating the sowing and reaping of crops.

Many of these advances, as might have been expected, came during the reign of the many-sided King Sejong (1418–1450). In 1433 a chart of the heavens was carved on stone after exhaustive consultation of all available astronomical records. In the same year the lunar calendar was reformed and regularized on the Chinese lines established during the Sung and Ming dynasties. In 1438 the two scholars Yi Ch'on and Chang Yong-sil, on the King's instructions, devised a whole series of astronomical instruments: a small and a large astrolabe, a celestial globe, a sun-dial and a water-clock. In 1442 a rain gauge was invented, the first such instrument recorded in history. Others were soon built and sent to each of the eight provinces so that records of the rainfall in all parts of the kingdom might be kept.

In addition to these technical advances, the government attempted to encourage agriculture in more direct ways. A book called *The Art of Farming* was published during this period which gave detailed information not only about farming but about sericulture as well. And the government could give practical help to farmers, as it did for an irrigation project in the Kimje district in Cholla Province, on which ten thousand soldiers are said to have worked. Water-wheels for irrigation were proposed at this time, but did not become so widespread as in China and Japan.

Technical and scientific progress depended, of course, on a knowledge of mathematics, and several texts on this subject were published. Of particular interest is one called *Sanhak kyemong* (Arithmetical Enlightenment) because it was based on mathematical knowledge gained during the Mongol rule of China from Arab mathematicians, the most advanced scholars in this subject in the world at that time.

Two special government institutions were established for medical care, one for the royal family and the higher bureaucrats and the other for the general population. The study of medicine was encouraged. At first the Yi dynasty was dependent on China for medicinal drugs, but local sources were developed and in 1433 a text appeared on the preparation of medicines from Korean products. Later an attempt was made to compile a text on all known theories of medicine, mainly, of course, the vast medical lore and *materia medica* of China. It was completed in 1445, an immense work of 264 volumes. Far too bulky and expensive for common use, it was provided only for certain government offices. The need continued to be felt for a long time for a more convenient medical reference book. Finally in 1596 King Sonjo ordered Ho Chun and his group to compile a briefer and simpler work, and after ten years it appeared under the title *Tongui pogam* (Treasures of Eastern Medicine). This book was so highly regarded that it was reprinted in both China and Japan during the eighteenth century.

The development of new military weapons was not so encouraging. The government experimented with gunpowder for artillery, but without any remarkable results. Explosives were used during the Japanese invasions but only on a small scale. As we have already pointed out, though the use of muskets was understood it was not possible to produce them in sufficient quantities to have any military effect.

The most important event for literature during this period was the invention of Han'gul, the Korean alphabet. This created an interesting division in Korean literature. Official records, government documents and all "serious" literature continued to be written in Chinese. There now began to appear, however, a kind of novel or romance, written in Korean and eventually using Han'gul exclusively. In addition, the Korean folk-songs of the past, which had been recorded in the clumsy *Idu* or *Kugyol* systems, could now be written in Han'gul, and contemporary songs and poems could be written down as well. A type of short poem in Korean called *sijo* became popular, and remains so today.

Writings in Chinese were varied. The composition of Chinese poetry was an accomplishment required of all scholars, and several anthologies of their poems appeared. Prose romances were at first written in Chinese and imitated Chinese tales from the Ming dynasty, but eventually developed into original Korean forms written in Han'gul. *Kumo sinhwa* was of particular importance because it served as a model for many tales in Korean. *The Tale of Hong Kil-tong* by Ho Kyun, a satiric novel protesting the discrimination against concubines and their children, was remarkable in that it was written in Korean, using Han'gul, and became the inspiration for many later works. Essays and historical records in Chinese were numerous, perhaps the most outstanding being Yu Song-yong's *Chingbi-rok,* a record of the Japanese invasions.

Almost all early writings using Han'gul were in verse, as we have seen. Many of the songs of Koryo times were now recorded in the convenient Han'gul form, as were the short poems called *sijo* and longer songs or odes called *kasa,* a form which had originated in Koryo times. The texts of songs accompanying palace rituals were also set down in Han'gul, as were poems on Buddhist themes, the latter two types being published in special collections. Another type of poem called *pyolgok* (special style, that is native as opposed to Chinese) appeared in a famous collection known as *Songgang's Songs and Poems* compiled by Chong Ch'ol in the later sixteenth century. It would appear that in the early years of its use Han'gul was confined almost entirely to poetry and song, that is, to forms of composition in which the sound of the Korean language was important.

The reason for this, of course, was the great prestige of

the Chinese language and literature. Government, education and literature had been so closely associated with Chinese for so many centuries that it was not possible to shift immediately to the new writing. Han'gul soon acquired class associations and was relegated pretty much to the use of ignorant persons and women. A compromise was eventually reached in which Chinese characters were used in association with Han'gul to write the Korean language. This has been the practice ever since, and the Chinese characters have never lost their prestige.

Music was closely connected with court rituals, which, as we have seen, were extremely important in the Confucian scheme of things, a separate ministry being devoted to them. One section of this ministry was charged with improving musical instruments, training musicians, and promoting the study of musical theory, all, of course, within the framework of Chinese court music. During Sejong's reign Pak Yon established a distinctive Korean court music on this Chinese base, revising and refining the Chinese models and adapting them to Korean method.s Musical sounds were represented in Han'gul. Later, during the reign of Songjong, *Akhak kwebom*, a musical encyclopedia was published dealing not only with specifically musical subjects but also with dance and with the proper costumes for musicians and dancers. This compendium has survived and is extremely valuable for the study of Oriental musicology. Korean court music underwent little further development after the reign of Prince Yonsan.

Folk music grew in popularity during this period, though not as much as during the later Yi dynasty. One of the most popular instruments to accompany singing was (and still is) a sort of long, flat-bodied lute called the *Kayagum*. Songs and dances accompanied the rituals of the shamans, hymns were chanted in honor of the Buddha, and farmers sang special songs at harvest-time, accompanied by instruments, and danced.

The fine arts also flourished during this period, most notably painting and calligraphy. Painting was of two sorts, amateur and professional. The professional painters were of a somewhat lower status than the yangban, who disdained professionalism in any form, and supplied pictures to order for court and government. They also supplied woodcuts for the illustrations in books published under government auspices. Their work consisted mostly of official portraits and landscapes, which were mainly rather slavish imitations of Chinese work, though a few landscapes of considerable originality did appear.

Amateur painting was closely associated with Chinese calligraphy, an important element in yangban education, and was widely practiced by the yangban. They were careful not to sign their pictures to avoid any taint of professionalism, but many of their surviving works have been identified. The most famous were An Kyon and Ch'oe Kyong. An Kyon's *Mongyu towon-do* (Dream of Paradise), which is said to have been painted from the description of a dream of Prince Anp'yong, one of Sejong's sons, is one of the best surviving paintings. The yangban Kang Hui-an (1417–1464) left masterpieces in both landscape and portrait painting.

A few fine artists of lower status also left great works. Yi Sang-jwa, who was employed as a government painter in the middle of the sixteenth century despite his ch'onmin status, also painted portraits and landscapes, and is especially admired for his *Songha powol-to* (Moon Walking in the Pine Trees). Sin Saimdang, the mother of Yi I, was an excellent painter, an unusual accomplishment for a woman.

Calligraphy itself, of course, had many practitioners. Calligraphers were much influenced during the period under discussion by the Chinese Yuan (Mongol) dynasty calligrapher Chao Meng-fu. Excellence in this art, unlike painting, was felt to be a mark of scholarship, and most yangban vied openly for it. The most famous were Prince Anp'yong, Kim Ku (1488–1534), Yang Sa-on (1517–1584) and Han Ho (1543–1605). They were known in later years as the Four Masters.

The architecture of the earlier Yi dynasty suffered greatly during the Japanese invasions. Both Kyongbok and Ch'angdok palaces, built soon after the founding of the dynasty, were burned, the present buildings having been constructed some time afterwards. Tonhwa-mun, the main gate of Ch'angdok, is still standing and gives a good idea of early Yi architecture, as does the towered side gate. Many of the old city gates have also been preserved in their original positions, most notably the Great South Gate of Seoul. Early Yi gates are also to be seen in Kaesong and P'yongyang. Some of the buildings of the private academies called sowon are still standing, notably Paegundong sowon built in 1542 at Yongju and Tosan sowon built in 1552 at Andong. These are rather more modest than the palaces and give us a notion of early Yi domestic architecture.

Because of the government's anti-Buddhist policy there was very little temple building during this period, and indeed many of the temples were destroyed. Even the few whose remote location in the mountains protected them from persecution were demolished by the invading Japanese. A few Buddhist buildings or parts of buildings remain from this period, however. The gate of Sogwang-sa in Anbyon is one such, as are the shrine of Silluk-sa in Yoju and the storehouse of Haein-sa in Hapch'on. The Yi dynasty style is also to be seen in Songgwang-sa in Sunch'on and T'ongdo-sa in Yangsan. The ten-storied pagoda built at the instance of Sejo now in Pagoda Park and the seven-storied pagoda at Silluk-sa are practically the only examples of Yi dynasty stonework in this form. A few fairly competent Buddha images in metal and wood remain, but in general the art of sculpture did not flourish during the Yi dynasty.

Korea retained her preeminence in ceramics, but a change in technique took place. The art of producing the Koryo celadons, the most widely admired of Korean ceramics, died out. Some efforts were made to produce similar wares early in the period, but they were not successful. The characteristic ceramics of the Yi dynasty were white porcelains called *paekcha*. This was at first influenced by the styles of Ming China, but developed its own characteristic forms. It is simple and elegant, but has a homely, familiar feeling quite different from the aristocratic celadons. Many examples have been preserved and are to be seen in the national art museum on the grounds of Toksu palace in Seoul.

Chapter 21

Political and Economic Change in the Seventeenth and Eighteenth Centuries

The Yi dynasty bureaucracy, already in some disarray because of factionalism, was thrown into complete confusion by the Japanese invasions. Practically the only group that was able to maintain any semblance of order was the army's Frontier Defense Command. Exercising at first purely *ad hoc* functions, it eventually emerged as an executive council of both military and civil officials. The members of the old State Council met regularly with this new group, which thus absorbed the council's functions. All important matters were dealt with by the new council, which continued to exist after the Japanese invasions and the Manchurian invasions which followed them.

This was an important change in the organization of government. The early Yi kings had striven to establish direct control over the country, and had eliminated or emasculated all offices which interposed themselves between the King and the conduct of affairs. This work was now undone to some extent, and a situation prevailed which resembled the later Koryo dynasty, with a council of high officials running the government on behalf of the King, whose power was in this way diminished. This council, called the *Pibyonsa*, became a permanent feature of Yi dynasty government and continued to function until the end of the nineteenth century.

One of the effects of the Japanese invasions was to expose with brutal thoroughness the fatal weaknesses of the Korean military organization. Using a famous Chinese work on tactics by Ch'i Chi-kwang, the Pibyonsa completely reorganized the army. Artillery, bowmen and spearmen were organized into special units, and private slaves, formerly exempt from conscription were pressed into service. The new army was put under the command of the Military Training Office. The new military administration also became permanent, and underwent no further significant changes until 1882.

Yi Kwal's uprising in 1624, which as we have seen was the forerunner of the Manchu invasions, brought further military changes. A permanent military base to guard Kyonggi Province, in which the capital was located, was set up in the same year and manned by about a thousand soldiers, including conscripted private slaves. Also in 1624 another permanent base was established on Mt. Namhan, near Kwangju, where a strong fortress was built. In 1652 a third base came into existence, and here were stationed the crack artillery and cavalry units which were to have participated in King Hyojong's planned assault upon the Manchu rulers of China, which was never executed. Finally in 1682 another base was established near the capital and picked cavalry and infantry units assigned to it. Troops for some of these bases were supplied by conscription, farmers from all the provinces serving in them on a rotation basis. With the addition of the royal guard in Seoul itself, these bases constituted the "Five Camp System" which was the backbone of the later Yi military organization. The main purpose, as is obvious from their location, was to defend Seoul and Kyonggi Province.

All this was vitiated, however, by the severe privation and social confusion that resulted from the invasions. The government was chronically short of funds, and the confusion occasioned by the destruction of many official documents enabled many farmers to evade conscription.

Consequently, the five bases were mostly undermanned and lacking in weapons and munitions.

The suffering and destruction caused by two foreign invasions, the confusion in government, and the lasting effects of the reduction in land under cultivation did nothing to mitigate the factional struggles of the yangban bureaucrats. On the contrary, factionalism became intensified during the post-invasion period, the old factions splitting and multiplying at a bewildering rate. They often centered around succession to the throne or points of Confucian ritual and etiquette, especially the proper period of mourning on the death of a royal personage, but their actual motivation was for the most part pure and simple greed for power.

The Northern faction which held power after the Japanese invasions soon split over the succession issue. Because King Sonjo's queen died without having borne a son, Kwanghae-gun, the son of one of the Kings's concubines, was made Crown Prince. But when the King married a second queen and she bore him a son, some of the Northerners held that this child had the legitimate right of succession. They were over-ruled, and Kwanghae-gun ascended the throne at his father's death with the support of the faction now called the Great Northerners, and proceeded to eliminate the Small Northerners who had opposed him, including his brother Prince Imhae and his half-brother Prince Yongch'ang, both of whom were executed for trying to prevent Kwanghae's accession. Yongch'ang's mother was closely guarded as well.

The Western faction then took advantage of the Northerners' disarray to depose Kwanghae by a *coup d'etat* in 1623, replacing him with his nephew, whose posthumous title is Injo. There was a fresh round of banishments and executions, particular resentment being felt against the Great Northerners' having deprived King Sonjo's second wife of her rights as queen. But internal quarrels arose almost immediately between the Westerners who had taken part in the coup and those who had not. The Northerners, however, never regained power.

Factional strife remained more or less quiescent during Injo's reign and that of his son Hyojong (1649–1659), but broke out again upon Hyojong's death. Hyojong had come to the throne as Kwanghae had, because of the untimely death of his half-brother, Crown Prince Sohyon. Ostensibly the argument was over how long his father's second legitimate wife, the Queen Mother (who was not his mother) should wear mourning for him. The faction leader Song Si-yol argued that since Hyojong had not actually been her son, the Queen Mother need only mourn for him for one year, as the Confucian regulations provided in the case of a relative not of one's immediate family. But two other leaders, Yun Hyu and Ho Mok, opposed this, holding that since Hyojong had replaced the dead Crown Prince before his accession he had in effect become the Queen Mother's son, and she should mourn for him for the full three years prescribed for a relative in one's immediate family.

These seemingly trivial arguments were in fact simply a cover for a factional power struggle. Limiting the length of the Queen Mother's mourning implied doubts of the legitimacy of Hyojong's succession. Yun Hyu, though descended from a line of Northerners, was suspected of having Western leanings because of his friendship with Song Si-yol. In fact, however, he sided with the Southerner Ho Mok. Song Si-yol's arguments ultimately won out, and the Westerners remained in power.

A similar struggle broke out when Hyojong's wife died in 1674, during the reign of his son Hyonjong. This time the Westerners and Southerners wrangled over how long the Dowager Queen Mother, Injo's second wife, should mourn for her daughter-in-law. The King sided with the

Southerners and the Westerners were at last displaced. Hyonjong died that same year and his son, a boy of fourteen succeeded him (posthumous title Sukchong), which meant an intensification of factional struggles until the King was old enough to choose sides.

The political pattern that emerged during the seventeenth century involved two important developments. In the first place, the factions, now permanent groupings although they frequently split, each insisted upon monopolizing the government whenever they took power, so that it was impossible for any but the members of a single faction to hold office at a given time. As a consequence of this, the King lost the power to make appointments freely, and was thus at the mercy of the faction in power, though he could at times decide between the factions when contention arose.

The Southerners who came to power at Sukchong's accession soon split over the degree of severity with which to treat the ousted Westerners. They were ousted by these same Westerners six years later, in 1680, and there was a great purge, ostensibly because a plot to usurp the throne had been uncovered. In 1689 a fiery dispute arose over the naming of a Crown Prince, and the Southerners temporarily returned, but five years later the Westerners again replaced them, and this time the faction was eliminated from politics for good.

The Westerners now split permanently into the *Noron* (Old Doctrine) and *Soron* (New Doctrine) factions, and their quarrels followed the same pattern as before. But during the reign of King Yongjo (1724–1776) the Noron faction managed to eliminate all the other groups and monopolized power from then on.

Under these circumstances the examination system could hardly be expected to operate as it had been intended to. The Confucian classics, which were supposed to be the

foundation of learning and of politics, were largely neglected, the examinations being largely concerned with Chinese
classics and composition, so that even successful candidates could not be expected to have much political skill.
Moreover, the examination questions were not adequately
guarded, nor were the examinations themselves impartially
supervised or marked. No one could hope to pass them
unless he belonged to the faction in power, and even if he
did pass he was not guaranteed an appointment, although
officially he was supposed to get one.

All these disputes and the ultimate establishment of a
single faction in power had serious effects upon the social
and economic position of the yangban class as a whole.
Large numbers of them now found themselves either
temporarily or permanently out of office, and thus unable
to depend on the government for their income. As a result
they turned their attention to enlarging their estates and
establishing local bases of power. In this process the sowon,
the private academies which we have previously discussed,
played a large part.

About a hundred sowon were in existence by the time of
Sonjo (1567–1608), each possessing a sort of charter in
the form of a sign-board in the King's calligraphy. During
Sukchong's reign, when factional strife reached a climax
with the victory of the Noron, there were 274 of them, of
which 131 had the royal authorization. Early in the reign,
when there were rapid shifts of power, each succeeding
faction tried to close its rival's sowon in order to sap its
strength. Until the Noron faction brought a degree of
stability to government there was a great deal of opening
and closing of sowon until a relatively stable pattern emerged. The yangban barred from office, as had been the case
before the invasions, were concentrated largely in Kyongsang Province, where accordingly the sowon were most
numerous. The Kyongsang scholars were descended mostly

from the old Southern faction, which as we have seen had long been eliminated from the political arena.

The long rule of the Noron faction brought about a further weakening of the royal power and destroyed the balance of power among the yangban groups. More fundamentally, it seemed to signal the complete collapse of the Confucian system by which government was supposed to be conducted. The uneasy conflict in the yangban soul between his aristocratic, not to say feudal proclivities and the allegiance which he felt he owed to Confucian principles, which lay at the heart of much of the conflict within Yi dynasty government came to the fore again. When personal animosities had had time to cool somewhat, during the reigns of Yongjo (1724–1776) and Chongjo (1776–1800), a new policy of impartiality was adopted, posts being awarded equally to Noron and Soron members. The factional feuding which had so impeded government was thus calmed to some extent, political stability was achieved, and Confucian consciences were salved.

But this was not the kind of basic reform that was needed to end the conflict between the aristocratic nature of Korean society and Confucian ideals of government. Although factionalism was for a time eliminated, power continued to depend upon wealth and position rather than talent, and the Confucian concepts that had contributed so much to Yi dynasty government and society no longer had any real influence on the actual practice of government.

While the factions succeeded one another in Seoul, new patterns of landholding and taxes were gradually emerging in the devastated countryside. With much land lying fallow and abandoned, its tillers dead or driven away, the royal family greatly enlarged its holdings. Palaces, government offices and military posts now became the King's personal property. Fisheries, salt-making and forests used as sources of firewood also came under the control of the royal household, as sources of income. Islets off the southern coast were taken over, and persons displaced by the invasions were invited to settle on waste lands and pastures owned by the royal family. The royal relatives, by now quite numerous, then began the purchase or outright seizure of farmland.

The yangban landlords were not idle while all this royal self-aggrandizement was going on, and the nongjang expanded in step with the royal estates. The economic problem which paralleled the political contradiction just discussed appeared once more: as land was taken over by the royal family and the great landlords, it disappeared from the tax rolls, and government revenue suffered.

The tax system itself had to be overhauled as a result of the invasions. The tax laws promulgated by King Sejong had stipulated that all taxable land be annually surveyed and the amount of tax determined by the size of the farms and the amount of each harvest, so that farmers would not have to pay disproportionately heavy taxes in bad years. This system had never been fully applied, and now it became quite impossible. Instead, the lowest tax imposed in the past on each plot of land became the fixed annual tax, regardless of the nature of the harvest. The government attempted to resurvey all farmland in order to impose this tax, but due to the expansion of the nongjang and the machinations of corrupt officials, much land was never registered and the amount of land officially taxable remained much less than it had been before the invasions.

While the basic land tax was much lower than it had been before the invasions, various other impositions made the farmer's burdens at least as heavy as before, if not heavier. In the first place, when paying the tax, he had also to pay a forwarding charge or custody fee. Moreover, he was obliged to indemnify the government for any losses of tax grain incurred in storage or transportation. Since the tax was assessed through the landlords rather than directly on the farmers, further exactions could be made. The actual amount the farmer paid, therefore, was several times the amount of the official land tax. In addition, the farmers of the five southern provinces, the richest agricultural region, had to pay a special tax for the support of a special army unit stationed in the area which eventually amounted to half the total charge on the land. Finally, the local tribute which had formerly been paid in the specialties of each region was transmuted into a further tax in grain. The lowering of the official tax was more than offset by all these other charges.

The commutation of the local tribute was a matter of some importance. It will be recalled that this had formerly been managed by tribute contractors who collected local specialties for the government. These people were still in business. Under the new system the government collected the tribute in grain, and gave some of it to the contractors to buy whatever local specialties were required, and remunerate themselves from the surplus. The system was first tried in Kyonggi Province, which was obliged to compensate for the impossibility of collecting tribute from Kyongsang Province because the southern area had been so ravaged by the Japanese.

From Kyonggi Province, where it was first tried in 1608, the practice spread to Ch'ungch'ong and Cholla Provinces in 1623, to Kyongsang in the mid-seventeenth century, and finally to Hwanghae Province in 1708. The system was not applied to P'yongan and Hamgyong Provinces in the mountainous north, where relatively little grain was produced. The importance of the new system was that it contributed to uniformity in taxation and that its restriction of taxes (in most cases) to a single medium of exchange opened the way for the development of a money economy.

The amount of tribute was computed on the basis of units of arable land, each one paying a fixed amount annually. Part of it went to meet the expenses of local administration, but most went to the capital. In a few instances the old tribute in local specialties was retained, but by and large payments were made in grain, or sometimes in textiles.

In addition to all this, the farmers still had to pay the charges for military exemption, which were fixed at two rolls of cloth for each man of military age. This system became well-nigh universal after the wars, so that the armed forces had to rely almost entirely on volunteers.

Two rolls of cloth for every man of military age (between sixteen and sixty) could be a very heavy burden, especially for a family with many sons, and the farmers had to bear it alone, for yangban families were exempt from the tax. Consequently, all sorts of expedients were tried to evade it. Farmers' sons would attempt to enter the local sowon, for example, or get into the local government schools, or by other means try to identify themselves as yangban and thus exempt. The local officials who collected the tax, on the other hand, were held strictly accountable for handing over the exact amount assessed upon their jurisdictions, so that they too were driven to various illegal devices. They would alter the age of children in order to make them appear qualified, for example, and even enroll the dead as a justification for collecting the tax. Sometimes whole families would simply decamp at collection time, in which case their payment would be exacted from their neighbors.

Although most responsible government officials realized the evils of the system, they dared not take the obvious course and alleviate the sufferings of the farmers by imposing the tax on the yangban. It was not until 1750 that a solution was sought. In that year the military tax was cut by half, the shortage to be made up by taxes on fisheries, salt-making and shipping, which were now returned from the control of the royal family to the government. This was to be supplemented by an additional land tax.

This was only partially successful. While the farmers were somewhat relieved, fishermen and salt-makers were virtually robbed of their livelihood, the yangban remained exempt, and the land tax went up. The net effect of the reform, clearly, was not to remove the evils of the older system, but simply to replace them with other evils. Taxes that had been formerly paid in local products were now paid in grain, textiles or cash, and that is about all that was achieved.

One reason the farming population could bear all these exactions was the improvement of agricultural techniques, which led to increased crops and a consequent increase in population. Since practically all transactions were carried out in grain, everyone concerned was anxious to increase the productivity of the land. The more efficient rice-planting methods of the southern provinces now spread to Kyonggi and Ch'ungch'ong, and two-crop farming appeared.

Two-crop farming was (and is) very important to the national economy, and deserves a paragraph to itself. After the rice harvest in the fall, the farmers would plant some of their fields with barley. The hardy barley seeds could survive the winter, and would begin to sprout in early spring. The barley would be harvested in May and June, in time for the fields to be planted with rice once more. To this day in Korea the seasons of late spring and summer are known as the "barley pass," because during those months the farmers, with the previous year's rice all consumed or paid out in taxes, had to depend upon the spring barley crop until the new rice was harvested in the fall.

In 1662 the government established an office of irrigation, in order to give government support to the improvement of irrigation systems, extremely important in the wet-field method of cultivation required for rice. Government support was also extended for the reclamation of land which had ceased to be cultivated because of the invasions. All these measures brought about a marked increase in agricultural production, which was able to support a much increased population.

The emergence of the tribute contractors in and around Seoul, meanwhile, was bringing about changes in the economy. These men were charged with obtaining various kinds of supplies for the court and government, which they did mainly by purchase. By tolerating their existence the government thus opened the way to the development of a commercial economy on a money basis, despite the official discrimination against commerce. The tribute contractors formed a very large proportion of the population of Seoul. There were about 300 firewood contractors during the eighteenth century, for example, and between thirty and forty ginseng contractors. When the wide variety of products in which the contractors dealt is taken into account, it can be seen that a large and growing number of people were obtaining their livelihood from what actually amounted to commerce.

The censuses taken regularly during the seventeenth and eighteenth centuries, mainly for tax purposes, while they cannot be regarded as accurate, give some idea of the growth of population during this period. The following table has been compiled from these census figures.

year	HOUSEHOLDS		ESTIMATED POPULATION	
	Seoul	nationwide	Seoul	nationwide
1657	15,760	658,771	80,572	2,290,083
1669	23,899	1,313,453	194,030	5,018,644

1717	28,356	1,560,561	185,872	6,846,568
1753	34,953	1,772,749	174,203	7,298,731
1786	42,786		199,227	

Official government policy permitted only two forms of commercial activity: the tribute contractors and government-licensed merchants. Each of the latter had what amounted to a monopoly, and it was thus in his interest to prevent non-licensed merchants from dealing in his specialty. The government tried in this way to limit commercial activity to a minimum while maintaining tight control over what it regarded as at best a necessary evil.

The tribute contractors were also under tight control. While they needed no investment capital, being paid in advance for procuring the items needed by the government, they often faced difficulties because the amount of their payment was fixed, while commodity prices frequently fluctuated, threatening them with heavy losses. Often they needed the collaboration of the local officials who resided in Seoul to provide liason with the central government. Licenses to collect tribute were themselves salable commodities.

The importance of the tribute contractors in developing commerce becomes clear when it is considered that, while the amount of tribute in various goods was fixed by law, the demand frequently exceeded this amount. A contractor who could get together sufficient capital to purchase the additional amounts needed might easily turn a profit. The tribute contractor was becoming a sort of wholesaler. Inevitably, persons not licensed to supply tribute tried to enter this field, and often succeeded despite government prohibitions. What we should regard today as brokers and commission agents made their appearance and commerce markedly expanded.

Since the tribute contractors purchased the goods they

supplied to Seoul mainly in provincial markets, these too were stimulated to expand. Groups of merchants began to emerge in various areas, notably those who lived on the banks of the Han River and controlled trade in Kyonggi Province and on the west coast. The merchants of Kaesong and Uiju, cities whose trade had early been stimulated by the fact that Chinese and Korean diplomatic missions regularly passed through them, also expanded their activities, especially in ginseng and border trade.

Things reached such a point that wholesalers in Seoul could corner a given commodity and force up the price. Government attempts to halt this practice were generally ineffective, especially when the wholesalers were military officers, or slaves acting on behalf of powerful families. In connection with their activities, extra-legal markets began to spring up here and there in Seoul to supplement the government-authorized market on Chongno.

After the invasions it was found financially impossible to continue the system of providing for court and government needs for handicraft items by supporting artisans out of government funds. The government artisans found themselves on their own, with no other recourse but to sell their goods wherever they found a market. While some of them managed to become tribute contractors in their own specialties, most of them became free craftsmen. While their chief customers remained the yangban class and the government, the demand for some artifacts was rising, and many of the craftsmen prospered. Brassware, porcelain and hemp cloth especially were in high demand in most cities, and the artisans found good business in the district markets that were held every five days. These also grew in numbers, until there were around a thousand of them in the eighteenth century.

The final ingredient in this greatly expanded commercial activity was coinage. Coins had been minted in the past but had never had a very wide circulation. The government saw the issuance of coins simply as an economic expedient in the straitened circumstances after the invasions, but the effects of a monetary medium of exchange went far beyond their expectations. Commercial transactions of all kinds were greatly facilitated by the replacement of such bulky items as grain or textiles with small, easily portable symbols of value. Most taxes were eventually commuted to cash payments, but the most important effect of coinage was that it made possible and stimulated finance. The practice of lending money at interest was deeply disapproved in Confucian doctrine, but even for many of the yangban class the temptation was too great. They were joined by wealthy merchants and even by some government offices, and the growth of commercial capital after the eighteenth century was largely owing to their activities. What was developing, in Western terms, was a laissez-faire capitalist economy, and what happened in the early stages of its development was a familiar phenomenon to economic historians: the rich got richer and the poor got poorer, and the traditional class structure of society was disrupted and confused.

The initial disturbance of the class system, however, was not caused by commercialism but simply by financial distress in the aftermath of the invasions. The government began offering promotion in social status and even government office to anyone who would supply it with funds or grain. The practice became widespread, the government, for example, sending blank certificates of appointment to provincial officials to be sold to the highest bidder in order to support local administrations. This practice did not cease after the country recovered from the wars, and with the rise of commercialism it became possible to buy one's self into the upper classes.

On the other hand, the factional struggles which followed

the wars and culminated in the triumph of the Noron faction forced all but a few yangban from office, and many of them found it impossible to maintain themselves on the scale to which they were accustomed. Yangban families long out of office came to constitute a class of their own, inferior in status to the actual ruling group. Worse yet, many of them lost their land when the royal family began accumulating estates in the confusion following the wars. The Seoul yangban, on the other hand, went into business in large numbers as we have seen, so that wealth rather than lineage began to be the criterion of social status.

Farm freeholds, which of course paid the heaviest taxes, all but disappeared. But a few farmers who had been able to take advantage of the new agricultural techniques had prospered, and many of them managed to buy or fabricate yangban status, thus escaping taxes altogether. In the countryside as in Seoul, wealth was becoming the sole criterion of status and the traditional constitution of society was breaking down. One symptom was that in Seoul the distinctive hats and clothing of the yangban were now worn by anyone who could afford them, and many persons produced false pedigrees showing yangban status, while others promoted themselves by conniving with census officials to alter the records. Traditional class distinctions were everywhere blurred or ignored.

One final and long-lasting effect of the invasions upon Yi dynasty society was that upon slave-holding. The number of slaves held by the government had been greatly increased at the outset of the Yi dynasty by the expropriation of many thousands of slaves held by Buddhist temples and monasteries. Their numbers increased through the following two centuries, at least partly because of the rule that the status of a person followed that of his mother. There were about 200,000 government slaves in 1420 and 350,000 in 1484, and later years showed a comparable increase. Slaves held by private individuals also increased.

This was a formidable number of people, and their resentment at their status was clearly demonstrated when they attacked government offices in Seoul during the Japanese invasion of 1592 and destroyed large numbers of the census registers in which their status was officially recorded. This, combined with the destruction of other records by the Japanese, resulted in many slaves escaping their bondage. Official records show only about 190,000 government slaves in 1655 and an earlier census gives 400,000 as the number of privately owned slaves throughout the country, also a significant decline.

But the loss of records was not the only cause for the decline in the numbers of slaves. Desperate not only for funds but also for manpower, the government pressed many slaves into military service during the invasions, and this often entailed an automatic rise in status. And when at last the country was at peace, many of the government offices found that they were unable to support as many slaves as formerly. The artisans already discussed, who had had slave status until the wars, are a case in point. Often the government had no option but to emancipate large numbers of slaves simply because it was unable to feed and house them. Many of the yangban were in like case, and large numbers of slaves became artisans or farmers.

The slaves themselves continued to work for emancipation, and made active efforts to raise their status once freed. Some of them found positions as menials in government offices, jobs formerly the prerogative of the yangmin (farmer) class. Some even managed to enter the lower ranks of the bureaucracy. Whenever the government encountered financial or military difficulty the slaves were eager to offer their services in order to improve their status.

Eventually it became government policy to give official yangmin status to all slaves who had served the government for two generations in positions formerly reserved for yangmin. Like the distinction between yangban and yangmin, the distinction between slaves and yangmin was fading.

Chapter 22

Intellectual Developments in the Seventeenth and Eighteenth Centuries

Perhaps the most portentous, if not the most pervasive phenomenon for Korea as for all Asia during the seventeenth and eighteenth centuries was the appearance of travelers from Europe, first explorers and traders, then missionaries, and then soldiers. The Portuguese arrived first, for it was they who pioneered the sea route around Africa to India. By the middle of the sixteenth century they had been granted the foothold at Macao which they still retain, and had established trading relations with the Japanese daimyo and brought in missionaries. They were soon followed by the Spaniards, and in the seventeenth century the Europeans were a force to be reckoned with throughout East Asia.

But two factors prevented immediate and significant contact between Korea and the West. First, Korea was geographically isolated. The main trade routes followed by the Portuguese and Spanish ships, as later by those of other European powers, ran north from Southeast Asia to Japan and to the southern ports of China. Few of them had any occasion to travel further northwest, and the occasional European ship that appeared in Korean waters had usually been blown off its course in a storm.

Second and perhaps more important was the cultural chauvinism and isolationism of the Korean ruling class. It was inconceivable to them that anything of value could be obtained from any foreign country except China, and indeed contacts with other foreign nations were strictly limited by law. The occasional shipwrecked Westerner was hustled off as soon as possible.

There are a few recorded instances of Western contacts of some duration during this period. A missionary named Cespedes accompanied Hideyoshi's troops in 1592, though he cannot have had very extensive contacts with Koreans. In 1628 a Dutch ship was wrecked and the three survivors, including one Jan Janse Weltevree managed to reach the shores of Cheju Island. They were sent to Seoul, where they were asked to help improve the weapons of the Korean army, which they did. Two of them died fighting the Manchurians, and Weltevree ended his days in Korea under the name of Pak Yon.

In 1653, as a result of another Dutch shipwreck, Hendrik Hamel and several others came ashore at Cheju. They too were detained by the Korean authorities, but after fifteen years some of them managed to escape and return to Holland. Hamel wrote a book about his experiences, the first information given the Western world about Korea, and it was translated into English, German and French, but aroused little interest.

The only other direct Western contact was hostile. The Russian empire was expanding into Asia during the seventeenth century, and made contact with the Manchu rulers of China (the Ch'ing dynasty) along the Amur River in northern Manchuria. The Ch'ing rulers asked Korea to help them in repelling the Russian invaders, and the Koreans, who, ironically enough, had been cherishing dreams of appropriating Manchurian territory for themselves, had no choice but to aid the Chinese.

Opportunities to benefit from direct contact with Europeans were thus let slip by the Koreans, and the only way in which Western thought could influence the country was an indirect one. Korea, of course, continued her relations with China, and the Western missionaries ultimately succeeded in gaining access to the Ch'ing court. Through the annual journeys of the Korean envoys between Seoul and Peking, a means of contact with Western thought was created.

Francis Xavier, one of the earliest Portuguese missionaries in Japan, had reached the conclusion that the best way to bring Christianity to Asia was to convert the rulers of China. Although he himself never managed to obtain permission to enter the country, one of his Jesuit successors, Matteo Ricci, after numerous difficulties and delays, not only preached Christianity at Peking but was allowed to build a church there and became an advisor to the imperial government.

Ricci and his successors ingratiated themselves at the Chinese court by learning Chinese ways and by introducing Western scientific knowledge. They aided the court in such matters as astronomy, the calendar, geography and mathematics, and also in the manufacture and use of firearms. They translated Western works on these subjects into Chinese, and these books were widely distributed. Inevitably copies were obtained by the Korean envoys who visited Peking annually, and taken back to Korea.

The first Western works to reach Korea are said to have been a map of Europe and a theological work by Matteo Ricci. Many more were to follow. In 1630 the Korean envoy Chong Tu-won became acquainted with Johannes Rodriguez, an Italtian priest in Peking. Rodriguez presented to Chong books on astrology, the calendar, and geography, and also a telescope, an alarm clock and a cannon, all of which were presented to the King on Chong's return. Again in 1644, Crown Prince Sohyon, while staying in Peking as a hostage, met the German priest Adam Schall and acquired from him a large number of Western books in Chinese including theological works, and a religious statue, all of which he took back to Seoul with him.

In 1720 the Korean envoy Yi I-myong became acquainted with the Jesuits Koegler and Saurez, who were supervisors of the royal astronomical observatory in Peking. He received books on the subjects already mentioned and read them diligently. He was particularly impressed by Ricci's *Outline of Arithmetic,* and took a keen interest in Western science generally. Numerous other Korean envoys visited the Catholic cathedral in Peking, where they were impressed by the Western-style statues and paintings, especially for the use of perspective, and where they heard Western music for the first time. A small but steady stream of Western works on religion and science, translated into Chinese, began to flow from Peking to Seoul.

All this Western learning made a considerable impression on the Korean scholars. A fairly typical example is that of Yi Ik, an out-of-office yangban during the first half of the eighteenth century. His father having been envoy to Peking in 1677, he had access to many Western books, and also read some of the translations brought back by Chong Tu-won. His reactions to Western ideas and techniques are interesting. He was fascinated by the manufacturing techniques which produced cannon and by the intricacies of astronomy. Of Adam Schall's work on the calendar he said it was the most perfect of all calendar systems, and contained no errors in its explanation of solar and lunar eclipses. He believed this system should replace the one currently in use, even though the book also taught that an ancient saint was to return to life, which seemed to him not sensible. He also accepted the idea that the earth is round, and asserted that the Western maps showing the continents surrounded by oceans had been made from actual observation and were therefore accurate. One of the more interesting books he read was Matteo Ricci's *Original*

Text of Geometry, a translation into Chinese of Euclid. He remarked of the use of perspective in Western painting that Chinese art could show nothing like it, and was also interested in Western methods of education. But—significantly—he utterly rejected the Christian doctrines of heaven and hell.

There were many men like Yi Ik among the Korean intelligentsia, and they could not help being impressed by Western accomplishments in science. Perhaps more important, having seen the Western maps of the world and having been convinced of its shape and size, they were forced to revise their world-view to the extent of admitting that China was not the center of it and that Korea was only a small corner of it. They were also impressed by the techniques of observation and induction by which scientific knowledge was obtained.

But it is sadly significant that the only practical result of all this knowledge was a calendar reform in 1654, following the example of the Chinese. Western knowledge in the seventeenth and eighteenth centuries remained a mere intellectual curiosity in Korea, with little or no effect upon government or society.

But if Western science and technology did not immediately take root in Korea, Western religion did. While most of the Confucian scholars took only an academic interest in Catholicism at first, we find it spreading among the farmers of Hwanghae Province in the second half of the eighteenth century, although no ordained priest entered the country until 1795. The disturbed state of society and the many factional disputes which we have discussed encouraged many people to accept the new religion as an alternative to traditional beliefs, especially the oppressed and the yangban of the long-defeated Southern faction.

The government did not at first interfere with the spread

of the Catholic faith because it was regarded as unimportant and as appealing only to foolish and ignorant persons. But during Chongjo's reign (1776–1800) it began to spread among the yangban. An official named Yi Sunghun, who had accompanied his father in the party of the envoy to Peking, was baptized there by Bishop Alexandre de Gouvea in 1783. He brought back several Catholic books and also ritual objects such as crosses. A group of several dozen yangban of the Southern faction began to hold regular services, performing the rituals as best they could from the books they had read. At the same time, the religion was growing popular among the lower classes, and before the first missionary arrived it was to be found throughout the country, except for the two northern provinces.

The rulers were eventually compelled to take notice of the rapid spread of this foreign cult, and what they discovered did not please them. In particular, the doctrine that this world is but a preparation for the afterlife and that worldly power and position are unworthy ends seemed to them subversive of the Confucian concepts of society and of the relationships between individuals in much the same way that Buddhism was. They were particularly shocked to find that Catholics disapproved of ancestor-worship, one of the most fundamental elements of Confucianism. In 1785 Catholicism was officially banned. The import of books from Peking was stopped, and envoys to the Chinese capital were warned to have no private contacts with Chinese and not to visit any Catholic church.

That these measures were not fully effective was demonstrated by an incident that must have seemed not only subversive but positively indecent to the Confucian officials. In 1791 the mother of Yun Chi-ch'ung, a yangban living in Cholla Province, died. Instead of performing the Confucian rites for the dead, Yun gave his mother a Catholic burial. The matter was reported to the authorities, who found to their horror that he had earlier burnt his ancestor-tablets because Catholicism taught that worshipping them was idolatry. This amounted to a rejection of the whole Confucian system, and was besides a crime against family and government and a breach of the cardinal virtue of filial piety. It was, in short, the gravest crime a person could possibly commit. Yun and the relatives who had assisted at the Catholic burial ceremony were arrested and executed. For good measure, in addition to banning the import of books, the authorities ordered the destruction of all the foreign books in the government library.

There was no further persecution during Chongjo's reign, and in 1795 the first ordained priest to enter Korea, a Chinese named Chou Wen-mu, was able to cross the Yalu and make his way to Seoul. There was a mood of reconciliation in government at the time, and several Southern scholars had been given posts. Since it was among the Southerners that Catholicism was most popular, the missionary was not molested for the time being.

Meanwhile, partly because of the stimulus of Western ideas, a new school of thought was growing up among the Korean intelligentsia. Called *Sirhak* (Practical Learning) it was directed primarily against the preoccupation among the bureaucrats either with Chinese literature or with the speculative side of Chu Hsi's neo-Confucianism. The Sirhak scholars demanded an end to empty formalism and concern with ritual trivialities and a return to the true spirit of Confucianism. They also demanded a practical, empirical approach both to government and to learning. The movement had its roots in the seventeenth century, but came to prominence in the eighteenth.

Resistance to Chu Hsi formalism began in the mid-seventeenth century with Yun Hyu, who did not achieve political office until late in life. He was a man of remarkably independent mind, who held that no doctrine, not even Chu Hsi's neo-Confucianism, deserved to be followed blindly and uncritically, and insisted that all ideas and practices be judged on their merits. He was joined in this attitude by Pak Se-dang, and the latter set out to examine impartially all the doctrines he was aware of, even Chinese Taoism, which the Confucianists condemned.

But when at last Yun Hyu achieved political office and tried to apply his ideas, the conservative members of the Western faction, led by Song Si-yol, were so scandalized at his lack of respect for venerated doctrines that they hounded him from office and ultimately executed him, and his colleague Pak Se-dang was also dismissed. The scholar-officials generally identified the Chu Hsi interpretation of Confucianism with the monarchy and the bureaucracy and regarded criticism of it as equivalent to treason.

But despite all this intellectual rigidity, the reigns of Yongjo (1724–1776) and Chongjo (1776–1800) constitute a period in later Yi dynasty history comparable in some ways to the reign of the great Sejong in earlier times. It was during this time, for example, that the Korean tax system came as near to being rationalized as it was ever to do, and political stability was achieved by breaking the monopoly of the Noron faction and giving posts to members of other parties. Both of the kings were intelligent and able, and Chongjo was as fine a scholar as any of his officials. As a consequence, scholarly activity flourished during their reigns.

One of the most important scholarly activities of Yongjo's reign was the revision and supplementation of the law code, an immense labor since the basic law of the kingdom had been codified some three centuries before and promulgated in 1470. Besides this, revisions were made of the textbooks of military strategy to bring them up to date and a new edition was made of the *Oyeui,* the simplified book on Confucian propriety which had been published in an earlier reign for the edification of the masses. King Yongjo also caused to be compiled and printed a historical record of the various calendrical systems, educational methods and types of administrative organization in use in Korea at various times in the past.

Under King Chongjo the law code was again revised. New books on the military arts appeared, and the documents showing precedents set by the boards of personnel and justice were published, as were a selection of diplomatic documents. A new dictionary on phonetic principles was made. As a by-product of all this compiling and publishing, the art of printing was further refined and new designs for both wooden and copper type appeared.

It must not be imagined that all this intellectual activity was carried on for its own sake, or merely in pious veneration of the past. Each of the publications we have mentioned had, at any rate in the minds of the scholars concerned with them, an intimate connection with the affairs and fortunes of the kingdom. The Confucians, true to their master's spirit, were still struggling to learn the lessons of history in order to solve the problems of their own time.

Most of the original ideas produced during the later Yi dynasty arose among yangban who were debarred from public office by factional strife. We have already mentioned the *Sirhak* school of thought which some of them developed, and it is now time to discuss it in detail.

The movement first appeared during the seventeenth century, and the reformers of the eighteenth based their ideas upon those of a few eminent thinkers. One of the most important of these was Yun Chung (1629–1714), who refused a government post even when it was offered to him, and devoted his long life to perfecting and teaching Sirhak ideas. He was deeply discontented with the empty formalism of the Chu Hsi philosophy, and believed that there must be a break with tradition if the government were to deal effectively with the harsh realities of the time. For him and for the group which followed his teachings the welfare of the people was the primary concern. The king, they asserted, could not exist without the people, but the people could exist without the king.

This was a startlingly democratic notion, especially at a time and in a society in which the hierarchical principle was believed to be inherent in nature itself. But the Sirhak scholars refused to accept the idea that men are born unequal, that their social status is predetermined. In practical terms, they asserted that the partial reforms carried out from time to time by the government were aimed not at improving the common lot but at perpetuating an oppressive system. They called instead for a root-and-branch reformation which would assure a decent livelihood to all the people.

The Sirhak scholars did not present all these radical notions merely as their own. Such a thing would have branded them as ignorant braggarts. Instead, like Confucius himself and like all other radicals and reformers in Oriental history, they asserted that they were trying to restore in their original purity the practices of ancient times. To find precedents for their ideas they turned to the *Chou li,* an ancient Chinese record of administrative practices which seemed to lend support to their equalitarianism. This did not mean that they wished merely to return to ancient ways, although it is necessary to point out that the Silhak scholars would not have seen the matter in quite that way. Even the most radical thinkers in this Confucian-oriented society held to the belief that the history of the past holds the solution to present problems.

Another strand in the fabric of Sirhak thought was contributed by Yu Hyong-won (1622–1673), whose collected essays were widely studied. He gave most of his attention to the landholding system, the bugbear of all reformers. He held, not unexpectedly, that the expansion of private estates should be prevented, and that a truly equitable system of taxation and government stipends should be established. He also said that the examination system should be replaced by a system of recommendation for government posts which should be based on the principle of equality of opportunity, regardless of social status, and that this should also apply to education. All this was hardly new, but it was certainly contrary to government practice (the officials in power dismissed it as the unrealistic vaporings of an idle scholar) and formed an important element of Sirhak thought in the eighteenth century.

The successor to Yu Hyong-won as the leading Sirhak thinker was Yi Ik (1681–1763). He was a widely cultivated thinker in many fields, including astronomy, geography, law and mathematics, and he too was much concerned with the landholding system. But in addition to land reform, he openly advocated the abolition of class barriers and of slavery. His famous *Collected Essays* not only give a good summary of Sirhak thought but also provide a valuable picture of the social conditions against which Yi Ik protested.

Chong Yag-yong (1762–1836) added to these elements of Sirhak thought the stimulus of Western learning. He eagerly studied all the Western books he could obtain, and in addition became a believer in Catholicism, for which belief he was banished in 1801 to a remote island where he remained for eighteen years. During his exile he worked out in detail his ideas for reform, including redistribution of land to the farmers and insurance to them of a fair share of their crops, reorganization of both central and local administrations, the abolition of slavery and the development of technical education.

These three thinkers and their disciples were not merely

theorizing or constructing Utopias. They were reacting to the misery and oppression which was plainly visible all around them. The devastation caused by the invasions, the rapacity of the landlords, the crushing burden of taxes— all these aroused their concern, not only because of the sufferings of the people but also because these conditions threatened to cause social collapse. It is significant that the three thinkers came from the two provinces where conditions were worst, Kyonggi and Cholla.

In addition to the works already mentioned, several books on farming were produced by the Sirhak scholars as a consequence of their emphasis on the practical as against the merely theoretical. The leading writers on these subjects were Pak Se-dang, Hong Man-son and So Yu-gu. Their books dealt mainly with crop management and animal husbandry, and give valuable insights into agricultural techniques and development during the seventeenth and eighteenth centuries.

But if the Sirhak thinkers were in some ways ahead of their time, in other ways they were behind it. The reforms which they envisaged were predicated upon the continued existence of a purely agricultural economy in which trade would be kept to a minimum as before. Yi Ik, seeing the many abuses of money-lending, went so far as to propose the abolition of money itself as a solution and adopted "Shun Usury" as his family motto.

In their detestation of commerce and the money economy which supported it the Sirhak thinkers were for once in agreement with the government, but both groups were out of tune with the times. We have already seen how the tribute contractors had developed into wholesale merchants, and how the government, in order to shore up its finances, had begun to coin money in large quantities and accept tax payments in cash. In Seoul even the yangban found that they could no longer depend solely upon the land for their income. Inevitably some of the more perceptive among them began to assert that commerce could be a useful source of revenue, and that it should be encouraged. Many went further and suggested that handicrafts and other forms of manufacturing should be developed for export trade, and that new forms of technology such as those of the Europeans should be imported.

Yu Su-won may be taken as representative of the Seoul yangban who favored encouragement of commerce during the first half of the eighteenth century. Kept in confinement for eight years because he was suspected of being involved in the treasonable plot of a relative, he wrote a book in which he set forth his solutions for the social and economic problems of his time. Like the Sirhak scholars, he argued for the breaking of class barriers and equality of opportunity in government and education. Unlike them, he argued for government promotion of commerce. He suggested that permanent shops be opened in the provinces, that transportation be improved, and that mining, fisheries, fruit culture and stockbreeding be encouraged. He wanted the smaller merchants to borrow from the larger ones so as to undertake large-scale trade projects, and favored extensive use of coinage and prohibition of counterfeiting.

These ideas were underscored during the second half of the eighteenth century by the lively development of commerce in China under the Manchu Ch'ing dynasty. Korean envoys to Peking returned home praising the prosperity which commerce had brought to the Chinese. Pak Chi-won urged that agriculture could benefit from the development of commerce, and that agricultural techniques used in China, especially in irrigation and sericulture, be imported, along with Chinese advances in porcelain and metallurgy. He was also in favor of improvements in transportation, both on land and by sea, for the encouragement of trade.

Pak Che-ga went even further. Having visited the Chinese court three times, he formally proposed to the government that Korea should send trading ships to China regularly, and that some of the Western technicians employed by the Chinese court should be invited to Korea to impart their knowledge to the young.

His proposition came at an unfortunate time. The government was then becoming aware of what it considered to be the menace of Catholicism. The Western technology which Pak so admired was, of course, closely associated with this religion. As we have seen, contact with Peking was reduced to a minimum, the importation of books was banned, and even the Chinese translations of Western books already in the country were destroyed.

We must add to our list of the perceptive men who advocated the use of Western technology the names of Hong Tae-yong and Yi Tong-mu, both of whom had visited Peking and been impressed by what they saw there. Collectively, this group came to be called the school of Northern Learning, since Korea's border with China was in the north. They are remarkable not only because they saw the advantages of Western technology but also because, although yangban themselves, they were willing to concern themselves with such matters as commerce and technology, things which it was supposed to be beneath a yangban's dignity even to know about. Although their ideas did not prevail, the very fact that such men could have such ideas shows that the old Confucian order, however slowly and reluctantly, was changing.

Parallel with this rising awareness of Western techniques and ideas there developed a new national consciousness and a new interest in the study of things Korean. This first manifested itself in the study and writing of history. Histories of the various reigns and dynasties had been compiled in the past as we have seen, but the notion of a general history of Korea as a nation and people was new. Stimulated by the development of new historical methods in China during the seventeenth century, Korean scholars began to turn their attention to the history of their own country.

One of the dominating and salutary influences on this new study of Korean history was the scholar Yi Ik, whom we have met before in another connection. He held that the duty of the historian was to portray the times of which he wrote as clearly and accurately as possible, and to avoid the anecdotal, moralizing manner of older Chinese historians. Inference and conjecture were to be avoided, and a critical, objective attitude was to be adopted toward sources. The fruits of this new historical method are to be seen in the work of one of Yi's disciples, An Chong-bok (1712–1791), whose *Tongsa kangmok* (Outline of the History of Korea) appeared in 1790. It was an important book, not only for its subject but also because it stimulated other scholars to study their nation's history and to produce other works using the new methods.

Another stimulus to Korean studies was provided by Han Ch'i-yun (1765–1814), the author of *Haedong yoksa* (A History of Ancient Korea). While this book still used the methods of the old Chinese compilations, it did provide a fresh look at the early history of the kingdom, which had not been much studied since Koryo times. Yi Kung-ik (1736–1806) wrote an unofficial history (i.e. compiled from sources other than the official chronicles) of the Yi dynasty, *Yollyosil kisul*, interesting in that it concerned itself with matters other than the official acts of kings.

One of the most significant developments in historical studies was the interest shown in the ancient state of Parhae (see Part III, Chapter Six). This state, it will be recalled, had occupied part of the old Koguryo territory in northern Korea and Manchuria during most of the United Silla period. Numerous works appeared concerning this kingdom, including even a special study of its geographical names. With the new national consciousness went a desire to assert Korea's ancient rights and powers. Parhae, the scholars said, had been Korean, and its history should be treated as an integral part of Korean history.

The interest in Korean history during the eighteenth century brought about a concern for geography, and works on this subject also appeared. The pioneer in this field was Yi Chung-hwan (1690–1760?), whose *T'aengni-ji* (Geographical Description of the Eight Provinces) showed the way to others. Specialized works on boundaries, roads, mountains, and rivers by Sin Kyong-jun and Chong Yag-yong followed. In conjunction with these works cartography was greatly improved and drawing to scale, which had been learned from Chinese translations of Western geographies, was employed. Surveys were carried out to make maps as accurate as possible and atlases were compiled. Large folding maps were made which began to approach modern scientific standards, the most famous of which was the *Taedong yojido* by Kim Chong-ho.

The national consciousness also revealed itself in studies of the Korean language, and especially of Han'gul, the Korean alphabet invented during the reign of Sejong. Sin Kyong-jun produced a valuable study of the proper use of Han'gul in representing sounds, and other scholars are known to have valued it highly, a new trend among the scholar class, who had traditionally valued Chinese writing and considered Han'gul beneath them. Yu Hui produced another study of Han'gul and also a book on the Korean vocabulary, called most appositely *Mulmyong-go* (On the Names of Things).

One of the most outstanding scholarly activities in the seventeenth and eighteenth centuries was the compiling of encyclopedias, both general and special. Yi Su-gwang (1563–1628) began the trend with a compilation called

Chibong yusol, covering a wide variety of subjects. Other scholars, notably Yi Ik, Yu Hui and especially Chong Yag-yong produced similar works, and a trend toward speciali-zation began. Kim Chong-hui (1786–1856), for example, wrote the first book on Korean epigraphy, a study of the monuments and inscriptions of the reign of King Chinhung of the Silla dynasty, in which he employed both historical research and textual criticism. Chong Yak-chon, exiled for sixteen years on the island of Chasan (now Huksan), beguiled the tedium of his lonely life by writing a study *Chasan obo* (On the Fishes of Chasan Island) in which he recorded in minute detail the names, distribution, shapes, habits and uses of 155 varieties of fish and seaweed in a manner which approached modern scientific method. Finally, Chong Yag-yong wrote *Makwa hoet'ong* (On Vaccination for Smallpox), marking a new era in medicine.

The new national consciousness also had its effect on literature. The development of a genuinely native literature, it will be recalled, had been impeded by the fact that Korea adopted the Chinese ideograms before she had developed a writing system of her own. Korean literature written in classic Chinese had such high prestige, moreover, that even after the invention of Han'gul in the fifteenth century literature using Korean themes and written in the Korean language was slow to appear. In the seventeenth century, however, native literature began an extensive development.

We have already explained how Korean poetry was the first to be recorded phonetically and how beneficial the invention of Han'gul was for this purpose. In the seven-teenth century two forms of poem were popular. There was the narrative poem called *kasa* and a much more popular form, the short reflective lyric called *sijo,* comparable in form to the Japanese *haiku.* While these forms were probably inspired by Chinese models, they came in-creasingly to be written in Korean and recorded in Han'-

gul. Those of the earlier Yi period often dealt either with loyalty or with the joys of scholarly seclusion, while those of the later period had a greater variety of themes, usually striving to convey the emotional essence of experience. Through the medium of Han'gul, *sijo* became popular not only among the yangban but also among commoners.

Prose narratives at first followed Chinese models even when written in Korean. Fiction came in time to be written exclusively in Han'gul, as it is today, and so had a much wider appeal than literature which used Chinese characters. The earliest novel recorded in Han'gul, Ho Kyun's social novel *Hong Kil-tong-jon* (The Tale of Hong Kil-tong), has already been discussed. Also notable in this period is Kim Man-jung's *Kuunmong* (The Nine Cloud Dream),which is still popular. Love stories and family chronicles supplied the main themes, with a strong admixture of fantasy, as in Chinese popular literature. The greatest of them all was the *Ch'unhyang-jon* (The Tale of Ch'unhyang). The author's name is unknown, unfortunately. It is a tale of two lovers, their separation and suffering and eventual reunion. While its themes are conventional, it is full of sharp observation, realistic and humorous. Retold in prose and verse, presented in drama and song, it has for the Korean people a special significance comparable to the story of Romeo and Juliet in the West.

Jokes and satires directed at the yangban class were another feature of later Yi dynasty literature. The yangban themselves were capable of poking fun at their class, though they usually did it in Chinese. The outstanding social satires of the time were written in Korean. One of the best satirists was Pak Chi-won, whose *Yangban-jon* (Tale of a Yangban) and *Hosaeng-jon* (Tale of Hosaeng) exposed the defects of yangban life and thought. The important thing to note about these satires aside from their subject-matter is style. The author abandoned Chinese models completely and created for himself a style appropriate to Korean themes and ideas. Together with other literary movements of the seventeenth century, this shows that Korea was at last developing a literature of her own, and one, moreover, which through the medium of Han'gul was available to the masses and not confined to the yangban alone.

Significant also of the national awakening was the recording and publication of folk-songs, often by persons of inferior social status. Several anthologies of this kind appeared. There were collections of *sijo* by authors known and unknown and also collections of *kasa* in both Chinese and Korean. Of special importance was the sijo collection *Ch'onggu yongon* (Eternal Word of the Green Hills, i.e. Korea) edited by Kim Ch'on-t'aek. In short, Korea had developed a national literature which truly belonged to all the Korean people, and this was made possible by Han'gul.

There were parallel developments in the fine arts. Korean painting, like other arts, followed the changing styles of China, adopting at this time the Southern style, refined and elegant, which had replaced the more ambitious and grandiose Northern style during the Ming dynasty. Painting continued to be closely allied to calligraphy, and ink drawings flourished.

This basically Chinese manner of painting was modified by knowledge of Western techniques as applied to portraiture and by the development of a genuinely Korean style in landscape and genre painting. Though the Korean painters often chose the same subjects as those treated by Chinese masters, their developing technique gave to their works a distinctive, original mood.

The pioneer in landscape was Chong Son (1676–1759), whose pen name was Kyomjae. He toured the country in order to paint landscapes from nature, and produced a series of vigorous, markedly original works, quite independent of Chinese style.

But the most notable development in Yi dynasty art was the appearance of genre painting. Sin Yun-bok (Hyewon) and Kim Hong-do (Tanwon), both of whom flourished during the later eighteenth century, were its leading practitioners. Sin's paintings portrayed the daily life of the urban upper class, while Kim pictured the manners and customs of farmers, shopkeepers and artisans in a robustly humorous style. These two and many like them made a complete break with the conventional Chinese subject-matter in order to portray realistically the life of their people. It is not to be imagined, however, that these pictures were mere cartoons or impromptu sketches. Kim Hong-do's paintings especially were carefully conceived landscapes, but with real people in them, so that the unreal, dreamy quality of Chinese landscape was replaced by a humanistic realism.

In the peculiarly oriental field of calligraphy there was also a move toward originality and independence of Chinese models. Kim Chong-hui (Ch'usa or Wandang), also known for his studies in epigraphy, was the leader in this field. His energetic, original style was so widely admired that he came to be regarded as the founder of a new school by other practitioners of the art.

In handicrafts, Yi dynasty artisans continued to be outstanding potters. The earlier ware was an undecorated creamy white. Later, when Korea had ceased depending on Chinese imports and learned to make her own blue pigment for glazes, white wares with elegant designs in blue appeared. Landscapes, birds and flowers ornamented vases, wine-bottles, jugs, jars, water-droppers and brush-holders in a wide variety of shapes of a simple and refined elegance. Wooden utensils and furniture were also skilfully made, especially lacquered pieces inlaid with mother-of-pearl, a characteristic Korean craft. These of course were confined to the upper classes.

Chapter 23

Resistance to Change: the Nineteenth Century

The reigns of Yongjo and Chongjo which filled most of the eighteenth century were, as we have seen, a period of relative political stability, first under the dominance of the Noron faction and then proceeding to the new policy of endeavoring to supercede the old factionalsm by a policy of making appointments on the basis of merit, regardless of party. Also, while there was resistance to Western notions such as Catholicism, it was moderated by the fact that many of the Southern faction, who were now gaining some degree of power, were either Catholics or strongly influenced by the religion.

But the latent quarrelsomeness of the bureaucrats was stirred anew by a particularly vicious intrigue toward the end of Yongjo's long reign. The King had chosen Prince Changhon, the son of a court lady, as Crown Prince. There was wide opposition to the choice: the legitimate Queen was angry; the members of the ruling Noron faction felt that the Prince might rob them of their privileged positions when he became king; and the wife of another prince wished her husband to be king. These parties plotted together to change the succession, and to this end laid false evidence before King Yongjo that the Crown Prince was plotting to overthrow him by force. The King believed them, and angrily ordered that Prince Changhon be executed at once. The plotters, however, could not bring themselves to shed royal blood, much as they desired the

Prince's downfall. The King thereupon ordered that the Prince be placed alive in a pine box and the lid nailed shut. This was done, and it was thus that the Prince died.

The crowning irony of this tragic story is that the next King was not the candidate of any of the plotters but Prince Changhon's son, whose posthumous title is Chongjo. Upon his ascension he purged all those who had been involved in his father's death or opposed his accession. He then conferred upon his father the posthumous title of Changjo, as if he had been a reigning monarch. For this reason, Korean historians have called him the "Coffin King."

This affair split the Noron faction into those who had favored Changhon's death and those who had not, with the usual bickering and maneuvering. Significantly the bureaucrats who had participated in the plot also favored a much stronger policy against Catholicism. Although they failed at this time to dominate the government, their dislike and suspicion of Catholicism and other Western ideas was to prevail in succeeding years.

Chongjo had come to power with the aid of a relative named Hong Kug-yong, who for a time dominated the government. Although Hong was eventually eliminated and Chongjo managed to maintain a reasonable degree of control over the government, this was the beginning of the dominance of the kingdom by relatives of royal spouses, facilitated by the fact that several of Chongjo's successors were children when they came to the throne. The practice began immediately upon Chongjo's death, for his son (posthumous title Sunjo) was only eleven. Chongjo had tried to insure his son's peaceful possession of the throne by placing him under the protection of a trusted retainer, Kim Cho-sun. Kim, however, proved ambitious. He managed to have Sunjo marry his daughter, occupied the leading posts in the government himself, and placed members of his family in most of the other important offices.

The Kim clan of Andong began its long ascendancy.

Perhaps it should be explained here that Koreans of the same surname thought of themselves as belonging to the same clan (they still do, to some extent), and that each clan was believed to have originated in a particular place, the name of which was always associated with the clan name. The case of the Kims, however, was unique. Instead of all belonging to the same clan, the Kims belonged to several different ones (Andong Kim, Kyongju Kim, Kimhae Kim, etc.). This perhaps accounts for the fact that so many Koreans are named Kim. The clan which dominated the government during King Sunjo's reign was the Andong Kim clan.

A similar thing happened when King Sunjo fell ill in 1827 and the Crown Prince was made regent. The Cho clan, from which the Crown Prince's wife came, replaced the Andong Kims. Their domination was made the easier by the fact that the Crown Prince predeceased his father and the throne went to his son, who ruled from 1834 to 1849 and is known as King Honjong.

Honjong died without male issue, and the throne went to King Ch'olchong, his uncle and a great-grandson of Yongjo. He was only nineteen at the time, and was under the guardianship of Sunjo's widow, the daughter of Kim Cho-sun. The Andong Kims returned to power, replacing the Cho family, and dominated the government for many years thereafter.

The repeated succession of minors to the throne and the domination of government by relatives of the queens resulted in a progressive weakening of royal power. Moreover, the efficient functioning of the bureaucracy was once more disrupted by favoritism and nepotism in appointments which made it impossible to choose officials according to merit. The examination system became an empty formality, the way to office being through bribes or through relationship to someone in high office. Able and competent young men developed such contempt for this corruption that few of them would even sit for the examinations.

The situation in provincial administration was, if anything, worse than that in the central government. District magistrates obtained their posts by bribery so commonly that regular prices were set for them. They in turn regularly received bribes from the local men they appointed to their staffs. Both then occupied themselves chiefly with extracting as much wealth as possible from the helpless farmers. The amounts collected for taxes were almost always considerably greater than the law provided, to the illegal profit of these officials, and various other pretexts were devised to collect more. The national finances were affected by these practices, and the government attempted to correct the situation by sending out secret inspectors with orders to report irregularities. But the inspectors proved just as susceptible to bribery as most other officials, and the scheme achieved no practical results.

During the nineteenth century all the various taxes and other government levies upon the population were unified in three categories: the land tax, the military exemption charge and the rice-loan system. This last, it will be recalled, had originally been devised in order to help the farmers through lean periods with interest-free loans, but had later developed into another means of taxing them when interest began to be charged. By the time we are discussing, the government was deriving more income from these loans than from the regular tax system.

The root of the government's financial problems was, as we have frequently pointed out before, the practice of exempting certain lands from taxation. Land belonging to the royal clan and land whose income was supposed to support government offices was exempt, and these lands grew as the royal clan proliferated and officials found ways to divert government income. Private individuals were continually getting their land withdrawn from the tax registers by bribing officials, especially in the southern provinces, which contained the best farmland. By the opening of the nineteenth century much regularly cultivated farmland was officially listed as wasteland, newly reclaimed land, or land uncultivated because of drought or flood, all of which were exempt from tax. The government land surveys which were supposed to determine tax obligations each year according to the land's ability to produce had become corrupt and ineffective.

Another difficulty was the rapacity of the local officials. The regular government land tax came to about a tenth of the harvest, which was not oppressive. But the local officials frequently invented taxes of which the central authorities had no knowledge, and the amount of his income that a farmer actually paid depended almost entirely on the district in which he lived. If his magistrate was an equitable man, taxes would be light and he could become relatively prosperous. If, as was more likely, his magistrate had obtained his position chiefly to enrich himself, the farmer might have to pay as much as a third of his harvest in taxes and charges of various kinds. Even after the tax in grain was commuted to a fixed amount in money, these practices continued. Frequently magistrates were forced into them because they had diverted government funds in their charge to private uses. Sometimes, reversing the practice of evading the land tax, even actual waste land was taxed.

The military exemption tax, generally paid in textiles, was cut in half about the middle of the eighteenth century, but still bore heavily on families with numerous men of military age. But the greatest confusion and corruption existed in the rice-loan system. The interest on these loans had been officially set at ten percent, and had originally been intended to defray the expenses of local administration. But when the central government demanded that it be sent to Seoul instead, various malpractices immediately set in. There was confusion over what proportion of the interest had to be paid to the central government. Various fees for carriage, storage and wastage were added, often unfairly, so that in these exactions also the amount a farmer was obliged to pay varied from district to district. If the loans were unpaid the interest on them was compounded, so that the amount demanded frequently rose out of all proportion to the amount of rice actually loaned.

Other forms of lending quickly developed with the coming of a money economy, and local officials took to lending out government funds at usurious interest for private gain. Many farmers were ruined by these loans and deserted their land in despair, taking to banditry or eking out a precarious living by farming hillsides in remote, mountainous areas. The financial structure of the kingdom verged on collapse, but no effective reforms were made.

All these evils could not but alienate the people from their government. There were ominous signs at the opening of the nineteenth century. Posters with anti-government slogans appeared mysteriously, and the popular custom of fortune-telling and divination was used to criticize the officials, some of these prophecies going so far as to foretell the downfall of the dynasty. The *kasa* folk-songs took on a menacing tone.

In P'yongan Province in the northwest there lived at this time a man named Hong Kyong-nae. He came of a yangban family, but he was poor and had not been given a government post. It was the general practice at the time to exclude most P'yongan scholars from the government, in fact, so that Hong found many kindred spirits in his province. Discontented and resentful, and possessing considerable abilities as a leader, he had soon assembled a large group who shared his feelings, and began to plot a rebellion. For three years he planned his moves and accumulated his forces. Discontented officials, merchants, scholars and fortune-tellers all joined him, and he found a ready supply of troops among the farmers who had been forced off their land by drought and put to work in the gold mines. The plan was that when all was ready, the rebels would strike simultaneously in all parts of the province, so that all the major towns would be taken at a single blow. Once this was accomplished, the rebel army would march on to Seoul.

The uprising began in 1812 with a rebel attack on the local government offices near Kasan. At the same time, Hong Kyong-nae led several hundred men in a successful attack on the neighboring town of Pakch'on and another rebel group took Kwaksan. Within six days, eight towns north of the Ch'ongch'on River were in rebel hands. Then, however, a rebel force was defeated by local government troops at Songnim-ni near Pakch'on, and Hong was forced to withdraw with his forces to the mountain fortress of Chongju.

Meanwhile, troops had been promptly dispatched from Seoul on receipt of news of the rebellion and these, on their arrival, soon recaptured the towns occupied by the rebels. Hong continued resistance as long as he could, but was ultimately killed in battle, after the fortress of Chongju had withstood a siege of a hundred days. Many of the rebels were taken captive. In all, the rebellion had lasted for five months.

There was some suspicion at the time that certain groups in Seoul might have collaborated with the rebels. Prince Unon, the second son of Prince Changhon (Changjo, the "coffin king"), was living in exile on Kanghwa Island, and there was a plot to depose King Sunjo and put this prince on the throne. Spies from the rebel army were supposed to have visited Seoul to coordinate their activities with those of the plotters. The intrigue was discovered and its leaders executed, however, and some scholars contend that it was this failure, together with the failure of some P'yongan towns to join the uprising, that led to its defeat. One of the ironic features of the defeat was that a group of artillerymen on their way to join the rebels was waylaid by government forces and forced to turn its guns against them.

The rebellion of Hong Kyong-nae was not an isolated incident but a plain indication that corruption and oppression had gone beyond tolerable limits. A whole province had risen in arms, and it had taken the government five months to suppress it. In 1813 it had to suppress another rising on Cheju Island, and in 1816 a Buddhist monk named Haksang began representing himself as a former comrade of Hong Kyong-nae, though he was really only a robber. Hong's name became a rallying cry for discontented people all over the country.

The suffering of the people was aggravated during the first half of the nineteenth century by a series of natural calamities. There were great floods in one or another of the southern provinces from 1810 to 1819, and in 1820 floods struck the whole country. Hwanghae suffered from floods in 1822, Kyongsang in 1823, Cholla in 1824, Hamgyong in 1829 and Ch'ungch'ong in 1832. Fires were frequent and no measures were taken to prevent them. In 1821 a cholera epidemic spread to Korea from China and ravaged the country for several years. Social unrest increased markedly.

There were no government relief measures after these disasters. Whole families wandered starving in the countryside, and the irrigation works that made rice culture possible fell into disrepair if the land was not seized by the royal clan or a local yangban. Destitute rural people poured into the cities or fled to the mountains, and as a result there were frequent forest-fires. Census registers ceased altogether to show the real population. For example, the census records show that in 1807 there were 1,764,504 households in the kingdom, and a population of 7,561, 403. The corresponding figures for 1837 were 1,578,823 and 6,755,280, indicating a decrease in population of some 800,000 in thirty years, an incredible figure even if re-bellions and natural calamities are taken into account. A similar startling decline is found in the figures for P'yong-an Province, where there appeared to be 260,000 fewer males in the second count. The logical inference from these figures is that many of the missing people were home-less vagabonds or bandits, and indeed there was an ominous increase in banditry and piracy during the period.

The farmers had no recourse. Appeals to the district magistrates went undelivered, or fell upon deaf ears. In Cholla Province most of the landlords were absentees, so that their tenants' troubles did not reach them. In Ch'ung-ch'ong, on the other hand, the violent rapacity of the local yangban was notorious, and the tenant farmers could hope for no relief from that quarter. All over the country dis-content was reaching the point of violence.

In the spring of 1862 a discontented ex-official led a farmers' uprising in the Chinju area of southwestern Kyongsang Province. The immediate cause was the ex-actions of the recently appointed military commander of the area, Paek Nak-sin. The rebels drove out the local magistrate, killed some of the petty officials, and sacked and burned houses. When this was reported to Seoul, the government dismissed Paek and another high provincial official and sent a special inspector to calm the people and determine the cause of the trouble. This official uncovered the illegal extortions of Paek Nak-sin and also found that similar small uprisings had taken place in numerous other towns in the province. The only result of this government action, however, was that numerous ringleaders of the rebellions were arrested and executed and nineteen were banished.

Only forty days after the Chinju uprising, another one took place at Iksan in Ch'ungch'ong Province in which three thousand people attacked the government office. At about the same time similar rebellions occurred at many locations throughout the three southern provinces, all following more or less the same pattern: several thousand people would attack the district government office, destroy tax records, drive the higher officials away, kill the magistrate's staff, who were the tools of his corruption, and sack and burn the houses of officials and the wealthy. The situation was compounded by the appearance of armed bandits who took this opportunity to carry off as much loot as they could find.

The ringleaders of most of these uprisings were arrested and executed, and the government did make some efforts to rectify the situation. All officials and Confucian scholars were invited to make suggestions for reform, and the government meanwhile attempted to curtail expenditures and find new sources of revenue. But the discussions of effective reforms came to nothing, and the office which had been set up to handle suggestions was eventually abolished.

When it became obvious that the government was not going to take action to redress the people's grievances, more uprisings followed throughout the country. They lasted all through 1862 and into the spring of 1863. The movement eventually burned itself out, but the grievances remained and there were no reforms. The social situation of the kingdom was still explosive.

It is quite possible that the alienation of the people because of economic distress was also at least partly responsible for the spread of Catholicism at this time. We have already noted how it came to Korea in the eighteenth century and how the government turned against it when it was found to conflict with Confucianism. The anti-Catholic measures had not been very severe, however, mostly because the religion had the sympathy of some members of the Southern faction, which then shared power with the Noron under the policy of opening careers to merit.

But with the death of King Chongjo, everything changed. The new King, Sunjo, was still a boy, and the court was dominated by his great-grandmother, who brought her family, the Andong Kims, back to power. The Andong Kims were members of the Noron faction, enemies of the Southerners, and strongly anti-Catholic. The new century opened with persecution.

Several prominent persons were executed for pro-Catholicism before the end of 1800. About three hundred of the several thouasnd Catholics in the country followed them to the block or died in prison. In 1801 the Chinese priest Chou Wen-mu (James Chou), the first ordained priest ever to enter Korea, gave himself up to the authorities in an effort to stop the persecution, and was executed.

But perhaps the most important incident in these persecutions was the case of Hwang Sa-yong. He had fled to a hiding-place in Ch'ungch'ong Province, and while there had written a letter to the French Bishop in Peking asking for help for the Catholics of Korea. But the letter, written in very small characters on a piece of silk cloth for easy concealment, was confiscated before it could be sent and read by the government authorities. What they saw gave them ample pretext for further suppression of the religion. After explaining why and how the persecution had begun and relating how it had proceeded and what the current situation was, Hwang requested that a French battleship be dispatched to Korea to protect Korean Catholics.

Catholicism had formerly been disliked because it seemed in conflict with Confucian propriety. Now it seemed also to involve the threat of a foreign invasion, a thing most dreaded by Koreans, who had plenty of bitter experience. Ever afterward the authorities would be able to point to this danger when anyone tried to explain the merits of Christianity to them. Although France was in no position to send a battleship to the Far East at that time, being embroiled in the Napoleonic wars so that the letter would probably have been ignored, persecution seemed more justified than ever, and it continued.

The situation was rendered even more difficult for the Catholics when, in 1805, the Manchu rulers of China also turned against Catholicism and began to persecute believers. But just as at its beginnings in ancient Rome, the church seemed to thrive on martyrdom. Suppressed in one place, it arose in another, and despite the danger thousands of people saw in it a release from the social and spiritual fetters imposed by Confucianism. Their faith was nurtured and sustained by the selfless devotion of a succession of French priests, who despite the near certainty of death continued coming to Korea to lead the faithful.

The French Foreign Mission Society (Société des Missions Étrangères) had been founded in Paris in 1651 and since that time had sent over 250 missionaries to Asia. In 1831, when Korea was removed from the jurisdiction of the Bishop of Peking and made a separate diocese, Barthélemy Brugière, who had been assistant to the Bishop of Siam, volunteered to serve as the new Bishop. His efforts to enter the country were unsuccessful, however, and he died of illness in Manchuria. It was not until 1836 that father Pierre Philibert Maubant managed to smuggle himself across the Yalu River and reach Seoul. Fathers Jacques Honoré Chastan and L.M. Joseph Imbert followed in 1837.

In order to conceal themselves from the authorities, the three French priests dressed in Korean mourning clothes, whose huge, wide hats completely hid their faces. Thus attired they went about their mission work to such effect that after only a year, in 1838, records speak of some nine thousand Korean Catholics. Communication with higher church authorities was maintained by sending secret messengers with the diplomatic missions to Peking.

The French priests were not left unmolested for long. In the spring of 1839 renewed persecution broke out. Many believers were arrested and eighty were executed. The three priests were seized one after another and put to death on the banks of the Han River. Of the eighty Koreans who died, fifty were women, an indication of the attractiveness of the new religion to people who were dominated and oppressed in practically all aspects of social life.

The Catholics were undeterred. In 1845 the first Korean priest, Kim Tae-gon (Andrew Kim), was ordained in Shanghai by Bishop Jean Ferréol after training in the Portuguese colony of Macao, the main base for Catholic missions in East Asia at the time, since it was ruled by a European Catholic power. In September of the same year Father Kim left Shanghai in a small boat, accompanied by Bishop Ferréol and Father Henri Daveluy. After six weeks they managed to enter Korea, where the horrors of the persecution of 1839 were still fresh in peoples' memories.

Meanwhile, news of the execution of the French priests had reached the Bishop of Peking through a letter written by Father Imbert just before his execution and smuggled out by one of the faithful. Three French warships which were cruising in Chinese waters were ordered to Korea to demand that amends be made. They arrived off the coast of Ch'ungch'ong Province in 1846, and the commander, Admiral Cécile, sent a letter to the King saying that he would return the following year and would expect an explanation of the deaths of French citizens. Two French ships did indeed arrive off Cholla Province the following year, but one of them was damaged by a rock on the coast and they left without fulfilling their mission.

The arrival of Bishop Ferréol and Father Daveluy with Father Kim Tae-gon reanimated the suppressed church. They were, of course, still forced to work in secret, for the authorities remained extremely hostile. In 1846 Father Kim was arrested while trying to contact a Chinese ship in order to send a letter to a French priest in China. He was executed after a short imprisonment, at the age of twenty-five.

But when King Ch'olchong came to the throne in 1849, the persecution slackened. Several more French priests entered the kingdom during his reign including Fathers Maistre, Jansou and Berneux. Bishop Ferréol and Father Jansou died of overwork during this period. Catholicism now began to expand vigorously. The French priests visited every district in Seoul, and began moving out to the villages of the surrounding area. Four more French priests arrived in 1861, bringing the number of missionaries to twelve. The number of Korean Catholics steadily increased, from around 11,000 in 1850 to some 23,000 in 1865. The extreme political confusion of Ch'olchong's reign made enforcement of the anti-Catholic laws difficult, and the authorities virtually ceased any effort to suppress the church.

In 1861 Seoul and the surrounding area were divided into parishes, each ministered to by one of the missionaries. Messages from higher church authorities, even from the Pope, were openly printed and distributed. There were converts even among the female attendants in the palace.

But this situation could not prevail for long. The mid-nineteenth century was a period of great instability for Korea as for the other nations of East Asia. With her social structure in a state of imminent collapse, so that the old norms and values seemed no longer to apply, she was being beset at the same time by the Western nations, which since the industrial revolution had far outstripped Asia in material power. For this reason the appeal of Christianity could not be considered simply on its merits, but was always associated with the Western powers. In many Korean minds it thus represented the encroachment of alien nations, something Korea had experienced many times before and of which she had a bitter hatred.

In order to understand the xenophobic isolationism which characterized Korean foreign policy in the later nineteenth century, it is necessary to give some account of the events during this period in other Asian nations, especially China and Japan, for it was partly from what happened to these two countries that Korea drew the conclusions on which that policy was based. These events mainly arose from the demands of Western nations for the opening of ports to trade. The dynamic growth of industrial capitalism demanded ever-expanding markets for the goods it produced, and many of the Western states were willing to back their demands with force if they felt it necessary.

The first major shock to East Asian states was the "Opium War" of 1839–42, in which the superior fire-power of British ships easily defeated the Chinese and forced them to sign a humiliating treaty. Resentment of this spread throughout China and finally brought about the T'ai-p'ing rebellion of 1850. This was a truly serious attempt at revolution, not a mere peasant uprising. The rebels wished to overthrow the Manchu Ch'ing dynasty and to expel the foreigners whom these rulers had admitted. They had made Nanking their capital by 1853, and controlled large areas of South China.

In 1856 a T'ai-p'ing port governor refused to allow a ship from Hong Kong to fly the British flag, and at about the same time a Frenchman was captured and killed by the rebels. The British and French, who had maintained neutrality in the conflict up to that time, sent a joint expeditionary force into China which took Kwangchou in January of 1858 and had occupied Tien-tsin by May of the same year. A new treaty was forced upon the Chinese under which the allied powers were allowed to maintain diplomatic missions in Peking, travel freely in China, carry on trade, and send Christian missionaries. Eleven new ports were to be opened to foreign ships, which were also to be permitted to travel up the Yangtze River, at that time under T'ai-p'ing control. When the Chinese attempted to violate this treaty in 1860 the allied forces of Britain and France reoccupied Tientsin and moved on to Peking. The Emperor fled to Jehol, leaving his brother, Prince Kung, to negotiate a fresh treaty. This time Tientsin itself became a treaty port, the Kowloon peninsula was added to the British colony of Hong Kong, and China was forced to pay the allies compensation for the war from customs duties. Similar treaties were concluded with Russia and the United States at this time.

In 1862 the T'ai-p'ing rebels moved into Kiangsi and Chekiang Provinces and began to threaten Shanghai, which was becoming one of the biggest centers of foreign trade. The Franco-British forces combined with those of the Ch'ing court in a concerted attack which drove the rebels back. By 1864 they had been completely defeated, and government control was restored throughout China.

Meanwhile, in July of 1853 an American flotilla under the command of Commodore Matthew Perry arrived at the Japanese port of Uraga with a letter from the President of the United States requesting that Japan open her ports to trade with the Americans and that diplomatic missions be exchanged. This created a national crisis. Japan had kept herself strictly aloof from almost all foreign contact ever since the beginning of the Tokugawa Shogunate more than two hundred years before. Many Japanese leaders favored refusing the request and driving the foreigners away by force on their promised return the following year.

But others were well aware of the Westerners' military power and had followed recent events in China. When Perry returned in 1854 a treaty was concluded which opened Japan to U.S. trade and granted extraterritoriality to U.S. citizens. By 1858 Japan had concluded similar treaties with Britain, Russia, France and the Netherlands. The preoccupation of the European powers with China and with Russian expansionism and the American Civil War saved Japan from the kind of foreign pressure experienced by China.

In Japan as in China there were rebellious feelings against the government for having yielded to the foreigners, and numerous anti-foreign incidents took place in 1862. There was no organized rebellion as in China, however, and by 1864 anti-foreign sentiment was fading. But there was a growing feeling that the Shogunate was corrupt and out of date. A movement began to restore the Emperor to his proper powers, which really meant to displace the Shogunate and install new and progressive-minded leaders. This movement culminated in 1867 when the last of the Shoguns yielded to the new leaders and abdicated. In the following year the Meiji Emperor left the old Imperial capital of Kyoto and was installed in the Shogun's palace at Edo, which was now renamed Tokyo, the capital of a renovated Japan.

The Korean government watched these developments in China and Japan with growing trepidation, and each new encroachment of the Westerners hardened their determination to allow no foreigners on Korean soil. Korea was not yet a target of foreign attention at mid-century, but there were clear signs that her turn was coming. An English ship had appeared off the Ch'ungch'ong coast as early as 1831 demanding trade, and in 1845 another English ship not only asked for trade relations but began surveying the coast in order to make charts. These ships and the increasing numbers that followed them were turned away with the information that it was illegal to allow foreigners to enter the country. The powers were occupied elsewhere in Asia, and for the time Korea was left in peace. But the news of the taking of Peking, the flight of the Chinese Emperor and the humiliating treaty forced upon China threw the court into a panic. Although no foreign troops had yet appeared, the frequent appearance of Western ships, the spread of Catholicism, and the mounting inflow of Western goods plainly showed that sooner or later Korea would share the fate of other East Asian nations.

With these external pressures building up around her, Korea was experiencing internal troubles as well. The gradual collapse of the traditional class structure which had been going on since the eighteenth century and the arbitrary rule of the King's in-laws which began in the nineteenth were rendering Korean political institutions ineffective. Confucianism, which assumed a static, hierarchical society, was becoming irrelevant to a society in a process of irrevocable change.

The yangban class was disintegrating. Those in office remained the aristocracy, but yangban out of office, and with no prospect of it in the faction-ridden government, sank to the level of commoners. Confucian thought made no provision for this, and indeed it was a sort of heresy even to admit the possibility of such a situation.

Buddhism, disdained by orthodox Confucians, had managed to survive but offered no alternative to the official philosophy. The women of the royal clan patronized it, as did women generally, and it had some appeal to the lower classes, but it had long lost any pretensions to intellectual respectability in Korea. It had assimilated numerous folk-beliefs and had itself become a kind of folk religion, remote from political realities.

The same was true of the Taoist beliefs which so strongly

influenced Korean thought, particularly through geomancy. The chief influence of Taoism at this time was a negative one, for the scholars who truly understood the doctrines of Lao-tzu and Chuang-tzu fastened upon the ideal of the scholar-hermit who attains superhuman powers through solitary study and meditation. In this way Taoism contributed to the alienation of yangban scholars, who abandoned Confucian political ideals completely. On the other hand, Taoism contributed to the body of folk-belief.

Among the majority of the people, the old animism prevailed, as it had since the beginning. The *mudang*, usually female shamans, were resorted to in all emergencies in a remarkable persistence of very primitive religious beliefs. Chinese influence had added to the basic Korean animism a belief in prophecy and divination by certain occult methods. This belief was very old, but in the nineteenth century centered on a book called, *Chonggam-nok*, which appeared sometime around the end of the seventeenth century. Since the fate of nations as well as the fate of individuals could be predicted by use of this book, or so most people believed, many groundless rumors and fantastic ideas were given substance by recourse to it. Popular uprisings resulting from injustice and oppression were frequently sparked by predictions based upon this book.

In reaction to the failure of the old values, a new religion appeared around 1860. Its founder was Ch'oe Che-u (1824–1864), a descendant of a fallen yangban family. He felt keenly the economic distress and moral decay of his society, and saw that only a new set of values relevant to modern conditions and having the sanction of religious belief could correct the evils of the time. After a period of wandering during which he tried many different ideas, he returned to his home in Kyongju and there announced the foundation of the new religion.

The new creed was called *Tonghak*, or Eastern Learning,

as opposed to *Sohak*, Western Learning (i. e. Catholicism), a clear indication of one of the purposes of the movement. Ch'oe made the usual claims of the founder of a sect, saying that he had received inspiration from heaven, that he was abused and misunderstood, and that he received revelations in his dreams. Tonghak had a special appeal to impoverished yangban and also to the farmers whose sufferings we have described in this chapter. It spread so rapidly that within three years there was a branch in nearly every district with its own leader chosen from among the local believers. All believers paid a sum in proportion to their income to support the sect and the local leaders were responsible for religious training and making converts.

The government looked with no particular favor upon a religion which condemned it in so many ways. In 1863, when it had become so widespread as to seem a serious problem, Ch'oe and twenty of his followers were arrested, and the following year Ch'oe was executed at Taegu. This, however, did not suffice to check the movement. A successor to Ch'oe Che-u, Ch'oe Si-hyong, quickly appeared and the movement went underground. When King Kojong came to the throne as a minor and the Taewon'gun (Regent) took over the government, the movement spread further, largely owing to the Taewon'gun's arbitrary suppression of the sowon and the yangban class and his opposition to all things foreign.

Ch'oe Si-hyong and his successor organized in writing the doctrines of the cult. These were in two parts, the *Yusa*, consisting mainly of hymns to be sung, and written in Han'gul, and the *Tonggyong taejon* or Great Eastern Scripture, the esoteric doctrines of the cult, written in Chinese. It is said that Ch'oe Si-hyong had to dictate the founder's poetic compositions because he was too ignorant to write them out himself.

Tonghak contained elements of many of the religions

and philosophies with which its founder was acquainted. It begins with reverence for "Heaven," that vague deity which figures in so many beliefs of Chinese provenance, and teaches also a kind of predestination. These ideas were drawn from two of the Confucian classics, the *Classic of Changes* and the *Record of Rituals*. From Taoism it borrowed the idea that men could develop superhuman powers and become immortal if they lived in accordance with the will of Heaven. Tonghak thought drew the conclusion that all men should be treated as potential immortals, heavenly beings. There is also a suggestion of Buddhism in the manner in which immortality is to be attained.

But these high-minded ideas were not sufficient to make the religion popular among the common people. It also contained elements of native Korean shamanism, such as the belief that illnesses could be cured by means of certain special Tonghak incantations, which were actually quite similar to those of the *mudang,* the female shamans who were a characteristic feature of this ancient Korean belief. Primitive animism was united with sophisticated Confucian and Buddhist ideas by means of the concept of *ch'i,* a Chinese term which translates into English, but only approximately, as *spirit.* A sort of pantheism was made a part of the religion, in which *ch'i* was said to be the creator of all things and immanent in all things, and the spirit of man was *chich'i,* the essence of *ch'i.* The spirits of Korean animism were subsumed under this concept as were the concept of Heaven and the order of the universe, which was taken over from Chu Hsi.

Tonghak was thus a syncretic religion. It even contained some Catholic elements. However, it strongly rejected all the religions from which it derived. It envisioned an earthly paradise which should come into existence when the corrupt bureaucracy had been overthrown and the foreigners, with their disruptive ideas and their crude commercialism, had been driven away. In many ways it resembled the beliefs of the T'ai-p'ing revolutionaries of China in its basic nationalism and opposition to foreign encroachments, features that were to make it a formidable element in the political developments at the close of the nineteenth century.

PART SIX

The Modern Period (II)

Chapter 24

Isolationism in the Later Nineteenth Century

King Ch'olchong died in 1864, leaving no male heir. This meant, of course, an immediate struggle over the succession, and this time it was a struggle which had fateful results for the kingdom. Ch'olchong's wife was an Andong Kim, and this powerful clan, which had dominated the government ever since Chongjo's reign, was naturally anxious to see a King of its choice on the throne. But it was the custom in the Yi dynasty that when the King died without issue the new King should be chosen by the Dowager Queen. The nearest thing to a Dowager Queen there was, was the wife of Ch'olchong's cousin Ikchong, who had a dynastic title but never reigned because he died before his father, King Sunjo.

This lady belonged to the Cho clan, the most powerful rival of the Andong Kims. She seized the opportunity which family custom offered and made an appointment which she felt would guarantee the Chos' domination of the court. Her choice fell upon the son of an obscure descendant of King Yongjo named Yi Ha-ung, who had managed to survive the various political conflicts by having no affiliation with any of the factions and by making himself appear of no account. The boy was only twelve, and so would not become a factor in politics for some time, while the father, the Cho clan felt, could easily be used as a tool for their domination of the court. They were in for a surprise.

The boy Yi Myong-bok duly ascended the throne in 1864 (posthumous title Kojong) and his father was made regent and given the title Taewon'gun (Prince of the Great Court), a title bestowed upon the living father of a King. He proved to be one of the most powerful personalities in the history of the Yi dynasty. Within a short time after his son's accession he was in complete control of court and government and no clan or faction could stand against him. So strong an impression did he make upon his contemporaries that his official title, Taewon'gun, though it had been given to other men at other times, became permanently associated with him, and he is known to this day as *the* Taewon'gun.

The Taewon'gun represented all the virtues of the Confucian tradition. He was uncompromising, honest, and dedicated to the creation of a society upon the lines prescribed by the great sage. Unfortunately, he also represented the defects of Confucian thought—the rigidity of mind, resistance to change, refusal to face realities which conflicted with his beliefs. It was the tragic irony of his life that he came to power at a time when the ideals in which he sincerely believed had become outmoded. Only a dynamic society with rapidly expanding commerce and industry could successfully oppose the mounting pressure from the West, as the example of Japan clearly showed. The Taewon'gun could not see this. His only answer to Western pressure was to attempt to isolate Korea completely from the outside world, refusing all foreign contact and violently repressing all foreign ideas at home. If in the process many people suffered and died, it was not primarily because the Taewon'gun was a power-hungry tyrant. His sins were the sins of an idealist, which unfortunately are often more serious and harmful than those of a mere criminal. History had passed him by before ever he was born, and he did not know it.

The new ruler first set about breaking the power of clans and factions at court and reestablishing royal authority and power. The Andong Kims were driven from the positions they had occupied in the previous reign and his own men were appointed in their place. Old government institutions which had fallen into abeyance under clan rule were restored, in particular the State Council, which went all the way back to the early Yi dynasty, and *Pibyonsa,* the civil-military council, was abolished. The law codes were newly revised, as were the household law of the royal clan and the rules of court ritual. As far as possible, the court was restored to its status and organization in the early years of the dynasty.

In order to break the power of the factions and prevent their re-emergence at a later time, all of the sowon were closed except forty-seven which had a legitimate function as shrines to famous scholars. The sowon had become not only factional bases but also means to evade military duty or taxes, and themselves possessed land and slaves. All this now became national property. Corrupt local officials were strictly disciplined and their illicit profits confiscated. The taxation for military funds was reorganized and for the first time imposed upon yangban as well as commoners. The rice-loan system, which had become a tool of exploitation, was abolished, and the original system of interest-free loans to farmers in time of need was restored.

All these measures served the royal dignity in practical ways and also benefited the kingdom, but in certain directions the Taewon'gun appears to have been fiscally blind. At a time when the government was chronically short of funds and new sources of revenue had to be found, Kyongbok palace, which had lain in ruins ever since the Japanese invasion of 1592, was rebuilt on a lavish scale. The land tax rose, a transit tax was imposed upon all persons entering or leaving Seoul, and huge exactions artfully designated "gift money" were made from both officials and commoners. The coinage was debased, which had the effect of encouraging counterfeiters and causing a sudden rise in prices. By the time the palace was finished in 1867, after two years of work, the government was on the verge of bankruptcy.

In 1866 the Taewon'gun had his attention drawn to the Catholics by a rash proposal from one of them, a former official named Nam Chong-sam, to appeal to France for help against the Russians, who were now appearing on Korea's northern border. Learning in this way of the numbers and influence of the Catholics in the kingdom, he launched a great persecution which lasted until 1872. Nine of the twelve French priests were captured and executed, only Fathers Ridel, Calais and Féron managing to escape. About eight thousand Korean Catholics lost their lives, and many more were imprisoned. This was the first evil fruit of the policy of Confucian orthodoxy and international isolation. There were to be more.

Just before and during the persecutions, and in some instances in relation to them, Western ships appeared on Korea's coasts with increasing frequency. However, their only effect seems to have been to increase the Taewon'gun's stubbornness. The occupation of Peking in 1860 by a Franco-British force had been a great shock, and many Korean officials anxiously counselled military preparedness. Foreign goods, especially British textiles, were appearing in Korean ports and border cities in increasing quantities, and this was felt to be an economic threat, draining off money and grain. Western vessels demanding trade were seen as threats to the kingdom and were rebuffed, sometimes with violence.

Russian warships had already appeared off the Hamgyong coast in 1865, indirectly touching off the persecution of the Catholics. In 1866 an American merchant ship, the

General Sherman, sailed up the Taedong River toward P'yongyang in defiance of Korean officials. It was attacked, burned and sunk with the loss of all of its crew, greatly to the delight of the Taewon'gun and his government, who were thus encouraged in the mistaken belief that foreign interlopers could easily be driven off by force.

News of the persecution of Catholics and the execution of French priests had reached Peking through the escape of Father Ridel. Bellonet, the French Minister to China, was for immediate retaliation and so informed the Chinese government. The French Far East Fleet, however, was at that time engaged in the fighting involved in the French colonization of Indochina, and its commander Admiral Ross could spare only three ships for the expedition to Korea. One of these was damaged near Kanghwa Island, and the other two were able to do no more than reconaissance before returning to report. In the following month, however, seven French ships with Admiral Ross in command appeared off Inch'on. A detachment of troops landed on Kanghwa Island and occupied Kanghwa city, which they looted. However, they found that five hundred picked troops armed with muskets had been stationed on the island in expectation of attack. The French retired under fire, suffering about thirty casualties. Unable to mount an effective attack with the men and equipment at his disposal, Admiral Ross and his seven ships sailed away.

The Taewon'gun was in high spirits, and proudly informed the governments of China and Japan of the failure of the French attack. Military preparations of all kinds were pushed forward, especially coastal defense and the casting of cannon, in the expectation that future foreign attacks could be driven off just as easily. The persecution of Catholics went on unabated.

A somewhat comical incident, but one with great significance for Koreans, occurred shortly after the French affair, in 1868, and served to intensify deeply the anti-foreign attitude of the government. A Shanghai-based German merchant named Ernest Oppert had been twice rebuffed in efforts to trade in Korea during the 1860s. Hearing of the French retreat and having learned of the persecutions from the escaped French priest Father Féron, Oppert devised a fantastic plan. Together with a few picked confederates, he would sail to Korea and enter the country secretly. Once there, he would dig up the tomb of the Taewon'gun's father, sail away with the relics, and refuse to return them until the country was open to Western trade.

That anyone could even conceive such a plan was sufficiently strange, but Oppert actually tried to carry it out. Father Féron was brought into the plot, together with six other Westerners, some Malays, and a few Korean Catholics to act as guides. The ship *China* was chartered, a Chinese crew engaged and in the early summer of 1868 this group set out on its bizarre mission. Reaching Asan Bay in Ch'ungch'ong Province, they embarked in a small boat and went up a river to Kaya-dong, the location of the tomb. They found, however, that the grave-mound was far too large for a few people with picks and shovels to despoil it in a short time, and they dared not linger for fear of being discovered, which would have meant certain death. Reluctantly they abandoned the project and returned to the ship in time to catch the ebbing tide.

This was not the end of the matter, however. Instead of returning immediately to China, Oppert sailed north to Kanghwa where he informed the astonished local authorities that he had profaned the grave of the Taewon'gun's father in retaliation for the execution of the French missionaries, and added to this a renewed demand that Korea be opened to Western trade. The Korean reaction was what might have been expected, and after a clash in which two Malays in Oppert's party were wounded, the *China* sailed for Shanghai.

A greater offense than this against a rigidly orthodox Confucian like the Taewon'gun could hardly be imagined. Fears of Western political domination were now reinforced by a hearty detestation of Westerners and all their ways. Oppert could have done nothing more calculated to intensify the persecution of Catholics and guarantee the exclusion of foreigners from Korea. When later he wrote a book about Korea, he had a great deal to say about the Taewon'gun's exclusion policy, but was strangely reticent about this particular incident.

Meanwhile, American diplomatic officials in China were becoming concerned about the fate of the *General Sherman*, which had sailed to Korea but never returned. When the French expedition returned with the news that a foreign ship had burned and sunk in the Taedong River, American Minister to China Anson Burlingame asked the Chinese government to inquire of the Koreans whether it had been the *Sherman*. The Korean government replied belligerently but vaguely that it had been an English merchant ship and that they were ready to repel any attack by Westerners. Dissatisfied with this reply, the Americans sent the naval ship *Wachusett* to Korea early in 1867. Frustrated in his attempts to gather information, the commander had to retire. Again in the following year the U.S.S. *Shenandoah* sailed up the Taedong River, but with no better results than its predecessor.

Now virtually certain that the Koreans had destroyed the *Sherman* and killed her crew, the Americans decided upon retaliation. After announcing their intentions to the Koreans through the American mission to China, they dispatched five ships under the command of the Admiral of the Asian Fleet John Rodgers. In 1871 these ships appeared off Kanghwa Island and sent out a small steam launch to survey the coast. The Kanghwa shore batteries promptly opened fire on it and a sharp artillery duel ensued, ending in the withdrawal of the launch.

The American ships then concentrated their fire on the island and succeeded in silencing the guns and landing troops, who occupied part of the island after overcoming the desperate resistance of the Korean soldiers under the command of O Chae-yon, who was killed in the fighting. There were fifty-three Koreans killed and twenty-four wounded, while the Americans counted three dead and nine wounded. Not having expected such strong resistance and judging it foolhardy to risk the loss of any more of his small force, Rodgers re-embarked his men and returned to his base in China.

The temporary success of the Koreans in repulsing Western attacks and incursions was not primarily attributable to Korean military prowess, as the Taewon'gun imagined. In the first place, none of the Western powers considered the opening of Korea important enough to send a large-scale invasion force against her. In the second place, all of the powers had more important preoccupations elsewhere—Britain in India, Russia in the Kurile Islands north of Japan, France in Indochina, and the United States with the aftermath of the great Civil War.

But the Taewon'gun exulted in these small victories, and proclaimed to the people that he would continue repulsing evil. As symbols of his determination, he erected monuments in all parts of the country with the following inscription: "Not to fight back when invaded by the Western barbarians is to invite further attacks, and selling out the country in peace negotiations is the greatest danger to be guarded against." The country was living on borrowed time.

While these events were going on in Korea, a process

was beginning in Japan that was to have the gravest consequences for all of East Asia, and ultimately for the whole world. After the Americans had pried her doors open in 1854, Japan concluded treaties with most of the other Western powers. At the same time, numerous Japanese leaders began taking a realistic look at Japan's situation with relation to these powers. They decided that the only chance for Japan to avoid the fate of China was to adopt Western technology as rapidly as possible, so as to make the country strong enough, both economically and militarily, to resist any threat of foreign domination. To this end the old, conservative government of the Tokugawa Shoguns had to be got rid of. We have already mentioned how, in 1868, the last Shogun abdicated and the Emperor became the figurehead of a new government intent on modernization.

The new government was also intent on enhancing its position as an Asian power. One of its first diplomatic actions was an offer to mediate between Korea and the United States in the *Sherman* dispute, an offer which the Taewon'gun of course refused. But the Japanese proved far more persistent than any Western power in their efforts to open Korea to diplomatic relations and trade. In 1870 a mission was sent to announce the establishment of the new regime and to present credentials to the Korean government as the first step toward setting up diplomatic missions. But the Taewon'gun's government, which disapproved of the removal of the Shogun, refused to accept the credentials, complaining that they were not written in sufficiently respectful terms, and the Japanese were compelled to return home. Again in 1872 a Japanese party appeared at the southern city of Tongnae, this time aboard two naval vessels. But the district magistrate would not even allow them to proceed to Seoul, and after a frustrating wait of some months they departed. Some Japanese leaders thereupon began demanding that Korea be made to submit to Japanese demands by force. But others, who had been to Europe and were aware of the great strength of the Western nations, contended that Japan was not yet strong enough for military adventures, and they won out. But the invasion of Korea in one way or another was only postponed, not abandoned.

The Taewon'gun and his government, for their part, seeing the Japanese wearing Western-style clothes and traveling in Western-style ships, concluded that the Japanese were the same as the "Western barbarians" and could be disposed of with equal ease. They were equally unrealistic in their relations with China, dutifully reporting all important events to the Chinese court as had always been done in the past, and requesting help and advice, ignoring the fact that since 1860 China had been in no position to help anybody, not even herself. Like the hero of a Greek tragedy, Korea advanced toward her inexorable fate with her eyes stubbornly and tightly closed.

Chapter 25

Early Relations with Japan

While the Taewon'gun's isolationist policy was generally popular, many of his other actions were not. The taxation which financed his building projects was widely resented, as was his debasement of the coinage. Imposing the military tax on the yangban made him unpopular in his own class, and his closing of most of the sowon was an added grievance. In the court itself the fall from power of the Andong Kims had made him powerful enemies and their rivals of the Cho clan were equally hostile. Finally, the persecution of the Catholics had filled the people with fear and horror.

Knowing the danger to a strong administration often posed by the relatives of queens, the Taewon'gun had chosen his son's wife with care. He selected a girl from the Min family, to which his own wife belonged, who had lost her parents as a child and would thus be unable, he reasoned, to form a strong faction at court. In this he was mistaken. Even without parents the intelligent, energetic and ambitious Queen Min was able to form a powerful faction as soon as she reached adulthood. In marrying her to his son the Taewon'gun had placed at the center of power the deadliest of all his many enemies.

This antipathy began when the son born to King Kojong and Queen Min died in childhood, and the Taewon'gun attempted to have a son born to the King and a concubine elevated to the rank of Crown Prince. The Queen's relative Min Sung-ho set about forming a faction, which he found easy to do. Many high officials openly pointed out that the King was, after all, twenty-two years old, and capable of ruling in his own right. Finally a scholar named Ch'oe Ik-hyon prepared a formal document of impeachment in which he set forth at length all of the Taewon'gun's shortcomings. This was the signal for all those who had hitherto remained silent to speak out against the Regent. He had no choice but to retire to his estate at Yangju. Queen Min and her family were supreme at court.

Japan had been anxiously following developments in Korea, watching for an opportunity to open the country. Japan needed markets for her new industries. She was also anxious to prevent Korea from being dominated by any other power, lest this prove a threat to her. There were even some Japanese who favored a military invasion, and there was considerable political conflict over the issue. When the Taewon'gun retired, renewed Japanese attempts were made to open relations. A Japanese envoy again appeared at Tongnae, a southern city near the modern port of Pusan, in 1875, carrying formal proposals from the Emperor. Once more, however, the local Korean officials objected that the messages were not written in sufficiently respectful terms, and the mission had to return empty-handed.

The Japanese now decided to apply the lesson they had learned from the Americans in 1854. On the pretext of surveying sea routes, the Japanese battleship *Unyo* and another ship sailed into Pusan and then north to the Bay of Yonghung. In September of 1875 the ship returned, this time to Yongjong Island on the west coast. The captain and twenty men landed on Kanghwa Island ostensibly to get drinking-water. Guards stationed there fired on them and they withdrew, returning the fire. Ships were then sent to Pusan and a contingent of marines landed. Armed clashes with Korean troops occurred once more. After they judged that the Koreans had been sufficiently impressed, the Japanese notified the Koreans that negotiations must now begin. Six naval vessels conveyed a Japanese envoy and his party to Kanghwa Island.

The Korean officials were in a dilemma. A majority of them still favored the absolute isolationism which had been the policy of the Taewon'gun. But the demonstrations of the Japanese ships had shown that Japan would use force if necessary, and that her military power was formidable. After many meetings and arguments, the Korean government very reluctantly sent negotiators to Kanghwa, where a treaty of amity was drawn up and signed in February, 1876.

That Korea would even reluctantly sign such a treaty was at least partly the result of the fact that King Kojong and Queen Min had been trying to keep themselves as well informed as they could on contemporary events through the Korean envoys in China. The information they received showed clearly the crisis which was developing as a result of the contact between the tradition-bound, slow-changing Orient and the powerful and dynamic civilization of the West. On the one hand, they heard with horror of the Western encroachments on Chinese sovereignty, which had grown to such an extent that the Emperor had been compelled to flee from his capital. They heard of the spread of Christianity, so subversive of Confucian ideals, the inflow of Western goods that was distorting the Chinese economy, and the opium evil that also resulted from Western trade. But they also heard of the wonders of Western technology, especially as it applied to military weapons, and they were introduced for the first time to the Western concept of diplomatic relations between nations on equal terms, instead of the suzerain-vassal relationship they were accustomed to. How to acquire the advantages of Western civilization without falling victim to the Westerners themselves was the dilemma of all the peoples of East Asia in the nineteenth century.

These ideas or something like them probably underlay the Korean agreement to the Kanghwa Treaty. A majority of the people, however, still disliked the idea, and had to be placated by the argument that Korea was not opening her doors to all the world, but only to Japan, a neighbor with whom the traditional relations of former days were now being restored. This was a feeble argument, however, for Korea had entered into a modern diplomatic relationship, not one of the traditional Chinese type, and the treaty she had signed was extremely disadvantageous.

The Kanghwa Treaty was modeled upon those which the Western powers had imposed upon China. It first declared that Korea entered into this new relationship as a free and sovereign state on an equal basis with Japan. The significance of this seemingly innocuous statement was that Japan was attempting to detach Korea from its traditional relationship with China. This would mean that Japan would have a free hand in the exploitation of Korea without any interference from the Chinese. The Japanese were to go on guaranteeing Korean independence and sovereignty down to the day they annexed the nation to Japan and snuffed out its sovereignty altogether.

The treaty also provided that diplomatic missions be exchanged and permanently maintained and that Pusan and two other ports be opened to Japanese trade. Japanese merchants were to be allowed to trade unhindered in these ports, and were also to be given the right to lease land and buildings for business purposes and for housing. Japanese vessels were to be allowed to conduct survey and mapping operations in Korean waters. Most importantly, Japanese nationals in Korea were to have the right of extraterritoriality, which placed them outside the jurisdiction of Korean courts. While in Korea they could be tried for crimes only by Japanese consular courts. This was the feature of the treaties with Western powers that was most widely resented, for it not only enabled foreigners to commit crimes with relative impunity but also implied that the nation's system of law was primitive or unjust.

The Japanese were quick to take advantage of the treaty. Agents of Japanese firms began acquiring Korean property, a process that was to impoverish the Koreans before it was over. Prohibited from making any effective regulations, Korean officials had to watch helplessly while Japanese goods overwhelmed what domestic industry there was and drained off Korean wealth. And the consular courts in which Japanese guilty of crimes were tried were seldom particularly severe.

The most disputed point was which ports beside Pusan should be opened. The Japanese had been busily gathering data on the military and economic advantages of various Korean ports, and proposed Wonsan on the northeast coast and Chemulp'o (Inch'on) on the west coast near Seoul. The Koreans objected that Wonsan was too near Yonghung, where the ancestors of King T'aejo, the founder of the dynasty, were buried, and that Inch'on was too close to the capital. Inconclusive negotiations continued for several years, but finally, despite strong public opinion against it, Wonsan was opened in 1880 and Inch'on in 1883.

A supplement to the treaty and regulations for trade were agreed to shortly after it went into effect. Japanese diplomats in Korea were to be free to travel throughout the country and were to have residences in each of the treaty ports. Japanese currency was allowed to enter Korea, and Japanese were allowed to take Korean currency to Japan. All articles imported from or exported to Japan were to be free of duty for several years, a provision which made it impossible to protect domestic industry and so prevented Korea's economic growth. It was conceded that in case of national emergencies such as invasions, the Korean government should have the right to prohibit the export of rice.

As the ports opened one by one, Japanese merchants flocked to them, and soon there were large numbers of Japanese residents. For the first few years they enjoyed a near monopoly of trade, and Korean merchants suffered serious losses. The Japanese penetration of the country had begun.

The Japanese minister arrived in Korea in 1879 and the legation was temporarily set up in the Ch'ongsugwan, a building just outside the Great West Gate. Korean envoys were sent to Japan, and thus for the first time Korea had a chance to observe at first hand how an Asian nation went about adopting Western technology. Kim Ki-su and others had visited Japan immediately after the conclusion of the treaty and returned with the information that Japan had adopted Western military weapons, telegraphy, steamships and agricultural techniques, and that young men had been sent to Western nations to study. In 1880 a more comprehensive mission headed by Kim Koeng-jip (better known as Kim Hong-jip) set out. Its specific purpose was to discover what were the Japanese intentions toward Korea, in negotiating the supplement to the treaty. The Japanese Minister of Foreign Affairs, Inoue Kaoru explained to the party that Japan expected Korean ports to be opened shortly to Western trade, and the supplementary regulations were to protect Japanese merchants against this competition.

While he was in Japan, Kim Koeng-jip had the opportunity to meet the Chinese Minister to Tokyo Ho Ju-chang and the councillor Huang Tsun-hsien and to discuss the international situation with them, particularly as it affected Korea. Councillor Huang took a particular interest in Korea, and on this occasion presented to Kim a book he had written called *Korean Strategy* (Chao-hsien T'se-lueh). Huang believed that the most serious danger for Korea at that time was the expansionism of the Russian Empire. He advised that Korea should adopt a pro-Chinese policy, but should retain close ties with Japan. He also advised an alliance with the United States in order to secure protection against Russia. He said that Korea should open trade relations with Western nations and should achieve prosperity by applying Western technology to domestic industry. He added that Korean youths should be sent to China and Japan to study, and that Western teachers of technical and scientific subjects should be invited to Korea.

When Kim Koeng-jip returned home, he gave this book to King Kojong. The King read it attentively and then asked that all the ministers of state read it also. It seemed to them clear that Korean policies would have to be changed to fit the changing international situation, and that Huang's book gave an accurate picture of this situation. They had it printed and distributed to yangban scholars throughout the nation, in the hope of securing a general consensus for policies which they felt Korea would be forced in one way or another to adopt.

This hope was vain. The scholars had been opposed to opening the country from the very first, and even the arguments of a shrewd Chinese diplomat could not change their minds. Ch'oe Ik-hyon, who had impeached the Taewon'gun, had asserted that the treaty with Japan would be against the national interest. He said the Japanese were just like the "Western barbarians," and that relations with them would mean the spread of subversive notions like Catholicism. He also said (and he was right) that the treaty would mean an inundation of Japanese goods and the outflow of Korean rice, which would surely ruin the economy. Most of the others agreed with Ch'oe.

The government knew through its envoys that the Japanese had wreaked a great deal more havoc upon China than was contemplated in the Kanghwa Treaty, including the building of Japanese-controlled railroads and outright invasions, such as that of the island of Taiwan. It was aware of the disadvantages of the Kanghwa Treaty, but had accepted it in order to stave off worse evils. It was also aware that the only hope for Korea was to adopt Western technology in order to make the nation powerful enough to withstand Japanese encroachments.

To the scholars, however, there was little to choose between the Japanese and the Western nations, and any change in traditional ways meant to them the destruction of the social order. The response to the distribution of *Korean Strategy* was a joint memorial to the throne from scholars in every province. It stated that the ideas in the book were mere abstract theories, unrealizable in practice, and that the adoption of Western technology was not the only way to enrich the country. The real objective of the policies the book recommended, the scholars thought, was the spread of Catholicism and the subversion of Confucian principles. They demanded that the number of envoys exchanged, ships engaged in trade and articles of trade be strictly limited, and that all foreign books in Korea be sought out and destroyed. One cannot doubt the scholars' sincere devotion to their country, but their attitude was extremely unfortunate.

Despite all these objections, the government did what it could to modernize the country. In 1881 a large fact-finding mission was sent to Japan for a stay of seventy days. They were to inspect Japanese government offices, factories, military and police organizations and business practices. They also obtained information about innovations in the Japanese government, especially the proposed constitution.

They were briefed on the manner in which Japan had been forced to open her doors to the United States in 1854, on the Japanese annexation of the Ryukyu Islands, and on the Russian encroachment on Hokkaido, the northernmost of the main Japanese islands. Each of the party duly prepared a report to the throne upon his return.

Partly on the basis of these reports, the government was reorganized. Under a sort of cabinet modeled after a Chinese institution there were now twelve bureaus. Of particular interest was the matter of foreign relations, for in this department one special bureau handled relations with China, whose suzerainty was still recognized despite the Kanghwa Treaty,while a separate one handled relations with other countries. There was a bureau for commerce (an innovation) and a renovated military department which endeavored to modernize the armaments of the army and navy. Civilian departments were also set up to import Western technology. As far as it could against widespread opposition, the government was trying to put into practice at least some of the ideas in Huang's *Korean Strategy*.

The modernization of the military involved much more than merely buying guns. The technology of weapon manufacture had to be learned, and men had to be trained in modern military tactics. King Kojong had set up an elite army unit soon after the Taewon'gun's retirement, and this unit supplied men to be trained in modern methods.

Here the rivalry between China and Japan began to show itself. The leading Chinese statesman Li Hung-chang, anxious about the threat to Chinese security implied by Japanese influence in Korea, proposed that the Korean government send a select group of men to China to study weapons technology and military skills. Korea, however, decided that the students should learn weapons technology only. Negotiations were started late in 1879, and the next year it was agreed to send Koreans to study in China.

The Japanese, too, were quick to see the advantages that training the Korean military would give them. Before students could be sent to China, Japan volunteered through her minister in Seoul to supply rifles and train a unit of the Korean army to handle them. Queen Min's faction acceded to this plan, with the reservation that students should still be sent to China. Eighty soldiers were chosen from the Five Camps and placed under the special guard unit established earlier, and a Japanese officer was assigned to train them. The unit came increasingly under the control of Queen Min and her group, and was given special privileges which aroused envy in the regular military. This was the meager result of the policy of increasing armaments and developing a powerful army.

But even this modest step aroused opposition because of the way in which it was done. The special treatment of the training unit caused resentment among the other troops, and the arrival of a Japanese officer to train it aggravated the resentment of the scholars who had opposed the Kanghwa Treaty. In September of 1881 a plot was uncovered to overthrow Queen Min's faction, depose King Kojong, and place the Taewon'gun's eldest illegitimate son, Yi Chaeson, on the throne. The plot was frustrated, but although the Taewon'gun was generally believed to be at the bottom of it, the fact that he was the King's father kept him safe.

Against powerful opposition, twenty yangban scholars and eighteen artisans were finally sent to Tien-tsin in China. There they studied the making of gunpowder and ammunition, electricity, chemistry, smelting, mechanical engineering, cartography, and other basic subjects related to military affairs. This was the first really effective attempt to modernize the Korean military, and it balanced to some extent the influence of Japan.

The government was now reorganized again, and the twelve bureaus all headed by protégés of Queen Min. They were mostly young men who had visited Japan and favored modernization. Somewhat later, under their influence, military administration was remodeled, the old Five Camps being abolished and the army organized in two main divisions. These moves, while fairly sensible in themselves, served to increase the resentment of the conservative scholars and of the soldiers, and all centered their hatred upon the Queen's faction, the Japanese training officer, and the Japanese minister in Seoul, who was felt to be behind it all.

In 1882 matters came to a head. The men of the old military units, already angry over the preferential treatment of the training unit and its much higher pay, had had their grain rations deferred for thirteen months. Their special hatred was directed at Min Kyom-ho, a relative of the Queen who was government paymaster-general and also administrative head of the training unit. When at last tax grain arrived from Cholla Province and the government was able to distribute some of the deferred rations, the officials in charge of issuing it mixed it with chaff in order to divert some of it to their own use. When the men discovered this, they were utterly enraged. Rebellion broke out at once.

A body of soldiers immediately attacked and destroyed the house of Min Kyom-ho. More importantly, they sent emissaries to the Taewon'gun to ask his advice. Publicly that wily gentleman deplored the revolt and asked the soldiers to return to their duty, but privately he encouraged them, and was soon controlling their actions behind the scenes.

The soldiers broke into arsenals to obtain weapons and proceeded to a general campaign against their enemies.

They attacked police stations to free comrades who had been arrested, destroyed the homes of many of the Queen's relations, killed the Japanese training officer, and narrowly missed killing the Japanese minister, who escaped with his staff to Inch'on at the beginning of the troubles and returned to Japan. They pushed through the gate of Ch'angdok palace and surrounded the private living quarters of the King and Queen. It was there that they caught and killed Min Kyom-ho and also Kim Po-hyon, the governor of Kyonggi Province, who was visiting the King. But Queen Min escaped in disguise and fled to her relative's house in Ch'ungju, where she remained in hiding.

There was now no choice but to recall the Taewon'gun to power, for only he could control the situation. The King sent for him and he was reinstated at the head of the government, after nine years in retirement. The riots subsided and the soldiers returned to their duties.

The military rebellion had aroused intense concern in both Japan and China. The Japanese minister Hanabusa returned to Korea with three naval vessels and three hundred soldiers. He arrived in Seoul with an armed escort, and tried to present to the government a Japanese demand for compensation for Japanese lives and property lost in the rioting. When the government refused to receive him, he delivered an ultimatum, stating that Japanese forces would attack Inch'on in three days if Japanese demands had not been met.

The Chinese, meanwhile, had already sent a party to investigate matters, and when they realized how serious things were, immediately sent ships and troops in large numbers, concentrating at Masanp'o in Kyonggi. The Japanese, outnumbered, had to withdraw, though they were paid an indemnity. The Chinese leaders then decided that China must exercise more direct control over Korea, to forestall further Japanese interference. By a ruse they kidnapped the Taewon'gun and sent him off to China. The leaders of the rebellion were hunted down and executed, Queen Min returned in triumph to Ch'angdok palace, and her faction was once again installed in office. A strong force of Chinese troops was stationed in Seoul.

The Japanese, however, did manage to secure some new advantages. The payment of the indemnity involved the negotiation of a new treaty known as the Treaty of Chemulp'o (the old name of Inch'on). In addition to the indemnity, to be paid in installments over five years, Korea now had to agree to allow Japanese merchants to travel within a stated radius of the treaty ports, open another of its ports to trade, and allow the Japanese minister and his staff to travel freely in Korea. The leaders of the riots were to be punished.

With the help of Chinese troops the soldiers' barracks were attacked and all those suspected of having killed Japanese were either banished or executed. King Kojong then requested that the Chinese release his father the Taewon'gun, but this was refused and he remained in Pao-ting near Tien-tsin. Chinese troops were stationed permanently in Seoul under the command of general Yuan Shih-k'ai, a formidable man whom we shall meet again. Korean diplomatic relations were now almost completely under the control of China.

Chapter 26

Foreign Relations
and the Failure of Reform

The Kanghwa Treaty seemed to the Western powers to be a break in Korea's long isolation, and they began once more to take an interest in relations with the kingdom. The first initiative came from the United States, whose government now decided that good relations with Korea would be advantageous, and sent Commodore Robert W. Shufeldt, in command of the U.S.S. *Ticonderoga,* to obtain the mediation of Japan in negotiating a treaty of friendship. Shufeldt sailed into Pusan harbor in May of 1880 and requested the assistance of a Japanese diplomatic official stationed there. This was refused, and Shufeldt sailed to Japan, where he obtained the good offices of the Japanese Minister of Foreign Affairs. This time the Korean government refused to accept the letter and returned it through a Korean envoy in Japan. It was clear that Japan would not willingly see her monopoly on Korean relations broken.

As we have seen, however, China retained considerable influence over Korea even after the Kanghwa Treaty. Li Hung-chang, China's leading statesman at the time, hearing of Commodore Shufeldt's difficulties, offered to try to obtain a treaty himself. Li conferred with Kim Yun-sik, the Korean representative in Tien-tsin, pointing out to him the advantages of an American treaty as a counterbalance to that with Japan. Moreover, Li felt, it would be advantageous to China to check Japanese power in Korea, and an American treaty seemed a good means to this end.

384

Shufeldt duly arrived in Tien-tsin in March, 1882 and a long series of conferences ensued between the two, carefully considering each article in the proposed treaty. Li repeatedly attempted to insert a clause implying that China still retained her old suzerainty over Korea, but without success. In May a draft was produced which was moderately satisfactory to all parties, and was formally accepted by the Korean government at Chemulp'o (Inch'on) shortly after. To this extent, the more enlightened members of the Korean government, who were becoming better acquainted with Western culture, prevailed over the conservatives and opened the way for other Western nations to begin relations with Korea.

The provisions of the treaty included extraterritoriality for U.S. citizens, the leasing of land for a legation and residence, and a most favored nation clause. A customs duty of ten per cent was placed upon import of necessities and of thirty per cent on luxuries, while commodities exported to the United States were to pay a duty of five per cent. One can see in these customs provisions the hand of Li Hung-chang, who attempted in this way to insure that American economic activities in Korea would not seriously compete with those of China. Lucius H. Foote was sent out as the first American Minister to Korea, while Min Yong-ik departed as Minister Plenipotentiary to the United States, accompanied by a party of observers including Hong Yong-sik, So Kwang-bom and others.

The treaty set a precedent which other nations were not long in following. Immediately after its conclusion, Sir Harry Parkes, British Minister to Japan, sent Admiral Willes to Chemulp'o to negotiate a treaty through the Chinese representative there, Ma Chien-chung. Following the lines of the American treaty, negotiations went quickly. The British government, however, refused ratification on the grounds that import duties were far too high and

British opium (the cause of the war with China some forty years before) was excluded. A new treaty was therefore negotiated and signed in November of 1883. The British government ratified it the following year. Opium was still excluded, but tariffs on various important commodities were drastically lowered, notably that on cotton textiles, which was only 7.5 per cent. Tariffs on American goods automatically followed suit under the "most favored nation" clause, and Li Hung-chang's efforts to protect Chinese trade were thwarted.

A treaty of the same type with Germany followed quickly, but with France matters were somewhat more difficult. The persecution of Catholicism and the execution of French priests have already been mentioned. Despite these events, French missionaries continued to come secretly to Korea. In 1876, perhaps encouraged by the fall of the Taewon'gun, Fathers Bland and Deguette arrived, and in the following year Father Ridel, who had escaped the earlier persecutions, returned accompanied by Fathers Doucet and Robert. But in January of 1878 Father Ridel was arrested and deported to China. The other French priests went into hiding, but in May of 1879 Father Deguette and several Korean Catholics were arrested in Kongju, and the priest was deported, also to China. This left only three French missionaries, but in November of 1880 Fathers Mutel and Louisville arrived.

The French attempted to contact the Korean government through the Chinese, but negotiations were far from smooth. In the first place, the French demand that Korea legalize the preaching of Catholicism was utterly unacceptable even to the most liberal Korean officials. Moreover, the Chinese themselves were wary of France because of the French colonization of Annam (modern North Vietnam) on her southeastern border. A French treaty was not accepted until 1886.

The Russian Empire had now extended itself all across north Asia to the Pacific Ocean, where its maritime provinces touched Korea's frontier a short distance from the Manchurian border. This frontier was as yet ill-defined, and numerous Korean and Russian subjects lived on both sides of the line. For these and other reasons Russia had been demanding relations with Korea ever since the 1860s, though without success. When the American treaty was concluded, the Russians again attempted to contact the Korean government, acting without the mediation of China, with which they were on bad terms. Finally in 1884 Karl Waeber, secretary to the Russian Minister in Peking, arrived in Korea, where he negotiated a treaty through the good offices of Paul Georg von Moellendorff, a German who had been sent to the Korean court as an advisor by Li Hung-chang. It was ratified in 1886, with the French treaty. At the same time, relations with Italy began.

All of these treaties followed the pattern that had been set by the agreements between the Western powers and China, which historians now lump together as the "unequal treaties." All included extraterritorial rights, the granting of leases for various purposes, and regulation of customs, so that in fact they violated Korean sovereignty. Most of them were negotiated through the mediation of China, which hoped in this way to keep Korea in her traditional vassal relationship and frustrate Japanese attempts to dominate the country.

China did for a time become the paramount power in Korea, thanks to her prompt action during the army revolt of 1882. Some officials had even favored a complete military takeover of the Korean government, but Li Hung-chang was content to support Queen Min's faction, which in return instituted policies favorable to China.

When negotiations with Western nations began, the Korean government found it necessary to get advice on how to conduct modern diplomatic relations, and turned to Li Hung-chang for help. He sent them Ma Chien-shang and Paul von Moellendorff, whom we have already met, and both were given posts in the government. Moellendorff also had a hand in organizing the customs.

It was also found necessary to replace the traditional government organs which the Taewon'gun had revived with more modern institutions. Specifically, a Foreign Affairs Ministry and a Home Ministry on modern lines were set up, while other government bodies were modeled on their contemporay counterparts in China. High posts went to Cho Yong-ha, Min Yong-ik, Kim Hong-jip, Kim Man-sik, Kim Ok-kyun, Min T'ae-ho, Kim Yun-sik, Hong Yong-sik and O Yun-jung, some of whom we shall meet again. Both Ma Chien-shang and Moellendorff were given posts equivalent to Vice-Minister of Foreign Affairs.

The Korean military organization was completely reformed by the Chinese. The Chinese troops who suppressed the rebellion were under the command of general Wu Ch'ang-ch'ing, but the job of hunting down and executing the rebels was given to his subordinate, Yuan Shih-k'ai. Once this job was done, Yuan took the Korean army in hand. Four elite groups of five hundred each were formed and trained by Chinese officers. Weapons and ammunition were supplied by China. In both government and military affairs, Chinese control was firmly seated in Korea.

Another important event of 1882 was the signing of a trade agreement with China. This had long been needed, for the inflow of Chinese luxuries had been seriously depleting Korean stocks of precious metals, and Chinese fishermen were making serious incursions into the Korean fishing grounds on the western coast. At the same time Korea hoped that the agreement would check Japanese commercial practices. China for her part wished mainly to reestablish her suzerainty over Korea officially and publicly, and managed to insert in the agreement the same clause to this effect which had been rejected by the Americans.

For some time after the rebellion Seoul was in the hands of Chinese troops, while Chinese merchants flocked to the city in a desperate attempt to replace the Japanese. Both of these groups treated the Koreans with scant respect, and there were numerous incidents and widespread resentment. Korea still disliked any hint of direct foreign rule, even by her traditional overlord, and a permanent revulsion against Chinese rule grew among the people, which was to play a part in future political developments.

The trickle of Western ideas that had been reaching Korea mainly through diplomatic missions to Peking now became a torrent as ports were opened and regular contacts with other nations began. Much of this Western influence still came through China, and a large share came, naturally enough, from Japan. Many of those who served in diplomatic missions to these two countries became leaders in the efforts to modernize the country, and there were suggestions that Korea should imitate Japan. These efforts faced the opposition of those who still believed that modernization would bring subservience to the Western powers as in China and those who felt that modernization along Japanese lines would mean domination by Japan.

Even those who most feared foreign domination, however, were forced to admit grudgingly that many Western goods and Western technology were superior to their own, and that such things were not mere playthings but could enhance everyday life in important ways. They continued, however, to oppose vehemently the importation of Western religion, especially Catholicism. Many began to suggest that Western technology could be accepted while retaining the traditional Confucian ethics and social structure. One Confucian scholar proposed a sweeping reorganization of the whole government, to include a chamber of commerce and industry, a national bank, a modern navy, a police force, a modern currency system, and drastic renovation of taxes and salaries. The government, of course, was not in a position to put such a radical reform into effect, but the very fact that such suggestions could be made is significant.

Most of these radical suggestions came from people who wanted to follow the example of Japan. The government, however, was controlled by Queen Min's faction, with Chinese support, and it followed a more moderate policy. Significant moves toward modernization were made, but they did not deeply affect the structure of government or society. A foreign language institute was set up for future diplomats, and a modernized publication bureau was organized. Coinage was reformed through the establishment of a new mint, and on ordnance office was added to the military organization. The first modern post-office was opened in Seoul. In addition, there were organizations to spread Western techniques of farming, sericulture, textiles, pottery, stock-raising and the manufacture of paper and tea. Forty students were sent to Japan in 1883, chosen from all classes of society though none was the son of an incumbent bureaucrat. About half of them were enrolled in the Japanese military academy, while the others attended various vocational schools.

The gradualism of the pro-Chinese Min faction aroused increasing impatience among the group which wished to follow the Japanese example, and sweep away the whole traditional structure of the Korean government and economy at a blow, to make Korea into a modern, self-reliant power like Japan. It became increasingly clear to this group that nothing short of a *coup d'etat* could displace the Queen's group, end Chinese hegemony, and open the way for genuine modernization. They began to organize and to plot. Their goals are suggested by the name by which they are generally known, the Independence Party.

Kim Ok-kyun, the leader of this group, went to Japan after the army revolt to pay the Japanese government some of the compensation it had demanded and also to try to raise a loan for his own government. In his absence, the Queen's faction, on the advice of Moellendorff, decided to issue a debased coinage in order to alleviate the government's financial difficulties. This, of course, caused an inflation which wiped out any gains the government might have made, as was to be expected. It was an old Chinese practice which had always had bad results, but this was one of the lessons of history that no East Asian government ever seemed to learn. When Kim Ok-kyun returned, having failed to raise a loan, it was decided that this was the last straw, and the Queen and her faction must be eliminated.

No doubt the Independence Party members were sincere in their desire to modernize Korea in order to secure her independence and prosperity, but they were playing into the hands of the Japanese. Many of the modernization projects previously mentioned had been carried out with Japanese help, but Kim Ok-kyun and his group failed to grasp the fact that Japanese motives were hardly altruistic. Many of the modernization projects involved sending Japanese officials and technicians to Korea, and these men acted as agents for their government.

While in Japan Kim Ok-kyun had been much influenced by Fukuzawa Yukichi, a prominent supporter of Japanese modernization and also one of the leading exponents of Japanese imperialism. Kim had become convinced that his movement could succeed only with Japanese help, but he had also imbibed the dangerous notion that Japanese support for Korea's modernization was disinterested, which of course it was not. The Independence Party made secret contacts with the Japanese Minister in Seoul in order to secure the support of Japanese troops when the time was ripe.

Large numbers of Japanese technicians had come to help in the laying of a telegraphic cable between Japan and Korea in 1883. That same year numerous disciples of Fukuzawa Yukichi arrived in advisory capacities and a number of Japanese military officers accompanied them. In 1884 news arrived of Chinese difficulties with the French in Indochina, which meant that the Chinese would be preoccupied for a time. The conspirators believed that their moment had arrived. The Japanese promised full support, seeing in this plot an opportunity to eliminate the Chinese influence on the Korean government and establish themselves in China's place.

The occasion chosen for the coup was a dinner party in celebration of the opening of the new post-office, at which most of the important government officials would be conveniently assembled. The Japanese Minister supplied necessary funds and Japanese troops stood in readiness. At the appointed time, a building near the new post-office was set afire. It was expected that the officials would leave the banquet to report to the King, as they were supposed to do when anything unusual occurred. Young military officers recently returned from study in Japan lay in wait for them, supported by troops from the Japanese-trained units. This part of the plot failed. Several of the officials were later killed, but Min Yong-ik, one of the most important of them, was able to escape, though severely wounded.

Meanwhile, Kim Ok-kyun and some of his followers went to Ch'angdok palace and reported to the King that Chinese troops were making a disturbance and he must be moved for his own protection. The King was escorted to Kyongu palace under Japanese guard, and here the plotters waylaid and killed some of the Min military leaders and some other civil officials who had somehow learned the King's whereabouts. Kyongu palace was ringed with

洋夷侵犯非戰則
和主和賣國
戒我萬年子孫
丙寅作辛未立

57. A Ch'okhwa Monument:
The inscription exhorts the
people to resist foreigners.

56. Yi Ha-ung (Hungson Taewon'-gun): 1820–1898. Father of King Kojong.

58. A Gathering of Catholics.

59. Kim Ki-su, the First Korean Envoy to Japan: Passing along a street in Yokohama, Japan.

60. Foreign Diplomats in Seoul (about 1896) : From left to right: Reinsdorf (Germany), Dr. Allen (U.S.A.), Kato (Japan), Plancy (France), Jordan (England).

61. A Copy of the Treaty Between Korea and America: The first page of the text agreed on at Chemulp'o, May 22, 1882.

62. *Four Leaders of the Independence Party:*
This picture was taken after they had
sought asylum in Japan following the
failure of the Kapsin coup of 1884.
From left to right: Pak Yong-hyo, So
Kwang-bom, So Chae-p'il, and Kim
Ok-kyun.

63. *A Village School (Sodang).*

64. *A Foreign Language School
in Seoul.*

65. *Ch'oe Che-u, the Founder of Tonghak:* 1824–1864.

66. *The Government Army:* Marching to fight against the Tonghak.

67. *Chon Pong-jun, the Tonghak Leader:* Arrested and escorted.

Japanese troops and the King held incommunicado.

These were the events of December 4, 1884. The next day the King was returned to Ch'angdok palace and the insurgents notified the diplomatic corps in Seoul that a new government had been established. The coup seemed to be a success. On the sixth, they announced their political program. Before anything else, the Taewon'gun was to be returned and Chinese dominance was to cease forthwith. The old class system was to be abolished and all people treated as equals. Corrupt officials were to be dismissed, taxation was to be reformed, and the national finances were to have a unified administration. The military forces were to be reorganized, a police force established, and criminal law revised. The government was to be headed by a policy-making council to be composed mainly of members of the Independence Party.

But the plan had one fatal flaw. The Independence Party had assumed that, faced with a *fait accompli* which had Japanese backing, the Chinese would acquiesce. However, there were only about two hundred Japanese troops in Seoul, whereas the Chinese had 1,500 soldiers. As soon as he heard the news, Yuan Shih-k'ai sent a contingent to Ch'angdok palace, and the Japanese guards were driven off with heavy casualties. Kim Ok-kyun and some other leaders were compelled to seek shelter in the Japanese legation. Other leaders, with the help of Japanese-trained officers, managed to escort the King to the place where Queen Min had taken refuge, but there Chinese soldiers caught and killed them and took the King into their custody. It was several days before he was able to return to Ch'angdok palace. Rioters and Korean soldiers attacked the Japanese legation, killing several Japanese, and the minister and his staff were compelled to flee to Inch'on and thence to Japan. They were soon followed by Kim Ok-kyun and those of his group who were able to escape.

The coup had ended in failure after only three days. The King cancelled all appointments made by the conspirators and rescinded all decrees made in his name during the three days. The reform program was scrapped and the situation was restored as far as possible to what it had been before the coup. This attempt is usually referred to by Korean historians as the *Kapsin* coup, after the year-name, and we shall use this handy reference hereafter.

The Korean government lodged a strong protest with that of Japan against the interference in its internal affairs by the Japanese Minister, Takezoe Shinichiro. It refused to be held responsible for the attack on the Japanese legation and demanded that Kim Ok-kyun and the others who had fled to Japan be arrested and returned for trial. The Japanese, however, declined in their turn to be held responsible and declared that Takezoe had been acting on his own initiative and not on government orders. Moreover, they demanded compensation for the loss of Japanese lives and property, and backed their demands with force. Japanese Foreign Minister Inoue Kaoru landed at Inch'on with two battalions of troops and marched into Seoul. The Koreans had no choice but to accept the terms he offered, and the result was the so-called Hansong Treaty, concluded in January, 1885. The Korean government was compelled to pay compensation for Japanese losses and build a new legation. Koreans who had killed Japanese were to be severely punished. A renewed demand that the coup leaders in exile be handed over was again rejected.

Japan had been prepared for this contingency. It was, of course, not true that the government had been ignorant of the plot, for they had encouraged it from the first. Should it have succeeded, Japanese dominance in Korea would have been assured. In case of failure, the Japanese knew, there would be a confrontation with China, and in this case they were sure China would not risk war and they would be able to conduct negotiations to their own advantage. This was indeed what happened. Japanese and Chinese representatives met at Tien-tsin and worked out the Tien-tsin Treaty. It provided that both Japanese and Chinese troops were to be withdrawn from Korea within the next four months. Should either country find it necessary to send troops back again to protect its interests, it was to inform the other before doing so, and withdraw the troops again as soon as possible. The Korean government was to be advised to employ at least one officer who was neither Chinese nor Japanese to train its troops.

This treaty was to Japan's advantage because there were far more Chinese than Japanese troops in Korea and China had easier access to the country. The Japanese, moreover, were in the midst of a vast military buildup that would enable them to face any military threat from China. The troops were withdrawn, but Yuan Shih-k'ai stayed on to protect Chinese interests. He was not called ambassador or minister, however, but given the title Supervisor for Foreign Affairs in Korea, an indication that China had still not given up its claim to suzerainty. Yuan continually interfered in domestic affairs, and was particularly active in trying to secure economic advantages for China.

For many reasons, the dreams of the Independents had been foredoomed to failure. In the first place, they had no political backing at home, and many of the reforms they proposed were abhorrent to large numbers of the bureaucrats. Though resentment of the Chinese was growing, it was not yet strong enough to form the basis of a coup. And the support of Japan only heightened suspicion. Although foreign troops were withdrawn, the result was a heightening of Sino-Japanese rivalry over Korea and interference in her affairs by both sides. A conflict was brewing, and Korea was helplessly caught in the middle of it.

Chapter 27

The Great Powers in Korea

The opening of Korea to diplomatic and commercial relations almost immediately involved her in the conflicts between Western powers with interests in East Asia. One of the most important of these was that between Great Britain and Russia. British power in Asia was chiefly center- ed in India, but the important British trade with China brought frequent and not always friendly contacts with the expanding Russian Empire. There had been chronic hostility between the two nations ever since the Crimean War of 1856, and Britain viewed the expanding power of the Russian Empire in Asia not only as a threat to her own interests but also as a threat to the balance of power in Europe. When the Russians reached the Pacific and set up the port of Vladivostok within easy reach of Korea's northeastern frontier in 1860, Korea inevitably became a factor in this rivalry.

There had been Russian demands for the opening of relations ever since this event, and Britain moved to counter Russian influence as soon as possible. She had sought to lease Komun Island (Port Hamilton) off the south coast as early as 1882, even before obtaining a treaty. When a treaty did become effective in April of 1884, British com- mercial interests immediately moved in. An office of the great British trading firm of Jardine, Matheson and Company had already been established at Inch'on. When Korea concluded a treaty with Russia the following year and Karl Waeber was sent as minister, the British took direct action to check the Russians.

Komun Island actually consists of three small islets ideally placed for defense against a Russian invasion by sea. Without making any request or even giving prior notice, the British navy occupied these islands and began to construct permanent bases and shore batteries. The Russians immediately protested, and threatened that, if this move had been made with Chinese approval, they would occupy another part of Korea as compensation. The Korean government also protested through China. Negotiations thereupon began between Britain and Russia with Chinese mediation, and Britain agreed to withdraw. She was very slow in doing so, however, and the last British forces did not leave Komun until 1887, after Russia had given assurances that she would not occupy any Korean territory and China had promised not to approve the occupation of any part of Korea by any nation.

The Korean court had been advised throughout the Komun affair by the Russian Minister, Karl Waeber, and the Koreans now began to see in Russia a countervailing force against China and Japan, both of which had intensified their efforts to dominate Korea after the failure of the Kapsin coup of 1884. Waeber gained increased influence with the court, and was even able to persuade Moellendorff, who ostensibly represented Chinese interests, that it was to Korea's interest to have good relations with Russia. In 18 85 it came out that King Kojong was conducting secret negotiations with Russia through Moellendorff. These had to be abandoned because of widespread opposition in the government, and Moellendorff's dismissal was called for.

These events and renewed rumors of secret negotiations with Russia caused much apprehension in the Chinese court. Li Hung-chang, in a bid to win back Korean sentiment, repatriated the Taewon'gun at this time. Moellendorff was recalled, and in his place Li sent two foreigners who had been working for the Chinese: O. N. Denny, an ex-American Consul General, to advise on foreign affairs, and Henry Merrill, to supervise the customs office. Chinese efforts to control Korean affairs were intensified. The customs office was largely staffed by Chinese, and when the Korean Telegraph Office was established under Chinese auspices it too had mostly Chinese employees. Yuan Shih-k'ai remained in Seoul as general overseer of Chinese interests, and was as violent and arbitrary as ever. When it was rumored for the second time that Korea was approaching the Russians he wanted King Kojong deposed, and though this plan was not adopted he continued to receive backing from Peking. When Korean ambassadors were sent out to Japan, the United States, and concurrently to Britain and France he objected that Korea could not afford all these diplomatic missions without financial support, in an obvious attempt to prevent an independent Korean foreign policy. The envoy to Britain and France, who had by this time reached Hong Kong, was intercepted and had to return home. The diplomatic corps in Seoul protested this high-handed behavior and asked the Chinese government to replace Yuan, but Li Hung-chang stood behind his man, and Yuan remained in Seoul.

In 1888 an overland trade treaty was concluded with the Russians and the northeastern border city of Kyonghung was opened to them. They also secured timber-cutting rights along the Yalu River. The Russians also wanted naval coaling stations at Wonsan and on Choryong Island near Pusan, but Chinese objections prevented their getting these. Chinese interference in Korean affairs, both foreign and domestic, continued to intensify, as did Chinese economic penetration. This last especially brought China into direct collision with Japan.

Although Japan had lost ground to China after the Kapsin coup, her economic exploitation of Korea was by no means stopped. She had secured fishing rights on the southern and eastern coasts in 1883, and in 1885 a new agreement enabled Japanese fishermen to purchase for a modest sum the right to fish within three miles of the coast. Japanese fishermen appeared on Ullung and Cheju Islands in such numbers that the inhabitants objected, and in 1891 the people of Cheju actually rose in revolt. In 1888 Japan obtained the right to fish along the coast of Kyonggi Province and thus confronted the Chinese who were also fishing there. The incursion of the Japanese into the important fishing industry threatened both the livelihood of Korean fishermen and an important part of the Korean food supply.

In the open ports the number of resident Japanese merchants increased rapidly, and there were whole communities living on leased territory, like the Western communities in Shanghai. Japanese ships, often escorted by naval vessels, began appearing at ports not open for trade, and illegal business grew. Japanese steamships quickly monopolized the carrying trade, and what few Korean ships there were, were forced out of business.

Korean exports were mainly rice, soybeans, ginseng and hides. Gold, unhindered by any laws or regulations, flowed out of the country in vast quantities, exceeding all exports in value. Imports were chiefly British cotton textiles, metals and manufactured goods. British consular reports for 1890 show that British goods accounted for fifty-seven per cent of imports, Japanese for nineteen, Chinese for twelve, and American, Russian and French for the rest.

Grain and gold were exported mostly to Japan, and Japan and China acted as middlemen in selling British textiles to Korea. But as Japan became increasingly industrialized, she gradually replaced Britain in the textile market. Branches of the Daiichi Bank of Japan were established in the treaty ports as soon as they were opened so that Japanese merchants had funds immediately available for buying up goods for export. The lack of tariffs and price differentials between Korea and Japan enabled many of them to make quick profits, especially in gold. Japanese retail stores began to appear in Seoul and other cities, in defiance of the treaty, and Korean retailers found themselves facing unexpected competition. Further treaty violations occurred when Japanese businessmen began buying mines, ginseng fields and farmland outside the leased territory. Japanese economic penetration spread through every trade and industry in Korea.

Quite a few of the Japanese merchants were unprincipled scoundrels attracted by the easy money and the fact that Japanese banks were willing to make loans to anyone who could show a profit, and no questions asked. Treaties and trade regulations were virtually ignored. Korean competition was negligible, but the Japanese did have to face the competition of the Chinese merchants under the powerful protection of Yuan Shih-k'ai.

In the period between 1884 and 1890 Chinese commerce enjoyed high prosperity in Korea. This, of course, was at least partly due to the strong influence of the Chinese government in this period. Yuan Shih-k'ai did pretty much as he liked in Seoul, and even the protests of Western diplomats could not shake his position. Chinese guards and officials in Korea were mostly army men whose main function was to protect Chinese commerce. Chinese merchants began to break treaty regulations as the Japanese were doing by engaging in trade of all kinds wherever they pleased. To get around the regulation prohibiting foreigners from travelling outside Seoul and the treaty ports without passes issued by the government, Yuan simply seized a quantity of blank passes by force and issued them at will. Chinese merchants spread through the countryside, selling silk and cotton cloth, kerosene, drugs, Western textiles and cosmetics. They bought hides, soybeans and gold. Chinese virtually took over the ceramic industry, and invested in sericulture, the raising of medicinal herbs and farming.

The high-handed behavior of the Chinese in Seoul was very widely resented, and there were numerous incidents. In 1888 and 1889 outright riots took place, and several Chinese shops were looted and burned. Yuan Shih-k'ai was compelled to decree that all Chinese reside in segregated areas. The Chinese merchants were gathered around the palaces within the Great East and South Gates, which became the original Chinese quarters of the city.

But the Chinese did not owe their success exclusively to the protection of their government. They were superior to the Japanese in several ways, especially in their banking system and their shrewd use of investment capital, which was loaned at a much lower rate of interest than Japanese money. Their retail business was much larger in scale than the Japanese, who had no shops the size of the Chinese ones in Seoul. Most of them worked under contract with home companies, but this did not keep them from showing initiative, cooperation, and frugality. Records show that they handled at times a much greater volume of trade in proportion to their numbers than did the Japanese. In Wonsan in 1891, for example, there were about a hundred families of Japanese (some six hundred persons) and only six Chinese families (about forty persons), yet the amount of business done by the two groups was about equal.

Chinese trade gained steadily on Japanese through the eighties and into the nineties. Between 1885 and 1892 the proportion of Korean foreign trade with China increased from nineteen to forty-five per cent, while Japan's share decreased from eighty-one to fifty-five. This change is also illustrated by the exports and imports passing through the port of Inch'on, for which British consular records are available. The unit here is the Mexican dollar, the currency mostly used for international trade in East Asia at the time. The value of Japanese trade passing through Inch'on in 1885 stood at $867,029, and this had climbed by 1892 to $2,262,417. Chinese goods passing through Inch'on were valued at $252,135 in 1885 and increased much more rapidly than Japanese volume, reaching $1,813,571 in 1892.

The Japanese became increasingly frustrated by this situation. Japan was industrializing rapidly and had embarked upon an ambitious program of military expansion. She was sorely in need of foreign markets in which to earn hard currency to finance her modernization. All sorts of expedients were tried. Japanese military men and secret agents were sent in large numbers to detect and root out anti-Japanese or pro-Chinese activities wherever possible. Political pressure was applied. But the Chinese continued their sway unchecked and at last it seemed that nothing short of open conflict could unseat them. Then in 1894 came the Tonghak rebellion, and the Japanese saw a golden opportunity.

Chapter 28

The Tonghak Revolt

The inequities of the tax system and land distribution have frequently been discussed. We must revert to them once more because they were an important cause of the fateful uprising known as the Tonghak revolt. The Tae-won'gun had tried to alleviate the suffering of the farmers somewhat by curbing the extortions of local officials and landlords and by trying to widen the tax base, but these gains had been largely wiped out by the financing of his ambitious building program and by debasement of the currency. The practice of selling government posts added to the difficulties, for the persons who bought these posts were intent mainly upon getting back their investments and making profits, and this resulted in further irregular exactions, and usurious loans remained common.

The opening of the country to Japan exacerbated this already intolerable situation. Large-scale Japanese fishing robbed Korean fishermen of their livelihood. Japanese shipping ruined the carrying trade. The government's use, at Japanese instance, of steamboats to transport tax grain cost many people their jobs and increased the cost of transportation into the bargain. But the greatest threat to the livelihood of the farmers was the mounting export of rice. The retail price of rice rose steeply, as did the cost of daily necessities, ·many of them now imported, such as textiles, kerosene, and kitchen utensils. On top of this there were disastrous droughts in 1876–77 and again in

1888–89 in Cholla Province.

The foreign treaties provided that Korea could stop the export of grain in times of emergency. This the governors of Hamgyong and Hwanghae Provinces now proposed to do in 1889 and 1890. The Japanese, however, protested that a month's notice was required before such a ban could go into effect, and demanded compensation for the rice which merchants had been unable to export. Several years of intermittent negotiations resulted only in the payment of damages by Korea. There were frequent conflicts of this kind between Japanese merchants and provincial officials, especially in the southern provinces.

The poverty of the farmers caused a decrease in tax revenue, which caused more exactions in a vicious circle. This was especially true in Cholla Province, which supplied a disproportionate amount of the government's income. The situation was not improved by the imposition of customs duties, for the income from these went almost entirely to modernization programs and the servicing of foreign loans. The situation of the Cholla farmers was such that a breaking point must soon be reached.

One result of the economic situation was an ominous rise in banditry throughout the eighties and early nineties. Farmers had turned bandit before in bad times, of course, but not to this extent. Well-armed and organized robber bands began to appear, with bases deep in the mountains, attacking shipments of tax grain and convoys of imported goods on their way to Seoul. Another result was a wave of local uprisings of various kinds, usually against corrupt officials. Miners revolted in Hamgyong and Kyongsang Provinces, and the fishermen of Cheju rebelled. There were peasant risings in almost every province, sometimes led by former officials or government slaves. Ruined yangban also organized revolts. After the drought of 1888–89 in Cholla the situation became really serious.

The Taewon'gun's isolationism and persecution of Catholics, and his attempt at a conservative revolution had served to stimulate the growth of the Tonghak sect, which was itself both anti-foreign and reformist. In the deepening economic crisis of the nineties, thousands began to see in this new religion the only means of salvation, not only spiritual but even physical. It had gone underground since the death of its founder Ch'oe Che-u, but under his successor Ch'oe Si-hyong had continued to make converts, meanwhile developing into an organized body with leaders who were the counterparts of priests and bishops.

In 1892 there were widespread Tonghak demonstrations in Cholla and Ch'ungch'ong Provinces demanding toleration for the sect and posthumous rehabilitation for Ch'oe Che-u, who had been executed as a criminal. The immediate cause was suppression of the sect by the newly appointed governor of Ch'ungch'ong, who used this as an excuse to confiscate property. Early in 1893 messages went out from the Tonghak leaders appointing times and places for believers in the two provinces to gather to present their demands formally to the two governors. This show of strength had the effect of eliciting a promise that the persecution would cease, but the governors said they had no authority to clear the name of Ch'oe Che-u. For this recourse must be had to the King himself.

Forty Tonghak leaders accordingly went to Seoul in April of 1893. For three days they knelt before the King's palace to present their petition. The petition was rejected, however, and government officials ordered them to return to their homes. They did so, but they left the city in a state of panic. Posters appeared on every corner demanding the expulsion of foreigners and the suppression of Catholicism. The foreign community locked its doors and stayed home at night. Rumors mounted that tens of thousands of Tonghak were converging on Seoul. Nervousness reached such a pitch that foreign warships were ordered to Inch'on to protect foreign residents in case of violence.

In the next month about twenty thousand did gather at Poun in Ch'ungch'ong, this time with more detailed demands. They wanted reform at home, expulsion of Westerners and Japanese, and an end to relations with foreign nations. The government managed to disperse them by a mixture of force and appeasement.

It is to be noted in all these events that the government did not resort to full-scale persecution. Tonghak had by now become so widespread in the south that this would have meant economically crippling the whole area. It is to be noted also that the movement's political aims coincided well with those of the Taewon'gun, a fact which was to become important later.

The leaders of the movement were mostly yangban who had been ruined by the social confusion and political conflicts of the eighteenth and nineteenth centuries, and the sons of yangban by concubines, whose status was ambiguous at best. Alienated by their own miserable circumstances and the failure of the Confucian social system, they turned to revolutionary action. Many of them had tried to save at least a few shreds of the dignity their class supposedly conferred upon them, and many were educated. It was they who gave coherent organization and purpose to what might otherwise have been just another peasant uprising. They had the two elements necessary for a genuine revolution: belief in the righteousness of their cause sanctioned by religion, and a political program which, if unrealistic, had clear and concrete aims.

The manner in which the revolt was touched off was illustrative of its cause. Cho Pyong-gap had been appointed district magistrate of Kobu in Cholla Province in 1892. He set about lining his pockets in the usual manner, but with unusual energy. Farmers were encouraged to bring waste land under cultivation by promises of tax exemption, and then taxed. The well-to-do were blackmailed by false accusations of crimes. Farmers were forced to work on irrigation projects without pay, the money they should have got going to Cho.

The people complained to Cho's superiors up to the provincial governor, but without success, the petitioners being dispersed by force. Chon Pong-jun, the local Tonghak leader, realized at this point that appeals to local officials were futile, and chose the only alternative. In February of 1894 he led about a thousand angry farmers in destroying the irrigation system they had been forced to build and then in an attack on the government office. They broke into the armory and took the weapons stored there, and then seized the tax grain in the government warehouse and distributed it to the needy.

When a report of this incident reached Seoul, a special inspector was sent out to appraise the situation and take appropriate action. Chon held his hand for the time being, perhaps hoping that the central government at any rate would deal fairly with the people. But the inspector blamed the whole affair on the Tonghak religion, and began arresting believers and having their homes destroyed. Chon Pong-jun, now feeling that there was no recourse but violence, sent messages to other Tonghak groups in the province urging them to rise against oppression as he had. Revolution had become irrevocable.

The flame spread all across Cholla. In district after district the officials were driven out, and always the people were careful to seize weapons, as Chon had advised them. Thousands gathered on the Paeksan near Kobu, where the revolt had started, some armed only with clubs and bamboo spears, but many carrying rifles and swords they had taken from the armories. By May the government was confronted not with a mere unruly mob but with a group that was beginning to form itself into an army.

Chonju, the seat of provincial government, was only about twenty-four miles from Kobu, and the governor was seriously alarmed. He sent a call for help to Seoul, and then ordered the local government troops to attack the rebels, who had meanwhile advanced northward and taken the town of Puan. This force the rebels easily defeated. The government had meanwhile dispatched 800 troops, but they arrived only the day after the engagement, cut almost in half by desertions on the way. Local officials began fleeing to Seoul, and four were caught and killed by the Tonghak. Chonju lived in terror of attack.

But the rebels, perhaps feeling that they were not yet strong enough to face government troops, turned south. They took every town in their path and grew daily in numbers, until by the time they reached Mujang they had increased to about ten thousand. The government troops in Chonju were reinforced and marched in pursuit, narrowly missing the Tonghak force at Yonggwang. After taking Hamp'yong, it turned north again, and the government troops attacked. The rebels beat them off and forced them to retreat to Yonggwang. This was May 27th, by which time the revolt had spread into Ch'ungch'ong and Kyongsang Provinces as well. On May 31 the Tonghak took Chonju, which offered no resistance.

The government, meanwhile, had at least partially come to its senses. The governor of Cholla had been dismissed and the magistrate of Kobu imprisoned. King Kojong promised that all corrupt officials would be dismissed and the grievances of the Cholla people redressed. On the other hand, the government troops reached Chonju and bombarded the town, and two Tonghak counterattacks were unable to drive them off. There were many casualties, and the rebels began to grow discouraged, some of them believing that, now that the King had given his promise, there was no longer any reason to fight. The government commander wisely promised good treatment to all who surrendered. At length there was a formal agreement, and the rebels withdrew from Chonju and returned to their homes.

While the grievances of the Tonghak were certainly genuine and many of their demands just, their attitude toward modernization and their hatred of foreigners placed the government in an extremely precarious position. If Korea was to escape foreign domination it was absolutely essential that she adopt Western technology, both to strengthen her armed forces and to develop a healthy economy. The rebels looked no further than their own immediate circumstances. The demands which they made, and their very success, involved Korea in a disastrous war.

The number of specific demands had grown with the success of the rebellion, but the two major ones were equitable taxation and the halting of rice exports to Japan. After they had withdrawn unmolested from Chonju and things had more or less quieted down, the government carried out its part of the bargain by setting up "Correction Offices" in each of the fifty-three districts of Cholla, staffed by Tonghak, under the general supervision of Chon Pong-jun, the leader of the revolt. They were to act in an advisory capacity to each district magistrate in order to prevent extortion and protect the farmers' interests.

Once the offices were organized, the Tonghak made their program public in a formal document of twelve items. It proclaimed that the oppression of officials and rich yangban would no longer be tolerated; that the slave-registers should be burned and the old system of status abolished; that widows should be allowed to remarry; that farmland should be redistributed on an equitable basis; and that those who collaborated with the Japanese should be punished. What this amounted to was a demand for the abolition of the aristocratic structure of society which had characterized (and frequently plagued) Korea throughout her history. What it resulted in was a foreign war.

When the seriousness of the situation was brought home to the Seoul government, there were doubts whether its forces could handle the rebels unaided. Against the advice of many officials, King Kojong appealed to China for help. Ships were immediately ordered to Inch'on, and in June a Chinese flotilla assembled in Asan Bay, after the Chinese had informed Japan of their action in accordance with the agreement between them.

The Japanese Minister in Seoul had been gravely concerned about the harm the revolt might do to Japanese interests, and had kept his government closely informed. When news of the Chinese move came, a Japanese ship sailed for Inch'on and landed troops there on June 10, ostensibly to protect the legation. This provoked a Chinese reaction, and troops of both nations began to pour into Korea in large numbers. The Korean government protested that the revolt had been quelled, and there was no justification for sending troops. China, satisfied that she still had the upper hand, proposed a mutual withdrawal.

But the Japanese saw in the situation an opportunity to drive the Chinese out of Korea. Moreover, they now felt strong enough to face China in a war if necessary. They therefore proposed that Japanese troops remain in order to "renovate Korean home affairs," a flimsy bluff which they did not expect the Chinese to accept. Japanese troops continued to arrive in Korea, China refused the Japanese proposal, and the situation became so tense that Yuan Shih-ka'i was forced to escape from Seoul in disguise. Japan continued to press Korea for "renovation" in order to prevent further rebellions, by which vague expression it presumably meant the adoption of policies favorable to Japan.

The Korean government continued helplessly to protest, and resisted also a demand that it scrap trade relations with China. The Japanese now flung aside all pretense and began openly to prepare for domination of Korea and war with China. At midnight on July 23 Japanese troops overpowered the guards at Kyongbok palace, occupied it, and so gained control of the King. Kojong was forced to call the Taewon'gun once more to power, and the man who had instituted a policy of strict isolation came back under the sponsorship of the Japanese. Queen Min and her group were driven out, and the pro-Chinese government was at an end. Meanwhile, the Japanese had disarmed all the Korean troops they could find and started stringing telegraph wires between Pusan and Seoul for military communications.

Open war began on July 25 with an unprovoked attack upon the Chinese ships in the Yellow Sea near Asan Bay, which were sunk or driven off. Simultaneously, Japanese troops marched south from Seoul to attack Chinese units in Asan and Kongju, which they defeated on July 29. The remnant retreated north by a circuitous route to P'yongyang, where they joined other forces sent from China. The Sino-Japanese war began with a swift series of victories for Japan.

With the Chinese gone and her own forces helpless, Korea was now forced to sign a series of agreements that placed her virtually under Japanese rule. The Japanese obtained rights to build railroads and telegraph systems. All ports on the Cholla coast were opened to Japan. A treaty of military alliance was signed which in effect made Korea a source of Japanese military supplies. All Chinese residents were to be deported. Korea was completely in Japanese hands.

To meet the Korean contention that the Tonghak rebellion had been suppressed so that there was no longer any need for foreign troops in the country, the Japanese minister had sent an inspector to Cholla Province to assess the situation. He had secret instructions to prolong his inspection as much as he could and finally to report that the rebels were still active. At the same time, secret agents were sent to the province, where they contacted Chon Pong-jun, the Tonghak leader, and tried to convince him that the Japanese were on his side against the corrupt and oppressive government in Seoul. The agents knew quite well, of course, that Tonghak was violently anti-Japanese, and were hoping to provoke another revolt, which would give them further reason for keeping troops in Korea.

Chon Pong-jun had been following events with deepening suspicion and dismay. He finally decided to lead a second revolt, and though evidence is lacking it seems probable that he did this with the secret encouragement of the Taewon'gun. The tough old statesman (he was by now 73) had accepted Japanese help in order to vanquish his enemy Queen Min, but now his hatred of foreigners reappeared, and he seemed willing to turn on the Japanese with any means that came to hand. Chon waited until after the harvest in October, and then raised the standard of revolt once more.

A hundred thousand farmers rose in Cholla Province alone. Ch'oe Si-hyong, the spiritual leader, came out of hiding to give his encouragement to the fight. Ch'ung-ch'ong Province rose likewise, and an immense force assembled at Nonsan. Meanwhile Tonghak farmers in other Provinces engaged in numerous harassing actions. Japanese supply bases were attacked and communications cut, and for a time the surprised Japanese, most of whose combat troops were pursuing the Chinese, suffered reverses. The Seoul government made various official gestures against the revolt, but since it controlled no troops these amounted to nothing.

The Japanese, on the other hand, acted with ruthless efficiency. A battalion was detached from the fighting front and marched south in three groups. In early November it encountered the Tonghak main force as it moved on the strategic town of Kongju. A desperate battle ensued that lasted for seven days. Even the immense numbers of the Tonghak could not stand against experienced troops with modern training and equipment, and they were finally beaten and retreated south, leaving many casualties behind. Chon Pong-jun attempted to appeal to the Korean soldiers who had been brought along by the Japanese, but they were helpless.

While measures were taken to suppress the Tonghak in other provinces, the Japanese continued their pursuit of the main force, which was now retreating in disarray and dispersing into the countryside. It soon became clear that the Japanese would not be content with simple suppression of the revolt, but were bent upon exterminating the Tonghak sect. Despite the fact that military resistance had ended the troops continued to capture and kill Tonghak wherever they found them, moving down through Cholla Province all the way to the southern coast.

Chon Pong-jun was arrested and sent to Seoul on December 28, and most of the other leaders soon after. The slaughter in the provinces continued until the end of January, and there were sporadic outbreaks throughout 1895, especially in the northern area, until Chon and his associates were put to death and the few remnants ceased resistance and crept away to hide.

The revolt had been one of the farmers, led by destitute yangban, and had been mainly a domestic affair. At one time it might actually have reformed and strengthened Korean society, but that time was long past, and the social evils against which it protested were overshadowed by the menace of Japan. Instead of securing freedom and justice for the oppressed, the Tonghak rebellion ironically played into the hands of a foreign power bent on conquest. Ch'oe Si-hyong and a few other leaders managed to escape arrest and went back into hiding, later to pass their beliefs on to succeeding generations.

Having dealt with the Tonghak, Japan proceeded to deal with the Chinese. The Chinese army was defeated at P'yongyang and driven out of Korea. Chinese naval forces were defeated in numerous engagements, and the Japanese occupied the strategic naval base of Lushun (Port Arthur) on the Liaotung peninsula, Weihaiwei on the Shantung peninsula, and the island of Taiwan. China was forced to ask for negotiations, and in April of 1895 the treaty of Shimonoseki brought the war to a close.

This agreement began by once more proclaiming the independence of Korea, the old Japanese tactics of detaching the country from its dependence on China. The other provisions gave ominous evidence of future Japanese intentions. Both the Liaotung peninsula and the island of Taiwan were to be ceded to Japan; several more ports were to be opened to Japanese trade; Japanese ships were to have free passage on all inland rivers; Japanese nationals were to be given additional rights of residence and trade in China; and finally, enormous reparations were to be paid to Japan. A threatening protest by Russia, France and Germany forced Japan to give up the Liaotung peninsula, but she kept Taiwan. The building of the Japanese Pacific empire had begun.

The Tonghak rebellion and the Sino-Japanese war had two important results in Korea. The obvious one, of course, was that the Japanese gained a free hand in the peninsula and could do with it pretty much what they liked. But while they slowly smothered and ultimately snuffed out Korean independence, the Koreans had at last begun to develop a true national consciousness, the first prerequisite for the building of a modern state.

Chapter 29

Reform and Japanese Domination

The Confucian conceptions of government and society which had played so large a part in Korean life for so long were made increasingly irrelevant to the actual situation by the accelerating pace of change during the nineteenth century. To give but one important instance, the tax system was based almost entirely on agriculture, and even then was for the most part inequitably administered. When reforms were called for, they were almost always changes of detail, the basic principles remaining untouched. When commerce began to expand the authorities attempted either to suppress or to ignore it, and serious economic distortions resulted.

But not all Koreans were blind to the times. The Sirhak scholars, it will be recalled, had taken a pragmatic view of affairs, and when they became aware of Western technology had eagerly advocated its adoption. But debarred as they were for the most part from putting their ideas into practice, they could not work out policies which could actually be applied to the realities of their society, and their thinking remained mostly theoretical.

Korea had a brief opportunity, after the opening of the ports in 1876, to take her place in the modern world. The most urgent matters were to encourage and develop commerce by means of Western technology so as to achieve prosperity and broaden the tax base and to adopt Western weapons and techniques in the armed forces so as to preserve independence. There were indeed various gestures in these directions while the Korean government still had freedom of action, and thinkers in the Sirhak tradition encouraged them as much as they could. But it was all too little and too late.

The root of the matter was political. As the tragic example of China shows, basic social and economic reforms cannot be achieved by a regime that is committed to an outmoded tradition. There must first be political reform and the establishment of a government whose reason for existence is to make the necessary changes. The example of Japan clearly shows this, as the examples of China and Korea show what happens when a political regime and a political philosophy outlive their usefulness. The Kapsin coup of 1884 should have corresponded to the Meiji revolution in Japan, bringing to power a group of men who understood the modern world at least to some extent and were willing to make a whole-hearted effort to bring their nation into it free and independent. Its failure brought ten years of turmoil and confusion during which reform was not possible even had the government been willing, and at the end the nation found itself in the gradually tightening grasp of Japan, which was not to relax for half a century. It was the tragedy of Korea that her modernization was achieved under the direction of a foreign power and so took a distorted form which served the real interests of the people only incidentally.

Even before the outbreak of the Sino-Japanese War Japan had presented a reform program to the Korean government and pressed for its adoption. While this contained most of what has been indicated above in the realms of politics and economics, it was so devised that it would result in rapid Japanese exploitation of the Korean economy. All sorts of mining, railway and communication concessions were envisioned. The Korean government responded by setting up a special organization for the purpose and devising its own reform program. This was the background of the Japanese coup which drove out the Min faction and brought back the Taewon'gun. A pro-Japanese government was established under him with Kim Hong-jip as premier, and after China had been defeated the reform program proceeded under Japanese direction.

A special Reform Council was first of all set up by the new government which was to deliberate all of the reform decrees. Kim Hong-jip presided, but took his cues from Otori Keisuke, the Japanese Minister. The decrees then went through the empty formality of the King's signature and duly became law. This group exercised the supreme power, and no decree was valid without its assent. It began functioning on July 26, 1894, and remained in existence for about six months, endorsing 208 pieces of reform legislation in the first three months.

These new laws were devised primarily to destroy the traditional Korean society and establish capitalistic institutions which the Japanese could exploit. There was even a decree against the traditional Korean costume. The laws were devised without any regard for Korean desires or sometimes even for the realities of the situation. Several of the decrees were quite unenforceable and became dead letters immediately. There were numerous contradictions and absurdities and the people were frequently compelled to obey laws they did not even understand.

The Taewon'gun, of course, was excluded from this process. He had been brought in to help defeat the pro-Chinese Min faction, but once he had served this purpose he was prevented from exercising any real power, and was compelled to preside helplessly over the foreign domination of his country, the very thing he had struggled all his life to prevent.

Before economic and social reforms could take place, the government itself had to be reorganized. Formerly there had been no clear distinction in financial administration between the expenses of the royal court and finances which could properly be called public. Two bodies were now set up, a Palace Council which attended to the personal expenses of the royal family and related matters such as royal tombs and shrines, and a State Council which headed the government proper. This now consisted of eight ministries: Home Affairs, Foreign Affairs, Finance, Military Affairs, Justice, Education, Industry, and Agriculture and Commerce. A Prime Minister was chief executive. There were also an Inspection Office, a Consultative Committee, the Treasury and Board of Audit, and a Police Bureau.

The old examination system was abolished, and a new one substituted. This was to choose junior officials only, however, the higher posts being filled by promotion or direct appointment. The new examination subjects were Korean, Chinese, calligraphy, mathematics, political science, international relations and composition, a radical shift away from the old emphasis on the Confucian classics and toward subjects important in modern government. There were also examinations in scientific and technical subjects for the various specialists required, for which candidates had to be recommended by the appropriate officials. Perhaps the most significant thing about the new system was that class distinctions were disregarded in selecting candidates.

Local administration was also reorganized. The old eight provinces were retained unchanged, but a new system of dividing them into counties and districts was adopted. Local officials were appointed by the King on recommendation of the State Council. New posts were created for the regulation of commerce in each of the treaty ports, of the same rank as the chief administrator of a district. Local magistrates no longer had the judicial and military powers of former times, these being delegated to the appropriate officials. Military affairs were negligible, however, all of the Korean armed forces except for the Royal Guard having been disarmed during the Sino-Japanese War.

Like the rest of the Japanese reform program, this reorganization of the government was carried out in a hasty and confused manner. Many of the old officials were simply turned out of office to fend for themselves, creating a large group of destitute and resentful yangban who constituted a serious social problem. High-ranking officials who lost their posts, as a sop to their vanity, were placed on the Consultative Committee attached to the State Council and told to await new assignments which never materialized. In effect, they too were unemployed.

This hastily assembled government then proceeded to take in hand the vast confusion of the nation's finances. Royal expenses were separated from strictly governmental ones, as we have seen, but this was only the beginning. In former times each government department had had its own treasury, causing great confusion because it was impossible to determine or control revenues and expenditures exactly. All this was ended with the establishment of the Ministry of Finance, which now controlled all government revenues and expenditures of whatever kind, and was also charged with accounting, government loans and coinage.

The many varieties of taxation were brought into a unified system and taxes were to be paid in cash. This was done so abruptly that it brought about many hardships. Even this late many taxes were still paid in kind, the circulation of money being limited. Farmers now had to sell their crops for whatever they would bring in order to obtain money for taxes. Eventually a government rice exchange was set up for this purpose, within the Ministry of Agriculture. Here again, however, haste and mismanagement vitiated an essentially good idea, for the exchange was inadequately financed.

One of the most urgent needs to make the new financial system work was a stable currency. Coins of all sorts had appeared during the nineteenth century, none of them with a universally accepted value. The old copper coins issued by the government varied greatly in weight. Later coins issued when the government was in financial difficulties had been debased and so fell in value. A certain number of Chinese coins had been imported after 1867, but this had ceased in 1874. In addition to all these, unauthorized coinage (not exactly counterfeit when there was no official standard) had appeared. The government had planned to establish a mint, but this was never done. In the port cities currency of many nations circulated, while on the northern borders Chinese and Russian silver coins were common. The most acceptable currencies for foreign exchange were Mexican dollars and Japanese currency. Foreign merchants would accept Korean currency only at the value of its metallic content, and could find no other use for it than paying for Korean labor or small purchases of Korean goods. Japanese traders in the ports and Chinese merchants in Seoul and elsewhere generally demanded payment either in hard currency or in precious metals, and Korean supplies of these were seriously depleted.

The reform administration brought some order into this confusion by issuing a new coinage similar to the Japanese. Silver was in such short supply, however, that few coins of large denominations could be minted, and the deficiency was made up by allowing the circulation of Japanese coins for the time being. Many of the old coins continued to circulate in smaller transactions, and the main effect of the new currency was to facilitate Japanese transactions.

The reform of the social system, at any rate on paper, was a sweeping one. The four classes into which society had formerly been divided were abolished, so far as the government was concerned, and appointments were to be made on the basis of merit only. Except for the lowest class these distinctions had long been blurred by the destitution of numerous yangban, who had perforce become no more than simple farmers. Slavery was abolished, and this too followed a tendency which had already begun, for government slaves had been freed in 1801 and hereditary slave status had been abolished in 1888. People in despised occupations, especially butchers and leather-workers, were declared the equals of other citizens, though old prejudices died hard. The official disapproval of commerce was abandoned and former yangban officials were free to go into business, which some of them did.

The new regulations also affected the old extended family system. Early marriage was prohibited, the minimum ages being twenty for men and sixteen for women. Widows were allowed to remarry, a grave sin according to Confucian views. The custom of criminal implication, whereby the whole family of a criminal was punished with him, was done away with.

In the upper ranks of society, the special privileges of class were abolished. Only high officials were to be accorded deference, while all others were to be treated equally regardless of class. The number of attendants upon ranking officials was reduced, and all of them were forbidden to ride in palanquins. All people had the right to appeal to the Reform Council for redress of grievances or to make suggestions for improvements in government. Official dress was much simplified and wide sleeves were banned, as were the long bamboo tobacco-pipes which had been a sign of rank.

Undeniably many of these reforms were good and necessary for the development of a modern state. They were carried out, however, not only carelessly and in haste but with complete disregard for the feelings and even the welfare of those whom they most affected. The Japanese simply made a list of desired reforms and set a time limit for their accomplishment which had to be rigidly adhered to. Reforms were instituted solely on the basis of whether they would benefit the Japanese, and this led to a distorted society and a government which ruled not on behalf of its own people but on behalf of a foreign power. Even the reform of dress was aimed at least partly at benefiting the Japanese textile industry.

As might have been expected, the Japanese Minister at whose orders the Reform Council acted found himself constantly at odds with the Taewon'gun. The old man had been shorn of political power, retaining only an empty title, and new decrees were no longer submitted to him, requiring only the King's signature, but he was still an influential man and commanded the respect of many. His deep dislike of the reforms and his antagonism toward the Japanese could be very embarrassing. Moreover, there were rumors, not altogether unfounded, that the Taewon'-gun had been in communication with the Tonghak leaders and had encouraged them to go to the aid of the Chinese army when it was besieged in P'yongyang.

When the war ended, Minister Otori Keisuke was called home and a new Minister, Inoue Kaoru, took his place to complete the reform program. One of his first actions was to force the Taewon'gun into retirement on the convenient excuse that he had encouraged the rebels. He then presented a fresh set of reforms to the government, mainly concerned with the completion of the government reorganization. First, laws and decrees were to be promulgated on the authority of the King and the King alone, a provision which prevented political opposition from Queen Min and her group. Secondly and even more important, foreign (i.e. Japanese) advisors were to be employed in each of the ministries. The judiciary, police and military were to be reorganized. Political power was to be centralized at the expense of the power of district officials. Lastly, the Ministry of Industry was no longer necessary and was to be disbanded.

Pak Yong-hyo and So Kwang-bom, two survivors of the Kapsin coup who had been living in Japan, were now summoned home and appointed to high posts. After the formation of this government, the Reform Council was at last abolished and the State Council transformed into a cabinet. Japanese officials arrived to take up their "advisory" posts, along with a military attaché.

All the basic principles under which the new government operated were now incorporated in a document of fourteen articles which was in effect a constitution for the reformed government. On January 7, 1895, attended by the Taewon'gun, the Crown Prince and civil and military officials, the King went to Chong-myo, which housed the Confucian shrines of all the Yi kings, to announce to his ancestors the establishment of the new form of government. The fourteen articles of the Constitution may be summarized as follows:

1. Korea is a sovereign nation completely independent of China.
2. The rules for succession to the throne are to be legally determined.
3. The King alone heads the government, and the Queen and other relatives are excluded from political power.
4. The finances and other affairs of the royal family are to be administered seperately from those of the government.

5. The powers and functions of each official post are to be clearly defined.
6. Taxation is to be imposed solely according to law.
7. All government financial affairs without exception are to be controlled by the Ministry of Finance.
8. The expenses of the various offices are to be reduced.
9. Annual budgets are to be prepared to regularize finances.
10. The functions and jurisdictions of local administrations are to be clearly defined by law.
11. Talented persons are to be sent abroad for study in order to develop and apply modern science and technology.
12. An army is to be established on the basis of conscription.
13. Reformed civil and criminal law codes are to be enacted.
14. Appointments to government posts are to be made on the basis of merit only, without regard to social status.

This constitution bears certain resemblances to the Japanese constitution which had been promulgated in 1889, notably in the fact that it presupposes autocratic rule and makes no guarantees of civil rights, nor does it even mention an elected legislature. Closer examination of the document, however, reveals that its creators were not merely slavishly following Japanese orders, for it does contain implications that Korea should be independent not only of China but of Japan also.

The Japanese continued to tighten their grip in 1895. The government was in financial difficulties because of the expenses involved in the Tonghak revolt and the Sino-Japanese war, during which Japanese soldiers had carried off, among other things, quantities of gold and silver bullion and one hundred thirty thousand *won* (the Korean unit of currency). Ironically, the first loan by Japan to Korea was one of one hundred thirty thousand won, the identical figure, to be paid from customs revenues with interest of eight per cent a year. In March a second loan of three million won was granted, to be paid from taxes and customs at five per cent over a period of five years. Then the Japanese decided to take over railway construction, telegraphy and mining in lieu of payment, and took over all of these except the telegraph system. Chinnamp'o and Mokp'o became open ports. A proposal to issue paper money was refused, however. To the political bonds in which Japan held Korea financial ones were now added.

The new reforms demanded by the Japanese were completed in April. One of their effects was that 16,000 of the 22,300 district officials were dismissed. As has been noted, the Ministry of Industry had been abolished. Its functions were now transferred to the Ministry of Agriculture and Commerce.

The Japanese had no particular interest in reviving the Korean military forces, and kept pointing out the expense involved whenever the subject came up. The palace guards, however, received training from General W. M. Dye, the American military attaché, and an American assistant. Two battalions were organized and put under the command of the Japanese army. There were also two battalions of royal bodyguards and small numbers of military engineers and cavalry.

An important part of the reforms was the modernization of the judiciary. New courts were established and an appeals system set up. A high court was organized in Seoul, with district courts in the provinces. There were also a special court for the treaty ports and a court for trying members of the royal clan. These were supported by national police, with central headquarters in Seoul and ice stations in all districts. Five of the eight provinces were divided into northern and southern sections, so that the provinces now numbered thirteen, and new district boundaries and designations were made.

The new examination system required a new system of education. It had already begun to appear before this period. The government had established a new school in 1886, and invited an American to help run it. That same year the American Missionary Society had founded Paejae [Paichai] School for Boys, Ihwa [Ewha] Girls' School, and Kyongsin School. Chongsin Girls' School was added in 1890. These were the beginning of the very significant contribution Christian missionaries were to make to Korean education. During the reforms the government established Hansong Normal School, a foreign language school, and a training school for various government officials and functionaries, including army officers, teachers and trade officials.

Chapter 30

Crossfire: Russia and Japan

It will be recalled that Japan's demand for occupation of the Liaotung peninsula as one of the terms of the Treaty of Shimonoseki after the Sino-Japanese war had evoked protests from Russia, France and Germany, and Japan had been compelled to give it up. Russia in particular had felt her interests threatened by this penetration, and the three nations were suspicious of a Japanese presence so near the capital of China. Japan received compensation of thirty million Chinese *liang* for this concession, but Japanese resentment was deep and lasting.

This resentment was not mollified when the three nations proceeded to secure for themselves the advantages they had denied to Japan. Russia leased Lushun (Port Arthur) and Dairen on the tip of the Liaotung peninsula in 1897 on a twenty-five-year lease. Germany secured interests on the Shantung peninsula in the same year, and got a ninety-nine-year lease on Kioachow. France obtained interests in Honan in 1896 and in 1899 took a ninety-nine-year lease in the Kwangchow Bay area in the south. Other nations were not idle meanwhile. Britain obtained a lease on Weihaiwei in 1898. The United States did not participate in these territorial encroachments, but its famous "open door" policy, demanding equality of opportunity for all nations in China furthered the policies of the colonial powers. Chinese sovereignty was deeply compromised, and the Russian advance brought her into direct confrontation with Japan.

The period after the Sino-Japanese war in Korea was one of great fear and unrest. The reforms instituted by the Japanese were not tamely accepted, and all sorts of rumors circulated. One was that the Taewon'gun was planning a coup which involved the assassination of all the ranking pro-Japanese officials, and indeed Kim Hag-u, the Vice Minister of Justice, was assassinated in November of 1894. Another rumor had it that the Taewon'gun was planning to depose King Kojong and his old enemy Queen Min and place his grandson, Yi Chun-yong, on the throne. This last was widely regarded as a fabrication of the Japanese, an excuse for arresting Yi Chun-yong and others in March of 1895, when they reshuffled the government and forced the Taewon'gun unto retirement. Kim Hong-jip was dismissed from the premiership, and other officials were replaced.

The Japanese yielding to the three powers in the Liaotung affair caused many Korean officials to turn eagerly to Russia for help against them. Karl Waeber, the Russian Minister, welcomed these overtures and was in frequent contact with the government. Queen Min saw in the situation an opportunity not only to counteract Japanese domination but to regain her old power, while King Kojong expressed regret that he had given his assent to the reform program. The Chongdong Club, a social organization of the Western community in Seoul, became an unofficial meeting place for Korean officials and Western diplomats, especially Russians. When they became aware of this tendency, the Japanese belatedly attempted to recoup by placing the Royal Guard and the Training Unit directly under Japanese command, but had to back down in the face of protests from both the Russian and the American Ministers. Pak Yong-hyo, who had replaced Kim Hong-jip as premier, was dismissed for his opposition to the Queen, and Kim returned to power in July of 1895, just after Inoue returned from leave. In August Inoue was replaced by Miura Goro, and the stage was set for one of the most despicable plots in modern history.

With Russian support, the Koreans became bolder. Pro-Japanese officials were dismissed, and a royal decree ordered that the old court dress again be worn, implying that the Japanese reform program would be repealed. There were rumors that the Japanese would attempt to dissolve the Military Training Unit, and there were clashes between soldiers and police. Tension between Japan and Russia mounted.

Japanese Minister Miura presented a conciliatory front to the Korean government during all this, but behind the scenes he was busy preparing to oust the pro-Russian group by violence. His plan was the same as that which had overthrown the Queen's faction just before the Sino-Japanese war, by occupying Kyongbok palace, seizing the King, and then placing tools of the Japanese in the government. This time, however, the Queen and her followers were to be eliminated permanently. They counted once again on the Taewon'gun's hatred of the Queen to secure his cooperation. As before, he was to head a government under Japanese auspices. The plot was to be disguised as a clash between discontented soldiers of the Training Unit, who were threatened with disbandment, and palace guards.

At three o'clock on the morning of October 8, 1895, a party of Japanese went to Kongdong-ni outside the Great West Gate to meet the Taewon'gun and escort him to the palace. On their way they were joined by Training Unit soldiers and a number of Japanese guards. A number of mysterious Japanese civilians, who appeared to be criminals of some sort, also came along. Reaching Kyongbok palace, they opened fire on the royal guards, who were no match for them.

There was no escape for Queen Min this time. The Japanese ransacked the palace, and, when they found her, immediately stabbed her. She was carried, dying, into the courtyard and there, even before she was fully dead, her assassins poured kerosene over her body and set it aflame, to hide the evidence of how she had been killed. The commander of the Training Unit, Hong Kye-hun, was killed in the fighting and the Minister of the Royal Household, Yi Kyong-sik, was beaten to death when the ruffians found him. The Japanese troops occupied the palace and seized the King. They were now ready to proceed to the restoration of a pro-Japanese government.

There were complications, however. General Dye, the American instructor of the Training Unit, and a Russian technician named Sabatine were both residing in the palace, and they saw what happened. They were quick to inform the diplomatic corps, which shortly called Minister Miura to account in a joint protest. None of them doubted for a moment that the murder had been carried out with official Japanese connivance. Miura tried to pretend that the whole affair had been simply a clash between the Training Unit and the palace guard. Contemporary Japanese documents which have recently been discovered, however, describe the plot in minute detail and give the names of the two Japanese who did the actual killing. They even note how, afterward, they tried to spread a rumor that the Queen had escaped and was in hiding.

This barbarous act provoked widespread indignation throughout the world. The Japanese government, pretending to know nothing about it, sent a special envoy to inquire into the matter. Miura and some forty others were arrested and imprisoned in Hiroshima, where they were put on trial. All of them were shortly freed, however, on grounds of "insufficient evidence." By this means the

Japanese government hoped to exonerate itself of blame, but the fact that the murderers and those who had employed them went unpunished is sufficiently significant.

Having punished the guilty with a slap on the wrist, the Japanese tried to continue with the reform program as before. The Training Unit and Royal Guard were integrated into a single command of four battalions, with two in Seoul and one each in P'yongyang and Chonju. The postal system was expanded, with post offices planned in most major cities. A primary education system was established and primary schools began to appear, mostly in Seoul at first. The solar calendar replaced the lunar one.

All this could be accepted, however reluctantly. But one of the reform laws, typical of the mechanical and insensitive approach of the Japanese, touched off an uproar. It was decreed that all Korean men should cut off their topknots and wear their hair short in Western fashion. This might seem trivial to an outsider, but to the Koreans it symbolized the denial of all their customs and traditions, and Confucian scholars especially were outraged. Their attitude is perhaps best summed up by the scholar Ch'oe Ik-hyon, who said that he would sooner have his head cut off than his hair.

Coming as it did on the heels of Queen Min's murder, which had also caused great resentment, the "bobbed hair" order proved one provocation too many. There were armed uprisings all over the country from January to April of 1896, and they only ended when the Japanese had suffered a serious setback. At the height of the turmoil, with Japanese attention focused mainly on the provinces, the Russian Minister Alexander de Speyer, who had replaced Waeber in January, summoned 120 sailors from a Russian ship moored at Inch'on on the pretext that he needed extra guards for the legation because of the revolts. With the secret cooperation of other legations, who contributed some of their guards, and acting in concert with some Korean officials, he took his force to the palace early on the morning of February 11, 1896. The King was more than willing to get away, and before the surprised Japanese could do anything about it he was safely ensconced in the Russian legation and the pro-Japanese government was without a legal head.

Though the King had not actually ruled for a long time, his seal on official documents was still necessary and the respect felt for him by both government and people was so great that orderly government without him was unthinkable. The only alternatives the Japanese had were either to disregard legal government altogether and rule Korea by military force or attempt to break into the Russian legation and seize the King, either of which acts would have provoked a war with Russia for which they were not ready. For the time being at any rate the Japanese had to back down and see Russia become the paramount influence on the Korean government.

Decrees now appeared labelling premier Kim Hong-jip and four other leading pro-Japanese officials traitors and calling for their arrest and execution. Premier Kim and Minister Chong Pyong-ha were arrested near Kwanghwamun, the main gate of Kyongbok palace and killed by an enraged crowd before they even reached the prison. Minister O Yun-jung was also killed by a mob while fleeing to his home for safety. The remaining two, Yu Kil-chun and Cho Ui-yon, managed to escape to Japan. A new, pro-Russian cabinet was immediately formed, and one of its first acts was to declare an amnesty for all acts of rebellion caused by the Japanese hair-cutting order and the murder of Queen Min.

The Japanese decided to make the best of things and come to an understanding with the Russians. Minister Komura therefore made contact with Waeber, who had stayed on to advise Speyer, and the two signed a memorandum on May 14, 1896. Its four articles provided that the King was free to return to the palace or stay in the Russian legation as he chose; that the King retained the right to appoint ministers from among suitable candidates; that Japan might station troops in the countryside to protect Japanese facilities such as telegraph lines, but that they should number not more than 200 and should be withdrawn when order was restored; and that Japan might station troops in Seoul to protect Japanese residents, but that these troops should not exceed two battalions of 200 men each. Two further battalions might be stationed in Pusan and Wonsan for similar purposes. The number of Russian troops was to be similarly regulated.

Soon after this agreement the Russians took advantage of the opportunity presented by the coronation of Czar Nicholas II, which was attended by high officials from many countries. In separate, secret negotiations, Russia promised China to protect Korea and Manchuria from Japanese encroachments and received in return the right to build a railway between Siberia and Manchuria, which would connect with the trans-Siberian railroad. Russia agreed with Japan on joint cooperation in advising the Korean government on reform and modernization. The establishment and maintenance of an army and police force was to be left to the Korean government. The Japanese would retain the right to control the telegraph lines they had already built, while the Russians would be allowed to construct telegraph lines on the northern border. If it became necessary for either or both nations to send troops to Korea there should be previous consultation as to their stationing so as to avoid armed conflict. The troops of both sides already in Korea would remain there until the Korean army was organized. It was also understood that the King would remain under Russian protection.

With the Korean officials attending the coronation the Russians worked out an agreement somewhat similar to the one the Japanese had had. Russian officers were to train the Korean army and Russian financial experts were to advise the government. The Russians would be responsible for the King's safety. The Russians would work out loan agreements for Korea in future discussions. Finally, both nations agreed to the construction of telegraph lines connecting them. This agreement was quickly carried out, the Russian officers and a financial expert named Alexieff arriving in October to replace the Japanese advisors in their respective departments. A Russian-language school had already been founded in Seoul the previous April with the help of a Russian officer.

With the Russians firmly entrenched, the Korean government now began to make economic concessions to various foreign powers, a thing it had previously managed to avoid except for the Japanese telegraph system, which had been built quite illegally though later legalized. An American named Morse obtained the right to build a railway from Inch'on to Seoul and also a mining concession in Hamgyong Province. In September another Russian obtained timber rights on the Yalu River and on Ullung Island. A French firm was to build a railroad from Seoul to Uiju. The British firm of Holmringer established a branch at Inch'on, acting as agent for the British-owned Hongkong and Shanghai Banking Corporation.

But these European and American investments in Korea amounted to little when compared with the economic penetration which Japan had made and retained in spite of her political reverses. There were twenty branches of Japanese banks in Seoul and the treaty ports. The Daiichi Bank of Japan had become virtually the central bank of Korea, handling customs duties, purchasing gold and silver, controlling government loans, managing the treasury and issuing currency. There were 210 Japanese firms operating in Korea by 1896, whereas firms of all other foreign countries amounted to only forty-eight.

The situation at the end of 1896 was only an uneasy truce. Japan was developing at a tremendous pace and her ambitions grew correspondingly. The easy defeat of China and the territory it brought had whetted her appetite for more, while the forced disgorging of the Liaotung peninsula still rankled. Her rapid industrialization had created a need for new markets while her growing population created a need for new sources of foodstuffs and raw materials. These the Japanese intended to have, quickly and by force if necessary. Forty to fifty per cent of the annual budget went to the military, while Japan took advantage of the shifting alliances and conflicts among the great powers to obtain loans, equipment and expert advice in a wide variety of technical fields. The primary goal was to get control of Korea and Manchuria, both for her own economic advantage and as insurance against any military threat from Russia. Korea once again became the victim of contending forces greater than herself.

PART SEVEN

The Contemporary Period

Chapter **31**

The Last Years of
Independence

Russian dominance afforded Korean government and society a brief period of freedom during which there were some notable achievements. One of the leading figures during the Russian period, a sincere patriot and an advocate not only of modernization but of the development of political democracy, was So Chae-p'il. He had been involved in the Kapsin coup of 1884, and had fled to Japan upon its failure. From there he had gone to the United States, where he had earned a medical degree from the University of Washington, married an American wife and acquired United States citizenship. In 1896 he returned to his native land, determined to help secure her independence and spread enlightenment among her citizens by whatever means he could. He was known to Westerners as Dr. Philip Jaisohn, but we shall use his Korean name in this work.

So Chae-p'il refused the offer of a government post when he returned, although he did consent to act in an advisory capacity. He wished to have freedom of action in his efforts to instil a desire for independence and belief in democratic principles in the hearts of his countrymen, and he chose the press as his medium. On April 7, 1896 appeared the first issue of the *Independent*, the first modern newspaper in Korea, printed in both Korean and English and appearing three times a week, later daily.

One of the first projects undertaken by the paper was the

439

establishment of some tangible symbol of Korean independence. So proposed that Yongunmun, the special gate where Chinese envoys had been received in the past, should be torn down, and in its place a new gate, to be called the "Independence Arch" should be erected as a symbol of Korean independence and the end of suzerainty to a foreign power. A few days later the "Independence Association" was founded.

Both of these ideas proved popular and received government support. The Independence Association announced as its purposes the reflection of public opinion in politics and the protection from foreigners of national resources. Within three months it had ten thousand members. These contributed money for the Independence Arch project, and a ground-breaking ceremony was held in November. Frequent meetings of the Association discussed democracy and ways to implement it in Korea. The Arch was completed and dedicated within a year.

It had been necessary for the King to take refuge in the Russian legation to escape the Japanese, but his continued stay there meant a loss of international prestige for the nation, and public opinion from the first called for his return to his palace. So Chae-p'il himself petitioned the King to leave the legation upon his return from America, but for some time this was not possible. After Russian dominance had become well established and it was generally agreed that the Japanese would not stage another coup, the King at last decided to come out, and on February 20, 1897, after more than a year with the Russians, he took up residence in Kyongun palace (now Toksu palace) in the legation quarter, so that he could easily return in case of trouble. Government officials who had stayed with him in the legation also moved out.

Attention now turned to the title customarily given the ruler. The word which we translate as *king* signified in the

Chinese language a ruler subordinate to the Chinese Emperor, whereas the title given the Japanese Emperor made him linguistically the equal of the ruler of China. It was now suggested that the Korean monarch also be called Emperor, to show that Korea was independent of both nations and entitled to equal treatment. This was accordingly done in August of 1897, at which time also the official name of the country was changed from Choson to Taehan Cheguk, meaning roughly the Korean Empire, using the old name *Han,* which had designated some Korean people in ancient times. On October 12 a coronation was held, after which the now Emperor Kojong received the congratulations of foreign diplomats, who came to the palace to deliver messages of recognition from their governments.

The independence movement went on against a background of rising foreign demands upon Korea. Immediately after the coronation, when the Russian financial adviser arrived, Russia demanded the use of Choryong Island as a coaling station, and England asked the lease of Komun Island for a similar purpose. In March of 1898 a Russian branch bank appeared in Seoul, and there were rumors that national treasury and tax funds would be transferred to it. In April of 1897 the German firm of Edward Meyer & Co. had obtained a gold mining concession in Kangwon Province, and another mining concession went to the English firm of Morgan in September. In December the American Standard Oil Co. constructed an oil storage depot on Wolmi Island in Inch'on harbor, and in February, 1898, an American firm obtained contracts to build a streetcar line, a water works and a power plant in Seoul.

Many of these foreign investments were relatively unsuccessful, and the firms wanted to give them up. This suited Japanese plans very well, and Japanese businessmen were always glad to buy up concessions and contracts from disappointed Westerners. In 1897 the American Morse conveyed his contract for a rail line between Seoul and Inch'on to the Japanese, and they also purchased from the French the contract to build a railway from Seoul to Uiju. In September of 1898 an agreement between the Korean and Japanese governments projected a rail line between Seoul and Pusan, to be managed jointly. Japanese fisheries now extended all the way up the west coast of Korea. Since the Japanese were really interested in conquest, which the other foreign nations were not, they were willing to accept economic liabilities which helped tighten their grip on the country.

The Independence Association initiated a popular movement to protect the nation's natural resources from foreign exploitation. On February 9, 1898, a mass meeting was held at Chongno intersection in Seoul, at which the truth about the Russian bank was revealed. The meeting demanded that the granting of concessions to foreigners be stopped, and that the Russian military and financial advisers be dismissed. It also criticized government policies in general. The pressure of public opinion generated by this meeting forced the government to dismiss the Russian advisers and close down the Russian bank.

These anti-government moves caused conflicts within the Association which resulted in the resignation from it of several government officials and a reshuffling of the leadership. Yun Ch'i-ho, who had attended the Czar's coronation and then toured Europe and America, was elected president. Another leading member at this time was Yi Sungman, or Syngman Rhee as he himself romanized his name, later to become the first president of the Republic of Korea.

The government reacted to the Association's activities by deporting So Chae-p'il, who was a United States citizen, probably at the instance of foreign diplomats who felt that the Association was inimical to their countries. The government then founded a rival group called the Imperial Association, which tried to rally popular support and counteract the criticisms of the Independence Association.

The Independence Association then held another mass rally at Chongno, this time with several high government officials in attendance, and passed the following resolutions: 1) We must support the Emperor by making the nation independent of all foreign powers; 2) All agreements with foreign nations concerning mining, timber, railways, loans, military aid and treaties must be endorsed by the heads of all ministries before going into effect; 3) Financial matters should be controlled by the Finance Ministry only, and other ministries and private firms should not be allowed to interfere; annual budgets and balance sheets should be made public; 4) All trials for felony should be open to the public, and grave offenders should not be brought to trial before confession; 5) Officials appointed by the Emperor should take office only with the concurrence of a majority of the government leaders; 6) These resolutions should be adopted by the government and put into practice.

The government, needless to say, did not adopt these resolutions. It did revise the membership of the Consultative Committee, making half of its members elective, the first appearance of elective office in Korea. However, this was simply a device to get members of the Imperial Association into the government by having them elected rather than appointed so that the Independence Association could not criticize their appointment. This strategy merely sharpened the antagonism between the two groups, and matters reached such a point that the government ordered the Independence Association dissolved and issued warrants for the arrest of its leaders. President Yun Ch'i-ho managed to escape but seventeen of the leaders were imprisoned.

The Association, however, refused to submit. Mass rallies

were held at Chongno day and night, demanding the release of the leaders and the repeal of the dissolution order. When the leaders were freed, the rallies shifted to the palace gate and pressed for government reform, even passing a resolution of no confidence in the Cabinet. The government pretended to make a compromise, but secretly mobilized the Imperial Association, whose members launched surprise attacks on the demonstrators. Numerous bloody clashes followed, until at length Emperor Kojong felt obliged to intervene personally. He first ordered the Imperial Association leaders arrested and the dissolution of the peddlers' guild which it controlled. This was followed by a second dissolution of the Independence Association, and this time the government meant business. Some of the leaders were imprisoned, while some managed to find asylum in other countries. For a brief moment it had seemed that the developing spirit of nationality in Korea might have included a desire for democracy, but the movement died of suffocation.

The clamor over foreign concessions subsided after the suppression of the Independence Association as events abroad began to loom large in Korean affairs. In 1900 occurred the Boxer Rebellion in China, a mass anti-foreign movement which had the covert support of the Chinese court. Numerous foreign nationals were killed, and the diplomatic corps in Peking was besieged in the legation quarter of the city. An allied expeditionary force was sent to put down the rebels and rescue the diplomats, including troops from Russia, England, Germany, France, the United States, Austria, Italy and Japan. The largest contingent in this force was Japanese. The Russians, however, in addition to their contribution to the allied force, sent a separate expedition to occupy Manchuria on the pretext of protecting Russian railways there.

In preparation for what now seemed an inevitable clash,

Japan in 1902 concluded an alliance with Britain, the traditional foe of Russian expansionism, while Russia on its part allied itself with France. In 1903 Russians crossed the Korean border at Yongamp'o at the mouth of the Yalu, and began purchasing land, and putting up buildings and telegraph lines. Russia failed to get a lease on the region due to the strong protests of Japan and Britain, but opened the city to trade.

Japan now felt strong enough to force the Russians either to back down or fight in Manchuria. She had the advantage of geographical position, while Russian lines of communication would be long. She had an army of 200,000 troops and a fleet of 260,000 tons, and her men were well equipped and trained. In 1903 negotiations were called for and Japan made her demands. The Russians were to withdraw their troops from Manchuria and recognize the paramountcy of Japan's interest in Korea. The Russians acceded to the Japanese interest in Korea so long as it was not used for military purposes but asserted that Manchuria lay outside the Japanese sphere and that the presence of Russian troops was not a Japanese concern. They even proposed to divide Korea into a Russian and a Japanese sphere at the thirty-ninth parallel.

When it became clear that the Russians were not going to back down, Japan struck without warning, just as she had struck China ten years before. On February 8, 1904, Japanese ships opened fire on Port Arthur, bottling up the Russian fleet at anchor there. War was officially declared on the tenth. The Korean government immediately declared complete neutrality, but this was a futile gesture. Japanese troops landed at Inch'on immediately and marched into Seoul. The government was forced to sign a protocol with the following provisions: Korea accepts Japanese advice on the improvement of facilities; Japan assures the Korean government of independence and territorial integrity; if and when there is danger to the personal safety of the Korean Emperor, the Japanese government will take such steps as the occasion demands, and the Korean government will give complete cooperation; the Japanese government may make use of any part of Korean territory for military operations in securing the Emperor's safety; the Korean government is to conclude no treaties with other governments without the consent of Japan.

The excuse of protecting the Emperor was fairly transparent. Japan plainly intended to use Korea as a military base in her war with Russia, and to this end would also deprive the nation of its sovereignty by taking control of foreign relations. When the war went favorably for Japan, she took the further step of abrogating all agreements between Korea and Russia and expropriating all concessions granted to Russians. In August a fresh protocol was signed which re-imposed the "adviser" system through which Japan was to control the government. In this first of a series of Korean-Japanese "agreements" Korea was to employ a Japanese as financial adviser and an American (D. W. Stevens, formerly employed as adviser to the Japanese Foreign Ministry) as adviser on foreign affairs. Other Japanese "advisers" soon followed for the royal court, the Bureau of Military Affairs, the Bureau of Police and the Department of Education. Korea was compelled to summon home her diplomatic missions, whose functions were taken over by their Japanese counterparts. In everything but name, Korea was a part of the Japanese Empire.

Meanwhile, Japan inflicted a series of decisive defeats on Russia. In March of 1905 the important Manchurian city of Mukden fell. In a desperate attempt to tip the balance, Russia sent her Baltic fleet all the way to Asia. It was denied the use of the Suez Canal by Britain and had to sail around Africa to reach its destination. Hardly had it arrived, however, than it was blown to pieces by the

Japanese navy off Tsushima Island in the Korea Strait. After this, Russian capitulation was only a matter of time, and Korean independence was doomed. As victory neared, Japan took a tighter grip on Korea in a fresh agreement giving her control of all Korean communications and freedom of navigation on inland waterways.

While the defeat of Russia was ensuring Japanese rule in Korea, Japan was busy making sure there would be no interference from Western powers. In July of 1905 Japanese Prime Minister Katsura Taro met secretly with William Howard Taft, the American Secretary of War, who was on a visit to Tokyo. The result of their deliberations was the Taft-Katsura Agreement, in which the United States recognized Japan's interests in Korea in return for a Japanese promise not to interfere or raise objections over American rule in the Philippines. In August a similar agreement was reached with Britain, with Japan promising to support British rule in India. The United States and Great Britain thus bargained away Korea's freedom to preserve their own colonial possessions from the rising power of Japan.

It was also in July of 1905 that Russia admitted defeat and consented to begin peace negotiations. These were initiated through the good offices of the President of the United States, Theodore Roosevelt, and conducted in the United States, so that the treaty which ended a war far off in Asia bears the name of the town of Portsmouth, New Hampshire. In this treaty Russia officially conceded Japanese political, military and economic interests in Korea, and in addition virtually gave up the effort to control Manchuria. All the Manchurian concessions acquired by Russia were now taken over by Japan, including railways, a lease on the Liaotung peninsula and fishery rights to the coast of Sikhote Alin. Russia also ceded to Japan the southern half of Sakhalin Island, just north of

Hokkaido. Most importantly, it was agreed that the sovereignty of Korea should not be mentioned in any international treaty, a public acknowledgement of Japanese control over Korean foreign relations. Japan now had guarantees from three of the world's great powers to do as she liked with Korea. The Korean people, against their will and without being consulted, came under the rule of Japan at least partly by the connivance of Western nations. It was a proceeding that did honor to none of the parties to it.

The Japanese moved quickly to reap the fruits of victory. In October of 1905 they presented to the Korean government a new agreement of five articles which placed all relations with other nations in the hands of the Japanese. Negotiations in the Emperor's presence were held under the eyes of Japanese guards, who removed anyone raising objections. After many altercations, during which many Korean officials were taken away by the guards, the agreement was signed on November 17. Its provisions were as follows: 1) The foreign relations of Korea are to be controlled and supervised by the Japanese Foreign Affairs Ministry, and the lives and interests of Koreans residing abroad are to be protected by Japanese consuls; 2) Japan undertakes to fulfill the conditions of all existing treaties between Korea and other nations, but Korea will not conclude any new international agreements except through the mediation of Japan; 3) A Japanese **Resident**-General is to reside in Seoul and have the right to consult the Emperor whenever he deems it necessary and Japanese commissioners under the Inspector-General's supervision are to reside in the open ports and any other places thought necessary; 4) All existing treaties between Korea and Japan are to remain valid unless they violate the spirit of this agreement; 5) The safety and dignity of the Korean Emperor are guaranteed by the Japanese government.

In December of 1905 Ito Hirobumi, a leading Japanese statesman, was named Resident-General of Korea, and by the end of January the twelve commissioners had taken up their posts, one in Seoul and the rest in the provinces. In March Ito himself arrived and all the foreign legations were withdrawn from Korea. The Resident-General was charged not only with overseeing Korean foreign relations but also with protecting and advancing Japanese interests generally. He was under the direct authority of the Japanese Emperor, and had the power to use Japanese troops at his discretion. The Korean army was disbanded except for one battalion of palace guards. The complete helplessness of the Korean government is shown by the fact that Japan arbitrarily transferred the Korean island of Tokto to the Japanese prefecture of Shimane immediately after the war, and in 1909 transferred the Kando (Chien-tao in Chinese) district to China as part of a railway concession.

The next objective was the Korean economy. Laws were revised so that Japanese could freely purchase land. In addition, land was often used as collateral for loans, and when the poverty-stricken Korean farmers could not pay, their land was taken over by Japanese money-lenders. By 1907 there were 7,745 Japanese land-owners in Korea, controlling an area of 230,803,000 *p'yong* (one *p'yong* is a little over four square yards). The Korean currency was reformed to conform with that of Japan so that financial transactions between the two countries would be facilitated. New methods were applied to increase rice production so as to make Korea a supplier to Japan, and the same policy was applied to silk and cotton textiles. Numerous Japanese left their over-crowded homeland for Korea, so that in addition to government officials and police there were merchants, financiers, money-lenders and farmers, subsequently joined by the unemployed and numerous undesirables who had been unsuccessful at home. The number of

Japanese increased from only 20,000 in 1897 to 170,000 in 1910. Korea had become a Japanese colony.

As might have been expected, neither the Korean people nor the government accepted the Japanese takeover without a fight. A portent of things to come had been a Japanese proposal during the Russo-Japanese War to allow Japanese farmers to take over uncultivated Korean land, which had resulted in such furious resistance that it had to be withdrawn. After the Agreement came into force the Emperor secretly sent Yi Sung-man (Syngman Rhee) to the United States to appeal to President Roosevelt to intervene on Korea's behalf, but Roosevelt was committed to the Treaty of Portsmouth and the appeal was ignored. Yi happened to come, unfortunately, just after the signing of the Taft-Katsura agreement.

At home Chang Chi-yon, editor of the *Hwangsong News*, wrote and published a leading article headed "Today is a Lamentable Day," appealing to the righteous indignation of the people. Numerous leading officials sent petitions of protest to the Throne. Min Yong-hwan was not content with a mere protest, and committed suicide rather than serve the Japanese. Several dozen others followed his example. The ministers who had given assent to the Agreement were labelled the "Five Traitors" by the people. Two of them, Yi Kun-t'aek and Kwon Chung-hyon, were shot and the homes of two others, Yi Wan-yong and Pak Che-sun, were burned down by furious crowds. Emperor Kojong secretly wrote to H. B. Hulbert, an American missionary who had returned home, asking him to appeal to the President once again, but this too was ignored.

In 1907 Emperor Kojong made one last effort to regain his country's independence. Hearing that the second World Peace Conference was to be held at the Hague in the Netherlands, he decided to send envoys secretly to plead Korea's cause. Yi Sang-sol and Yi Chun were given letters and credentials signed and sealed by the Emperor and made their way across Russia to St. Petersburg (Leningrad) where they were joined by Yi Wi-jong, a former member of the Korean diplomatic mission to Russia. The three reached the Netherlands safely and in time for the conference and immediately contacted the Chairman, a Russian, and requested that they be permitted to participate in the Conference as representatives of Korea. The Chairman, however, said that they could not be admitted because Korea had no rights to diplomatic representation. The three envoys remained, however, visiting the delegations of all the countries represented to explain how their country's sovereignty had been destroyed against its will, and also participated in meetings sponsored by the International Press Club. While they received considerable sympathy, none of the nations was willing to intervene in any effective way, and their mission was a failure. Beset by vexation and despair, Yi Chun became ill and died.

Although this mission achieved no practical result, Korea's plight and the greed and injustice of Japan had been put fairly before the world, and there was considerable criticism. Infuriated, the Japanese reached by forcing the abdication of Emperor Kojong, which took place on July 19, 1907. The Crown Prince (posthumous title Sunjong) took his place, becoming the last monarch to reign in Korea. Officials who opposed the abdication were banished by the Japanese.

Yet another "agreement" was now forced upon the Korean government, to ensure complete Japanese control. Conventionally called the "New Agreement," it gave the Resident-General control of all appointments to government posts. The vice-minister of each ministry was to be Japanese, and the Korean government was forbidden to employ foreigners of any other nationality. By 1909 about 2,000 of the officials high and low in the government were

Japanese.

The abdication and the New Agreement provoked the Korean people to a wave of violence. An angry crowd attacked and destroyed the building of a pro-Japanese newspaper. Another crowd clashed with Japanese guards outside the palace and did not disperse until the guards began firing on them. In 1908 in San Francisco Chon Myong-un and Chang In-hwan shot and killed D.W. Stevens, an American who had been employed by the Japanese in setting up the Resident-General's government. And on October 26, 1909, at the Harbin railroad station in Manchuria, An Chung-gun assassinated Ito Hirobumi, the elder statesman who had masterminded the Japanese takeover and become the first Resident-General. In Seoul, Yi Chae-myong fatally wounded Yi Wan-yong, the official who had been made premier under Ito.

There was popular resistance to Japanese rule in the countryside from the very beginning, much of it led by Confucian scholars, who had always been opposed to any relations with Japan. Min Chong-sik, formerly an important official, organized a force of about five hundred men in North Ch'ungch'ong Province and secured seventy-five old cannon in the spring of 1906, caused the Japanese considerable trouble before he was defeated. Ch'oe Ik-hyon, who had been banished for his opposition to the Kanghwa Treaty in 1876, now an old man of seventy, also organized a rebellion and wrote a detailed indictment of the Japanese, calling upon the people to rise against them, which was widely distributed. The revolt spread to Kyongsang and Kangwon Provinces.

The revolts intensified when, at the time of Kojong's abdication, the last remaining Korean military unit was disbanded. Pak Song-hwan, commander of one of the two battalions of the Royal Guard, killed himself in protest, and the majority of the soldiers fought a pitched battle with the Japanese in Seoul. When they were defeated, those who could escape fled to the provinces and joined the rebels there. The local militia forces went over to the rebels, bringing their weapons with them. The rebel forces established bases in inaccessible mountain regions and conducted regular raids on Japanese installations, destroying railroad tracks and cutting telegraph lines.

The rebels quickly found that they were no match for the well-armed Japanese in pitched battles, and confined their efforts mostly to guerrilla warfare. The Japanese response was indiscriminate slaughter and destruction. Nevertheless, the rebels received considerable support from the people and continued harassing the Japanese all through 1907 and into 1908. After that their efforts declined somewhat, and many of them crossed the border into Manchuria to attack the Japanese there.

To minimize rebel attacks and to control the people in other ways, Japanese military and civilian police networks were quickly set up. A Japanese-supervised Department of Police was added to the government of each of the thirteen provinces, and twenty-six police detachments and one hundred and twenty-two branch police stations appeared, all commanded by Japanese. There were about 2,000 Japanese military policemen by 1907. By 1908 4,234 Koreans had been recruited to serve the Japanese in subjugating their countrymen. Even this early the rise of militarism in Japan was blurring the distinction between civilian police and military organizations, and the Japanese police system was in effect a military occupation of the country.

In the brief period between the opening of the country and the Japanese victory of 1905 modern cultural institutions had begun to appear in Korea which might have served the country well had they been allowed to flourish in freedom. As it was, they became centers of resistance to the Japanese and created a tradition of democracy.

The first regular newspaper in Korea was the *Hansong Sunbo,* which appeared in 1883 and was published every ten days. However, this was only an official gazette, and real credit for the beginning of Korean journalism must go to the *Independent,* which has already been discussed. This paper, and the Independence Association which it sponsored, were very important in fostering among the people a spirit of independence and democracy. The mass meetings which the Association held were of particular importance in making the people aware of civil rights and in creating a spirit of nationalism. The suppression of the Association through the puppet Imperial Association was a very unfortunate step by the government.

Other papers appeared after the example of the *Independent.* In 1898 the *Hwangsong News* appeared, printed in a mixture of Chinese characters and Han'gul as Korean newspapers are today. It followed a more conservative line than the *Independent,* and appealed to upper-class readers. In the same year another paper, the *Imperial News* appeared, printed entirely in Han'gul. In 1905 E. T. Bethell, an Englishman, together with Yang Ki-t'ak, founded the *Taehan Daily News,* published in both Korean and English. All of these papers strongly criticized the New Agreement with Japan and stirred up public opinion against it.

Another sign of developing national consciousness and desire for freedom was the appearance of a number of political organizations for the study and dissemination of democratic ideas and resistance to the Japanese. In May of 1905 the Constitutional Government Research Body was formed to work for the extension of civil rights and in April of 1906 the Korean Struggle Society appeared to oppose a pro-Japanese organization named, with unconscious humor, the One Step Forward Society. The Struggle group was reorganized in November, 1907, in an effort to turn it into a true mass movement against the Japanese. The Forward Together Society and the Popular Representation Society also appeared during this time.

As soon as the Japanese Resident-General's regime was fully established and the police organization began to function in 1905, the Japanese authorities undertook the suppression of the free press and the various political organizations. In one notable action, E. T. Bethell, editor of the *Taehan Daily News* was deported to England after his paper published articles critical of the Japanese regime. A pro-Japanese paper, the *People's News* was organized to support Japanese rule. As late as 1909, however, yet another political organization, the Korea Society, began publication of the *Korean People's News*.

The Japanese suppression of freedom of speech and assembly drove many of the Korean intellectual and political leaders out of Seoul. Quite a few of them formed educational and cultural organizations in the provinces which, though not really political, did undertake the preservation and development of Korean culture. Schools were founded and journals appeared dealing with cultural matters.

Until their publications too were suppressed by the Japanese, the true state of affairs in Korea was reported to the world by American missionaries. The *Korean Repository*, a monthly in English, appeared as early as 1892, and after a brief suspension continued publication until 1898. It was edited and mostly written by F. Oblingers, H. B. Hulbert and H. G. Appenzeller. In 1906 Hulbert began publication of the *Corea Review*. The missionaries generally opposed the Japanese rule and supported Korean independence movements.

Another development that showed considerable promise before being blighted by the Japanese was the establishment of modern educational institutions. After the opening of the country, officials trained in modern subjects and modern languages were urgently needed to deal with foreign relations and trade. In 1886 the Royal English School was opened to the sons of high officials and prominent yangban. It had three American missionaries on its staff and taught English, mathematics, natural science, history, world geography and political science, using English as the medium of instruction. It continued in existence until 1894 but achieved no outstanding results, most of the yangban being somewhat less than enthusiastic about new-fangled notions.

Among the Japanese-inspired reforms of 1894 was a new educational system, and schools at every level were founded in Seoul, including primary schools, middle schools, teacher-training institutions and foreign language schools. The chief purpose of the system, it should be borne in mind, was to produce future officials and experts of various kinds. Universal education, free and compulsory, was not envisaged at this time.

Perhaps the most significant contribution to modernization of Korean education was that of the Christian missionaries. The private schools which they founded had an influence out of all proportion to the number of their graduates, and several of them are still in existence today. Most of these missionaries were Americans, and their schools roughly followed American models. Paejae Boys' School was founded in 1886, to be followed later in the same year by Ihwa Girls' School and Kyongsin Boys' School, all in Seoul. There were two further girls' schools established in Seoul, Chongsin in 1890 and Paewha in 1898, while the Sungsil Boys' School and Sungui School for Girls appeared in P'yongyang in 1897 and 1903 respectively, and also Hosudon in Kaesong in 1904.

Students were admitted to these schools without regard to class or status, and in them they imbibed, along with modern subjects, a spirit of democratic independence. Many of them went on to become leaders of their people in the struggle against Japanese domination. This process began very early, many of the leaders of the Independence Association, for example, being graduates of Paejae School.

During the years between the New Agreement of 1905 and the annexation of 1910 many Korean leaders, blocked in direct efforts to oppose the Japanese, turned to education as a means of fostering the national spirit, and numerous private schools were founded by them. In Seoul Posong, Yangjong, and Hwimun schools were founded in 1905, Chinmyong and Sungmyong girls school in 1906, and Taesong school at P'yongyang and Osan at Chongju in 1907. By 1910 there were about 3,000 private schools in Korea, an impressive demonstration of the people's faith in education.

But the education laws promulgated by the Japanese-backed government aimed at spreading a submissive attitude. Japanese teachers were assigned to all government schools, and the curricula of private schools were strictly regulated. No school could be established without government permission and existing schools had to be licensed. This meant, of course, the distortion or suppression of much that had been promising in the new education. Modern subjects such as ethics, history, geography, law, economics and mathematics were taught, replacing the old Confucian studies. Before the Japanese took complete control, however, a spirit of independence permeated Korean education. One result was a number of studies of Korean language and culture and biographies of national heroes. Numerous foreign books dealing with the rise and fall of nations and with revolution and independence were translated into Korean and widely read, particular interest being centered on the American and French revolutions and on the history of Switzerland, a small country which had managed to remain independent of greater powers and so in some ways was comparable to Korea. All this, of course, the Japanese suppressed as soon as possible.

The effect of Japanese domination on religion was to give most religious movements a political flavor. Tonghak, of course, had had political aspects from the first. The Japanese managed to win over one of its leaders, Yi Yong-gu, and attempted to use him in controlling the country and maneuvering for annexation. The chief Tonghak leader Son Pyong-hui was not deceived, however, and the majority of Tonghak remained firmly anti-Japanese. The authorities attempted to suppress the sect and refused to recognize it as a genuine religion, but it continued to spread nevertheless. Its name was changed at this time to Ch'ondogyo (Religion of the Heavenly Way), and it developed many social institutions of its own. Several schools were founded and a newspaper, the *Mansebo News* was established specifically to attack the Japanese. By 1910 the sect claimed three hundred thousand believers.

The progressive, democratic spirit of American Protestantism made the institutions founded by missionaries the natural breeding places for leaders of the resistance. With practically all public institutions controlled by Japan, large numbers of young people turned to the Protestant churches and the mission schools. The American Presbyterian Mission, North, and the American Methodist Episcopal Mission, North, were the most active groups at this time, having founded most of the schools mentioned earlier.

In addition to establishing modern education and fostering the democratic spirit, the American missionaries also brought modern medicine to Korea. In 1885 the American missionary doctor Horace N. Allen founded the Kwanghyewon Hospital with Korean government support, the first Western medical institution in Korea. In 1886 the hospital opened a medical school for a few students.

Renamed Chejungwon in 1887, it was taken over by the American Presbyterian Mission, North, and has been managed by that mission ever since. A regular medical school was added in 1899, and in 1908 its first class graduated. It is known today as the Severance Hospital and Medical School.

Other Christian groups made contributions to Korea, notably the Y. M. C. A. The Hwangsong Y. M. C. A. was founded in 1903 and sponsored numerous social service groups, generally against Japanese opposition. Resident-General Ito at one time had the curious notion that the spread of Christianity would weaken the spirit of Korean independence, perhaps because Christianity was thought subversive of Japanese society, but the passionate patriotism of Korean Christians soon disabused him of this idea. Generally speaking, the Christian churches of Korea, especially the Protestant ones, were opposed to Japanese rule and gave whatever help they could to the struggle against it. None of the oppressive Japanese measures ever overcame this resistance and the Japanese, at any rate in the early years of their rule, dared not suppress the missionaries for fear of offending the Western powers.

The political turmoil of this period did not permit much attention to literature, but even so new tendencies began to appear as a result of Western contact. This too first came about through missionaries. The Gospels of Luke and John from the New Testament were translated into Korean in 1882, and a complete Korean translation of the Bible appeared soon after. The first modern Western work to be translated was John Bunyan's *Pilgrim's Progress*, translated by the Canadian missionary James Scarth Gale. Others followed rapidly, mostly children's favorites such as *Aesop's Fables, Gulliver's Travels, Robinson Crusoe, William Tell,* and so on. The influence of these books on Korean literature was reinforced by that of Yu Kil-chun, who on his return from a tour of Europe published *Soyu kyonmun* (A Record of Personal Experience in Europe), written in a fresh and attractive style.

As the spread of Christianity and modern education increased knowledge of Western literature, new tendencies began to appear in Korean writing, especially in poetry, drama and the novel. The outstanding pioneer in the new literary movement was undoubtedly Yi In-jik, who created what came to be called the "New Novel" and was also active in drama. After studying law and political science in Japan he returned home to become a reporter for the *Mansebo News,* and later was president of the *Taehan News.* His *Hyol ui nu* (Tears of Blood), the first New Novel, was published in 1906. Numerous others followed.

The innovations in the New Novel were two. First, the old literary style, remote from everyday life, was discarded, and the common speech was adapted to literature. Second, fantastic and legendary themes were replaced by stories confined to the real world and written in a realistic style based upon observation. The New Novel was thus not only a literary innovation but a means of enlightenment and progress. Another writer of the time, Yi Hae-jo, translated numerous Western novels and wrote several of his own, including one called *Chayujong* (The Bell of Freedom).

The Koreans have always been a singing people, and Western vocal music had an immediate appeal. Many of the hymns learned in mission churches were soon put to secular use by writing didactic or patriotic Korean lyrics for them. A New Poetry in the Western manner also developed at this time, the first examples being published in a magazine called *Sonyon* (Boys) in 1909.

Innovations in drama also deserve special mention. Korea had a dramatic tradition of sorts, and a kind of informal musical play, usually presented in the open, but Western-style plays require theaters with special facilities.

The redoubtable Yi In-jik appealed to the Emperor Kojong for funds, and as a result a National Theater, in the style of a Roman amphitheater, was built. One of the first plays to be presented there was Yi's *Sol chung mae* (Plum Tree in the Snow), in 1909. Though the theater was also used for more traditional forms of entertainment, it served for some time to help develop modern tendencies in drama, and a number of new dramatic groups sprang up.

But foreign countries provided more than mere literary influence during the last years of Korean independence. For many patriots they were places of refuge and bases from which to continue the struggle against Japan. As Japanese oppression intensified and annexation neared, an increasing number of Koreans fled abroad. Many of them were not content merely to have escaped, but maintained contacts with the homeland as best they could and organized themselves into anti-Japanese groups in the hope of liberation.

The most numerous refugee groups went to countries that could be reached by land, and especially to Sikhote Alin on the Siberian Pacific coast and the Kando area of Manchuria. This was made easier by the fact that the northern borders had not been very tightly policed in the past and numerous Koreans already inhabited these regions. There were estimated to be 100,000 of them in the Kando area in 1903 and about 32,000 in Sikhote Alin in 1902. This last figure rapidly increased after the turn of the century, also reaching about 100,000 by 1910, as farmers who had lost their land and political refugees streamed across the border at the time of the annexation.

Many of those who participated in the struggle against Japan after the disbanding of the Korean armed forces in 1907 were based in Sikhote Alin and conducted numerous raids into Hamgyong Province until the establishment of a Japanese police network forced them to move their base to the western Kando region, then to the eastern part, from which the Japanese had withdrawn at the instance of China.

Numerous schools were founded in the Kando after 1905 to keep Korean culture alive and foster the spirit of resistance. Many noted Korean leaders taught in these schools and many of their graduates fought for national independence. In Sikhote Alin two anti-Japanese newspapers appeared, and though they were forced to suspend publication because of financial troubles and Japanese interference in 1909, one of them, the *Taedong Kongbo,* reappeared after the annexation and continued to inspire the emigrants.

The first Koreans arrived in Hawaii in 1903 and by 1905 there were 7,226 of them there, mostly farmers whose land had been appropriated in one way or another by the Japanese. This emigration soon extended to the United States mainland, where many of the political exiles took refuge, most notably Syngman Rhee. They became the leaders of Korean emigrant organizations which were active in public criticism of Japanese rule in Korea. In 1906, when Japan took over Korean diplomatic relations, these organizations jointly issued a bitter denunciation. The assassination of D. W. Stevens in 1908 gave more serious evidence of the depth of their resentment.

Korean organizations abroad continued to multiply as emigration increased. In Hawaii Korean schools were set up and a Korean-language newspaper appeared. In San Francisco a Cooperative Society was formed which also published a paper. In July of 1907 the majority of these groups were united in the Combined Society which published yet another paper. Branches of this society were set up in other countries, notably Russia and Manchuria. One of its leaders, An Ch'ang-ho, returned home in 1907 to found the New People's Society.

In the summer of 1908 there was a fresh reorganization, and all the anti-Japanese groups in the United States were combined into a single organization under the leadership of Pak Yong-man, Syngman Rhee and others. It stated purpose was "to regain the independence of the fatherland by promoting education and business, advocating freedom and equality, and enhancing the honor of our countrymen." Branches soon appeared in Mexico, and also in Vladivostok, Shanghai, Harbin, and many other cities all over the world. In June of 1909 Pak Yong-man and others established the Korean Youth Army School at Kini Farm, Nebraska, to train freedom fighters.

Chapter 32

Japanese Annexation and Resistance

Japanese policy in Korea after the Russo-Japanese war was clearly directed toward eventual annexation of the country to the Japanese Empire. The Japanese, as we have seen, quickly became the rulers of Korea in all but name, and only delayed making their rule official in order to make sure that there would be no interference from the Western powers and in order to subdue Korean resistance as far as possible. When Ito Hirobumi was appointed Resident-General in 1906 these were his objectives. When he was assassinated at the Harbin railroad station in 1909 by An Chung-gun he was on his way to Russia to confer with Russian officials.

Ito was replaced by Sone Arasuke who in turn gave way to Terauchi Masatake, a general who had previously served as Minister of War. Terauchi moved quickly toward formal annexation of Korea. Police surveillance was intensified to forestall the inevitable public indignation, and Japanese military police were empowered to extend their activities into the sphere of the civilian police, so that the country was under the direct control of the Japanese army. During the summer of 1910 he had a series of secret consultations with Yi Wan-yong, one of the leaders of the rubber-stamp Korean government, out of which came the so-called Korean-Japanese Annexation Draft. This Draft was signed by Terauchi and Yi on August 22 in a ceremony guarded by awesome numbers of Japanese troops. The full text need not to be discussed, since it consisted mainly of empty phrases intended to disguise the naked aggression of the Japanese. When these are winnowed out, its real effect is as follows: the Emperor of Korea is to be reduced to his former rank of King and the name of the country is to be changed from Taehan to the old name, Choson; all treaties between Korea and other nations are to become null and void, while all treaties between Japan and other nations shall now apply also to Korea; the Government-General of Korea shall be organized as an agent of the government of Japan to rule the peninsula. Korean independence was finally and officially at an end.

Terauchi became Governor-General after the annexation, and began the exercise of his new powers by banning the publication of several newspapers and suppressing the Sobuk Hakhoe, a political society opposed to Japanese rule. The military police were in complete control of all social activities. In the provinces, rebel groups were driven back and ultimately forced across the borders into Siberia and Manchuria, as we have seen, though this did not end their activities.

The Japanese government of Korea was carried out by five ministries: General Affairs, Home Affairs, Finance, Agriculture-Commerce-Industry and Justice. There were also the nine sections of the Governor-General's Secretariat, the General Police Bureau, the Investigation Bureau, the Court of Justice, the Railway Bureau, the Monopoly Bureau and the Temporary Land Survey Bureau. Perhaps the most striking thing about this government was the role of the military police. They were given control of the civilian police at the outset as already noted, and soon set up stations in all areas of the country. Each province had a military police commander. In 1910 there were 2,019 military and 5,693 civilian police in Korea, assigned to 640 civilian and 480 military stations. By 1914 the number of military stations had increased to 528, while civilian stations declined to 108, striking proof of the military nature of the colonial government. The number of police officers in Korea rose from 1,120 in 1910 to 1,825 in 1918. From the beginning, police expenses were the largest item in the Government-General's budget.

The functions of this large police force included not only ordinary police work and suppression of Korean independence movements but also guarding roads and forests, protection of the mails, enforcement of all tax collections, and even the spread of the Japanese language. It also enforced laws specially aimed at blocking nationalist movements, including the Peace Law (1907), the Assembly Control Act (1910) and the Guns and Ammunition Control Act (1912).

Beginning in 1906, one and a half divisions of regular Japanese army troops were stationed in Korea on a rotation basis. This was increased to two divisions in 1915. Most of them were sent to the northern provinces, both to check the Korean rebel groups in Siberia and Manchuria and to be ready to invade Manchuria itself when the time was ripe. The Japanese fully intended to follow the example of the European powers in the past, and to acquire a colonial empire second to none in Asia.

Attempts were made, though often without success, to win over Korean intellectual leaders by what amounted to bribes. Particularly eminent persons might be offered titles of nobility, while others were given pensions and "Imperial Gifts," and aged Confucian scholars were offered "Age Grants." The Consultative Committee was retained from the former government and staffed exclusively by Koreans except for its president. Membership was an empty honor, however, for it had no real power in government and was only a front for Japanese policy. In the end some seventy-six persons accepted titles of nobility and about 9,000 yangban Confucians were given various pensions and gifts.

One of the main purposes of the Government-General, of course, was to exploit the Korean economy for the benefit of Japan. This had already begun before the annexation, when Japan had taken over fishery rights on the northwest coast, railway concessions, communications and timber and mining rights. After the annexation the main concern was land ownership and agriculture. Laws were made to enable Japanese firms and individuals easily to acquire land in Korea, but the main instrument for depriving Koreans of their farms was what was called the Land Survey. Ostensibly, the purpose of the survey was simply to set up a modern system of land ownership, with title deeds recording the necessary information filed with the appropriate government office. A date was set by which all landowners had to report the location of their land, its precise size and its quality, together with their names and addresses. Korea had never had such a system before, and many of the ignorant farmers did not understand it. The effect of the survey, as the Japanese must have known it would be, was that many farmers failed to report to the government before the deadline, and were deprived of land they and their ancestors had farmed for centuries. In addition, all village common land was nationalized and the government now exercised the right to develop all arable uncultivated land. This it had not dared to do before the annexation because the mere suggestion had nearly started a revolt. A quarter of the nation's land was undeveloped, and Korean farmers were keenly aware of what the loss of this resource would mean. The Government-General eventually owned fully a twentieth of all arable land, and this does not count land owned by Japanese firms and individuals. The farmers took what recourse they could, and by 1913 20,148 complaints had been filed with the

Land Survey Bureau.

The land survey was completed in 1918, having cost the colossal sum of 20,500,000 won. The Government-General then proceeded to dispose of the land it had acquired to Japanese at bargain prices. Much of it went to the notorious Oriental Development Company, some to other Japanese firms, and some to Japanese individuals. The survey's real purpose had been to provide a legal basis for the seizure of Korean land by Japanese, and in this it succeeded. The chief beneficiary was the Oriental Development Company, which, with government patronage, extended the holdings acquired from the survey by large-scale leasing and purchasing. Its holdings totalled over 27,000 acres.

Another device used by the Japanese during the period of the survey was the seizure of land for non-payment of taxes. That this was not a legitimate operation but simply a method of expropriation is shown by the statistics. In 1912 less than a hundred persons lost their land in this way, but by 1914 the figure had risen to over 13,000 and did not thereafter fall below 6,000 annually. By the end of the Land Survey the number of Korean-owned family farms had declined by nearly 40,000. The farmers thus deprived had either to accept the status of tenants, eking out a bare subsistence while most of the profits from the land went to the landlords, become homeless wanderers, or emigrate to Manchuria or Siberia, which last many of them did.

Japanese hegemony was also established in the area of commerce and finance. Laws regarding the establishment of commercial enterprises were written and interpreted in such a way that, while Japanese firms could easily be established, it was virtually impossible for Koreans to set up businesses. Such laws had appeared even before annexation. Of one hundred and seventeen applications by Koreans to establish companies between 1907 and 1909, ten were granted and the rest rejected. In 1911 a law was promulgated giving the Government-General the power to close any firm which violated in any way the conditions under which it had been granted permission to do business. If the Japanese wanted to take over a Korean firm, in other words, they now had the power to do so.

The Oriental Development Company benefited enormously from these conditions, as did numerous other Japanese concerns. Many of these companies were new establishments based in Korea, while others were branches of Japan-based firms. The grip which Japan took on the economy is again shown by figures. Of the 110 companies in Korea after 1911, 101 were owned by Japanese and only nine by Koreans. Nineteen Japan-based firms had branches in Korea, and most of the capital invested in banks, electric companies, gas companies and railways, which are not included in these figures, came from the two giant Japanese industrial combines, Mitsui and Mitsubishi. On the other hand, the Government-General closed down the very prosperous Korean Land and Maritime Transportation Company and the Korea Hide Company. Ginseng and mining became government monopolies. Hardly any of the profits to be made in Korea went to Koreans, and as the Japanese prospered the Korean standard of living fell.

Most of this business activity was financed by Japanese banks, which had begun opening branches in Korea very early, soon after the Kanghwa Treaty of 1876. By 1910 they had appeared in almost all Korean cities of any size. In 1909 the Bank of Korea was established by the Japanese to handle government finances and in 1918 the Korea Industry Bank, another Japanese institution, took over provincial finances from the Agriculture-Industry Bank.

The natural resources were also diverted into Japanese hands. A forestry bureau was established to exploit the timber resources along the Yalu and Tumen Rivers. About 90,000 Japanese fishermen appeared in Korean coastal waters every year, and some 30,000 of them actually lived in Korea. Perhaps most important of all, increasing quantities of rice were shipped to Japan to feed her growing population. The Korean people were completely excluded from their own economy, which now became simply a source of profits and supplies for Japan.

In matters of education and religion the Japanese used a combination of ingratiating gestures and strict control and suppression. They were particularly anxious to prevent the growth of nationalism and of democratic ideas. For these reasons all religious organizations were carefully watched, while all but a few Koreans were prevented from receiving a modern higher education.

The Japanese attempted to ingratiate themselves with the Confucian scholars who had opposed them so bitterly in various ways. The grants to aged scholars have already been mentioned. Confucian institutions were respected. Songgyun'gwan, the Confucian training school for officials in former times, was renamed the School of Chinese Classics and allowed to continuing holding the spring and autumn ceremonies in honor of Confucius. The *hyanggyo*, Confucian schools in the provinces, were also allowed to continue, although part of their income was appropriated to finance the new public school program, thus undercutting the power of local Confucian leaders. The *sodang*, village schools where children made their first acquaintance with Chinese characters, were left untouched. Traditional and modern education went along side by side. Japanese efforts to educate the people were not particularly strenuous, however. By 1916 there were in the country 447 primary schools, seventy-four vocational school, three high schools and four colleges. Many Korean children never attended school at all, and few got beyond the elementary level.

Education for the children of Japanese residents, of course, was a different matter. A special section of the

government was responsible for them, and their parents
formed school associations in each district to found schools.
Japanese teachers were brought in and funds were provided
by the government. The low proportion of Koreans attending school and the high proportion of Japanese is
shown in the figures for 1919. In that year 42,767 Japanese
children were attending 379 schools. At the same time,
84,306 Korean children attended 498 public schools and
4,521 attended thirty-three private schools. When it is
taken into account that there were only 336,812 Japanese
residents at this time, while the Korean population was
approximately twenty million, the disproportion is obvious.

Taking account of the fact that many of the younger
Buddhist monks were anti-Japanese, the government
passed the so-called Temple Act in 1911. This provided that
temples and monasteries be used for religious purposes
only and that property owned by Buddhist organizations
could not be disposed of except by permission of the
Governor-General. The temples still owned a good deal of
farmland, and the Japanese wanted to make sure they did
not grow too wealthy or become centers of resistance.
Organizations such as the United Association of Buddhists,
the Buddhist Youth Association, the Buddhism Promotion
Society and the Buddhist Women's Charity Society
founded educational institutions and undertook various
innocuous good works.

But Buddhism, despite its long history in Korea and its
strong influence on the people's minds, was a declining
force, and could not serve as a rallying point against the
Japanese. Ch'ondo-gyo(the later form of Tonghak), on the
other hand, had been anti-foreign and nationalistic from
the beginning, and it continued to grow and prosper despite
persecution during the Japanese occupation. This was
particularly true in the northern provinces, where Confucian opposition to the new movement had been weaker

than in the south. So strong did the independence movement become in this area that the Japanese fabricated an "incident" which gave them an excuse to arrest its leaders and disrupt its activities. Ch'ondo-gyo by this time was organized into 185 parishes of about 100 households each, with nine further parished in the Manchurian border area, and it had its own newspaper.

Another force striving for independence was Protestant Christianity, brought to Korea largely by American missionaries. While missionaries and mission schools and other institutions did not participate directly in the struggle, the spirit of independence and democracy which they instilled in the people inspired many of them to fight against the Japanese. Many of the people who resisted Japanese domination and suffered at Japanese hands as a consequence were either Christians or inspired by Christian teaching. This is revealed in a whole series of incidents which took place at the time of the annexation and shortly thereafter.

In 1911 An Myong-gun, a cousin of the patriot An Chung-gun, was betrayed while attempting to reach Manchuria after a fund-raising expedition in aid of the independence movement in Sinch'on. The Japanese authorities took advantage of this opportunity and arrested numerous other leaders, among them some of the founders of the Yangsan School in Hwanghae Province who had been teaching the virtues of independence not only at the school but also in meetings of local Christians. Seventeen persons were imprisoned and forty banished to Cheju Island.

In P'yongan Province An Ch'ang-ho founded the Sinminhoe (New People's Society), a secret independence group that had close connections with Protestant organizations and itself sponsored a youth group and a school. It endeavored to cultivate nationalism in education, business and culture. In December of 1910 the Japanese pretended

68. So Chae-p'il and the Independent *Newspaper.*

69. The Independence Arch: Built in 1896, Seoul.

70. The Great West Gate, Now Demolished, and a Tram-car.

71. *The Royal Family:* From right to left: Princess Tokhae, Crown Princess, King Kojong, Crown Prince (later Sunjong), and Prince Yong (later Crown Prince).

72. *Japanese Troops in Seoul:* Demonstrating their military power.

73. *Korean Soldiers at the End of the Yi Dynasty.*

74. *The Rebel Army (Loyal Army) at the End of the Yi Dynasty.*

77. *Son Pyong-hui:* 1861–1921. The chief Ch'ondo-gyo leader.

75, 76. *The March 1 Movement and Massacre:* (Above) A demonstration held at Toksu palace, Seoul. (Below) Korean patriots massacred by Japanese military police.

78. *An Ch'ang-ho:* 1878–1938. The founder of Sinmin-hoe.

80. *Syngman Rhee, the First President of the Republic of Korea:* Taking the inaugural oath.

79. *Kim Ku:* 1876–1949. The President of the Provisional Government.

81. *Korean War:* Thousands of north Korean crossing a partly destroyed bridge on the Taedong River, south of P'yongyang, fleeing Communist troops.

82. *April Revolution:* Young lions of Korea University, demonstrating in angry protest against the corrupt Rhee regime, on April 18, 1960.

to have uncovered a plot to assassinate the Governor-General and arrested the Sinminhoe leaders and about 600 Christians. Of these 105 were brought to trial and found guilty. But the defendants were so vociferous in their own defense during the trial and the Japanese accusations so patently false that ultimately only six of them received prison sentences in 1913.

In 1917 students at Sungsil School, a Protestant foundation in P'yongyang, founded the Kungminhoe (People's Assembly) together with local Christians, and made contact with exile independence groups. This also was exposed by the Japanese, who arrested most of the members. The Japanese police were on the whole fairly successful in detecting and destroying resistance movements, but they were totally unable to destroy the desire for freedom and self-government among the Korean people.

Resistance was driven underground in Korea, but it was by no means crushed, and exile groups continued to expand. Raids were launched from time to time from Siberia and Manchuria, while groups in other countries sought the support of public opinion for Korea's cause. Japan's economic exploitation only intensified resistance, and though Western governments remained aloof Japan gained no popularity among the people of the world by her actions.

At the outbreak of World War I, Japan saw an opportunity to renew her incursions into China. Acting on the terms of her treaty with Britain, Japan occupied the German-leased territory on the shore of Kiaowchow Bay on the Shantung peninsula. In January of 1915 the infamous "Twenty-one Demands" were presented to the then weakened and divided Republic of China, which had come into being after the revolution of 1919. These demands amounted to complete Japanese domination of Manchuria and Mongolia. The Chinese response was a nation-wide anti-Japanese movement. In addition, Britain and the United States felt that their interests were threatened by Japanese expansion in China, and though they took no concrete action at the time, the former cordial relationship with Japan cooled markedly. In 1917 the Communist revolution in Russia toppled the Czars. After Germany surrendered in 1918, the American President Woodrow Wilson proposed at the Paris peace conference that the treaties of peace be based upon his famous "Fourteen Points."

These events all had an influence on Korea and Japan, but the most important in Korean eyes was the last. Among Wilson's fourteen points was the principle of self-determination, according to which the existence of a nation and the manner in which it was governed were to be freely determined by its people, and no people were to be dominated by others against their will. It was on the basis of this principle that the old empire of Austria-Hungary was broken up and new nations such as Czechoslovakia, Hungary, Bulgaria and Romania came into existence.

The relevance of self-determination to the Korean situation was obvious, and the exile independence groups especially seized upon it eagerly. Koreans residing China were especially active, sending a representative to the World Socialist Conference in Stockholm in 1917 and another to the Conference of Small Nations in New York in the same year, to plead Korea's cause. When the peace conference opened in Paris in 1919 the Korean group in Shanghai sent Kim Kyu-sik to represent them. They also sent Yo Un-hyong to seek support from the Soviet Union and Chang Tok-su to Japan to contact Korean students there. Kim Ch'ol secretly returned to Korea to aid the underground movement, while Yi Tong-hwi in Siberia and An Ch'ang-ho and Syngman Rhee in the United States prepared their groups for concerted action.

The first overt action occurred on February 8, 1919, in Tokyo, when 600 Korean students led by Ch'oe P'al-yong gathered at the Tokyo Korean Y.M.C.A. and tried to present a manifesto demanding Korean independence to the Japanese government. The movement had no practical effect, but it was a portent of things to come.

Fighters for Korean independence both at home and abroad reasoned that a nationwide demonstration for freedom from Japanese rule would focus world attention on Korea and bring heavy pressure on Japan to give up its colonial rule and allow Korea to rule herself just as the Allied Powers had recognized the rights of the peoples of Europe to self-determination. In cooperation with leaders abroad the Korean independence movement planned a national protest which was to begin with the reading of a declaration of independence drawn up and signed by thirty-three of their number. The demonstration was planned for March 3, 1919, the day of the funeral of deposed Emperor Kojong, whom many suspected had been poisoned by the Japanese. This was later put forward to March 1, and this date (*Sam-il* in Korean, i.e. "three-one," the first day of the third month) is celebrated to this day as a national holiday in the Republic of Korea.

Arrangements for the demonstration were quick and efficient and the secret was remarkably well kept, the Japanese authorities being taken completely by surprise. At two p.m. on March 1, 1919 the thirty-three signers assembled at T'aehwagwan in Seoul while the demonstrators assembled in Pagoda Park. Young students, who could move with comparative freedom from Japanese observation, served as liaison with the provinces, so that people all over the nation began demonstrating simultaneously. Copies of the Declaration were printed by the Ch'ondo-gyo organization and sent to each area, and also to the Paris peace conference, the President of the United

States, and to the Japanese government. It is worthy of remark that of the signers of this document fifteen were adherents of Ch'ondo-gyo, sixteen were Christians and two were Buddhists.

When all was ready, the Declaration of Independence was publicly read by the leaders in Seoul and by the organizers in other areas of the country. It proclaimed to the world that Korea had the right to exist as a free and independent nation, and that she had been annexed to Japan unjustly and against her will. This done, the demonstrators marched into the streets, not only in Seoul but in every community in Korea. The demonstration was a peaceful one, and no armed revolt or violence had been planned. The signers of the declaration made no attempt to hide and allowed themselves to be arrested. Thousands of national flags appeared, and people who had come to Seoul for Kojong's funeral immediately joined the movement. Koreans abroad immediately followed suit, and it must have seemed that every Korean alive was demanding his nation's freedom.

The Japanese were badly frightened by this demonstration, and reacted as frightened people often do, with violence. Japanese police and soldiers fired into the unarmed crowds, killing and wounding many. Thousands more were arrested and tortured. When angry mobs began to attack police stations as a result, the Japanese resorted to burning down houses and churches indiscriminately. It was estimated that 2,000,000 people took part in 1,500 demonstrations. Although accurate statistics are not available, it is generally agreed that about seven thousand people were killed and fifteen thousand wounded. Seven hundred and fifteen private houses, forty-seven churches and two school buildings were destroyed by fire. About 46,000 were arrested, of whom around 10,000 including 186 women, were tried and convicted. The largest demonstrations were in P'yongan, Kyonggi and Kyongsang Provinces, which suffered the greatest casualties. People of all ages, occupations and creeds took part. Seldom in history has an entire nation so unanimously expressed its desire for freedom.

In the most important sense, the March 1 movement was a failure, for the Japanese were not moved to grant Korea freedom, nor did other nations offer practical support. Japan at the time was coming increasingly under the rule of a military clique bent on conquest to which democratic principles were anathema. It was hardly to be expected that they would be moved by a peaceful protest. However, the March 1 movement was of great historical significance, and in some ways it did succeed.

First and most important, the March 1 movement greatly developed the spirit of national unity. Other attempts to resist the Japanese had been made always by particular groups for special reasons—the Confucian scholars in 1876, the soldiers in 1882 and the Tonghak in 1894 had reacted to pressures on their particular interests, and had mostly desired the restoration of the traditional order of society, in which nationalism in the modern sense played no part. But the March 1 movement embraced people of all classes and ages, and the Declaration of Independence with which it began envisioned a modern, independent state with a democratic government. From this time on Koreans thought of themselves as citizens of a nation with a common loyalty and a common desire for freedom which only increased under Japanese oppression. Though they were unable to free themselves unaided, the Korean people never acquiesced in Japanese rule and never abandoned their hope of independence.

Second, the March 1 movement revealed to world opinion the nature of Japanese rule in Korea. Never again would the Japanese be able to pretend that their rule was benevolent or that the annexation had been desired by Korea. Moreover, the Japanese pretension that the Koreans were a spiritless people lacking the intelligence and energy to rule themselves was shown up for the lie it was. Especially in the Western democracies, suspicion of Japanese motives began to grow, and though for reasons of national self-interest none of them made any direct moves against Japan, there was a cooling in relations that left Japan without allies in the Pacific when her imperialistic designs got into high gear, pushed her into alliance with the Axis powers in Europe, and ultimately brought about her defeat in World War II.

Finally, the March 1 movement brought home to the Japanese the fact that they could not rule Korea by mere force alone, that without at least some good-will and cooperation from the Korean people they would be in constant difficulties and the advantages they had hoped to gain from the annexation of Korea would be lost. Thus, though it failed to gain its objectives, the March 1 movement did bring the Koreans some practical advantages and also climaxed the formation of a national consciousness. From then on, though under foreign rule, Korea was a nation.

Chapter 33

Exploitation and Resistance between the Wars

Though the March 1 movement did impress the Japanese sufficiently to cause them to make certain gestures in the direction of liberalizing their rule of Korea, the net effect of the changes they made was not to make oppression less intense but to make it more subtle. First of all, they appointed admiral Saito Makoto Governor-General in August, 1919. Saito announced that he would respect Korean culture and customs and work to promote the happiness and well-being of the Korean people. As an initial conciliatory move, he withdrew the military police from some of their more obviously oppressive functions and abolished the wearing of uniforms and swords by civilian officials.

But this was superficial. The real effect of the reorganizing of the police was actually to increase the number of Japanese policemen in Korea. It was true that these were now civilian police under the control of provincial governors rather than military police under direct army command, but the tight control of all Korean activities was only less obvious, not less real. There were now police stations in every *myon* (the smallest provincial administrative unit) and the number of police increased by 10,000. A few Koreans were employed by the government in line with Saito's conciliatory policy, but they were in minor posts only and most of them were simply subservient tools used by the Japanese to help control the country. The same was true with the extension of the education system. It was proposed to make elementary school universal and compulsory, and to employ Koreans as school principals. The curricula of these schools, however, aimed at glorifying the Japanese Empire and subverting Korean nationalism. Education, too, was a tool of oppression.

A Japanese promise to allow a certain amount of freedom of expression proved equally meaningless. The *Choson Ilbo* and the *Tonga* [*Dong-A*] *Ilbo* were duly founded in 1920, the first newspapers to appear after the annexation. But they were subject to Japanese censorship from the outset, and there were frequent seizures of editions containing anti-Japanese sentiments and suspensions of publication, and finally both of them were completely suppressed. The Japanese had been made wary by the March 1 movement, but their policies remained unchanged.

One of the most important of these policies was economic exploitation. The rapid growth of the Japanese population, coupled with increasing industrialization, resulted in a food shortage. This was to be supplied from Korean rice. A fifteen-year plan to increase Korean rice production was instituted in 1920. The objective was to increase the annual rice crop by 45,000,000 bushels, 25,000,000 of which were to be exported to Japan. This proved an unrealistic goal, but nevertheless the planned quantity of rice was exported to Japan every year. By 1933 more than half of the annual rice crop was being sent to Japan, while rice consumption by the average Korean dwindled in proportion. By the end of the 1920s the average Japanese consumed almost twice as much rice as the average Korean, who had to supplement his diet with millet, maize and barley, mostly imported from Manchuria.

The rice-export policy had an unfortunate effect on Korean agriculture quite aside from the deprivations in diet, for it created a one-crop economy so that farmers were without recourse if the rice crop was not abundant. While new and more efficient techniques were introduced so that production increased, the farmer did not benefit. Taxes ate up much of his profit and land rents accounted for the rest, for the transfer of land from Korean to Japanese hands continued at an accelerated pace, and the majority of Korean farmers became tenants. Most of them had to give half of their crop to the landlord as rent, and in addition paid fertilizer expenses, transportation costs, and the government land-tax. Large numbers left their farms in despair to eke out a precarious existence in the mountains, using the slash-and-burn technique to grow crops on the dry hillsides, then moving on when the land became infertile. By 1939 the number of such nomad farmers had increased to 340,000 households, and thousands more had emigrated to Manchuria or managed to go to Japan. Further testimony to the ruthless Japanese exploitation of Korean agriculture is hardly necessary.

Japan did not at first pay much attention to Korean industry, being content with the traditional colonial policy of using the conquered land as a market for manufactured goods and a supplier of raw materials and food. But as a consequence of the economic depression following World War I, Japanese industrialists became interested in Korea as a likely source of profit. Laws regarding manufacturing were suitably changed and customs regulations were altered so as to favor Japanese manufacturing in Korea, and an industrial base began to appear.

First of all, a power source was needed. In 1926 the Korea Hydroelectric Company was established on the Pujon River in Hamgyong Province. In the following year a large factory was built for the Korea Nitrogenous Fertilizer Company, to make use of this power. Low wages and long hours assured the investors good profits. After Japan took control of Manchuria and installed a puppet government there another incentive was added for investment in Korean industry; Japan needed large supplies of munitions and other military necessities for the coming war with China, and Korea was a convenient location. Between 1925 and 1931 manufactured goods rose from 17.7 per cent of Korean industrial output to 31.3 per cent. The emphasis on Japanese military needs is also apparent from the fact that, while other industries grew slowly or even declined during this period, the chemical industry increased its output nearly four times. Gold mining declined, while iron, coal, tungsten and black lead boomed as the Japanese military machine grew.

Most of these industries were subsidiaries of the giant Japanese industrial combines such as Mitsui and Mitsubishi. There were few opportunities for Korean businessmen except in small-scale enterprises such as brewing, rice processing and textiles. There was no thought of Korean capital formation or the balanced development of Korean industry. Nor were Koreans trained in basic sciences or management. Some technical education was allowed to train workers for the factories, but that was all. There were less than 50,000 industrial workers in Korea in 1911. By 1933 there were 250,000, two years later there were 300,000, and by the end of the war in 1945 there were 1,500,000. Chronically overworked and underpaid, they engaged in perpetual labor disputes, always futile.

It must not be imagined that Koreans submitted tamely to this exploitation. Immediately after the March 1 movement, resistance leaders including Syngman Rhee, An Ch'ang-ho and Kim Ku met in Shanghai and organized a provisional government of Korea. There was no thought of reestablishing the Yi dynasty; Korea was to be a modern republic, and to this end a democratic constitution was drawn up. It provided for a freely elected president and legislature, guaranteed freedom of speech, press, religion, assembly and petition, and abolished patents of nobility. Church and state were to be separated and there was to be a national militia in place of a standing army. The rights of minorities were to be protected, an independent judiciary was to be established, and education was to be especially fostered. Resistance to Japan now had a regular organization and a modern democratic basis.

The new Provisional Government immediately made contact with Korean resistance groups in Manchuria, and through them with groups inside Korea. In 1920 an Officers Training School was established in Shanghai to train Korean military leaders. In 1922 all of the various Korean groups in Manchuria were unified under the authority of the Provisional Government. A newspaper, *Independence,* began publication, and a historical commission under An Ch'ang-ho commenced compilation of materials relating to Korea, especially the facts of the Japanese seizure of the country, so that both the Koreans themselves and the world at large should know the truth. Representatives were sent to all international conferences. While these activities were a great stimulus to Korean resistance against Japan, the international situation and the indifference of the great powers did not permit any significant changes in the situation.

Another significant event of 1920 was the foundation of the Korea Communist Party in Shanghai. This caused disagreements in the Provisional Government and hampered its efforts to some extent, but resistance continued nevertheless. Often it took the form of violence. Na Sok-chu smuggled himself into Seoul and attempted to destroy the office of the notorious Oriental Development Company with bombs. Unfortunately the bombs did not go off, and Na killed himself with his pistol before he could be captured. One of the members of Kim Ku's group went to Tokyo in 1932 and attempted to assassinate the Emperor.

He was caught in the act of throwing a bomb and later executed. In April of the same year Yun Pong-gil bombed a Japanese ceremony in Shanghai, inflicting numerous casualties. He was also arrested and shot.

To escape Japanese surveillance the Provisional Government moved to Nanking in 1932, and in 1935 to Chinkiang. When Japan launched a full-scale invasion of China in 1937 and Nanking fell in November, it moved to Changsha in Honan Province. When it became clear that China was in for a long war, it joined the Chinese government in Chungking in 1940.

After the March 1 movement numerous Koreans fled to the Kando area of Manchuria where, together with Koreans already there, they formed military organizations to resist the Japanese and protect Korean residents. There were several of these, and they had numerous encounters with Japanese troops. As early as 1920 one such group trounced a Japanese battalion at Fengwu-tung. Later, at Ch'ing Shanli near Kirin, a whole Japanese regiment was defeated in a four-day battle. The Japanese reaction to defeat was to arrest and execute innocent civilians and burn their homes. Ultimately the military groups had to move north to avoid such consequences.

An increase in Japanese troops in Manchuria managed to limit these conflicts somewhat, but in 1922 large-scale self-governing military groups began to appear, and there were three of them by 1925. Japan attempted to crush them through the cooperation of the puppet regime it had set up to govern Manchuria. Their response was to combine into the Korea Independence Party and the Korea Independence Army. In 1929 another group, the Korea Revolutionary Party, also with an army, was formed. Both groups were joined by Chinese in fighting Japanese occupation forces.

Many of the Koreans in the Russian Sikhote Alin territory joined the Russian Communist troops who were fighting the Japanese forces that had attempted to take over the Siberian railway after the Russian revolution. Their numbers grew to about three thousand. Supplied and instructed by Russian forces, they later attacked and disarmed non-Communist Korean resistance forces in the area and drove some of them to Manchuria.

Independence organizations appeared in other countries as well. In Los Angeles An Ch'ang-ho formed a party called the Kungminhoe, while in Honolulu Syngman Rhee set up the Tongjihoe and merged with an earlier organization which had been founded there by Pak Yong-man in 1919. In Japan the independence movement was carried on mainly by Korean students, who became divided during the 1920s into the Socialist and the Nationalists. They became more or less united under the influence of the international Communist United Front movement which attempted to make common cause among all left-wing political groups, but the Socialists continued attempting to take leadership away from the Nationalists. In 1929 they were absorbed into the Japanese Communist Party and in 1931 intensified Japanese police activity broke up the other Korean groups.

In Korea itself, meanwhile, the Korea Communist Party founded at Shanghai was making its influence felt. The increasing number of labor disputes after 1925 quite probably arose under its influence, and a number of Communist leaders were arrested by the Japanese. There were other anti-Japanese movements as well, which attempted to halt the inflow of Japanese capital investments, to boycott Japanese manufactured goods, and to encourage temperance. The Japanese countered this resistance by allowing the organization of a combination of rightist and leftist groups called Sin'ganhoe in 1927, through which they hoped to keep watch over and render innocuous the resistance to their rule. By 1929 it had 138 branches and about 37,000 members. It sponsored studies of the Korean language and attempted to mitigate as best it could the Japanese colonial policies and education system, while demanding freedom of thought and supporting scientific research.

As might have been expected, this organization was never very effective. The authorities would not allow it to hold national conferences and it was rent by internal dissension, caused mainly by Communists. When the Comintern, the international Communist organization, abandoned the united front policy the Korean Communists ceased all cooperation with other independence groups. Sin'ganhoe also lost several leaders who were arrested on suspicion of having taken part in the Kwangju student uprising of 1929. It was dissolved in 1931.

Because of tight Japanese control and the exile of most of the leaders, it was not possible to organize an independence movement with any hopes of success. This did not mean an end to resistance and protest however, for Korean resentment grew greater as Japanese control tightened. The students now made their appearance on the political scene, showing, among other things, that the Japanese education policy was a failure.

In April of 1926 Emperor Sunjong, the last reigning monarch of the Yi dynasty, died. His brother, the Crown Prince, had been taken to Japan in childhood, and the Japanese did not intend that he should reign. The passing of this last symbol of independence aroused great indignation, particularly among the students, who began to plan a demonstration in Seoul on the occasion of the Emperor's funeral, planned for June tenth. Leaflets attacking the Japanese rule and demanding independence were secretly printed and distributed, along with the forbidden national flags. When the day came, and Seoul was jammed with people attending the funeral, the leaflets and flags appeared on every corner of the city, and the people lining the streets as the bier was carried by began to chant patriotic slogans. The Japanese police, however, had uncovered the plot in advance and numerous student leaders were arrested. Since several of these students had been in contact with the Communists, quite a few of them were also imprisoned. The demonstration was thus a failure in the sense that the Japanese were able to stop it from spreading to the rest of the country.

A more serious demonstration broke out spontaneously three years later. On October 30, 1929, in Kwangju, South Cholla Province, a group of Japanese youths attempted to force their attentions on some Korean girls. When Korean boys came to their defense, the Japanese police intervened, and the Koreans were arrested, while the Japanese went unpunished. The news spread quickly through Kwangju and in no time practically every Korean student in the city was demonstrating. Before the Japanese authorities could stop them sympathetic demonstrations sprang up in other cities and soon the whole country was in an uproar. The disorders lasted for four months and involved 54,000 students from 194 schools, of whom 1,642 were imprisoned, 2,330 were suspended from school indefinitely, and 582 were permanently expelled.

The Sin'ganhoe organization mentioned earlier sent investigators to Kwangju to learn the truth about the initial incident. As a result, it secretly planned a mass meeting in Seoul which, it was hoped, would be the start of another nation-wide demonstration. The Japanese police got wind of the plan, however, cancelled the meeting and arrested the leaders. Another attempt in December, 1929, was similarly frustrated. The Japanese had had almost twenty years in which to persuade the Korean people to accept their rule, and they had signally failed.

The history of the press in Korea tells a similar story. A few Korean-language newspapers were allowed to exist—

the *Choson Ilbo* and *Tonga Ilbo* have already been mentioned and there were others—but only under the strictest Japanese surveillance. In spite of this, the Korean journalists were perpetually trying to serve the cause of national independence. They reported as much of the Japanese activity as they could, gave accounts of Koreans arrested by the police, and dwelt with emphasis upon the nationalist movements of other oppressed peoples. In addition they launched campaigns for poor relief and for the preservation of Korean cultural relics and sponsored public lectures counselling mutual trust and national awareness. In its first leading article the *Tonga Ilbo* proclaimed itself the voice of the national will and swore to preach and uphold democracy and Korean culture. The *Choson Ilbo* made similar claims.

Naturally all this did not go unnoticed by the Japanese authorities. Hardly an edition appeared of either of the two leading papers without some material removed by the censors. In the two years 1929 and 1930 alone 142 complete articles were refused publication and ninety-six whole editions were suppressed. There were also frequent arrests of reporters, suspensions of publication, and outright suppression of newspapers.

One of the most significant activities of these papers was the sponsoring of summer schools to teach and encourage the use of Han'gul, the Korean alphabet. These were aimed both at eliminating illiteracy and preserving the Korean language against the onslaught of Japanese. They were extremely popular, especially among students, who undertook to spread literacy in the countryside during their summer vacations. This was begun in 1928 and continued until it was stopped by the Japanese in 1935. The newspapers attempted to continue the work in other ways until they were all finally suppressed in 1940.

About thirty monthly magazines were established in

1920 and 1921, but few of them lasted more than a few months, either being suppressed by the Japanese or succumbing to financial difficulties. Among the most long-lived was *Kaebyok*, a magazine affiliated with the Ch'ondo-gyo sect which published seventy-two issues between 1920 and 1926. It was heavily censored, suspended thirty-two times, and finally ordered to cease publication. Other monthlies came and went in rapid succession, although the number in existence at a given time grew slowly. What is significant here, however, is the comparison with Japanese-owned publications both in the Korean and the Japanese languages. In 1931 there were 582 of these, as against only eighty-three Korean-run magazines. The Japanese were attempting by every means possible to overwhelm the Korean language and culture by the dessemination of huge numbers of newspapers, magazines, books, songs and films. That Korean culture emerged intact from this inundation is a tribute to its durability and to the stubborn loyalty of the Korean people.

One of the means to spread Japanese culture, of course, was education. We have already seen how at first the Japanese authorities did not concern themselves very much with how many Koreans got an education. The March 1 movement made them reconsider, however, the number of primary and middle schools was extended and their curricula reformed. When some Korean leaders who were concerned about the preservation of their culture attempted to found a private university in 1920 the authorities forbade it. Instead they made plans for a Japanese university. The preliminaries for this were announced in 1924, and in 1926 Keijo Imperial University admitted its first students, offering courses in medicine, law and the humanities. Almost all the students were Japanese, however, for very few Koreans were admitted. The only chance most Koreans had for higher education was to attend private universities in Japan, which were not so choosy. By 1930 there were about 3,000 of them there, in addition to the few who had managed to go to Europe or America. From these came many of the intellectual leaders of the future.

As an aid to their rule during the twenties and thirties, the Japanese government began sponsoring scholarly research into Korean history and culture, and in 1925 a Korean History Compilation Bureau was set up in the Government-General. Archeological investigations were made and monographs appeared on Korean folklore, social structure, religion and superstitution. The purpose of all this, it soon became clear, was to create a distorted picture of Korean history and society so as to convince the world that Korea was unfit for self-government and in need of the guiding hand of Japan. The Japanese scholars and investigators also showed their superior civilization by stealing as many Korean cultural relics and art treasures as they could and carrying them off to Japan.

Resistance to this and to the Japanese attempts to displace the Korean language took the form of the national language movement. The Korean Language Society was founded in 1921 and set out to standardize Korean grammar and Han'gul spelling and to compile a Korean dictionary. It also helped sponsor the spread of literacy in Han'gul. It became an effective resistance movement to the Japanese language policy and at the same time laid the foundation for modern scientific study of the Korean language.

Intellectual leaders had early recognized the need to preserve Korean culture and present an accurate picture of Korean history. As early as 1910 Ch'oe Nam-son had organized a group to publish and distribute Korean classical literature. He also did important research on Korean cultural origins and the background of Korean thought. Sin Ch'ae-ho and Pak Un-sik, exiles in China, devoted their whole lives to the writing of Korean history despite financial difficulties. In 1934 the Chindan Hakhoe (Korean Academic Society) was organized by scholars who had studied in Japan for the express purpose of conducting and publishing research on Korean history. Efforts were made to counteract the distortions and inaccuracies of Japanese publications on the subject, and some valuable work was done despite the usual harassment. In 1940 the group was dissolved by the Japanese, although they pretended that the dissolution was voluntary.

Resistance to the Japanese and a desire for freedom, together with the economic exploitation which was ruining the country combined to produce in the Korean literature of the twenties and thirties a mood of desperation and agony. In form and method it began to be influenced by European literary movements of the previous century, mostly through students who encountered modern Western literature while studying in Japan. Yi In-jik, as we have seen, introduced Western-style fiction to Korea. As early as 1908 Ch'oe Nam-son published the poem "From the Sea to the Boys" in his periodical *Sonyon,* beginning a new trend in poetry. In 1915 Yi Kwang-su published a short story, "To the Young Friends," in the same magazine and brought Korean fiction a long step closer to modern styles. Both men wrote in modern, colloquial Korean and their works were imbued with a hopeful, idealistic spirit. They were also somewhat didactic and tended to ignore the grim realities of the present.

After the failure of the March 1 movement, however, Korean literature, like other aspects of Korean life, was plunged in gloom. One of the first and most influential literary movements to emerge at this time was one which took its inspiration from the European naturalists, of whom Emile Zola is the prime example, and attempted to give in their writing a precise picture of society as it existed, without moral comment. This work appeared in the magazine *Ch'angjo* (Creation), which first appeared in February, 1919. Another group started the magazine *P'yeho* (Ruins) in July, 1920. Though the title of the publication signified a fresh start from the ruins of the past, they, like the *Creation* group, seemed more interested in describing the ruins than anything else.

In 1922 the magazine *Paekcho* (White Tide) introduced another group who wrote in a style of romantic decadence reminiscent of the *fin-de-siecle* school of England and France in the 1890s. They wrote of unknown worlds and morbid dreams, of nostalgia for the past and longing for death. Like their exemplars they were much concerned with style and there was much discussion of the proper choice of words.

In reaction to these groups, a school of proletarian literature appeared in the middle twenties, inspired by international Communism and its doctrine that the function of literature is to serve the cause of the masses. They were opposed by another group, of purely national-istic inspiration and thus opposed to the Communist variety of internationalism, who concentrated on the renovation of the traditional forms of Korean literature, especially the *sijo* form of poetry. They also devoted considerable at-tention to the spread of Han'gul.

As the Japanese penetration of China moved toward full-scale war during the thirties, the "assimilation" policy was born and applied to Korea with increasing severity. The Koreans, the Japanese decided, were now to become Japanese. The Korean language and culture were to be eradicated and the rising generation was to be taught to think, act and speak just as native Japanese did. Among its other unfortunate effects, this cruel and unrealistic policy brought great confusion to Korean literature and a desper-ate unrest to Korean writers. The various schools and tendencies disappeared or blended into each other. In 1941 the last two literary periodicals in existence were suppressed.

Chapter 34

War, Liberation, and the Birth of the Republic

While intensifying her oppression of Korea, Japan was beginning the series of military conquests that brought her into World War II and finally resulted in her defeat and Korea's liberation. Deliberate military provocations in Manchuria in 1931 resulted in the setting up in the following year of the puppet kingdom of "Manchukuo" under Japanese rule and also in placing the leading militarists in complete control of the Japanese government. Clashes with China increased until a state of all-out war was reached in 1937. Taking advantage of the preoccupation of the Western powers with the threat of war in Europe, Japan began to move into Southeast Asia, and when France fell in 1940 occupied French Indochina and Siam, threatening British positions in Burma and Malaya. Then began the farce of the "Greater East Asia Co-Prosperity Sphere," with Japan posing as the liberator of the Asian peoples from Western colonialism while treating those she conquered just as badly and sometimes worse that ever the Westerners had. The nationalist movements that were about to break out on every land in Asia were ignored or suppressed.

In 1940 Japan took another step toward world war by concluding a military alliance with Germany and Italy. At the end of 1941, frustrated in her attempts to obtain American sanction for her conquests and angered by the United States' refusal to continue supplying her with war materials, Japan took the fateful step of provoking war by the attack on Pearl Harbor, Hawaii, December 7, 1941. The United States Navy was badly hurt, and at first Japan swept all before her. In 1942 the Americans were driven out of the Philippines and the British strongholds of Hong Kong and Singapore fell. Japanese troops fanned out to northern New Guinea and most of the adjacent smaller islands and took the strategic American base on Guam. There seemed no stopping them.

But the turning point had already come, with the battle of Midway Island, in June, 1942, from which a severely mauled Japanese navy limped home in secrecy. Japanese expansion in the Pacific was stopped at that point, and in the following year the tide began to turn. One by one, the conquered islands were retaken and the Japanese forces pushed back. Meanwhile, the dictator Mussolini was overthrown in Europe and Italy surrendered to the Allies. With prospects of victory good in both theaters of war, the leaders of the United States, Great Britain and China met at Cairo at the end of November, 1943, to confer on strategy and post-war policy. In the Cairo Declaration which embodied the results of this conference, they announced that the war would continue until Japan surrendered unconditionally, that all Japanese territory acquired since 1894 should be returned to its previous owners, and that Korea should in due time become a free and independent nation.

In 1944 came the invasion of Normandy, opening the last chapter of Hitler's mad career in Europe. Germany surrendered in May of 1945, and the Allied Powers turned their full attention to Asia. On July 26 the leaders of the United States, Great Britain, the Soviet Union and China met at Potsdam and issued the Potsdam Declaration, again demanding the unconditional surrender of Japan. The Japanese, determined to struggle to the bitter end, refused. On August 6 the first atomic bomb obliterated Hiroshima, and on August 9 another fell on Nagasaki. Russia declared war on Japan on August 9, and within five days was in full control of northeastern Manchuria and northern Korea. Japan finally surrendered on August 15.

The war in the Pacific involved great suffering for Korea, especially in its later stages, for as Japan's defeat drew nearer her exactions and oppressions increased. Korea began being used as a supply base with the outbreak of war with China in 1937. In addition, as Japanese rice production fell because of a manpower shortage, more and more Korean rice went to Japan. Between 1917 and 1938 Korean rice exports rose tenfold, finally reaching over fifty million bushels. In addition, cattle were confiscated for meat and metal objects of all kinds, including scrap iron, brass pots and dishes, and even metal spoons and chopsticks were seized for the munitions factories. Japanese soldiers were everywhere. There were 46,000 of them in 1941 and 59,000 in 1943. By 1944 they had increased to 68,000, and in the disastrous year of 1945 the number leaped to 300,000.

A Japanese general, Minami Jiro, was appointed Governor-General in 1936. In 1937 the notorious "assimilation" policy was put into effect. Henceforth all educational institutions were to use the Japanese language exclusively. In 1940 the leading Korean-language newspapers were suppressed and in 1942 the last two literary magazines in Korean disappeared. In October of 1942 most of the members of the Korean Language Society were arrested and imprisoned on the pretext that they were secretly fomenting a nationalistic movement against Japanese rule. Scholarly and literary groups were dissolved.

From then on, all meetings and ceremonies in Korea began with an oath of allegiance to the Japanese Emperor, and Koreans were compelled to worship at Japanese Shinto shrines. In 1939 the assimilation movement reached a height of absurdity when all Koreans were ordered to change their names to Japanese ones.

As the war extended, Japan ran short of manpower and Korea was forced to supply the need. In 1938 a "volunteer" system, which was anything but voluntary, began conscripting Korean youths. In 1939 the Japanese began using forced Korean labor in mines and factories and military construction abroad. By the end of the war 2,616,900 persons were engaged in forced labor in Korea, while 723,900 had been sent abroad. Japanese patriotic societies were set up and Koreans forced to join them. In 1942 Korean men began being drafted into the Japanese army. As the strain on Japanese resources reached the breaking point and defeat loomed over her, the actions of her government in Korea become more and more desperate and cruel.

Korean reactions to this oppression were many and varied. One of the most important was that of the Christians, many of whom refused to obey the order to worship at Japanese Shinto shrines. In 1937, the year this order was promulgated, the minister and many members of a Presbyterian church in P'yongyang were arrested for refusing to obey. In 1939 all Christians who would not worship the Shinto gods were imprisoned, and many of them were tortured. In 1940 a number of Christians were accused of campaigning against the war and put in prison, and in March of 1941, even before the United States entered the war, several dozen British and American missionaries were arrested and secretly interned in a remote area of Kangwon Province.

Many Korean youths attempted to evade conscription, and were sent to the coal mines and munitions factories when caught. Many who were conscripted deserted at the first opportunity. As the situation worsened it became increasingly clear even to many Japanese that the defeat of Japan was inevitable.

The Japanese takeover of Manchuria in 1932 had greatly hampered the activities of patriot groups there. Many of them retreated into China proper, where some joined the forces of the Provisional Government, while others were won over by the Communists. In 1940 the Provisional Government removed to Chungking, where the Chinese government was then operating, and brought a great many Korean patriot groups under its control. In 1941 it organized a single military force from these, with Yi Pom-sok, a patriot fighter from Manchuria, as commander. At the same time, Korean units were set up within the Chinese Communist forces, which were based at Sian in the northwest. All these forces fought the Japanese side by side with the Chinese, and one Korean unit was even dispatched by the Chinese leader Chiang Kai-shek to aid the the British in Burma.

After the Japanese attack on Pearl Harbor brought the United States into the war, the Provisional Government began to make diplomatic contact with the Allied Powers with a view to ensuring Korea's independence after the war. As the Japanese suffered defeat after defeat, hope and joy rose in the hearts of Koreans both at home and abroad. The day of liberation was surely coming soon.

Driven back from all her Pacific conquests, pounded by perpetual Allied bombing raids and appalled by the tremendous destruction of the atomic bombs dropped on Hiroshima and Nagasaki, the Japanese at last surrendered unconditionally on August 15, 1945. The provisions of the Cairo and Potsdam declarations immediately came into force, and after forty years of struggle against the oppression of rulers who had tried to obliterate her very identity, Korea was free once more. For about three weeks, the Korean people lived in a state of happy confusion, and for many of them it was an emotional experience too deeply felt to be adequately described. Their happiness was soon overshadowed, however, by domestic political differences and the collision of the United States and Soviet Russia.

Tens of thousands of political prisoners came out of the jails as the Japanese relinquished control, and political and social organizations appeared in bewildering variety. The chief differences were between the Nationalists, who were awaiting the return of the Provisional Government leaders, and the Socialists and Communists, who wished to set up a Socialist state. All the differences which had rent the independence movement in the past and even divided the Provisional Government on occasion reappeared in aggravated form once independence became a reality.

Meanwhile, arrangements made among the victorious Allies were developing in such a way as to have the gravest consequences for Korea. One of the agreements reached after Russia's entry into the war against Japan had been that, upon a Japanese surrender, Russian troops should occupy Korea north of the thirty-eighth parallel, while those of the United States should occupy the area south of it. On the part of the United States, at any rate, this was thought of as a purely temporary arrangement, until such time as a Korean government could be formed and national elections held under the supervision of the United Nations. It was soon to become clear that the Russians saw it differently.

With the Russian forces already occupying the north, the troops of the United States Eighth Army under the command of Lieutenant General John R. Hodges began to arrive at Inch'on on September eighth. On the following day the Japanese forces officially surrendered in Seoul. The Governor-General was dismissed and the Japanese flag hauled down from the Government-General building. General Archibald V. Arnold was appointed military governor and a military government was organized. The American authorities made it clear from the outset that freedom of political activity was guaranteed and that they would observe strict neutrality in all arrangements made by Koreans in the process of organizing a government and holding elections.

In the north meanwhile, the Russians hastened to set up a Communist government led by Koreans. Cho Man-sik at first headed the Council of People's Commissars, but was soon replaced by Kim Il-song, who then began his long dictatorship. The Korean Provisional Council of People's Commissars was then set up and a Russian-style Communist regime organized. The nature of its rule could easily be judged by the fact that tens of thousands of people fled to the south, accompanied by every Japanese soldier or resident who could escape. Their numbers increased daily, and as the Russians guarded the thirty-eighth parallel more closely their efforts became more desperate.

Members of the Provisional Government now began to arrive in Seoul. Syngman Rhee returned in the middle of October, after a thirty-three-year absence from his homeland. In the latter part of November President Kim Ku and other important leaders arrived. All the nationalist groups supported them, and the people were anxious for the promised elections which were supposed to end the division of the country. They had to declare that they had returned in the capacity of private citizens, however, for the American military government recognized neither the Provisional Government nor the People's Republic which had been set up in the south.

Immediately upon his return, Syngman Rhee said in an interview, "When I heard there were some sixty political parties in Korea while I was preparing to return, my heart ached." He added that the first task for the Korean people was to unify the country and terminate the American and Russian military governments as quickly as possible. As soon as he could, he contacted General Hodges and

Military Governor Arnold to urge upon them the importance of a free and united Korea.

The division of the country was widely resented, and many of the political parties pressed for an end to it. One of them, the People's Party, even sent a resolution to general MacArthur demanding its abolition. But the Koreans were in for worse trouble. In October came the shocking news that the Allied Powers had decided that Korea was to be ruled by a trusteeship system for a maximum of five years. A provisional government was to be formed under the trusteeship of the United States, Britain, the Soviet Union and China. A conference of the foreign ministers of the United States, Britain and the Soviet Union was to be held in December in Moscow, and two weeks later the American and Russian commanders in Korea should proceed to carry out the arrangement.

Resistance was instantaneous and practically unanimous. After all the years of longing and fighting for independence, the Korean people simply could not accept the idea of even benevolent foreign rule. All the political parties agreed on this point and issued public statements opposing trusteeship. Demonstrations were practically continuous during the last months of 1945, and the press encouraged them in every paper that appeared. The trusteeship arrangements continued, however, and on the last day of the year the streets were still filled with angry people and the shopkeepers had closed their stores in protest.

Then on January 2, 1946, the Communist groups in Korea, doubtless on Russian instruction, suddenly changed their attitude and came out in favor of trusteeship. Well-rehearsed demonstrations in favor of trusteeship were held in north Korea and leftist groups in the south dutifully fell into line, while the nationalists stubbornly maintain their opposition.

In the midst of the continuing political turmoil, preparations went on for a Russo-American conference to organize a provisional government and a House of Representatives was appointed with Syngman Rhee as speaker, to act in a consultative capacity to the U.S. military government. This helped solidify the nationalist groups while the leftists were still trying to organize opposition to them. The trusteeship issue thus had the effect of creating a clear division between left and right.

After several preliminary meetings, the formal conference was held at Toksu palace in March, and almost immediately reached an impasse. The Russian side insisted that no political group or leader that had participated in the anti-trusteeship movement should be allowed to take part in forming the new government, hoping in this way to exclude the nationalists and set up a leftist government which they would be able to control. The American side refused to accept this provision and insisted that, to be truly democratic, the new government should consult all leading groups and shades of opinion. After weeks of fruitless argument, the conference was suspended *sine die* on May eighth.

General Hodges and his staff had not expected to rule a whole nation for any length of time, and despite their goodwill they faced problems with which they were ill prepared to deal. Japanese exploitation and concentration on munitions industries during the war had left the Korean economy a shambles, and in any case most of the nation's heavy industry was in the north and so controlled by the Communists. In addition, some 2,000,000 refugees had poured into the south, mostly from the north but many from China and Japan. Many of what factories there were stood idle because of lack of technical or administrative skills.

The American authorities did what they could, taking control of mines, reforming farm rents, and prohibiting the buying and selling of Japanese property. But they lacked detailed knowledge of civil administration and economics, and their regulations were made on a trial-and-error basis and frequently changed, creating more confusion. The political uproar over trusteeship and the Russo-American Conference was a constant and perplexing problem.

The political situation did clarify somewhat. The Korean People's Party led by Syngman Rhee pushed strongly for national unification and withdrawal of the trusteeship plan. The Korean Independence Party under Kim Ku and other members of the former Provisional Government wanted a national assembly elected and cooperation of all parties against trusteeship. A middle-right group led by Kim Kyu-sik and a middle-left group led by Yo Un-hyong both tried to heal the rift between left and right. But the left, especially the Communists, refused to give up support of trusteeship and demanded that the Russo-American Conference be resumed. When warrants were issued for the arrest of leading Communists on criminal charges, they went under ground and began fomenting strikes and riots, the most serious of which were the railway strike in Pusan and the riot of workers in Taegu.

In December of 1946 the Interim Legislature was formed under the American Military Government. Of the forty-five elected members the majority were from the Korean Democratic Party and the People's Council, which was led by Syngman Rhee. An additional forty-five were appointed by the Military Government, mainly from the groups led by Kim Kyu-sik and Yo Un-hyong. It was to propose urgently needed legislation in consultation with the Military Government.

During its first year, the American Military Government used a dual system with joint American and Korean heads of each department. When this proved ineffective, the Americans were changed from heads of departments to advisers. In February, 1947, An Chae-hong was appointed Civil Governor, the highest post. In June the military government was officially designated the south Korean Interim Government. A committee on government reorganization was established. A little later So Chae-p'il, who had supported Korean independence fifty years before, returned to offer his services as adviser, and was of great help in establishing a civilian administration. But the Interim Government was subject to many strains and stresses, and there were many problems with which it could not cope. It became daily more obvious that the formation of an independent Korean government was a necessity for the welfare of the people.

The Russo-American Conference meetings were resumed in Seoul in May, 1947, at which time the leading political parties presented to it in writing their suggestions for the formation of a provisional government. These suggestions differed so widely and contradicted each other in so many ways that the Conference could find no common ground on which all of them could be included. Moreover, the Russians renewed their insistence that all groups which had opposed the trusteeship plan must be excluded, a position which remained unacceptable to the United States. No real discussions were held, the two sides simply issuing statements from time to time.

Judging that negotiations must be held at a higher level if any progress was to be achieved, the United States proposed calling a foreign ministers' conference of itself, Britain, China and the Soviet Union for the settlement of the Korean problem. When Russia officially refused to accept this proposal, the United States placed the Korean question before the United Nations on September 17, 1947. The United Nations agreed, despite Russian objections, to attempt a solution.

The committee appointed to work on the problem laid

before the General Assembly a plan which called, first of all, for general elections throughout Korea under U.N. supervision. When a Korean government had been formed, both Russia and the United States were to withdraw their troops. At the same time, the United Nations Committee for the Unification and Rehabilitation of Korea (UNCURK) was to be organized to advise and consult with the new government. Over continuing Russian objections this plan was accepted by the General Assembly with some slight alterations.

UNCURK began to function in January, 1948 and immediately found itself excluded from north Korea by the Russians. In February it was decided to hold elections in the south in accordance with the U.N. resolution. These were held on May 10, when 198 representatives were elected to the National Assembly, 100 seats being left vacant in case of possible future elections in the north. The Assembly held its first session on May 31, and declared that from henceforth the official name of the nation was Taehan Minguk (freely translated as the Republic of Korea) and then set about drawing up a constitution, which was promulgated on July 17. Under this constitution, the Assembly elected Syngman Rhee as the first president of the Republic, and he immediately formed a government. On August 15, 1948, the third anniversary of liberation, the newly formed Republic of Korea was proclaimed to the world. It soon received diplomatic recognition from the United States and about fifty other countries. In December the United Nations proclaimed it the only legitimate government on the Korean peninsula.

While these events were going forward the last feeble gesture toward peaceful unification ended in failure. Having founded the Korea Council of People's Commissars as a step toward establishing a permanent Communist regime, the north Koreans proposed negotiations between representatives from north and south Korea at P'yongyang in April of 1948. This turned out to be simply a brain-washing operation on the part of the north Koreans, and nothing was achieved. Matters had gone too far for Korea to be unified through negotiations. For the time being, however, there was no overt conflict. The Russo-American Conference was dissolved and by June, 1949, both Russian and American troops had been withdrawn.

In defiance of the U.N. resolution the so-called People's Republic of Korea was formed in September, 1948. Almost immediately it began harassing guerrilla raids on the south, together with a propaganda campaign and fomenting of riots. Behind the scenes, serious military preparations were pushed forward as fast as possible.

In the south, the new government was having a difficult time. Communist-inspired strikes and riots were frequent, and so much money had to be spent on maintaining public order that shortages of essential goods and inflation followed. A majority of the Assemblymen elected were without political party affiliations, a clear sign of public disenchantment with the politicians. And the Republic's armed forces, which possessed no tanks and no warplanes, were far inferior in strength to the north Korean forces.

It was under these circumstances that early on the morning of June 25, 1950, without any warning or declaration of war, masses of north Korean troops crossed the thirty-eighth parallel and swept down upon the unprepared south. The Republic's troops fought bravely, but proved no match for the heavily armed Communists and the Russian T-34 tanks. The government was forced to move to Pusan and thousands of Seoul citizens fled before the advancing invaders. They were not checked until they reached the Naktong River near Taegu.

The Republic of Korea immediately protested to the

United Nations. In response, the Security Council passed a resolution ordering the Communists to withdraw to the thirty-eighth parallel and encouraged all member nations to give military support to the Republic. United States troops soon began to arrive, and were subsequently joined by those of many other nations, including Britain, France, Canada, Australia, the Philippines and Turkey. Under the command of General Douglas MacArthur they began to take the initiative, and after the surprise landing at Inch'on pushed the Communists out of south Korea and advanced into the north. Some units reached the Yalu River, and it seemed unification would at last be realized.

But in October the Communist Chinese intervened. Chinese troops appeared in such large numbers that the U.N. forces were compelled to make a strategic retreat, and Seoul once again fell into Communist hands on January 4, 1951. The U.N. forces regrouped and mounted a counter-attack which re-took Seoul on March 12. A stalemate was reached roughly in the area along the thirty-eighth parallel, where the conflict had begun.

At this point the Russians called for truce negotiations, which finally began at Kaesong in July of 1951 and were transferred to P'anmunjom in November of the same year. These talks were once suspended and dragged on for over a year before agreement was finally reached on July 27, 1953. Against the will of the Republic of Korea, it was agreed that each side should pull its forces back behind a demilitarized zone that was to follow the battle line at the time the armistice went into effect. Prisoners were exchanged and a neutral Supervision Committee was set up to ensure that both sides abided by the agreement. The three years of struggle had resulted in no thing but loss of life and property for both sides, and unification had been rendered virtually impossible without a radical change in the world situation.

The casualties and damage inflicted by the war were heavy. On the U.N. side 150,000 people were killed, 250,000 wounded, 100,000 kidnapped to the north, 200,000 missing and several million homeless. Precise figures are not available for the Communist side, but it is probable that their casualties were far greater. Taken and retaken four times, Seoul lay in ruins, as did most of the other cities of the south. More than half of all industrial facilities were inoperative, countless numbers of roads and bridges were destroyed and whole villages had been wiped out in many areas. But the gravest damage was to the Korean dream of unification. This was no longer a matter only of Korean concern, but had become an issue in the world conflict known as the Cold War. Once again Korea was compelled to suffer from the clash of powers greater than herself.

In the aftermath of the war, not only economic but very serious social and political problems appeared. These mainly centered around the Liberal Party regime of President Syngman Rhee. The old patriot, unable to see that he had outlived his usefulness, clung tenaciously to power. It was at least partly this refusal on the part of Rhee and his associates to let democratic processes take their normal course that was at the heart of the social and political unrest that followed the war.

The rehabilitation of the prostrate Korean economy was hampered by the fact that capital was monopolized by a very small group which had, of course, important political connections. This situation had arisen because industrial investments before liberation had been over 90 per cent Japanese. When the Republic of Korea government took over this property, it disposed of it in a very unfair and irregular manner to a few favored people. This favored few were interested only increasing and retaining their wealth, not in investing in the country's industrial development. As a result, the growth of small and medium industries was checked and heavy industry stagnated. Low productions meant shortages, which in turn meant inflation. Prices rose, but wages and salaries did not keep pace, while the fall in the real price of rice threatened farmers' livelihoods. A small rise in the price of rice meant little, for example, when the price of fertilizer rose by 500 per cent between 1953 and 1959.

This result was social disorders and hostility to the government and the monopolists, which complicated the already staggering social problems created by the war. There were many thousands of war-widows, over 100,000 orphans, and thousands of unemployed, whose numbers were swelled by farmers leaving their land to seek work in the cities. Exact statistics are not available, but in 1961 it was estimated that there were about 279,000 unemployed, of whom 72,000 were university graduates and 51,000 were discharged soldiers and laid-off workers. Here was a powder-keg of anger and resentment that waited only for a spark to set it off.

The spark was provided by President Rhee and the Liberal Party, whose maneuvers to retain power finally became intolerable. As early as 1952, with the country still at war, Rhee had managed to get the Constitution changed so as to have the President elected directly by the people instead of by the National Assembly. This seems a reasonable change, but was really motivated by the fact that Rhee was in danger of losing in the Assembly, while he was very popular with the people, who didn't know him as well. Martial law had to be declared before the Assembly gave in and passed the amendment.

In 1954 Rhee began to dally with the idea of again amending the Constitution, this time to repeal the provision limiting presidents to two terms in office. Once again the Assembly was bullied into compliance and the Rhee regime perpetuated in power. Democracy in Korea seemed to be rapidly disappearing.

The breaking point was reached with the elections of 1960. Realizing its unpopularity, the Liberal regime used every means at its disposal, legal and illegal, to rig the elections in its favor. Demonstrations broke out almost at once, especially among students. The first one occurred at Taegu on February 28, 1960, protesting political interference with schools. On March 15, election day, there were student demonstrations against the elections, and this time police fired into the crowd. In early April the body of a student who had been killed by police was found on the seashore at Masan. A riot followed.

The most serious demonstrations were in Seoul. Responding to the Masan affair, practically all the students in the capital poured into the streets. Again police fired on them as they neared the presidential residence, and there was bloodshed. Martial law was imposed and troops dispersed the crowds. This respite was only temporary, however, and on April 25 came the decisive action. All the university faculties in Seoul gathered on the campus of the Seoul National University Medical School and issued a statement demanding that the government pay compensation for students killed in the demonstrations. The professors then launched a demonstration of their own, which was rapidly joined by students and citizens. Troops sent to stop them joined them instead, while others would not attack the demonstrators.

The old President had no choice but to step down. His desire for power had overcome his patriotism in the end, and he had failed to meet the expectations of the people. The students had led the people into a democratic revolution. It was the first successful democratic revolution in Korean history. It showed that Korean democracy was alive and healthy, and none doubted that it would continue to grow and prosper.

Appendix I

The Rulers of the Three Kingdoms & Parhae

KOGURYO		PAEKCHE		SILLA	
Tongmyong	37B.C.–19B.C.	Onjo	18B.C.–A.D.27	**Pak clan**	
		Taru	28–76	Hyokkose	57B.C.–A.D.3
Yuri	19B.C.–A.D.18	Kiru	77–127	Namhae	4–23
Taemusin	18–44	Kaeru	128–165	Yuri	24–56
Minjung	44–48	Ch'ogo	166–213	**Sok clan** T'alhae	57–79
Mobon	48–53	Kusu	214–233	**Pak clan**	
T'aejo	53–146	Saban	234	Pasa	80–111
Ch'adae	146–165	Koi	234–285	Chima	112–133
Sindae	165–179	Ch'aegye	286–297	Ilsong	134–153
Kogukch'on	179–197	Punso	298–303	Adalla	154–183
Sansang	197–227	Piryu	304–343	**Sok clan**	
Tongch'on	227–248	Kye	344–345	Porhyu	184–195
Chungch'on	248–270	Kunch'ogo	346–374	Naehae	196–229
Soch'on	270–292	Kungusu	375–383	Chobun	230–246
Pongsang	292–300	Ch'imyu	384	Chomhae	247–261
Mich'on	300–331	Chinsa	385–391	**Kim clan** Mich'u	262–283
Kogugwon	331–371	Asin	392–404	**Sok clan** Yurye	284–297
Sosurim	371–384	Chonji	405–419	Kirim	298–309
Kogugyang	384–391	Kuisin	420–426	Korhae	310–355
Kwanggaet'o	391–412	Piyu	427–454	**Kim clan**	
Changsu	413–491	Kaero	455–474	Naemul	356–401
Munja	492–519	Munju	475–476	Silsong	402–416
Anjang	519–531	Samgun	477–478	Nulchi	417–457
Anwon	531–545	Tongsong	479–500	Chabi	458–478
Yangwon	545–559	Muryong	501–522	Soji	479–499
P'yongwon	559–590	Song	523–553	Chijung	500–513
Yongyang	590–618	Uidok	554–597	Pophung	514–539
Yongyu	618–642	Hye	598	Chinhung	540–575
Pojang	642–668	Pop	599	Chinji	576–578
		Mu	600–640	Chinp'yong	579–631
		Uija	641–661		

Sondok,[1] Queen		Hungdok	826–835	**PARHAE**	
	632–646	Huigang	836–837		
Chindok, Queen		Minae	838	Ko	698–719
	647–653	Sinmu	839	Mu	719–737
Muyol	654–660	Munsong	839–856	Mun	737–794
UNITED SILLA		Honan	857–860	Wonui	794
		Kyongmun	861–874	Song	794
Munmu	661–680	Hon'gang	875–885	Kang	794–809
Sinmun	681–691	Chonggang	886–887	Chong	809–812
Hyoso	692–701	Chinsong, Queen		Hui	812–817
Songdok	702–736		888–897	Kan	817–818
Hyosong	737–741			Son	818–830
Kyongdok	742–764	Hyogong	898–912	Yijin	830–857
Hyegong	765–779	Pak clan			
Sondok[2]	780–784	Sindok	913–916	Konhwang	857–871
Wonsong	785–798	Kyongmyong	917–923	Kyong	871–893
Sosong	799	Kyongae	924–926	Wigye	893–906
Aejang	800–808	Kim clan		Ae	906–927
Hondok	809–825	Kyongsun	927–935		

1, 2. These two titles have the same pronunciation but are written with different Chinese characters.

The Genealogy of the Koryo Dynasty

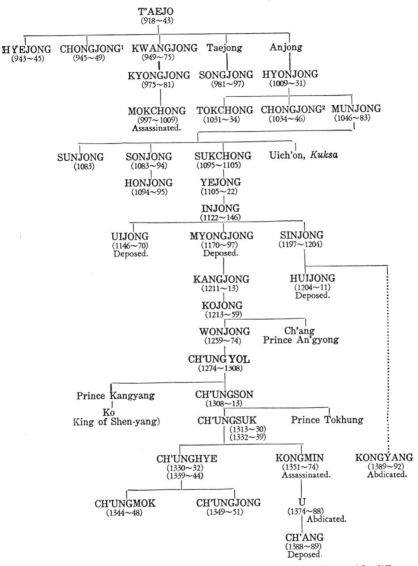

1, 2. These two titles have the same pronunciation but are written with different Chinese characters.

514

The Genealogy of the Yi Dynasty

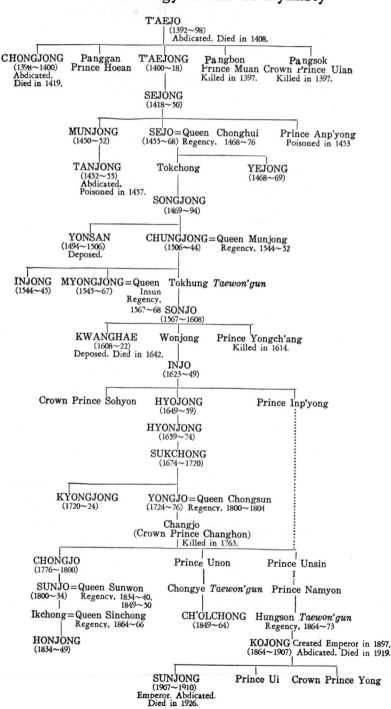

T'AEJO
(1392~98)
Abdicated. Died in 1408.

CHONGJONG (1398~1400) Abdicated. Died in 1419. — Panggan Prince Hoean — **T'AEJONG** (1400~18) — Pangbon Prince Muan Killed in 1397. — Pangsok Crown Prince Uian Killed in 1397.

SEJONG (1418~50)

MUNJONG (1450~52) — **SEJO**=Queen Chonghui (1455~68) Regency. 1468~76 — Prince Anp'yong Poisoned in 1453

TANJONG (1452~55) Abdicated. Poisoned in 1457. — Tokchong — **YEJONG** (1468~69)

SONGJONG (1469~94)

YONSAN (1494~1506) Deposed. — **CHUNGJONG**=Queen Munjong (1506~44) Regency, 1544~52

INJONG (1544~45) — **MYONGJONG**=Queen Insun (1545~67) Regency, 1567~68 — Tokhung *Taewon'gun*

SONJO (1567~1608)

KWANGHAE (1608~22) Deposed. Died in 1642. — Wonjong — Prince Yongch'ang Killed in 1614.

INJO (1623~49)

Crown Prince Sohyon — **HYOJONG** (1649~59) — Prince Inp'yong

HYONJONG (1659~74)

SUKCHONG (1674~1720)

KYONGJONG (1720~24) — **YONGJO**=Queen Chongsun (1724~76) Regency, 1800~1804

Changjo (Crown Prince Changhon) Killed in 1763.

CHONGJO (1776~1800) — Prince Unon — Prince Unsin

SUNJO=Queen Sunwon (1800~34) Regency, 1834~40, 1849~50 — Chongye *Taewon'gun* — Prince Namyon

Ikchong=Queen Sinchong Regency, 1864~66 — **CH'OLCHONG** (1849~64) — Hungson *Taewon'gun* Regency, 1864~73

HONJONG (1834~49) — **KOJONG** Created Emperor in 1897. (1864~1907) Abdicated. Died in 1919.

SUNJONG (1907~1910) Emperor. Abdicated. Died in 1926. — Prince Ui — Crown Prince Yong

Appendix II

A Note on Pronunciation and Proper Names

All Korean words in this book have been transcribed according to the McCune-Reischauer system of romanization, except that diacritical marks have been omitted. Vowels generally should be given their Italian rather than their English values. An apostrophe after a consonant indicates that it is aspirated, so that *P'yongyang*, for example, has a harder *p* than *pyong*. Exceptions have been made in cases where variant spellings have become familiar and customary, such as *Seoul*. As a general rule, Chinese words and names have been given in their Korean pronunciations, occasionally with the Chinese form in parentheses when this has seemed appropriate.

Koreans always put surnames before given names, and this practice has been retained here. In the name Yi Sun-sin, for example, Yi is the family name. An exception has been made in the case of Syngman Rhee, whose name is more familiar to Western readers in the form he gave it during his residence abroad.

As noted in the text, Korean kings were usually given posthumous titles after their deaths, and are generally referred to by historians under these names. A living king, however, could not be referred to either by this title (which he would not acquire until he died) or by his personal name, but by his title as king. For the sake of consistency, kings are referred to in this book by their posthumous titles, except for Yonsan and Kwanghae, who were never given such titles.

A somewhat similar practice was applied to Buddhist monks, who were given religious names on entering the order, and they are accordingly referred to here by their religious names.

Korean place-names have changed from time to time for various reasons. In all important cases, an effort has been made to give both the old and the modern place-name, so that places referred to here can be identified on modern maps.

Bibliography

[IN KOREAN]

BOOKS

Chindan Hakhoe. *Han'guk-sa* (History of Korea), Eul-Yoo Publishing Co., Seoul, 1959—1965.

Vol. 1 (Ancient Korean History, Yi Pyong-do).

Vol. 2 (Medieval Korean History, Yi Pyong-do).

Vol. 3 & 4 (Modern Korean History, I & II, Yi Sang-baek).

Vol. 5 & 6 (Recent Korean History & Contemporary Korean History, Yi Son-gun).

Ch'oe Chun. *Han'guk Sinmun-sa* (History of Korean Newspapers), Ilchogak, Seoul, 1960.

Ch'oe Ho-jin. *Kundae Choson Kyongje-sa Yon'gu* (The History of the Modern Korean Economy), Minjungsogwan, Seoul, 1947.

_____. *Han'guk Kyongje-sa Kaeron* (The Outline of Korean Economic History), Pomun'gak, Seoul, 1962.

Cho Ki-jun. *Han'guk Kyongje-sa* (Korean Economic History), Ilsinsa, Seoul, 1962.

Chon Hae-jong. *Han-Jung Kwan'gye-sa Yon'gu* (Studies in the History of Sino-Korean Relations), Ilchogak, Seoul, 1970.

Chon Pong-dok. *Han'guk Popche-sa Yon'gu* (A Study of Korean Legislative History), Seoul National University Press, Seoul, 1968.

Chon Sang-un. *Han'guk Kwahak Kisul-sa* (A History of Science and Technology in the Yi Dynasty), Kwahak Segyesa, Seoul, 1966.

Han Woo-keun. *Han'guk Kaehang-gi ui Sangop Yon'gu* (Studies in Korean Commerce during the Port-Opening Period), Ilchogak, 1970.

_____. *Yijo Hugi ui Sahwoe wa Sasang* (Society and Culture: 18th Century Korea), Eul-Yoo Publishing Co., Seoul, 1961.

Hong I-sop. *Choson Kwahak-sa* (A History of Korean Science), Chongumsa, Seoul, 1946.

_____. *Chong Yag-yong ui Chongch'i-Kyongje Sasang Yon'gu* (The Politic-Economic Thought of Chong Yag-yong (1762–1836)), The Korean Research Center, Seoul, 1959.

Hyon Sang-yun. *Choson Yuhak-sa* (History of Korean Confucianism),

516

Minjungsogwan, Seoul, 1949.

Kim Chae-won. *Tan'gun Sinhwa ui Sin-yon'gu* (A New Study of the Tan'gun Myth), Chongumsa, Seoul, 1947.

———— and Yun Mu-byong. *Han'guk Chisok-myo Yon'gu* (Studies of Dolmens in Korea), National Museum of Korea, 1967.

Kim Pyong-ha. *Yijo Junggi Tae-Il Muyok Yon'gu* (A Study of the Trade between Korea and Japan during the Middle Yi Dynasty), The Korean Research Center, Seoul, 1969.

Kim Tu-hon. *Han'guk Kajok Chedo Yon'gu* (A Study of the Korean Family System), Eul-Yoo Publishing Co., Seoul, 1949.

Kim Tu-jong. *Han'guk Uihak Palchon e taehan Kumi mit Sonambang Uihak ui Yonghyang* (The Influence of Western and Middle Asian Medicine on the Development of Korean Medicine), The Korean Research Center, Seoul, 1960.

————. *Han'guk Uihak-sa* (Korean Medical History), T'amgudang, Seoul, 1966.

Kim Won-yong. *Han'guk Ko-hwalcha Kaeyo* (Early Movable Types in Korea), National Museum of Korea, 1954.

Kim Yong-sop. *Choson Hugi Nongop-sa Yon'gu* (Studies in the Agrarian History of the Late Yi Dynasty), Ilchogak, Seoul, 1970.

Ko Pyong-ik. *Tonga Kyosop-sa ui Yon'gu* (Studies in the History of East Asian Interrelations), Seoul National University Press, Seoul, 1970.

Ko Sung-je. *Han'guk Kumyung-sa Yon'gu* (A Study of the History of Korean Banking Organs), Ilchogak, Seoul, 1970.

————. *Kunse Han'guk Sanop-sa Yon'gu* (A Study of the Industrial History of Modern Korea), Taedong Publishing Co., Seoul, 1959.

Ko Yu-sop. *Han'guk T'appa ui Yon'gu* (Studies of the Korean Stupas), Eul-Yoo Publishing Co., Seoul, 1948.

Pak Won-son. *Kaekchu* (The Commission Merchants in Korea), Yonsei University Press, Seoul, 1968.

————. *Pobusang* (The Peddlers in Korea), The Korean Research Center, Seoul, 1965.

Sin Ch'ae-ho. *Choson Saron* (Korean Historical Treaties), Kwanghan Book-Store, Seoul, 1964.

————. *Choson-sa Yon'gu-ch'o* (Studies of Korean History), Choson Toso Co., Seoul, 1929.

So Il-gyo. *Choson Wangjo Hyongsa Chedo ui Yon'gu* (A Study of the Penal System in the Yi Dynasty), 1968.

Son Chin-t'ae. *Choson Minjok Munhwa ui Yon'gu* (A Study of the Korean Natonal Culture), Eul-Yoo Publishing Co., Seoul, 1948.

Yi Chun-yong. *Yijo Nongop Kisul-sa* (A History of Agricultural Technology in the Yi Dynasty), The Korean Research Center, Seoul, 1964.

Yi Han-gi. *Han'guk ui Yongt'o* (The Territory of Korea), Seoul National University Press, Seoul, 1969.

Yi Hong-jik. *Han'guk Ko-munhwa Non'go* (Studies of the Ancient Korean Culture), Eul-Yoo Publishing Co., Seoul, 1954.

Yi Hyon-jong. *Yijo Junggi Han-Il Kyosop-sa Yon'gu* (Studies of the Korea-Japan Relations in the Middle Yi Dynasty), The Korean Research Center, Seoul, 1964.

Yi In-yong. *Han'guk Manju Kwan'gye-sa ui Yon'gu* (Studies of the Relations between Korea and Manchuria in the Early Yi Dynasty), Eul-Yoo Publishing Co., Seoul, 1954.

Yi Ki-baek. *Koryo Pyongje-sa Yon'gu* (Studies of the Koryo Military System), Ilchogak, Seoul, 1968.

Yi Kwang-rin. *Han'guk Kaehwa-sa Yon'gu* (Studies of the History of Enlightenment in Korea with Reference to the 1880's), Ilchogak, Seoul, 1969.

———. *Yijo Suri-sa Yon'gu* (History of Irrigation in the Yi Dynasty), The Korean Research Center, Seoul, 1961.

Yi Pyong-do. *Koryo Sidae ui Yon'gu* (A Study of the Koryo Period), Eul-Yoo Publishing Co., Seoul, 1948.

Yi Sang-baek. *Yijo Kon'guk ui Yon'gu* (Study of the Founding of the Yi Dynasty), Eul-Yoo Publishing Co., Seoul, 1949.

Yi Son-gun. *Choson Ch'oegunse-sa* (Recent History of Korea), Hansong Toso Co., Seoul, 1931.

Yu Hong-yol. *Han'guk Ch'onjugyohoe-sa* (A History of the Korean Catholic Church), Catholic Publishing Co., Seoul, 1962.

———. *Kojong Ch'iha Sohak Sunan ui Yon'gu* (Studies of Catholic Persecutions during King Kojong's Reign (1863–1907)), Eul-Yoo Publishing Co., Seoul, 1962.

Yu Won-dong. *Yijo Hugi Sanggongop-sa Yon'gu* (History of Commerce and Industry in the Later Period of the Yi Dynasty), The Korean Research Center, Seoul, 1968.

ARTICLES

An Kye-hyon. "Wonhyo's Rebirth-Thought of Mit'a-Chongt'o," *Yoksa Hakpo*, Nos. 16, 17, 18, and 21, 1961–63.

Ch'a Mun-sop. "Commoner Labor Service after Hideyoshi's Invasions and the Establishment of the Equal-Service System," *Sahak Yon'gu*, No. 10, 1961.

———. "On the Royal Court Guards of the Early Yi Dynasty,"

Sahak Yon'gu, No. 18, 1964.

Ch'oe Sung-hui. "A Study of the Chiphyonjon, Royal Academy in the Early Yi Dynasty," *Yoksa Hakpo,* Nos. 32 & 33, 1966–67.

Ch'oe Yong-hui. "The Nature of the Volunteers during the Japanese Invasion of 1592–98," *Sahak Yon'gu,* No. 8, 1960.

Cho Ki-jun. "A Study of the Loans Provided by Japan to Korea in the Late Yi Dynasty," *Asea Yon'gu,* Vol. 8, No. 2, 1965.

Cho Myong-gi. "The Ch'on-T'ae Thought of Priest Taegak and his Achievements in Scripture Collection," *Essay Collection in Commemoration of the 60th Birthday of Dr. Paek Song-uk,* 1959.

Ch'on Kwan-u. "The Formation of the *O-wi* of the Early Yi Dynasty," *Yoksa Hakpo,* Nos. 17 & 18, 1962.

_____. "A Study of *Han-in*—A Social Class in the Koryo Dynasty," *Sahoe Kwahak,* No. 2, 1953.

_____. "A Study of Yu Hyong-won—An Analysis of Yi Dynasty Society in Relation with the Origin of the Sirhak School, Practical Learning School," *Yoksa Hakpo,* Nos. 2 & 3, 1952.

Ha Hyon-gang. "A Study of the Local System in the Koryo Dynasty," *Sahak Yon'gu,* No. 13, 1962.

Han Woo-keun. "The Transformation of Thought in the Late 19th Century: Crisis-conscious versus Modernization," *Han'guk-sa Yon'gu,* No. 2, 1968.

_____. "A Study of Komgyo, an Honorary Official Post," *Chindan Hakpo,* Nos. 29 & 30, 1966.

_____. "A Study of the Causes of the Tong-hak Revolt," *Asea Yon'gu,* Vol. 7, No. 3 and No. 4, 1964.

_____. "A Study of the Mobile Corps in Late Koryo and Early Yi Dynasty," *Chindan Hakpo,* No. 22, 1961.

_____. "Yun Chung's View on Sirhak (Practical Learning)," *Tongguk Sahak,* No. 6, 1960.

Han Yong-guk. "On the Great Harmony System, or the Tribual System in Ch'ungch'ong Province in 16th Century Korea," *Yoksa Hakpo,* Nos. 13 & 14, 1960 and 1961.

Han Yong-u. "A New Interpretation of the Policies of Private Land Control during the Reign of Kings T'aejong and Sejong," *Han'guk-sa Yon'gu,* No. 3, 1969.

Hong I-sop. "On the Formation of Anti-Catholicism in Korea," *Inmun Kwahak,* No. 4, 1959.

Hwang Won-gu. "A Study of Confucianism in the Yi Dynasty: Its Development as Scholarship," *Tongbang Hakchi,* No. 6, 1963.

Im Pyong-t'ae. "A Study of the Auxiliary Capital System of the Silla

Dynasty," *Yoksa Hakpo*, Nos. 35 & 36, 1967.

Kang Chin-ch'ol. "A History of the Korean Land System," Part 1, *Han'guk Munhwa-sa Taegye*, Vol. 2, 1965.

_____. "A Study of the Military Farmland in the Early Koryo Dynasty," *The Sungmyong Women's University Essay Collection*, No. 3, 1963.

Kang Man-gil. "Growth of Commercial Capital in 18–19th Century Korea, with Emphasis on Wholesale Trade in the Capital and Songdo Area," *Han'guk-sa Yon'gu*, No. 1, 1968.

_____. "A Study of Handicrafts in the Early Yi Dynasty," *Sahak Yon'gu*, No. 12, 1961.

_____. "A Study of the Local Ceramics Office," *Asea Yon'gu*, Vol. 8, No. 4, 1965.

Kim Ch'ol-chun. "Lineage and Kinship of the Silla Social Organization," *Han'guk-sa Yon'gu*, No. 1, 1968.

_____. "The Role of the Ruling Clans in Silla Society," *Inmun Kwahak*, No. 7, 1962.

_____. "A Study of the Beginning and the Era of the Genealogy of Chiefs in the Early Silla Society," *Yoksa Hakpo*, Nos. 17 & 18, 1962.

_____. "A History of the Development of Korean Ancient States," *Han'guk Munhwa-sa Taegye*, Vol. 1, 1964.

_____. "On the Characteristics of the Ruling Power in the Period of the Later Three Kingdoms," *Essay Collection in Commemoration of the Late Yi Sang-baek*, 1964.

Kim Chong-hak. "Problems of Black Pottery in Korea," *Taedong Munhwa Yon'gu*, No. 4, 1967.

_____. "A Study of the Ungch'on Shell-mound," *Asea Yon'gu*, No. 10, 1967.

Kim Sang-gi. "On the Tung-i, Hsu-i and Hau-jung: Aboriginal Peoples of the Past Recorded in Ancient Histories of China," *Tongbang Hakchi*, Vols. 1 & 2, 1954 and 1955.

_____. "A Study of the Trade between Koryo and Sung China," *Chindan Hakpo*, No. 7, 1937.

Kim Won-yong. "An Archeological Study of Korean Culture," *Han'guk Munhwa-sa Taegye*, No. 1, 1964.

Kim Yong-dok. "A Study of Hyang, So and Pugok, the Three Kinds of Slums in Ancient Korea," *Essay Collection in Commemoration of the 60th Birthday of Dr. Paek Nak-chun*, 1954.

_____. "A Study of the Kyujanggak, Yi Dynasty Royal Library," *The Chungang University Essay Collection*, No. 2, 1957.

Kim Yong-ho. "A New Development of Seoul Merchants' Activities during the Late Yi Dynasty," *Han'guk-sa Yon'gu*, No. 2, 1968.

Ko Pyong-ik. "A Study of the Cheng-tung-hsing-sheng of the Koryo Dynasty," *Yoksa Hakpo*, Nos. 14 & 19, 1961 and 1962.

Pak Pyong-ho. "A Study of Landownership Rights in Recent Korean History," *Seoul University Law Journal*, 8–1, 1966.

Pak Song-su. "An Analysis of the Anti-Japanese War of the Korean Ui-byong, Righteous Army during the period 1907–1910," *Han'guk-sa Yon'gu*, No. 1, 1968.

Pyon T'ae-sop. "The Provincial Offices and Bureaucracy of the Early Koryo Dynasty," *Han'guk-sa Yon'gu*, No. 2, 1968.

_____. "A Study of the Military Officials in the Koryo Dynasty," *Asea Yon'gu*, No. 8–1, 1965.

_____. "The Growth and Development of Silla Society in terms of the Changes of Monument System," *Yoksa Kyoyuk*, No. 8, 1964.

Sin Ch'ae-ho. "The Largest Incident in 1,000 Years of Korean History," *Choson-sa Yon'gu-ch'o*, 1929.

Son Po-gi. "Pebble Chopping-tools; Industry of the Stratified Paleolithic Culture of Sokchang-ni, Korea," *Han'guk-sa Yon'gu*, No. 1, 1968.

_____. "Stratified Paleolithic Cultures Newly Excavated in Korea," *Yoksa Hakpo*, Nos. 35 & 36, 1967.

Song Ch'an-sik. "A Study of the Hwan-ja System, under the Yi Dynasty," *Yoksa Hakpo*, No. 2, 1965.

Won Yu-han. "The Currency Policy in the 18th Century," *Sahak Yon'gu*, No. 19, 1967.

Yi In-yong. "Northward Emigration Policy of King Sejo in the Yi Dynasty," *Chindan Hakpo*, No. 15, 1947.

_____. "A Study of the Trade with the Jurchen Tartars in the Yi Dynasty," *Chindan Hakpo*, No. 8, 1937.

Yi Chae-yong. "A Study of the Ch'eajik (Pension System) of the Early Yi Dynasty," *Yoksa Hakpo*, Nos. 35 & 36, 1967.

Yi Ki-baek. "On Sangdaedung," *Yoksa Hakpo*, No. 19, 1962.

_____. "The Introduction of Buddhism to the Three Kingdoms and its Social Impact," *Yoksa Hakpo*, No. 6, 1954.

_____. "The Formation of the Silla Administrative Organ," *Chindan Hakpo*, Combined edition of No. 25, 26, and 27, 1964.

Yi Kwang-rin. "Paper Manufacturing in the Buddhist Temples in the Late Yi Dynasty," *Yoksa Hakpo*, Nos. 17 & 18, 1962.

_____. "A Study of the 'Four Capital Schools' in the Early Yi Dynasty," *Yoksa Hakpo*, No. 16, 1961.

_____. "A Study of the Foreign Language School Established by the

Government in the Late Yi Dynasty," *Hyangt'o Seoul*, No. 2, 1961.

Yi Pyong-do. "A Study of the Ancient Nam-dang in Korea," *Inmun Sahoe Kwahak*, Seoul National University Essay Collection, No. 1, 1954.

————. "A Study of the Rise and Fall of Wi-ssi Choson," *Inmun Sahoe Kwahak*, Seoul National University Essay Collection, No. 4, 1958.

Yi Song-mu. "A Study of the Songgyun'gwan, National University in the Early Yi Dynasty," *Yoksa Hakpo*, Nos. 35 & 36, 1967.

Yi T'ae-jin. "A Study of the Discriminative Treatment against Concubinary Children," *Yoksa Hakpo*, No. 27, 1965.

Yi U-song. "A Study of the Han-in and Paek-chong in the Koryo Dynasty," *Yoksa Hakpo*, No. 19, 1962.

————. "The Urban Aspect of Seoul in the 18th Century," *Hyangt'o Seoul*, No. 17, 1963.

Yi Yong-hui. "Diplomacy respecting the British Occupation of Port Hamilton," *Essay Collection in Commemoration of the 60th Birthday of Dr. Yi Sang-baek*, 1964.

Yu Hong-yol. "The Formation of *Hyangyak* (Community Guilds) in the Yi Dynasty," *Chindan Hakpo*, No. 9, 1938.

Yun Mu-byong. "Classification of Forms of Korean Bronze Daggers," *Chindan Hakpo*, Nos. 29 & 30, 1966.

Yun Pyong-suk. "Japan's Request for the Privilege of Reclamation of Waste Land in Korea," *Yoksa Hakpo*, No. 22, 1964.

[IN WESTERN LANGUAGES]

BOOKS

Emile Bouraret. *En Coree*, Paris. 1904.

The British Consular Reports, Foreign Affairs. *Corea* (1883–1910).

China Imperial Maritime Customs. Appendix, *Korea*, Shanghai, 1927.

Allen D. Clark. *History of the Korean Church*, Seoul, n. d.

Allen D. Clark and Donald N. Clark. *Seoul, Past and Present*, Seoul, 1969.

William Craig. *The Fall of Japan*, New York, 1967.

George N. Curzon. *Problems of the Far East*, London, 1894.

Charles Dallet. *Histoire de l'Église de Corée*, Paris, 1874.

Tyler Dennett. *Americans in Eastern Asia: A Critical Study of the United States with Reference to China, Japan and Korea in 19th Century*, New York, 1922.

O. N. Denny. *China and Korea*, Shanghai, 1888.

Sukumar Dutt. *The Buddha and Five After-Centuries*, London, 1957.

Andreas Eckart. *Geschichte der Koreanischen Kunst*, Leipzig, 1929.

Everret Frazar. *Korea and her Relations to China, Japan and the United States*, New Jersey, 1884.

Siegfried Genthe. *Korea, Reiseschilderungen*, Berlin, Zweite Auflage, 1905.

Frans Goosens. *La Corée*, 1902.

Andrew J. Grajdanzev. *Modern Korea*, New York, 1944.

William E. Griffis. *Corea, the Hermit Nation*, New York, 1882.

Hakwon-sa. *Korea: Its Land, People and Culture of All Ages* (various contributors), Seoul, 1963.

Hendrick Hamel. *An Account of the Shipwreck of a Dutch Vessel on the Coast of the Isle of Quelpart, together with a Description of the Kingdom of Korea* (Transactions of the Korean Branch of the Royal Asiatic Society), No. 9, 1918.

Fred. H. Harrington. *God, Mammom and the Japanese*, Madison, 1934.

Ha Tae-hung. *Korea-Forty-three Centuries*, Seoul, 1962.

William E. Henthorn. *Korea: the Mongol Invasions*, Leiden, 1963.

Homer B. Hulbert. *The History of Korea*, 2 Vols., Seoul, 1905.

Kim Che-won and Kim Won-yong. *The Arts of Korea*, London, 1966.

Kim Che-won and St. G.M. Gomperts. *The Ceramic Arts of Korea*, London, 1961.

Adrien Launay. *Martyrs, Français et Coréens, 1838-1846*, Paris, 1925.

Lee Chong-sik. *Politics of Korean Nationalism*, Berkeley, 1965.

Lee Hoon-koo. *Land Utilization and Rural Economy in Korea*, Chicago, 1932

Lee In-sang. *La Corée et la Politique de Puissances*, Paris, 1965.

Peter H. Lee. *Korean Literature: Topics and Themes*, Tucson, 1965.

Joseph H. Longford. *The Story of Korea*, New York, 1911.

Andrew Malozemoff. *Russian Far Eastern Policy, 1881-1904*, California, 1958.

Eveline McCune. *The Arts of Korea*, Rutland, 1961.

George M. McCune. *Korea's Postwar Political Problems*, New York, 1947.

———. *Korea Today*, Cambridge, 1950.

Shannon McCune. *Korea's Heritage*, Rutland, 1956.

Frederick A. Mckenzie. *Korea's Fight for Freedom*, London, 1920.

———. *The Tragedy of Korea*, London, 1908.

Rosalie von Moellendorff, P. G. von Moellendorff. *Ein Lebensbild*, Leipzig, 1930.

Robert T. Oliver. *Syngman Rhee, the Man behind the Myth*, New York, 1954.

———. *Verdict in Korea*, Lebanon, 1952.

Ernest Oppert. *Ein Verschlossenes Land, Reisen nach Korea*, Leipzig, 1880.

———. *Voyage to Corea: A Forbidden Land*, London, 1880.

Cornelius Osgood, *The Koreans and their Culture,* New York, 1951.

George Paik. *The History of Protestant Missions in Korea, 1832–1910,* Pyongyang, Korea, 1929.

W. D. Reeve, *The Republic of Korea,* London, 1963.

Edwin O. Reischauer and John K. Fairbank. *East Asia: The Great Tradition,* Boston and Tokyo, 1965.

Edwin O. Reischauer, John K. Fairbank and Albert M. Craig. *East Asia: The Modern Transformation,* Boston and Tokyo, 1965.

B. A. Romanov. *Russia in Manchuria, 1892–1906,* 1928. Translated from the Russian by Susan Wilbus Jones, Ann Arber, Michigan, 1952.

W. Sirozewski. *Korea,* Berlin, 1906.

Theodore S. Soltau. *Korea: the Hermit Nation and its Response to Christianity,* London, 1932.

Harold W. Sonu. *Korea: A Political History in Modern Times,* Seoul, 1970.

Ssu-Ma Chien (translated by Burton Watson). *Records of the Grand Historian of China,* 2 Vols., New York, 1961.

Suh Dae-sook. *The Korean Communist Movement,* Princeton, 1967.

Horace H. Underwood. *Modern Education in Korea,* New York, 1926.

Benjamin B. Weems. *Reform, Rebellion and the Heavenly Way,* Tucson, 1966.

William H. Wilkinson. *The Corean Government: Constitutional Changes, July 1894 to 30th June 1896,* Shanghai, 1897.

Yi Kyu-t'ae. *Modern Transformation of Korea* (Translated by Song Tong-man, Kim Sun-sin, Charles Goldberg and Pak Nam-sik), Seoul, 1970.

Youn Eul-sou. *Le Confucianism en Corée,* Paris, 1939.

ARTICLES

Cho Soon-sung. "Korea in War-time Conferences: Cairo, Teheran and Yalta," *Journal of Asiatic Studies,* Vol. 5, No. 1, 1962.

Tyler Dennett. "Early American Policy in Korea, 1883–87," *Political Science Quarterly,* No. 38, 1923.

G. St. G. M. Gompertz. "The Development of Koryo Wares," *Transactions of the Oriental Ceramic Society,* 1948–49.

Augustine Heard, D. W. Stevens and Howard Martin. "China and Japan in Korea," *The North American Review,* 159, 1894.

William B. Honey, "Korean Wares of the Koryo Period," *Transactions of the Oriental Ceramic Society,* 1946–47.

Gari Ledyard. "The Mongol Campaigns in Korea and the Dating of the Secret History of the Mongols," *Central Asiatic Journal,* 9–1, 1964.

T. C. Lin, "Li Hung-Chang, his Korea Policies, 1870–1885," *The*

Chinese Social and Political Science Review, Vol. XIX, 1935–36.

George McCune. "The Exchange of Envoys between Korea and Japan during the Tokugawa Period," *Far Eastern Quarterly,* No. 5, 1946.

Glenn D. Paige. "Korea and the Comintern, 1919–35," *Journal of Social Sciences and Humanities,* No. 13, 1960.

Charles O. Paullin. "The Opening of Korea by Commodore Shufeldt," *Political Science Quarterly,* 25–3, 1910.

Robert T. Pollard. "American Relations with Korea, 1882–1895," *Chinese Social and Political Science Review,* No. 16, 1932.

Michael C. Rogers. "Sung-Koryo Relations, Some Inhibiting Factors," *Orient,* No. 11, 1958.

Richard Rutt. "An Introduction to Sijo," *Transactions of the Korea Branch of the Royal Asiatic Society,* No. 34, 1958.

Sohn Pow-key. "Early Korean Printing," *Journal of the American Oriental Society,* No. 79.

Payson J. Treat. "China and Korea, 1885–1894," *Political Science Quarterly,* Vol. XLIX, 1934.

_____. "The Good Offices of the United States during the Sino-Japanese War," *Political Science Quarterly,* Vol. XLVII, 1932.

Edward W. Wagner. "Recommendation Examination of 1519," *Chosen Gakho,* No. 15, 1960.

William Wetson. "The Earlier Buddhist Images of Korea," *Transactions of the Oriental Ceramic Society,* 1957–59.

Mary C. Wright. "The Adaptability of Ch'ing Diplomacy, the Case of Korea," *Journal of Asian Studies,* 17–3, 1958.

[IN JAPANESE]

BOOKS

Akiba Takashi and Akamatsu Chijo. *Chosen Fuzoku no Kenkyu* (A Study of Korean Shamanism), 2 Vols., Osakaya-shoten, Seoul, 1937.

Arimitsu Kyoichi. *Chosen Kushime-mong Toki no Kenkyu* (A Study of the Korean Comb-Ceramics), Kyoto Taikaku Kokogakudanwakai, Kyoto, 1962.

Fujita Ryosaku. *Chosen Kokogaku Kenkyu* (Korean Archaeology), Koto-shoin, Kyoto, 1948.

Mikami Tsugio. *Man-Sen Genshi Funbo no Kenkyu* (A Study of the Primitive Tombs in Manchuria and Korea), Yoshikawa-kobunkan, Tokyo, 1961.

Mishina Akihide. *Shiragi Karow no Kenkyu* (A Study of Silla Hwarang Knights), Sanseito, Tokyo, 1943.

Okudahira Takehiko. *Chosen Kaikoku Kosho Shimatsu* (Korea's Intercourse with Foreign Countries for the Opening of Korea), Toko-shoin, Tokyo, 1935.

Paek Nam-un. *Chosen Hoken Shakai Keizai-shi* (The Feudalistic Socio-Economic History of Korea), Kaizosha, Tokyo, 1937.

Suematsu Yasukazu. *Shinra-shi no Shomontai* (Problems of the Silla History), Toyo-bunko, Tokyo, 1954.

Tagawa Kozo. *Licho Konowsei no Kenkyu* (A Study on the Tribute System of the Yi Dynasty), Toyo-bunko, Tokyo, 1964.

Tahobashi Kiyoshi. *Kindai Nissen Kankei no Kenkyu* (A Study of Recent Japan-Korea Relations), 2 Vols., Government-General, Consultative Committee, Seoul, 1940.

Umehara Sueji. *Chosen Kodai no Bosei* (The Tomb System of Ancient Korea), Zaubogankokai, Tokyo, 1947.

Watanabe Katsumi. *Chosen Kaikoku Gaiko-shi Kenkyu* (The Diplomatic History of the Opening of Korea), Tokodo-shoten, Seoul, 1941.

ARTICLES

Fukaya Toshigane. "The Transition of the Land System in the Early Yi Dynasty," *Shigaku Zasshi*, Vol. 51, No. 9 and No. 10, 1940.

Hanamura Yoshiki. "A Study of the Laws of Koryo," *Chosen Shakai Hosei-shi Kenkyu*, 1930.

Hatada Takashi. "A Form of the Gung-ken (County and Prefecture) System in the Koryo and Yi Dynasties," *Oriental Historical Essay Collection in Commemoration of the 70th Birthday of Dr. Wada*, 1961.

_____. "Local Offices and Local Clans at the Outset of the Koryo Dynasty," *Hosei-shi Kenkyu*, No. 10, 1960.

_____. "The Villages of Silla," *Rekishigaku Kenkyu*, Nos. 226 & 227, 1958 and 1959.

Ikeuchi Hiroshi. "The Daizokyo (Collection of the Buddhist Scripture of Koryo)," *Toyo Gakuho*, Vol. 14, No. 1, 1924.

Mikami Tsugio. "The Political and Social Nature of Wei-ssi Chosen," *Problems in Ancient Chinese History*, 1954.

Shikata Hiroshi. "A Study of Population in the Yi Dynasty," *Chosen Shakai Hosei-shi Kenkyu*, Tokyo, 1937.

_____. "Investigation of Yi Dynasty Population in Terms of Status and Class," *Chosen Keizai-no Kenkyu*, Tokyo, 1938.

Shuto Yoshiyuki. "Land Reform in the Period from Late Koryo to Early Yi Dynasty," *Toa-gaku*, No. 3, 1940.

_____. "A Study of the Slaves in the Period from Late Koryo Early Yi Dynasty," *Rekishigaku Kenkyu*, Vol. 9, Nos. 1,2,3,4, 1939.

Shuto Yoshiyuki. "A Study of Land Deeds in the Late Yi Dynasty,"
Rekishigaku Kenkyu, Vol. 7–7, 8, and 9, 1937.

Yamaguchi Masayuki. "The Introduction of Catholicism to Korea,"
Seikyu Gakuso, No. 6, 1931.

──────. "Prince Shoken and Johan Adam Schall von Bell," *Seikyu
Gakuso,* No. 5, 1931.

Yu Hong-yol. "The Formation of Sowon, Private Institutes in the Yi
Dynasty," *Seikyu Gakuso,* Nos. 29 & 30, 1937 and 1939.

──────. "Private Schools in Late Koryo and Early Choson," *Seikyu
Gakuso,* No. 24, 1936.

INDEX